To Carlotta

Reminded of your
Matchless kindness in
June, forty-eight,
With gratitude and love,
Hortense.

ALBERT SCHWEITZER

By ALBERT SCHWEITZER

———

THE PHILOSOPHY OF CIVILIZATION

I. THE DECAY AND THE RESTORATION OF CIVILIZATION

II. CIVILIZATION AND ETHICS

Vol. III in preparation

THE QUEST OF THE HISTORICAL JESUS

THE MYSTERY OF THE KINGDOM OF GOD

PAUL AND HIS INTERPRETERS

THE MYSTICISM OF PAUL THE APOSTLE

J. S. BACH

ON THE EDGE OF THE PRIMEVAL FOREST
& MORE FROM THE PRIMEVAL FOREST

MEMOIRS OF CHILDHOOD AND YOUTH

MY LIFE AND THOUGHT

FROM MY AFRICAN NOTEBOOK

ALBERT SCHWEITZER

From the drawing by Daniel Wohlgemuth, 1929

ALBERT SCHWEITZER
The Man and His Mind

BY

GEORGE SEAVER

WITH THIRTY ILLUSTRATIONS
FROM PHOTOGRAPHS

HARPER & BROTHERS PUBLISHERS
New York   London

ALBERT SCHWEITZER: THE MAN AND HIS MIND

Copyright, 1947, by Harper & Brothers
Printed in the United States of America

To
The Hospital at Lambaréné

CONTENTS

PART I. *HIS LIFE*

PART II. *HIS THOUGHT*

x CONTENTS

APPENDICES

ACKNOWLEDGMENTS

Most of the photographs appearing in this book have been supplied by friends and helpers of Dr. Schweitzer, who have asked for no recognition; acknowledgment is made to these, and to any copyright owners of photographs whom it has not been possible to trace. For permission to quote from his several books acknowledgment is due to Dr. Schweitzer and to Henry Holt and Company, Inc. as follows:

From *Out of My Life and Thought* by Albert Schweitzer. Copyright, 1933, by Henry Holt and Company, Inc.

From *Indian Thought and Its Development* by Albert Schweitzer. Copyright, 1936, by Henry Holt and Company, Inc.

From *The Mysticism of Paul the Apostle* by Albert Schweitzer. Copyright, 1931, by Henry Holt and Company, Inc.

From *The Forest Hospital at Lambaréné* by Albert Schweitzer. Copyright, 1931, by Henry Holt and Company, Inc.

From *African Notebook* by Albert Schweitzer. Copyright, 1939, by Henry Holt and Company, Inc.

ILLUSTRATIONS

ILLUSTRATIONS

xvi

PART I

HIS LIFE

CHAPTER I

MEMORIES OF CHILDHOOD AND YOUTH

ALBERT SCHWEITZER is probably the most gifted genius of our age, as well as its most prophetic thinker. A Doctor four times over—in philosophy, in theology, in music, and in medicine—he was earning three of these distinctions while in his twenties, at an age when most men are still serving their apprenticeship in one; and for him they are but incidental to the classic contributions which he has made to each of these subjects. What is rarer still, his practical achievements and manual skill have kept pace with his scholarship: a surgeon, a self-taught architect and builder, an agriculturalist, an organist and a consultant in organ-craft, he has further proved his ability as an administrator in founding, organizing, and maintaining a hospital in the tropics. As an independent thinker, he foresaw the collapse of western civilization at a time when sociologists were confidently heralding its advance, and at the same time he was proposing a deeply-considered remedy for its eventual restoration.

An Alsatian born and bred, an alumnus of Strasburg University, and thereafter pursuing his studies in the Universities of Paris and Berlin, he is a product of Franco-German culture, but by every instinct of temperament and in every direction of outlook he is cosmopolitan. Preserving as he does the qualities of sturdy independence characteristic of his race, he takes pleasure in the thought that his remote ancestors were Swiss. His skill as an organist, his aptitude for teaching, and his devotion to the work of an evangelist, were all inherited: his father, Louis Schweitzer, who lived to a ripe old age, was recognized as a Nestor among the pastors of Alsace; his grandfather was a schoolmaster and an organist, as were also his grandfather's brothers; whilst his maternal grandfather, Pastor Schillinger, was an organist of repute with a gift for improvisation.

Born on January 14, 1875, at Kaysersberg in Upper Alsace, he was removed in infancy to the village of Günsbach in the Münster Valley which was thenceforth his family's permanent home. Through all the many vicissitudes of a long career, made up of self-imposed

3

and strenuous labours in diverse fields of thought and action, he has retained the deepest affection for the low hills of the Vosges wooded with fir and beech, oak and chestnut, and the peaceful valley that slips away between them to the Rhine; and even more for his early friendships, and the homely ways and pastoral simplicity of the kindly folk of the upper Rhineland. As a native of Alsace he was bilingual from his earliest years, but although in his home-letters he has always used French since this was the custom of his family, and German generally for his books and lectures, he regards the Alsatian dialect which is allied to German as his mother tongue, since this is the language in which he thinks, counts, and also dreams. He maintains that belief in the possession of two mother tongues is a delusion, although one may be equally fluent in both, and also that an adequate translation of one language into another is an impossibility, since, not only do the differences of idiom conceal different forms of thought, but also the cadences required by one language cannot be reproduced in the cadences peculiar to another. He finds a proof of this in his own experience, for having written his great work on Bach in French, and being requested for a translation of the same work into German, he soon felt obliged to give up the attempt and re-wrote the whole. When reading or writing in French he says that he seems to be "strolling along the well-kept paths of a fine park"; but in German to be "wandering at will in a magnificent forest."

As the eldest son of the local pastor, he was sent to school with the village boys, a circumstance which caused his boyish sensitiveness some embarrassment. For although robust beyond his years and able to hold his own with the best of them when it came to a rough-and-tumble, and though by nature friendly and desiring to be a friend to all, he found that his young companions could not treat him as one of themselves. He was the parson's son, "a sprig of the gentry." It cost him pains to live this down—to him it was an epithet of opprobrium; his soul revolted from the steaming mug of good broth at home which his school-mates never got; he refused to wear the winter overcoat (made from an old one of his father's) which they never wore; he would only wear fingerless gloves, and wooden clogs on week-days, and a common brown cap, because they could wear no others. In all things he wanted nothing so much as to be like them; and when his father boxed his ears and shut him up in the cellar for showing himself before visitors "unsuitably dressed to his station in life," he suffered these pains and penalties in

Aged 8

SCHWEITZER AS A BOY

Aged 11

THE VILLAGE OF GÜNSBACH, ALSACE

silence. He has never regarded his rustic education as other than a salutary boon, however, in that it left him without doubt that some of his school-mates "had at least as much in their heads as I had in mine"; and in after life when he meets one or another of them at work in the village or on a farm, "I at once remember vividly the points in which I did not reach their level." Thus early there awoke in him that sense of respect and consideration for his fellows, that inward courtesy and modesty, which was so marked a characteristic of his later life and thought.

During a happy childhood he showed no signs of precocity in any direction, except in one. The exception was in music. At the age of seven he surprised his teacher by strumming hymn tunes on the harmonium to self-invented harmonies; at eight, when his legs could scarcely reach the pedals, he began to play the organ; at nine he could play it well enough to deputize for the organist in the village church. This talent was inborn in him, a free gift, and budded early (he believes that he inherited it from his maternal grandfather); it blossomed from the age of eighteen under the tuition of Widor, the celebrated Parisian organist, "when there dawned on me, thanks to him, the meaning of the architectonic in music." Even in his boyhood there were occasions when the charm of a two-part harmony thrilled him with such intensity of pleasure that he had to cling to something solid to prevent himself from falling.

But his other intellectual gifts were latent in his youth, they grew with his growth and were acquired and developed by dint of patient industry till they reached fruition in his manhood. He tells us that it cost him trouble to learn to read and write; that he mastered classics and mathematics with difficulty; that he was much given to day-dreaming. The habit of day-dreaming received an unexpected corrective, however, when at the age of nine he entered the Gymnasium at Mülhausen, where he lived with an uncle and aunt whose discipline was kind but stern, and was taught by a master to whose example he owed one of the strongest influences of his life. This was due to the high standard of conscientiousness which the master set himself in preparing and conducting the lessons for his class, a standard which could not fail to influence his pupils, even though unconsciously, and foster in them a sense of the value of inner discipline. "That a deep sense of duty, manifested even in the smallest matters, is *the* great educative influence, and that it accomplishes what no exhortations and no punishments can, has, thanks to him, become my firm conviction, a conviction the truth of which I have tried to prove in practice in all that I have had to do as an educator." Thereafter he reserved his habit of day-dreaming for his solitary two-mile walks schoolwards, back and forth across tree-clad hills in all seasons and in all weathers, walks in which his heart was free to commune with Nature. Before he left school the new-fashioned velocipedes called bicycles had reached his valley and, investing the modest fees he had received from coaching backward scholars in mathematics, he purchased one and put it to strenuous use forthwith —not without severe physical strain.

The two chief interests of his boyhood were for History and Natural Science. The critical acumen of the future author of *The Quest of the Historical Jesus* is well exemplified by the following:

"When I was eight my father, at my own request, gave me a New Testament, which I read eagerly. Among the stories which interested me most was that of the Wise Men from the East. What did the parents of Jesus do, I asked myself, with the gold and other valuables that they got from these men? How could they have been poor after that? And that the Wise Men should never have troubled themselves again about the Child Jesus was to me incomprehensible. The absence, too, of any record of the Shepherds of Bethlehem becoming disciples, gave me a severe shock." And at the Mülhausen Gymnasium he found that "it was for History alone that I had any real ability," the only subject that he mastered without effort; he ascribes this partly to his passion for reading, and partly to the fact that his Professor, a distinguished historian, treated him more like a friend than a pupil. On leaving the Gymnasium he attracted the notice of the President of the board of examiners by the accuracy and extent of his knowledge of history and also by his historical judgment. But he soon came to realize that history is too full of riddles to be more than a bare approximation to fact, and that "we must abandon forever the hope of really understanding the past." His interest in the trend of contemporary events, even if as inexplicable as those which were passed, was equally keen and absorbing: a passion for reading the political news in the daily papers to the apparent neglect of his lessons earned him severe rebukes from his uncle.

Natural Science provided another wholesome stimulant to his mind, but the complacency of the text-books "which professed to explain everything" in a world so fraught with mystery, were pain and grief to him. "It hurt me to think that we never acknowledge the absolutely mysterious character of Nature. . . . Even at that age it became clear to me that what we label Force or Life remains in its own essential nature forever inexplicable. Thus I fell gradually into a new habit of day-dreaming about the thousand and one miracles that surround us. . . . The habit is with me still, and gets stronger. If during a meal I catch sight of the light broken up in a glass jug into the colours of the spectrum, I at once become oblivious of everything around me, and unable to withdraw my gaze from the spectacle."

His sense of awe in face of the beauty and mystery of the natural world impelled him to try his hand at poetry and sketching, but they were failures: "only in musical improvisations have I ever felt myself to have any creative ability." Here we see an anticipation of the idea which he develops with eloquence and conviction in his work on Bach: the idea, namely, that there is a blending of several arts in the artist's receptive imagination until the moment comes in which he chooses the "language" that suits him best.

When he left the Gymnasium and was required, with his fellow-scholars, to describe precisely how the Homeric heroes beached their ships, and could not do so, their ignorance was denounced by the examiner as a serious defect in culture. "For my part I thought it a far greater defect in our culture that we were leaving the Gymnasium without knowing anything about Astronomy or Geology."

These two sciences, then, the human and the natural, enhanced his growing sense of the overwhelming mystery of life which deepened with the years, and inclined him towards a mental attitude of reverent agnosticism.

Sincerely religious both by temper and parental training, he took his preparation for confirmation very seriously, and had the benefit of careful instruction from a good old pastor for whom he had a great respect. But it gave him no answer to the deep questions that were already kindling in his mind. Towards the end of the course the pastor found time to question each candidate individually, but "when my turn came, and he tried by affectionate questioning to learn of my thoughts and resolutions during that holy time, I began to hesitate and to answer evasively. It was impossible for me, much as I liked him, to let him look right into my heart." Here we have a sign of the first apparent stirrings of that strong individualism and deep reserve which marks the future exponent of the philosophy of

Reverence for Life, and which regards any intrusion of one mind into the private sanctuary of another as in the nature of a sacrilege. The interview had an unhappy ending: the good old pastor dismissed him with coldness, and informed his aunt that he feared the boy was one of the "indifferent" candidates. "In reality I was so moved by the holiness of the time that I felt almost ill." When a pastor himself and with ten years' experience of preparing lads for confirmation, Schweitzer had frequent occasion, if any of them seemed "indifferent," to recall that interview with the dear old pastor and himself, and to remind himself "how much more goes on in a child's heart than others are allowed to suspect."

During his first years in the larger school he sadly missed the services in his father's little church at Günsbach, and especially his father's sermons. These impressed him deeply because of their intense conviction, as being "of a piece with his own life and experience," and because of the evident "effort—I might say struggle" which for the same reason went into their utterance. "I still remember sermons that I heard from him while I was at the village school." He missed also the feeling of solemnity which those village services gave him, and "the need for quiet and self-recollection without which I cannot realize the meaning of my life." In his view it is not at all necessary that a child shall understand all that takes place in a church service for adults: the main thing is that they shall feel "the sense of something that is serious and solemn." For this reason too he has a rooted aversion to the Protestant type of church building which aspires to embody a "preacher's church," where the eye of the worshipper is brought up in every direction by short walls. "A church is much more than a building in which one listens to sermons"; it is intended primarily for the purpose of worship, and for this purpose it should be designed. The architecture should be adapted to the sense of distance and of spaciousness, so that the outward gaze can reflect the inner aspiration of the worshipper—"a complete whole, in which the service becomes as much a part of the soul's experience as the words heard, or the singing, or the prayers." Some of the churches of Alsace still retain a peculiarity which is unique in Christendom: they are Catholic-Protestant combined. The priest says mass in the choir, and the pastor says prayers and preaches in the nave, at different times by mutual arrangement every Sunday. This practice, introduced by Louis XIV for the benefit of Catholics in districts where their own places of worship were too few, was widely observed in old days and is still maintained in several of the Lutheran churches of which Günsbach is one; and, though originally due to "the irresponsible edict of a ruler," is for Schweitzer "something more than a historical phenomenon": it is the mark of a signal Christian grace —the grace of religious tolerance. These churches are for him a symbol of the Church of the future, "a prophecy and an exhortation to a future of religious unity, upon which we must ever keep our thoughts if we are really and truly Christians." As a boy he loved to let his gaze rest awesomely upon the gilded altar and the glittering images of the Virgin and St. Joseph flood-lit between the chancel windows, and feel a community of spirit in worship with his fellow-worshippers of both denominations, present and absent. Modernity has since then "improved" upon that simple setting, but not upon its spirit.

Now when I go and sit in Günsbach Church, I shut my eyes in order to see the choir again in that homely magnificence which once so enchanted me. As my mind's gaze lingers in the past, I can see again in their places figures that were once there in the flesh, but are there no more, because they have been carried out into the churchyard. And the remembrance of the departed who once worshipped with us is for me one of the most heart-gripping parts of the services in the village church of my home. How solemnly they sat there: the men all in black, the women in their simple Münstertal costume; much more solemn in dress, in behaviour, and in character than we of the new generation![1]

The boy that was native to a Franco-German province, and within that province the child of a Protestant-Catholic Church, has made of the man a unifying influence, political, religious, and in all other ways.

As to his faults, there were two which caused him special watchfulness and pains to try to cure—a passionate temper and an eager disputatiousness. The former evinced itself at games—"I played every game with terrible earnestness, and got angry if anyone else did not enter into it with all his might"—and is natural enough as the ebullition of youthful spirits accompanied by an unusually high degree of nervous vitality and moral and physical stamina. The latter fault is not surprising in a lad of an alert and vigorous intelligence, but by dint of careful observation of himself and others he outgrew his argumentative temper before he had grown out of his teens.

[1] *Memoirs of Childhood and Youth*, p. 68.

He was so quick to laugh at the funny side of things that risibility was almost an affliction, and one which his schoolfellows mercilessly exploited during lessons, nicknaming him "the Laugher." Yet on his own confession he was by no means a merry character, since he inherited from his mother a temperamental shyness and reserve.

But there were other and more important reasons to account for the fact that the young Schweitzer was not so merry a character as he seemed to be. "As far back as I can remember I was saddened by the amount of misery I saw in the world around me." (He adds the reflection that this is probably the case with many children who appear outwardly happy and care-free.) Human affliction was in itself a grim and saddening spectacle enough, but that the dumb creation should also be tormented with such excess of pain and cruelty was heart-rending. "The sight of an old limping horse, tugged forward by one man while another kept beating it with a stick to get it to the knacker's yard at Colmar, haunted me for weeks." It passed his childish understanding that such things could be taken by his elders and betters as a matter of course.

"It was quite incomprehensible to me—this was before I began going to school—why in my evening prayers I should pray for human beings only. So when my mother had prayed with me and had kissed me good-night, I used to add silently a prayer that I had composed myself for all living creatures. It ran thus: 'O heavenly Father, protect and bless all things that have breath; guard them from all evil, and let them sleep in peace.'"

He recalls occasions in his childhood when the obligation to prevent cruelty to the dumb creation was irresistibly borne in upon him with all the force of a moral law. Once on a fine spring morning, reluctantly obedient to the "terrible proposal" of a playmate to go bird-shooting with the catapults they had made, he went, but shooed the birds away from the leafless boughs before they could come to any harm, and then fled home. Again, when to show off his skill with reins and whip he overdrove an old asthmatic horse, and noticed when he unharnessed it at the journey's end the exhausted heaving of its flanks—"what good was it then to look into his tired eyes and silently ask him to forgive me?" Again, when driving a snow sledge in the winter, a vicious dog ran alongside and sprang at the horse's head. "I thought I was fully justified in trying to sting him up with the whip, although it was evident that he only ran at the sledge in play. But my aim was too good; the lash caught him in the eye and he rolled howling in the snow. His cries of pain haunted me; I could not get them out of my ears for weeks." Such and similar experiences moved him to a conviction which steadily strengthened as he grew older: "that we have no right to inflict suffering and death on another living creature unless there is an unavoidable necessity for it," and that most people feel the same but are deterred from expressing the conviction, or from carrying it into practice, either by the fear of ridicule or else by thoughtless indifference. "But I vowed I would never let my feelings get blunted or be afraid of the reproach of sentimentalism." These scruples caused him to give up shooting and fishing while in his teens; the captivity of wild animals in a menagerie was a horror to him second only to the training of tamed animals for an exhibition, and the sight of thirsty frightened cattle cramped together in a jolting railway truck was a nightmare. Thus in these early reflections he was laying the foundation of another aspect of that ethical philosophy to which he afterwards gave the name of *Reverence for Life*.

In this acute sensitivity to animals' pain there is evident an early recognition of the indissoluble alliance between gentleness and good sense, or reason. In other words, mercy is the twin-sister of truth. In the bird-shooting episode the young Schweitzer discovers a rational principle for conduct which is humane, even though it is not accepted by the majority; and determines thenceforth to do wanton injury to no living thing, for this is an offence against conscience and reason and natural good feeling. This discovery and this resolve are an integral part of his passion for ultimate truth.

But, arising from this there is another and more difficult problem to be solved. All life lives at the expense of other life: this is an obvious law of the natural world; and man—an ethical and spiritual being—is forced by the selfsame horrible and incomprehensible law to prey on other life, whether animal or vegetable, in order to maintain his own. No one has yet found the thought that will give the answer to this dark and inscrutable riddle of existence; but at least it is possible to adopt a sane and rational attitude towards it also: never to destroy life unless it is unavoidable. And by going out of our way to help any living creature in distress we are helping to discharge a debt—a debt of honour—which we owe to the rest of creation for its vicarious sacrifice to our needs. It is after all the only sane and reasonable course we can adopt.

For a long while a shadow lay across his boyhood years which were otherwise so sunny. The upkeep of a large unwholesome manse shut out from sunshine by surrounding buildings, a growing family of five children, his father's frequent illnesses—these things made life a hard struggle for his mother, and rigid economy a necessity for the household. "I took a pride in making my wants as few as possible. . . . There comes up even now the memory of my mother's eyes, so often red from weeping." He was no stranger to youthful hardships and tribulations. But before he left school a welcome change of fortune came with the family's removal to a new manse, his father's improved health, financial help from a bequest, "and there was again unclouded sunshine over our home."

His growing sense of responsibility for life, reverence and respect for all things living, wonder at all the mystery and beauty and tragedy of life, were henceforth accompanied by a new-found sense of gratitude for his own happy lot—to his parents most of all, to his aunt and uncle, to his many friends, and even to those chance acquaintances who never knew how much he felt he owed them.

Of his parents he says: "they trained us for freedom." Of his father: "he was my dearest friend." Of his mother: "we did not possess the faculty of expressing in words the affection we had for each other, and I can count on my fingers the hours in which we really talked to each other heart to heart. But we understood each other without using words." And of the others he has in effect this to say: "they never knew how much I owed them."

He reproaches himself for this, ascribing it to "youthful thoughtlessness which takes its benefits for granted," or perhaps—he adds as an afterthought—to that constitutional shyness "which prevented me from expressing the gratitude that I really felt. But down to my twentieth year, and even later, I did not exert myself sufficiently to express the gratitude which was really in my heart."

The most moving and the most eloquent of meditations are to be found in those passages where a profound mind releases itself in the most homely utterance. And among Schweitzer's musings few are to be found more eloquent in their simplicity than the sentences in his *Memoirs of Childhood and Youth* where, in his reflections upon gratitude for friendship, he recalls occasions when he has said quietly to himself over a grave in his native Günsbach the words which his lips should have spoken in gratitude years before. He takes comfort from the thought that "a great deal of water is flowing underground which never comes up as a spring," but "we ourselves must try to be the water that does come up,—a spring at which men can quench their thirst for gratitude."

And not only friends, but also chance acquaintances, and others too with whom he never exchanged a word, and still others of whom he had only heard things by report,—they too "entered into my life, and became powers within me." Their influence may have come home to him unconsciously, to be awakened consciously years later, "just as the beauty of a piece of music or of a landscape often strikes us first in our recollection of it."

Much that has become our own in gentleness, modesty, kindness, willingness to forgive, in veracity, loyalty, resignation under suffering, we owe to people in whom we have seen or experienced these virtues at work, sometimes in a great matter, sometimes in a small. A thought which had become act sprang into us like a spark, and lighted a new flame within us. . . . If we had before us those who have thus been a blessing to us, and could tell them how it came about, they would be amazed to learn what passed over from their life into ours.[1]

These then were the twin graces—the grace of Compassion and the grace of Gratitude—which, simultaneously engendered in Schweitzer in his tender years as by a kind of rational intuition (to which the majority of mankind are strangers), grew side by side to their flowering in his youth, to bear fruit in his manhood. They determined his whole attitude to life, and being the foundations of his ethical philosophy they shaped the course of his subsequent career in the fields both of thought and action.

[1] *Memoirs of Childhood and Youth*, p. 90.

CHAPTER II

WORK AT STRASBURG UNIVERSITY

WHEN Schweitzer at the age of eighteen, already a competent scholar in classical Greek and Latin, entered Strasburg University, he set himself to read Theology and Philosophy concurrently. One of the subjects required in the Divinity syllabus was Hebrew, of which he had learnt the elements at school. He found it irksome and passed the preliminary examination "with much effort. Later, spurred on again by the endeavour to master what did not come easily to me, I acquired a sound knowledge of that language."

But the subject which of all others most fascinated him, at the outset and increasingly, was the study of the synoptic—the first three —Gospels. In this he had the benefit of instruction from Heinrich Julius Holtzmann, whose lectures he attended with zeal and enthusiasm. Holtzmann's reputation among scholars was established by his elaboration of the theory that the second Gospel is the oldest and that its plan forms the basis for the contents of the other two. When, only a few years later, Schweitzer entered the lists with a wholly original proposition in this field of enquiry he dedicated the treatise, *The Mystery of the Kingdom of God*, to his old tutor, even though he disagreed with the conception of the life of Jesus which Holtzmann maintained; and when he enlarged upon it in his epoch-making *The Quest of the Historical Jesus* he wrote: "The ideal life of Jesus at the close of the nineteenth century is the life which Holtzmann did not write. . . . He provides the plan (the Life) and the building material (the Teaching) so that anyone can carry out the construction in his own way and on his own responsibility. The cement and the mortar are not provided by Holtzmann; everyone must decide for himself how he will combine the teaching and the life, and arrange the details within each."

In 1894 he began his year of military service and went off to manœuvres in the autumn with a Greek Testament in his haversack. It was then that he made the momentous discovery which proved the clue to the solution for him of the riddle of the Gospel narratives.

This discovery was an intuition of the significance of two chapters in the first Gospel which are not recorded in the second, and which effectually put out of court the previously entertained theory that the activities of Jesus can be understood wholly from St. Mark. He read them at first "with astonishment, sorely puzzled."

In Matthew x. the mission of the Twelve is narrated. In the discourse with which He sends them out Jesus tells them that they will almost immediately have to undergo severe persecution. But they suffer nothing of the kind.

He tells them also that the appearance of the Son of Man will take place before they have gone through the cities of Israel, which can only mean that the celestial, Messianic Kingdom will be revealed while they are thus engaged. He has, therefore, no expectation of seeing them return.

How comes it that Jesus leads His disciples to expect events about which the remaining portion of the narrative is silent?

I was dissatisfied with Holtzmann's explanation that we are dealing not with an historical discourse of Jesus, but with one made up at a later period, after His death, out of various "Sayings of Jesus." A later generation would never have gone so far as to put into His mouth words which were belied by the subsequent course of events.

But this was not the only conundrum.

Matthew xi. records the Baptist's question to Jesus, and the answer which Jesus sent back to him. Here too it seemed to me that Holtzmann and the commentators in general do not sufficiently appreciate the riddles of the text. Whom does the Baptist mean when he asks Jesus whether He is the "one who is to come"? Is it then quite certain, I asked myself, that by the Coming One no one can be meant except the Messiah? According to late-Jewish Messianic beliefs the coming of the Messiah is to be preceded by that of his Fore-runner, Elijah, risen from the dead, and to this previously-expected Elijah Jesus applies the expression the Coming One, when He tells the disciples that the Baptist himself is Elijah who is to come. Therefore, so I concluded, the Baptist in his question used the expression with that same meaning.

But why does Jesus not give him a plain answer to his question? To say that He gave the evasive answer He did give in order to test the Baptist's faith is only an outcome of the embarrassment of commentators, and has opened the way for many bad sermons. It is much simpler to assume that Jesus avoided saying either Yes or No because He was not yet ready to make public whom He believed Himself to be.

I was also driven into new paths of interpretation by Jesus' saying to the disciples after the departure of the Baptist's messengers, that of all born of women John was the greatest, but that the least in the Kingdom of Heaven was greater than he.[1]

"When I reached home after the manœuvres entirely new horizons had opened themselves to me."

He now began to occupy himself, "often to the neglect of other subjects," with independent research into the problems connected with the historical life of Jesus, "coming more and more confidently to the conviction that the key to the puzzles that are awaiting solution is to be looked for in the explanation of the words of Jesus when He sent out the disciples on their mission; in the question sent by the Baptist from his prison; and, further, in the way Jesus acts on the return of the disciples."

The investigation was given a welcome impetus for him when at the end of his fourth year the subject set for the preliminary thesis in theology was "Schleiermacher's teaching about the Last Supper compared with conceptions of it embodied in the New Testament and the Confessions of faith drawn up by the Reformers." Schleiermacher had drawn attention to the fact that, according to the accounts of the Last Supper as recorded by the first two evangelists, Jesus did not charge His disciples to repeat it; therefore the repetition of the festal meal in the primitive community, and thereafter perpetuated in the Church, must have been derived from the disciples only, and not from Jesus Himself. This set Schweitzer thinking hard. Schleiermacher had not pursued the historical significance of his own conclusions. What were its implications for a true understanding of the life of the historical Jesus?

If, I said to myself, the command to repeat the meal is absent from the two oldest Gospels, that means that the disciples did in fact repeat it, with the body of believers, on their own initiative and authority. That, however, they could only do if there was something in the essence of this last meal which made it significant apart from the words and actions of Jesus. But, since no explanation of the Last Supper which has been current hitherto makes it intelligible how it could be so adopted in the primitive community

[1] *My Life and Thought*, pp. 18-19.

without a command from Jesus to that effect, they all alike, so I had to conclude, leave the problem unsolved. Hence I went on to investigate the question whether the significance which the meal had for Jesus and His disciples was not connected with the expectation of the Messianic feast to be celebrated in the Kingdom of God, which was to appear almost immediately.[1]

Meanwhile he was pursuing his acquaintance with Philosophy with an ardour second only to his study of the Gospels. The tutorial instruction which he received in Plato and Aristotle he regards as the finest among his memories of his student days. And indeed his later work on the Ethics of Civilization shows how much he was indebted to Greek philosophy. But the dissertation which he chose for the degree of Doctor of Philosophy was the Religious Philosophy of Kant. It was suggested to him by one of his tutors, Ziegler (who had himself renounced dogmatic theology for ethics and the philosophy of religion), "in a conversation on the steps of the University under the shelter of his umbrella"; and it strongly attracted him.

The works of Kant, as is well known, are prolix and in many respects obscure, because his thought is not clearly systematized at least in its presentation, whilst the literature upon his philosophy is enormous. It is characteristic of Schweitzer that, finding access to the literature on Kant hampered by the regulations of the National Library in Paris, he decided to ignore it entirely "and to see what results I could get by burying myself in the Kantian writings themselves." It is a task which few would have the intellectual courage and independence to tackle unaided, but one which by its very originality brought him fresh discoveries. It affords too a striking example of the keenness of his critical acumen; his unerring instinct for essentials; his capacity to grasp and comprehend a subject in its entirety, and discrimination in weighing the possible significance of every slightest detail; the penetration and discernment that make his final judgment on any matter so impressive and convincing. He first detected in Kant an ambiguity in the use of terms ("intelligible" and "super-sensible"), and thereupon tracked through the whole series of his works to ascertain in what sense each is used. This enabled him to establish the discovery that there is embedded in Kant's first major work on metaphysics a large section of an earlier work, religio-philosophical in character, which is out of harmony both in thought

[1] *Ibid.* pp. 25-26.

and diction with the former, the removal of which from the main text would go far towards clearing up the apparent obscurity. He next discovers that the implications of this religio-philosophical insertion were never worked out, having no correspondence with the ideas developed in Kant's second major work on ethics where one would naturally expect to find it. There remains therefore a dualism in Kant's philosophy which is unresolved, that namely between his critical idealism on the one hand and the religio-philosophical claims of the moral law on the other. Kant originally believed himself able to reconcile them into a unity, but his scheme for doing so proved incapable of execution because of his ever-deepening conception of the moral law over against the claims of his critical idealism. This then is the explanation of Kant's apparent inconsistency.

Nevertheless, there is no philosopher ancient or modern with whose central thought the mind of Schweitzer can be more akin, or feel in closer sympathy. Inherent in all his thought is the philosopher's insistence upon the primacy of the practical over the theoretical reason; the autonomy and integrity of the Good Will which is inviolable against any failure or miscarriage in results; his vindication of the truth that obedience, and no sort of doctrinal shibboleths whatsoever—metaphysical or theological—is the organ of spiritual understanding; that the moral law is categorically binding and also absolutely free; that obligation to obey it implies ability, and with it the compulsion of an *inner* necessity: "I ought, therefore I can. . . . I ought to make my actions in the phenomenal world conform to the autonomy of the Timeless Will."

It was partly in Strasburg where he lived in a room in the Old Fish Market formerly occupied by Goethe in his student days (a fact of which he only became aware later), but chiefly in Paris, that Schweitzer studied for his Doctorate in Philosophy. All this while, he had been as diligent in cultivating his talent for music, both in theory and technique, as in pursuing his purely academic studies. Having familiarized himself with the whole of Wagner's works except *Parsifal*, it was for the express purpose of hearing the first repetition of the *Tetralogy* at Bayreuth in 1896 that he went there, contenting himself with one meal a day to balance the cost of the journey.[1] Equally careless of his sleep, he could work all day and all

---

[1] It was on this occasion that he first saw Cosima Wagner, and eight years later, at Heidelberg, first made her acquaintance. A singular friendship then began between this *grande dame*—with the haughty distant bearing of a queen—

night without intermission except to eat. Blessed as he was with an unusually robust constitution, a sturdy frame, and immense reserves of energy, he was—for all the exacting demands his will made upon his body—a stranger to fatigue. "I worked much and hard, with unbroken concentration, but without hurry. My thesis for the Doctorate suffered in no way through the demands made on me, either by my art or by society, for my good health allowed me to be prodigal with night work. It happened sometimes that I played to Widor in the morning without having been to bed at all."

His teacher in piano-playing was Marie Jaell-Trautmann, a former pupil of Liszt. Her theory in technique was the psycho-physiology of the piano-touch, in which "the finger must be conscious—both in the depression and in the releasing of the keys—not only of the movement intended but also of the kind of tone it desires." Under her guidance he completely altered his hand.

It is to his first music-master at Mülhausen, Eugène Münch, that Schweitzer owes his earliest introduction to the music of Bach. He was then fifteen years old. Three years later, when a student at Strasburg, his acquaintance improved when Eugène's brother, Ernest Münch, initiator and conductor of the Bach concerts at St. Wilhelm's in that city, entrusted him with the organ accompaniment of the Cantatas and the Passion Music.

This appreciation at such an age of the most recondite of all musical composers is remarkable enough, but even more so is the fact that together with his veneration for John Sebastian Bach went an equal veneration for another whose genius stands at the opposite end of the pole from his, Richard Wagner. When at the age of sixteen Schweitzer first heard *Tannhäuser*—"this music overpowered me to such an extent that it was days before I was capable of giving proper attention to the lessons in school."

In his Preface to Schweitzer's *Bach*, Widor recalls that in 1893 a young Alsatian introduced himself and requested an audition at the organ. "What will you play?" asked Widor. "Bach, of course!" was the reply. For six years thereafter Schweitzer was Widor's pupil —gratuitously, and the acquaintance thus formed ripened into a friendship that lasted for life. "I have him to thank," wrote Schweitzer, "for my introduction to a number of interesting and important

and the rugged young Alsatian scholar. It grew with her interest in his views on the music of Bach, and deepened after a discussion on problems of theology. Years later Schweitzer contributed to *L'Alsace Française* (February 12, 1933) his memories of her and of Siegfried Wagner and their cultured circle.

personages in the Paris of that day. He was also concerned for my material welfare. Many a time, if he got the impression that owing to concern about the slenderness of my purse I had not allowed myself enough to eat, he took me with him after my lesson to his regular haunt . . . that I might once more at any rate eat my fill!"

But there came a day when "the scholar ran afore the master," as Widor thus relates:

> One day in 1899 when we were going through the chorale preludes, I confessed to him that a good deal in these compositions was to me enigmatic. "Bach's musical logic in the preludes and fugues," I said, "is quite simple and clear: but it becomes obscure as soon as he takes up a chorale melody. Why these sometimes almost excessively abrupt antitheses of feeling? Why does he add to a chorale melody contrapuntal motives that have often no relation to the mood of the melody? Why all these incomprehensible elements in the design and the working out of these fantasies? The more I study them, the less I understand them."—"Naturally," said my pupil, "many things in the chorales are bound to seem obscure to you for the simple reason that they are only explicable through the texts which belong to them."
>
> I showed him the movements that had puzzled me the most; he translated the poems into French for me from memory. The mysteries were all solved. During the next few afternoons we played through the whole of the chorale preludes. While Schweitzer—he was the pupil it must be remembered—explained them to me one after the other, I made the acquaintance of a Bach of whose existence I had previously had only the dimmest inkling. In a flash it became clear to me that the Cantor of St. Thomas's was much more than an incomparable contrapuntist to whom I had formerly looked up as one gazes up at a colossal statue, and that his work reveals an unparalleled desire and capacity for expressing poetic ideas and for bringing word and tone into unity.

With characteristic consideration, desiring to extenuate his tutor's lack of comprehension, Schweitzer afterwards commented upon this: "Widor did not know enough German to understand the text of the old Lutheran hymns. That is why he could not solve the riddle. But I knew those texts." The Paris Bach Society was founded in 1905 by six musicians, including Widor and Schweitzer. Its conductor, Gustave Bret, made it a stipulation that the organ-part in every concert should be entrusted to Schweitzer. He was also appointed organist for the Bach Concerts of the Orféo Català at Barcelona. These appointments incurred for him the loss of much valuable time during all the years of his medical studies, not only in journeys but in rehearsals and performances.

By the early spring of 1899 Schweitzer has finished his thesis on Kant, and his Doctorate in Philosophy was conferred in the summer —at the age of twenty-four. After such intensive reading most students would feel justified in a well-earned respite, or at least in a change of mental occupation; but Schweitzer, for whom time was a most precious gift, immediately went to Berlin to continue his studies in Philosophy, ancient and modern, and also to hear what the German professors of Theology had to say on their subject. Among the latter was the great Harnack.

> I was so overawed by his knowledge and the universality of his interests that embarrassment used to prevent me from answering his questions when he spoke to me. Later in life I received from him many friendly postcards, full of information—for the postcard was the missive which he used more than any other for his corre-spondence. Two very full ones which I received at Lambaréné about my just-published book, The Mysticism of Paul the Apostle, belong to the year 1930 and must be among the last that he ever wrote.[1]

As compared with Paris, "the world-city," Schweitzer was dis-appointed in the organs and, on the whole, with the organists in the German capital; but was very much more favourably impressed with the standard of its high thinking, plain living, social ease and simple hospitality, and happy confident temper of the Berliners of that day, as of a people sure of themselves and with faith in their destiny. His best friends there were the family of the late scholar of Hellenism, Ernst Curtius, whose home was a centre of intellectual life. It was at this house that the chance remark of a fellow-guest, during a general conversation in the summer of 1899, gave a new impetus to the trend of Schweitzer's thought. "It struck home with me," he says, "like a flash of lightning, because it put into words what I myself felt." The remark was this: "Why, we are all of us just nothing but Epigoni!"—Nothing but Epigoni, nothing but a race of after-born, nothing but the inheritors of a great past. Even as early as his first years at Strasburg University, the young Schweitzer had sensed, below the confident slogan of "the march of

[1] My Life and Thought, pp. 33-34.

progress," symptoms of a kind of pernicious anaemia which was sapping the life of western civilization, which he describes himself as "the growth of a peculiar intellectual and spiritual fatigue." It was evidenced by a decline in idealism, and a contentment with a spurious "realism." The ethical was in danger of being ousted by the expedient or the opportunist, as a norm for conduct both personal and political. The slogan *Realpolitik*, originating in Germany, was being adopted by other countries, as the watchword of short-sighted policies of nationalism; whose Governments he saw pursuing, and their peoples listlessly condoning, courses of action which were fundamentally inhumane: everywhere the sacredness and freedom of human personality was being violated. There were other symptoms too.

When about the end of the century men began to take a retrospective review of every field of human activity in order to determine and fix the value of their achievements, this was done with an optimism that seemed to me incomprehensible. It seemed to be assumed everywhere not only that we had made progress in inventions and knowledge, but also that in the intellectual and ethical spheres we lived and moved at a height which we had never before reached, and from which we should never decline. My own impression was that in our mental and spiritual life we were not only below the level of past generations, but were in many respects only living on their achievements . . . and that not a little of this heritage was beginning to melt away in our hands.[1]

For many years after this incident his mind, he tells us, was inwardly occupied with a book to which he would give the title *Wir Epigonen*, in criticism—destructive criticism—of modern civilization. Not till the outbreak of the first world war, however, when the first manifestation of its collapse was obvious to all, did he begin to commit the book to writing, since not till then was he in a position to propose a remedy for its eventual restoration.

Returning to Strasburg in the summer of 1899, his former tutors advised him to qualify as a *Privatdozent* in the Faculty of Philosophy, but he decided for the Faculty of Theology as being the more suitable for the post which he was offered as Preacher at the Church of St. Nicholas. "For to me preaching was a necessity of my being. I felt it as something wonderful that I was allowed to address a

[1] *My Life and Thought*, p. 174.

congregation every Sunday about the deepest questions in life." But —"even today I am never quite free from shyness before a large audience."

He wrote his sermons in full, revising them two or three times, and committing the outline to memory; but when in the pulpit he frequently put it from his mind and delivered his discourse extemporaneously in a different form. He also took the Children's Services and the Confirmation Classes for boys: "the activities thus allotted to me were a constant source of joy." In the evangelical churches of Alsace preparation for Confirmation is a serious matter and is continued for two years, with hourly lessons thrice a week and home work. Schweitzer's aim was to foster in his pupils a real love for the Church; a sense of the solemnity of Sunday services; and a respect for traditional doctrines, and at the same time to impress on their minds the truth of the saying that "where the spirit of the Lord is, there is liberty." And he took care to reduce the time allotted for home work to a minimum, by trying to make the lessons themselves "a time of pure refreshment for heart and spirit," and would end them by requiring the candidates to repeat after him, and so to remember, Bible sayings and verses of hymns "which they might take away to guide them throughout their lives. The aim of my teaching was to bring home to their hearts and thoughts the great truths of the Gospel, in such a way that in later life they might be able to resist the temptations to irreligion that would assail them." In after years he was often encouraged by the thanks he received from old pupils who had reached manhood, for having instilled into their hearts the fundamental truths of the teaching of Jesus in such a way that they had been absorbed into their minds with lasting results. His afternoon discourses to adults were also deliberately devotional in character, and very brief; so brief that certain members of the congregation complained to the "Inspector in Spiritual Matters," who was obliged to summon him for an explanation. "But when I appeared he was as much embarrassed as I was. When he asked me what he was to reply to the aggrieved members, I replied that he might say that I was only a poor Curate who stopped speaking when he found he had nothing more to say about the text.—Thereupon he dismissed me with a mild reprimand, and an admonition not to preach for less than twenty minutes."

With this congenial pastoral background to his academic life he settled down to lecture in his own university, and chose for his study "the room looking on the garden with its big trees—the room in which I had passed so many happy hours as a student—as the fittest place for the work which now lay before me."

In Strasburg, as in German universities, the Licentiate ranks as a grade higher than the Doctorate, and carries with it the distinction of a full Professorship, as the Doctorate, which is conferred *honoris causa* for a work of signal scholarship alone, does not. In French universities the opposite of this is the rule. (It was not till 1919 that Schweitzer received his first Doctorate in Theology—from the University of Zürich.) He was unselfishly resolved to get his Licentiate within a year[1] so as to leave his Goll "travelling" scholarship open for another candidate, though he would personally have preferred to "travel slowly" and to complete his studies at an English university. In the summer of 1903 he was also appointed Principal of the Theological College of St. Thomas attached to the University, a position which he had filled temporarily during a vacancy two years earlier. The appointment of so young a Principal was due to the fact that there happened to be no one else at the time with the necessary academic qualifications, and also that all the clergy of Alsace, liberal and orthodox alike, requested his nomination. It was a position for life; with roomy comfortable quarters overlooking the sunny St. Thomas Embankment, a generous stipend, complete independence, agreeable companionship, the charge of an ancient and excellent library, and the prospect of a lifetime of congenial study. Schweitzer's special task was to lecture the advanced students for their final course in the Old and New Testaments. He continued to use as his study the room which he had occupied as a student, overlooking the trees which he loved in the quiet walled-in garden.

We know, though without his telling us, that he was immensely popular with the students and with his colleagues alike. His sanity and normality, his modesty and quiet geniality, his ready sympathy, his transparent sincerity and simplicity, his tremendous vigour and vitality, his love of fun and sense of humour, his bigness of mind and of body, and the fact that a man of such erudition and artistic attainments could wear his learning so lightly—all these qualities endeared him to young and old, and the college took him to its heart. Nowhere is his own sense of the value and inner meaning of human relationships more felicitously expressed than in the concluding sections of his *Memoirs of Childhood and Youth*.

[1] He obtained his Licentiate in July 1900.

Not one of us knows what effect his life produces, and what he gives to others; that is hidden from us and must remain so, though we are often allowed to see some little fraction of it, so that we may not lose courage. The way in which this power works is a mystery.

After all, is there not much more mystery in the relations of man to man than we generally recognize? None of us can truly assert that he really knows someone else, even if he has lived with him for years. Of that which constitutes our inner life we can impart even to those most intimate with us only fragments; the whole of it we cannot give, nor would they be able to comprehend it. We wander through life together in a semi-darkness in which none of us can distinguish exactly the features of his neighbour; only from time to time, through some experience that we have of our companion, or through some remark that he passes, he stands for a moment close to us, as though illumined by a flash of lightning. Then we see him as he really is. After that we again walk on together in the darkness, perhaps for a long time, and try in vain to make out our fellow-traveller's features.

To this fact, that we are each a secret to the other, we have to reconcile ourselves. To know one another cannot mean to know everything about each other; it means to feel mutual affection and confidence, and to believe in one another. A man must not try to force his way into the personality of another. To analyze others—unless it be to help back to a sound mind someone who is in spiritual or intellectual confusion—is a rude undertaking, for there is a modesty of the soul which we must recognize, just as we do that of the body. The soul, too, has its clothing of which we must not deprive it, and no one has a right to say to another: "Because we belong to each other as we do, I have a right to know all your thoughts." Not even a mother may treat her child in that way. All demands of that sort are foolish and unwholesome. In this matter giving is the only valuable process; it is only giving that stimulates. Impart as much as you can of your spiritual being to those who are on the road with you, and accept as something precious what comes back to you from them. . . .

It was perhaps a result of my inherited reserve that from my youth up reverence for the personality of others was to me something natural and a matter of course. Since then I have become more and more confirmed in this view through seeing how much sorrow, pain, and mutual estrangement comes from people claiming the right to read the souls of others, as they might a book that belonged to them, and from wishing to know and understand where they ought to believe. We must all beware of reproaching those we love with want of confidence in us if they are not always ready to let us look into all the corners of their heart. We might almost say that the better we get to know each other, the more mystery we see in each other. Only those who respect the personality of others can be of real use to them.

I think, therefore, that no one should compel himself to show to others more of his inner life than he feels it natural to show. We can do no more than let others judge for themselves what we inwardly and really are, and do the same ourselves with them. The one essential thing is that we strive to have light in ourselves. Our strivings will be recognized by others, and when people have light in themselves, it will shine out from them. Then we get to know each other as we walk together in the darkness, without needing to pass our hands over each other's faces, or to intrude into each other's hearts.[1]

Good health, good friends, congenial work, the background of a happy home—all these advantages were his: he recognized them with profoundest gratitude, but always there was a question, knocking with unceasing insistency at the door of his mind, "What have I done to deserve this?"—and with it the answering thought, "To whom much is given of him shall much be required." The following meditation shows how the question shaped itself in his mind:

The thought that I had been granted such a specially happy youth was ever in my mind; I felt it even as something oppressive, and ever more clearly there presented itself to me the question whether this happiness was a thing that I might accept as a matter of course. Here, then, was the second great experience of my life, viz. this question about the right to happiness. As an experience it joined itself to that other one which had accompanied me from my childhood up; I mean my deep sympathy with the pain which prevails in the world around us. These two experiences slowly melted into one another, and thence came definiteness to my interpretation of life as a whole, and a decision as to the future of my own life in particular.

It became steadily clearer to me that I had not the inward right to take as a matter of course my happy youth, my good health, and my power of work. Out of the depths of my feeling of happiness there grew up gradually within me an understanding of the

[1] *Op. cit.* pp. 91-94.

saying of Jesus that we must not treat our lives as being for ourselves alone. Whoever is spared personal pain must feel himself
called to help in diminishing the pain of others. We must all carry
our share of the misery which lies upon the world. Darkly and
confusedly this thought worked in me, and sometimes it left me,
so that I breathed freely, and fancied once more that I was to
become completely the lord of my own life. But the little cloud
had risen above the horizon. I could, indeed, sometimes look away
and lose sight of it, but it was growing nevertheless; slowly but
unceasingly it grew, and at last it hid the whole sky.[1]

He awoke one fine spring morning in 1896 at his home in Günsbach during the Whitsun holidays to the song of birds and the glory
of sunshine and "to the thought that I must not accept this happiness
as a matter of course, but must give something in exchange for it."
Proceeding to think this matter out "with calm deliberation" (a
characteristic touch), he resolved that he was justified in devoting his
life to science and music till he was thirty and from that time onward
to the direct service of suffering humanity, in some form or other
which circumstances would indicate, "as man to my fellow-men."
Already he had been an active member of a student association for
visiting and relieving poor families in the city, a service which involved begging appeals from the well-to-do. "To me, being rather
shy and awkward in society, these begging-visits were a torture."

He also interested himself in the welfare of tramps and discharged
prisoners, joining forces with a pastor who was similarly alive to the
evils connected with vagrancy, and together they scoured the byways
of the city on bicycles for the purpose of relieving this distress. But
he came to the conclusion (as others have done since) that this kind
of work can only be accomplished with success if it is properly
organized, and while he was willing to volunteer his services to any
such organization that could be formed and conducted efficiently, he
nevertheless knew in his own heart that that kind of method was not
his. "I never gave up the hope of finding a sphere of activity to which
I could devote myself as an individual and as wholly free."

How this hope was eventually realized will be told in its place.
Meanwhile he went on quietly to work with his labours in preparation of the work *The Quest of the Historical Jesus*, a great part of
which consisted in working through the numerous Lives of Jesus,

[1] *Op. cit.* pp. 81-82.

summarizing them, and grouping the summaries into chapters in his
book. The task was attended by difficulties in the economy of space
in more ways than one.

After attempting in vain to do this on paper, I piled all the Lives
in one big heap in the middle of my room, picked out for each
chapter a place of its own in a corner or between the pieces of
furniture and then, after thorough consideration, heaped up the
volumes in the piles to which they belonged, pledging myself to
find room for all the books belonging to each pile, and to leave
each heap undisturbed in its own place, till the corresponding
chapter in the Sketch should be finished. And I carried out my
plan to the very end. For many a month all the people who visited
me had to thread their way across the room along paths which ran
between heaps of books. I had also to fight hard to ensure that the
tidying zeal of the trusty Württemberg widow who kept house
for me came to a halt before the piles of books.[1]

[1] *My Life and Thought*, p. 58.

CHAPTER III

ORGANS AND ORGAN-BUILDING

"WHEN in Africa he saves old negroes; when in Europe he saves old organs."—That is what his friends say of Schweitzer, and it is aptly and truly said. Indeed, it would seem an extension of his philosophy of Reverence for Life from the animate to the inanimate that he should regard the life of an old organ as valuable as that of a human organism, and regard it as a real part of his own life's mission to rescue these instruments of living sound from death. For they too are the ministrants of another kind of life. It is a task that has involved him in as much labour and worry as his medical profession, and has cost him so much time and trouble that he has sometimes wished he had never undertaken it. His reason for not having given it up in despair long ago is that "the struggle for the good organ is to me part of the struggle for truth." The organ, for Schweitzer, is nothing if it is not a sacred instrument. Every organ recital which he gives, it has been well said, is "not merely a display of brilliant technique, but an act of worship and a sacrament." It was after his first visit to Bayreuth in 1896 to hear Wagner's *Tetralogy* that Schweitzer purposely broke his journey at Stuttgart in order to test the qualities of the new organ that had been installed in one of the great concert halls there. "When I heard the harsh tone of the much-belauded instrument, and, in the Bach fugue which Lang (organist of the Stiftskirche at Stuttgart) played to me, perceived a chaos of sounds in which I could not distinguish the separate voices, my foreboding that the modern organ meant a step not forward, but backward, suddenly became a certainty."—He determined to use his spare time thenceforth in improving his acquaintance with as many organs as possible, old and new; he also discussed their merits and demerits with all the organists and organ-builders with whom he came in contact. This investigation occupied him for intervals during the next ten years. His essay on the subject was published as a pamphlet in 1906, and republished in 1927 with an Appendix on the present state of the organ-building industry.[1]

[1] *The Art of Organ-building and Organ-playing in Germany and France.*

Here, stated very briefly, are the leading points which he makes:

The old organ-builders knew, by the collective experience of generations, the best proportions and the best shapes for their pipes, and for their materials used only the best wood and the best tin. Factory-built organs lack resonance because the diameter of their pipes is too small and their walls too thin.

The old wind-chest has some technical disadvantages compared with the new, but in quality of tone it is far superior; the old was round and soft, the new is harsh and dry. "The tone of an old organ laps round the hearer like a gentle flood; that of the new rushes upon him with the roar of surf."

What the modern electrically-driven apparatus gains in volume is lost in quality. The wind is driven out at too high a pressure: "the sound now blusters boisterously out instead of issuing in a steady stream."

Either the mechanical connection of keys with pipes, or failing that, the pneumatic, is preferable to the modern cheap electric system, because the latter needs constant care in maintenance, and it is unreliable.

Modern organs contain too many pipes which imitate stringed instruments. Certainly tones which resemble the violin, 'cello or double-bass, should be allowed,—but in moderation; their quality of tone should only be hinted at and not obtruded in the combined sounds of the whole instrument. "Just as the strings are the foundation of the orchestra, so are the flutes the foundation of the organ."

The position of the organ in the church is very important. The best position, if the nave is not too long, is above the entrance opposite the chancel. If the nave is very long, then half-way along its side wall, to avoid echo. Further, "an organ standing on the ground never produces the same effect as one which delivers its sound from a height, especially if the church is full."

There are many other ways of getting the choir and organ close together than by placing the organ on the floor of the chancel. In recent times architects and organ-builders have begun to take advantage of the abolition of the distance difficulty by electric connection between keys and pipes, to split up an organ into parts which are fixed in separate places and sound simultaneously though played from a single keyboard. Effects made possible by this arrangement may impose on the crowd, but the work of an organ can be truly artistic and dignified only if the instrument is one single-sound-personality, which sends its music down to flood the nave from its natural place above its hearers.[1]

It is not by any means that Schweitzer is what is called "reactionary"; as a scientist and a doctor he hails with joy any modern invention or discovery that makes life more livable. But in all ways he has a sense of proportion, a feeling for the fitness of things; and his discrimination in respect of the fitness of organs reminds one of the gospel apothegm: "No man having tasted old wine straightway desireth new, for he saith, the old is better."

The old organs were the productions of the reverent handiwork of the old organ-builders; the new are the machine-made products of the factory. Modern technical skill can, however, be used in the service of craftsmanship; and Schweitzer regards the peak period in the industry as having occurred between 1850 and 1880 when technical invention enabled organ-builders, who were also artists, to realize the ideals of Silbermann and the other great craftsmen of the eighteenth century.

Neither is Schweitzer at all impressed by the modern craze for size. He has much the same feeling about organs as the wise and experienced master-mariner has about ships—"that we are building them nowadays too large."

The building of the so-called giant organs I consider to be a modern aberration. An organ should be only so large as the body of the church requires, and the space which is allotted to it allows. A really good organ with fifty or sixty stops, if it stands at a certain height and has open space all round it, can fill the largest church. . . . It is not so much on the number of the stops as on how they are placed that the effect of an organ depends. . . . Because they have no Choir Organ, modern instruments are incomplete, however many stops and keyboards they may have. . . .

The small organs which make up the instrument as a whole are individualities if they are allowed their special requirements as to space and sound. The speciality of the Great Organ is that its stops occupy the lower part of the main case, and have a full round tone. That of the Choir Organ is that it is an organ by itself with clear-voiced stops which sings out freely into the church under the Great Organ. That of the Swell Organ is that it is housed in the upper part of the main case, and from the highest and furthest point of

[1] *My Life and Thought*, pp. 88–91.

the instrument sends out an intensive tone which can be modified as desired.

The organ is a trinity in which these three tonal individualities make a unity. The better the special character of each organ is secured, and the better the three combine into a unity, the finer is the organ.

The old organ is incomplete because there is no Swell Organ in it, the new because it no longer has a Choir Organ. It is by a combination of the old and the new that we produce the complete organ.[1]

Schweitzer considers the organ of St. Sulpice in Paris, completed in 1862, as the finest creation that he knows, and next to it that of Notre Dame, though the latter suffered from exposure during the first Great War when the stained-glass windows of the church were removed for safety. Both were the work of Cavaillé-Col, the venerable organist and organ-builder whom he is proud to have known, and whose maxim was: "An organ sounds best when there is so much space between the pipes that a man can get round each one."

Holland is in his opinion the country where there is most appreciation of the value and beauty of old organs. Dutch organists have conscientiously refrained from sacrificing magnificence of tone to securing the abolition of technical defects. In this they set a good example to those philistines who require of an organ every possible modern arrangement for altering the stops, and the maximum number of stops at the minimum price. "With an incredible blindness they tear out the beautiful old works of their organs, instead of piously restoring them with the care they deserve, and replace them with products of the factory."

Gradually the ideas which Schweitzer put forward for reform in organ-building gained recognition; the subject was ventilated at the International Musical Society's Congress in Vienna in 1909, when members who shared his views joined him in drawing up a set of *International Regulations for Organ-Building*. But advance in the practical application of these principles has proved very slow, because "commercial interests obstruct artistic ones."

How far we are still from having the ideal organ I have had to realize again and again on my concert tours, which gave me opportunities of getting to know the organs of nearly every country in

[1] *My Life and Thought*, pp. 98-99.

SCHWEITZER AT THE ORGAN
From the painting by Johanna Engel, about 1928

BARTHOLDI'S AFRICAN NEGRO AT COLMAR

See page 54. The monument was destroyed during
the German occupation, 1940–45, but this head is preserved

THE PRESBYTERY AT GÜNSBACH

Europe. Still, the day must come when organists will demand really sound and artistic instruments, and so put organ-builders in a position to give up the turning-out of factory articles. But when will it come to pass that the idea triumphs over circumstances? . . .

To the struggle for the true organ I have sacrificed much time and much labour. Many a night have I spent over organ designs which had been sent to me for approval or revision. Many a journey have I undertaken in order to study on the spot the question of restoring or rebuilding an organ. Letters running into hundreds have I written to bishops, deans, presidents of consistories, mayors, incumbents, church committees, church elders, organ-builders, and organists to try and convince them, it may be, that they ought to restore their fine old organs instead of replacing them by new ones, or it may be to entreat them to consider the quality, not the number, of the stops, and to spend in getting the best material for the pipes the money they had ear-marked for equipping the console with such-and-such superfluous arrangements for the alteration of the stops. And how often did these many letters, these many journeys, and these many conversations prove ultimately in vain, because the people concerned decided finally for the factory organ, the specification of which looked so fine upon paper!

The hardest struggles were for the preservation of the old organs. What eloquence I had to employ to obtain the rescinding of death-sentences which had already been passed on beautiful old organs! What numbers of organists received the news, that the organs which on account of their age and their ruinous condition they prized so little were beautiful instruments and must be preserved, with incredulous laughter! What numbers were changed from friends to foes because I was the obstacle to their plan of replacing their old organ by a factory one, or was guiltily responsible for their having to cut out three or four of the stops they wanted so that the rest might be of a better quality!

Even today I have sometimes to look on helpless while I see noble old organs rebuilt and enlarged till not a scrap of their original beauty is left, just because they are not strong enough to suit present-day ideas; yes, and to see them even broken up, and replaced at heavy cost by plebeian products of the factory!

The first organ that I rescued—and what a task it was!—was Silbermann's fine instrument at St. Thomas's, Strasburg.

.   .   .   .   .   .

The work and worry that fell to my lot through the practical interest I took in organ-building made me sometimes wish that I had never troubled myself about it, but if I did not give it up, the reason is that the struggle for the good organ is to me part of the struggle for truth. And when on Sundays I think of this or that church in which a noble organ is sounding because I saved it from an ignoble one, I feel myself richly rewarded for all the time and trouble which in the course of over thirty years I have sacrificed in the interests of organ-building.[1]

So he wrote in 1931; and still he continues the struggle, against long odds.

Once when invited to preach at Zutphen in Holland on Christmas Day, which fell on a Saturday, and having arrived at the manse on the Monday of the same week, nothing was seen of him during the day-time until Christmas Eve. If asked how he had been employing himself he would no doubt have replied that he had been having a look at the organ, and yet no audible sounds had issued from the cathedral. But eventually he was discovered in the organ-loft, covered with grime and sweat, cleaning the pipes of the accumulated deposit of years. Pierre van Paassen, one of his fellow-guests, recalls that when on Christmas Day the worshippers entered the cathedral, they looked up in amazement on hearing the prelude and exclaimed: "Is that our old organ?" Van Paassen adds: "Archbishop Söderblom told me that Schweitzer did the same thing once in Upsala, but that there he worked for two months before he had the organ back to what it should have been."

His views on the merits, and otherwise, of the organs of this country are clearly expressed in an interview which he gave to a reporter of the *Manchester Guardian* on June 20, 1932, when he gave a recital in the Cathedral of that city. He began by explaining that he played only in churches, never in concert halls, partly because the organs of concert halls have by comparison with those of churches "a harsh sound," and partly because an essential requisite for organ music is "the material presence of stone." He maintains that "it is for the physical shaping of a church that the organ was made, and it is only in a church that one finds the music has its proper richness."

The old English organs are very fine indeed. They are not loud, and they are mellow. The most monumental of organs are the Dutch, but they are built in that way because many of their

[1] *My Life and Thought*, pp. 95-101.

churches are lofty and can assimilate the sound.[1] Loudness is not necessary in churches of less height, and it would be a mistake here. I think that the modern English organs are inclined to be too hard and piercing. The contrast between bass and treble is too well marked sometimes, but I have some hope that English organ-builders will soon begin to modify those distinctions. I like the Cathedral organ here, except, of course, that it is new.

The real need in an organ is an instrument in which the voices are well blended; an instrument whose music will flow with even balance throughout its church. [Instancing the compositions of César Franck as examples which clearly indicated this quality, he added:] One does not want one voice speaking high and another low, so much as a weaving together of sounds; nor need the organ be loud. With a loud organ one may have cause to fear echoes in a church, but one of moderate power will make no disturbing echoes.

In his *Bach* he affirms that the finest old English organs are frequently deprived of voicing their quality by their unsuitable position at one side of the chancel.

His method in practising on an untried organ is to descend from the loft at intervals, proceed to the far end of the nave, and listen critically to the effect of his stops while someone else plays. It is only during these intervals that an interviewer may be lucky enough to snatch brief moments of rapid conversation with him; and if anyone is bold enough to ask to carry the precious package containing his organ-shoes to or from the sacred edifice, the offer is courteously but firmly declined.

But indeed it is at the organ that one sees Schweitzer at his best. As Professor Kurth of Berne has written:

The impression of tremendous energy that he creates accords with his outward appearance: a tall, broad-shouldered, robust figure, to which it is easy to ascribe intellectual as well as physical heroism; it is an unforgettable sight to see this tall, powerful man approach the organ, put on his glasses, and bend lovingly over the keys of the instrument in devoted service to his great master Bach. To see him thus is to see him suddenly transformed into the simple earnest organist of bygone times.[2]

[1] The magnificent old organs at Haarlem, Amsterdam, the Hague, Rotterdam, Utrecht, Deventer, Arnheim, are those he loves best in Holland.

[2] Quoted by Oscar Kraus in *Albert Schweitzer: His Work and his Philosophy*, pp. 55-56.

And Carl Dyrssen:

The effect of the printed word, which in any case is never so powerful as the spoken one, pales and fades into insignificance in the presence of this dynamic personality whose every fibre is penetrated by all that is ineffable and sublime. The spoken word, the warm vibrant voice with all its magic power, its infinite modulations from the gentlest whisper to a veritable tempest—in short, its whole gamut of tones, which he as a master of the organ has at his command—that is Schweitzer! [1]

[1] *Loc. cit.*

CHAPTER IV

DECISION FOR SERVICE

WHEN on October 13, 1905, in Paris, as the result of many years' deliberation culminating in a hidden fixed resolve, Schweitzer was about to embark on the adventure of Christian discipleship, and acquainted his friends and kinsfolk with his decision, at the same time resigning his post as Principal of St. Thomas' College, he found himself exposed to a hurricane of expostulations. Chief among these was the reproach that he had not shown them so much confidence as to consult them about it first. It was of no use to rejoin that, in common with his hero in the field of missionary enterprise, the apostle Paul, it had not occurred to him as necessary "to confer with flesh and blood beforehand about what he would do for Jesus." One of the many specious and time-serving arguments adduced to deflect him was—that a man of his academic attainments would do much more for the cause of medical missions by lecturing on their behalf than by actually engaging in them himself. But the genuine solicitude of those nearest and dearest to him was much harder to bear. He was like a man, they told him, who was burying the talent entrusted to him and who wanted to trade with false currency.

In the verbal duels which I had to fight, as a weary opponent, with people who passed for Christians, it moved me strangely to see them so far from perceiving that the effort to serve the love preached by Jesus may sweep a man into a new course of life, although they read in the New Testament that it can do so, and found it there quite in order. I had assumed as a matter of course that familiarity with the sayings of Jesus would produce a much better appreciation of what to popular logic is non-rational, than my own case allowed me to assert. . . . In general, how much I suffered through so many people assuming the right to tear open all the doors and shutters of my inner self! [1]

When, goaded at last to do violence to this natural repugnance, he

[1] *My Life and Thought*, pp. 108-109.

was driven to appeal simply to the act of obedience enjoined by the
direct commandment of Jesus, it was to be met with the accusation
of conceitedness; or with the hint that he was disappointed in the
recognition accorded to his work; or even with the suggestion that
perhaps he had been crossed in love. Kinder than these well-meant
insinuations on the part of those who "tried to dig their fists into my
heart" was the affectionate raillery of others who opined that much
learning had made him mad, and who treated him accordingly.

Having run this gauntlet (a long double row, for he had a host of
friends), and much bruised inwardly from the experience, he had to
take stock of his interior resources. He fully appreciated the solicitude
of his relations and friends, and their anxiety to put before him anything that told against the *reasonableness* of his project. "As one who
demands that idealists shall be sober in their views, I was conscious
that every start upon an untrodden path is a venture which only in
unusual circumstances looks sensible and likely to be successful." He
felt like the man in the parable who, intending to build a tower,
sitteth down first and counteth the cost, whether he have sufficient
wherewithal to finish it. He was well aware that the next few years
of study in medicine would entail for him a tremendous effort: "I
did in truth look forward to the next few years with dread." What
were his assets?—"Good health, sound nerves, energy, practical
common sense, toughness, prudence, very few wants, and everything else that might be found necessary by anyone wandering along
the path of an idea. I believed myself, further, to wear the protective
armour of a temperament quite capable of enduring an eventual
failure of my plan."—This latter qualification, it must be remarked,
is a very rare one.

But why, he was asked, why not go simply as a missionary? Why
must he put himself to the enormous labour of qualifying in a subject
of which he had none but the slightest knowledge, and no particular
aptitude, and this too at the age of thirty?

I wanted to be a doctor that I might be able to work without
having to talk. For years I had been giving myself out in words,
and it was with joy that I had followed the calling of theological
teacher and of preacher. But this new form of activity I could not
represent to myself as talking about the religion of love, but only as
an actual putting of it into practice.[1]

[1] *My Life and Thought*, p. 114.

Besides, the appeal from Equatorial Africa had been urgent for more and more doctors. So whenever Schweitzer was tempted to feel that the years of his probation for this form of ministry were too long, he reminded himself that Hannibal had prepared for his march on Rome by the slow and tedious conquest of Spain and then by the crossing of the Alps!—How many disciples of Jesus are there, it may be wondered, who are willing to recognize that He whom they seek to follow was a Healer of the Sick as much as a Preacher of the Kingdom of Righteousness, or to remember that His last command to His disciples was this: "Preach the word, heal the sick, cast out devils. Freely ye have received, freely give"?

But why go to the length of undertaking the whole course for the degree of a Doctorate in Medicine? Why not be content with qualifying simply as a practitioner, with of course the necessary specialization in tropical diseases?—That, though he does not mention it at all, is the artist's secret: the inner compulsion to bring every work he undertakes to the utmost possible completion. In every field of knowledge that he had set his mind to—Biblical Criticism, History, Theology, Philosophy, Literature, Languages; Music, both in theory and technique; Organ-building, both in its science and its craft— Schweitzer had been a serious explorer, no mere visitor in any of those realms. There is no need to specify the particular branches which the study of each of these general subjects must involve. But it may be as well to set beside them the several branches of the science which he now set himself to master with equal thoroughness and zest. The subjects of his pre-clinical course were as follows: Anatomy, Physiology, Chemistry, Physics, Zoology, Botany. And in his clinical course these: Medicine, Surgery, Gynaecology, Psychiatry, Bacteriology, Pathological Anatomy, Pharmacology. Taken in conjunction with his former studies, it may be said that this represents a mental and moral achievement that can scarcely be paralleled. And the tale of his practical achievements as an architect and builder has yet to be told.

Schweitzer, who has never been a stranger to hard work, looks back upon this period of seven years as the most strenuous of his life. "Now began years," he tells us, "of continuous struggle with fatigue." He spent the next six years of his life as a medical student in the university which he had adorned by his learning as a Professor. Coincidently with his attendance at lectures in Medicine, he continued for the first four months to deliver lectures in Divinity. But in addition to this, he preached almost every Sunday: undertook the organ part of the Paris Bach Society's concerts each winter, as well as those of the Orféo Català in Spain, employing the time back and forth between Strasburg and Paris or Barcelona in composing his sermons; and accepted several other concert engagements in France and Germany, in order to make good the loss of his stipend as Principal of the Theological College. At the same time, too, he was writing his Essay on Organ-building, and the final chapter of his *Quest of the Historical Jesus*, and actually completed his first work on the history of Pauline doctrine, *Paul and his Interpreters*, during his first few years as a medical student.—As a feat of sheer will-power alone, there is something almost superhuman about this.

But now, having surmounted his first difficulty, the opposition of his family and friends, Schweitzer encountered another obstruction to his plan from an unexpected quarter. This was from the very Mission to which he offered his services. The Director of the Mission, Monsieur Boegner, confided to him that serious objections would be raised by certain members of the committee on the ground of the "incorrectness" of his theological position. On being assured by the young volunteer that he wanted to help "merely as a doctor" the kindly Director was personally satisfied, but later was obliged to inform him that certain members still objected "to the acceptance of a mission doctor who had only correct Christian love, and did not, in their opinion, hold also the correct Christian belief." It was agreed between the two of them, however, that seven years might be long enough for these objectors to attain a state of "truly Christian reasonableness." Moreover Schweitzer, though he well knew that another Society (the German-Swiss Evangelical Mission) would have accepted him without hesitation, either as missionary or doctor, was resolved to persist in getting a decision from the Mission through whose appeal his call had come, as to whether it, or any Missionary Society, "had the right to refuse to the suffering natives in their district the services of a doctor, because in their opinion he was not sufficiently orthodox.—But over and above all this, my daily work and daily worries, now that I was beginning my medical course, made such demands upon me, that I had neither time nor strength to concern myself about what was to happen afterwards."

He was enrolled as a medical student in the autumn of 1905, and resigned his Principalship in the spring of 1906. The thought of having to turn out of the building which had been his academic home since his student days, and the room with its windows over-looking "the trees with which I had for so many years conversed while I was working," was a sad one. But he was happily spared this wrench. For the college building included in its precincts a large official residence allotted to the President of the Lutheran Church in Alsace, Frederick Curtius [1] and his family, and there were four small unoccupied attics above it under the gables. To Schweitzer's great joy, these were now placed at his disposal. "I was thus enabled to continue living under the shadow of St. Thomas's. On the rainy Shrove Tuesday of 1906 the students carried my belongings out through one door of the house on the St. Thomas Embankment and brought them in through another." He regarded it as a piece of great good fortune, and also as a privilege to be prized, that he was given the freedom of a household in which the aristocracy of learning united with the aristocracy of birth, and of which the aged Countess of Erlach was "the spiritual centre."—"This distinguished noble-woman gradually acquired a great influence over me, and I owe it to her that I have rounded off many a hard angle in my personality." It was the Countess of Erlach too who made him promise never to go with his head uncovered in the tropics even after sundown. This promise he has faithfully kept; and often since, when he has longed for the play of the evening breeze round his head after a hot day on the equator, his denial of the wish has called to mind this early friendship, in itself a sufficient compensation.

Now at last in 1906, with the responsibilities of his Principalship and his lecturing behind him, he could devote himself without dis-traction to the science which had fascinated him from boyhood: "I was at last in a position to feel the firm ground of reality under my feet in philosophy!" In the studies in which he had been

[1] Frederick Curtius was the son of Ernst Curtius, the Hellenistic scholar (1814–1896) who, after resigning his post at Berlin University and completing his excavations in Greece, became private tutor to the Crown Prince Frederick. His son Frederick played an important part in the German administration of Alsace and so endeared himself to its inhabitants that when, in 1905, the position of head of the Lutheran Church in that province became vacant, by general request it was offered to him. He fulfilled his duties in an exemplary manner and was universally beloved. During the first Great War he was dismissed because he opposed the German Government's ban on the preaching of sermons in French, though several parishes in the Vosges valleys were entirely French-speaking. Services were always conducted in German in the majority of the parishes. Curtius desired that the freedom of French-speaking communities should be respected during the war, and in doing so was maintaining the legitimate right of the Church for which he was responsible.

immersed hitherto, even in historical criticism, he had found it "not a little depressing" that men so often made a selection of facts · subserve their preconceived theories; and that in philosophy, most notably in Hegel's Absolute Idealism, the results of abstract thinking, which can never be verified, have been raised to the pinnacle of Truth. His observations on the point are worth quoting.

> . . . But the study of the natural sciences brought me even more than the increase of knowledge I had longed for. It was to me a spiritual experience. I had all along felt it to be psychically a danger that in the so-called Humanities with which I had been concerned hitherto, there is no truth which affirms itself as self-evident, but that a mere opinion can, by the way in which it deals with the subject-matter, obtain recognition as true. . . . Now I was suddenly in another country. I was concerned with truths which embodied realities, and found myself among men who took it as a matter of course that they had to justify with facts every statement they made.[1]

Nevertheless, refreshed as he was in mind by "the delight of dealing with realities determinable with exactitude," as by the stimulus of an intellectual tonic, he did not for that reason (as others have done who have undergone the same experience) incline to undervalue the Humanities. On the contrary, he recognized that knowledge which results from a creative act of the mind is on a higher plane than knowledge which is based only on facts. But the combination of these two methods of knowing—the subjective which seeks to know pure Being, and the objective which seeks to know manifestations of Being in the realm of phenomena—laid the foundations of that whole philosophy to which he afterwards gave the name of Reverence for Life. There is more than a hint of it in these reflections.

> The knowledge that results from the recording of single manifestations of Being remains ever incomplete and unsatisfying so far as it is unable to give the final answer to the great question of what we are in the Universe, and for what purpose we exist in it. We can find our right place in the Being that envelops us only if we experience in our individual lives the universal life which wills and rules within it. The nature of the living Being without me I can understand only through the living Being which is within

---

[1] *My Life and Thought*, pp. 126-127.

me. It is to this reflective knowledge of the Universal Being and of the relation to it of the individual human being that the Humanities seek to attain. The results they reach contain truth so far as the spirit which is creatively active in this direction possesses a sense of reality, and has passed through the stage of gaining a knowledge of facts about Being to reflection about the nature of Being.[1]

The conclusions of a philosopher who is also a scientist are always worthy of respect; but when that philosopher-scientist is also one to whom the Christian ethic (though not its doctrine) is unique and a necessity for thought, his conclusions should awaken reverent curiosity in the mind of anyone who thinks.

In the spring of 1908 he entered for examination in the pre-clinical course. But, apart from the fact that the memory of a man in his mid-thirties is not that of a twenty-year-old, the conscientious scruples of the pure scholar in quest of knowledge for its own sake nearly ruined his chances in a test designed for students who are up to all the tricks. "I had stupidly got into my head the idea of studying pure science only right to the end, instead of preparing for the examination. It was only in the last few weeks that I let remonstrances from my fellow-students make me become a member of a cramming-club, so that I got to know what sort of questions, according to the records kept by the students, the professors usually set, together with the answers they preferred to hear."—But the result far surpassed his expectations, though he confesses that those last few weeks cost him "the worst crisis of fatigue that I can recall during the whole of my life."

The three years' clinical course proved less of a strain because the various subjects were more closely allied to each other. He found a special interest in the practical and theoretical instruction in pharmacy. His tutor in the theory of drugs was Schmiedeberg, an authority on the derivatives of *digitalis*, to whom, years later, he was thankfully enabled to render a good service. Another source of relief was the fact that he was under less strain financially owing to the success of the German edition of his work on Bach, and the fees which he earned from his organ recitals. In the autumn of 1911 he entered for the finals of the State Medical Examination, paying the fee for it from his remuneration as organist at the French Musical Festival held in Munich the previous month. The theme for the

[1] *Ibid.* pp. 127-128.

recital was his old friend Widor's *Symphonia Sacra*, who himself conducted the orchestra. His last examination, in surgery, took place in mid-December of the same year. When it was over, and he strode out of the hospital into the darkness of the winter evening, side by side with his examiner the surgeon Madelung—"I could not grasp the fact that the terrible strain of the medical course was now behind me. Again and again I had to assure myself that I was really awake and not dreaming. Madelung's voice seemed to come from some distant sphere when he said more than once, as we walked along together, 'It is only because you have such excellent health that you have got through a job like that.' " But excellent health is only half the story; grim determination is the other. Madelung was probably unaware of all the extra-collegiate activities of this particular candidate, as that, for instance, he had during the last year of his course in surgery undertaken with Widor to prepare a complete edition of Bach's music, with directions for rendering it; and that he had given up many precious days to visit his collaborator in Paris for the purpose. This work was to comprise five volumes to begin with, in three languages, French, German, and English; and the directions concerning the Preludes and Fugues are all from Schweitzer's pen, those for the Sonatas and Concertos from Widor's: each composition is analyzed separately and in detail. Schweitzer made one stipulation: the Master's score itself must remain untouched.

Since I am continually annoyed by being compelled, with almost every edition of musical works, to have before my eyes the fingering, the phrasing, the fortes and pianos, the crescendos and decrescendos, and not infrequently even the pedantic analyses of some editor or other, even when I entirely disagree with them, I insisted on our observing the principle which, it is to be hoped, will some day be universally acted on, that the player must have before his eyes in print, as part of Bach's or Beethoven's or Mozart's music, only what was written by the composer himself.[1]

Three further volumes containing the Choral Preludes were, so it was agreed between them, to be left over until Schweitzer's first return to Europe for future compilation from his own rough drafts to be made by him in Africa. The outbreak and aftermath of the war prevented their completion, and various circumstances subsequently

[1] *My Life and Thought*, p. 159.

conspired to their indefinite postponement. Schweitzer continued these labours during his last year at Strasburg whilst he was preparing his thesis for the medical Doctorate; simultaneously with practical work in the hospitals, specializing in the study of tropical diseases and their cure, and collecting funds for his mission. The subject which he submitted and which was accepted was an unusual one. His published work on the Synoptic Problem had already contributed towards exploding the theory of the "Christ-myth"—that Jesus as a historical person never existed—by proving the two oldest records of His life to be genuine historical documents. Now he set himself to demolish on scientific grounds the argument that Jesus, in His Messianic consciousness, was the victim of the psychic disturbance known as *paranoia*. He found little difficulty in disposing of this theory, but, in order to do so thoroughly, he immersed himself in the study of psychology in general and of "the boundless problem of *paranoia*" in particular, "and thus a treatise of forty-six pages took over a year to write." [1]

On June 18th of 1912 he married Helene Bresslau, daughter of the Strasburg historian.[2] She had already been a valuable collaborator with him in his literary work, and was to prove still more so in his medical labours, since she had been trained as a nurse. With her help he now began to put together all the impedimenta required for his hospital and for housekeeping in the jungle swamps. The mass of detail inseparable from such an undertaking was irksome to a scholar's temperament at first, but he schooled himself to it with such a right good will that in course of time it became a pleasure.

> This, too, was an experience for me. Till then I had been engaged only in intellectual work. But now I had to make out from catalogues lists of things to be ordered, go shopping for days on end, stand about in the shops and seek out what I wanted, check accounts and delivery notes, fill packing-cases, prepare accurate lists for the custom-house examinations, and occupy myself with other similar jobs. . . .
>
> At first I felt occupation with such things to be something of a

---

[1] For a good short summary of his thesis see Professor J. D. Regester, *Albert Schweitzer*, pp. 68-72.

[2] Harry Bresslau (so named because he was from Hanover, where English traditions were maintained) began his university career in Berlin, and was afterwards called to Strasburg. He was a specialist in the history of the Middle Ages. He devoted the last years of his life to his *Monumenta Germaniae Historica*—a collection of the sources and documents for the history of the German Empire in the Middle Ages—which is a recognized classic on the subject.

burden. Gradually, however, I came to the conclusion that even the practical struggle with material affairs is worthy of being carried on in a spirit of self-devotion. Today I have advanced so far that the neat setting-out of a list of things to be ordered gives me artistic satisfaction.

The annoyance, which I do feel again and again, is only at the fact that so many catalogues, including those of chemists, are arranged as unclearly and unpractically as if the firm in question had entrusted the compilation to the porter's wife.[1]

When all his preparations were complete, and he was financially in a position to equip a small hospital, he made a definite offer to the Paris Missionary Society to serve at his own expense in its Mission on the Ogowe River. Apart from his own resources, derived from his organ recitals and work on Bach, financial help for his mission came in good measure from his congregation at St. Nicholas's and from other Alsatian parishes, as well as from the entire proceeds of a concert given by the Paris Bach Society on its behalf. But what moved him even more deeply was the fact that the German professors at Strasburg gave so generously to an enterprise to be founded in a French colony, because it accorded so well with his own conviction that no national or denominational barriers should stand in the way of the simple promulgation of the gospel of Jesus.

Monsieur Boegner had meanwhile been succeeded as Superintendent of Missions by Monsieur Bianquis, who fully concurred with the former's views and strongly represented to the Society its duty to accept this offer of the gratuitous services of a Mission doctor who was so urgently needed. But still the recalcitrant objectors continued to object. It was therefore resolved to invite Schweitzer to attend the committee and to conduct an examination into his beliefs. But this he declined to do, on the ground that Jesus required of His disciples no doctrinal test but only the will to follow Him. He added that a Missionary Society would be in the wrong if it rejected even a Mohammedan who offered his services for the treatment of their suffering natives! He suggested that instead of an official interview he would personally visit each member of the committee, "so that conversation with me might enable them to judge clearly whether my acceptance really meant such terrible danger to the souls of the negroes and to the Society's reputation."

[1] *My Life and Thought*, pp. 135-136.

My proposal was accepted and cost me several afternoons. A few of the members gave me a chilly reception. The majority assured me that my theological standpoint made them hesitate for two chief reasons: I might be tempted to confuse the missionaries out there with my learning, and I might wish to be active again as a preacher. By my assurance that I only wanted to be a doctor, and that as to everything else I would be *muet comme une carpe* ("as mute as a fish"), their fears were dispelled, and these visits actually brought me into quite cordial relations with a number of the Committee members.[1]

Schweitzer's offer was thus gratefully accepted on his own terms, though indeed one member sent in his resignation as a result of it; the committee agreed to place at his disposal one of their houses at the Lambaréné Mission Station, and to allow him to build his hospital there, with promise of help in the way of necessary labour. He on his part undertook to defray the expenses of founding, equipping, and maintaining the hospital, as well as all his own. The committee gave him a free hand, their only stipulation being that he should not preach. As it transpired, however, he was soon to be relieved of even this prohibition, by the general request of his fellow-missionaries a few months after his arrival among them.

The theological fence having been thus surmounted there remained one other to negotiate, the national. Though a German subject, Schweitzer was enlisting his services in association with a French Mission, because it is his settled conviction—and this he made clear—that "the humanitarian work to be done in the world should, for its accomplishment, call upon us as men, not as members of any particular nation or religious body." Now he had to obtain permission from the Colonial Department to practise medicine in a French colony, holding only a German diploma. Influential friends in both countries came to his rescue, and the difficulty was removed. "At last the road was clear!"

To the majority, the most serious loss that exile entails, whether it be voluntary or due to the exigencies of their profession, is lack of the material amenities of life, the social intercourse, the gentle recreations of civilization. But there is frequently compensation to be found for these in another set of similar or novel interests. It is seldom that a man finds himself quite cut off from association with

[1] *Ibid.* pp. 138-139.

his kind or at least from the opportunity of renewing it from time to time. Or if he does so, it is usually for him a matter of choice: he prefers his own company.

In trying to assess the nature and extent of Schweitzer's decision one must set his temperament and attainments against his environment on the edge of the primaeval forest. Although he has that passion for learning which is the scholar's pure delight and can cheerfully immerse himself in books for days together, he is by no means a recluse. His human sympathies are keen, and in Europe he had a host of friends, gentle and simple, to whom he was devoted and they to him. Further, he is by every instinct of his temperament and mental training cosmopolitan, and though the trend of European civilization towards its decay had, it is true, for years depressed him, he had loved to live in the exciting march of events, of which not least was the march of scientific discovery and mechanical invention. He might have chosen another country, such as India or China, where at least there is a native culture, an intellectual and religious tradition, and a background of history—all, centuries old. His omnivorous reading has in fact made him almost as familiar with the religious philosophies of Asia as of Europe. But with the primitive negro there is no culture, no tradition beyond an uninspired and uninspiring folk-lore, no history beyond the memory of their grandfathers. Or he might at least have chosen a healthier climate for the field of his labours, instead of one which is by common consent among the unhealthiest in the world.

The "choice" of a non-historical background for his labours has in fact been assumed, by two able and sympathetic commentators on Schweitzer's life and thought, to have been deliberate on his part. Thus, Albers writes:

It is surely symbolical that Schweitzer did not stay in Europe, where there is indeed enough misery to alleviate, but chose the African forest for his labours. It was the lack of a historical past, the primitiveness of Africa, that appealed more to his new intellectual phase than the super-historical background, the over-sophisticated, age-old atmosphere of Europe.

And Dyrssen:

The fundamental significance of Schweitzer's action lies in the fact that he turned his back on Europe after having shown her the tragic state of her civilization. Knowledge is nothing, and deeds can only bear fruit and bring about a transformation, if they are inspired by sacrifice,—a transformation which will give birth to a new and better reality.[1]

There is deep truth in these observations; and yet the point which they make was not the point that impelled Schweitzer in his "choice" of Africa. For the choice was not his; it was made for him, simply by an appeal for help. Like a man who feels himself to be bound under "holy orders," and that in no meretricious conventional sense but in stern and sober earnest, he was not disobedient unto the heavenly vision, but went out not knowing, or not caring, whither. He had no interest whatever in the African jungle swamps, or even in the negro as such; he only knew that there were primitive people there, his brother-men, suffering and dying of diseases caused by the neglect, and worse than the neglect, of white men who were also his brothers. It was this thought, when he deliberated the matter from every point of view, which weighed so heavily in his mind and on his conscience that "other considerations were as dust in the balance."

His departure was called a breach with civilization, a flight from reality. But the contrary was true.

He did not formulate his plans. He did not say that he wanted to save souls or to bring joy and relief into the lives of the most under-privileged of human beings. He went away silently. But in his mind was the feeling that he went to do his part in atoning for the western world's treatment of the natives of the most ruthlessly exploited continent in the world. . . .

In that sense Schweitzer's work should be evaluated: as that of a silent protective spirit who goes his way unobserved, whether he is misunderstood or not. Compassion and a profound feeling of responsibility for the harrowing condition of the peoples of Africa, drove him to abandon his position in Europe and to take up the cause of "the Brotherhood of those who are marked by suffering."

The right of the western nations to dominate peoples who stand on a lower cultural level is accepted by Schweitzer, but only on condition that there is a serious intention to educate those peoples morally and materially. For Schweitzer, missionary endeavour depends neither on dogma nor doctrine, but on the simple Gospel

[1] Quoted by Oscar Kraus in *Albert Schweitzer: His Work and his Philosophy*, pp. 28 and 66.

that teaches the liberation of the world through the Spirit of Jesus, as it went out to man in the Sermon on the Mount. . . .

There is no sentimental piety in Albert Schweitzer, no fanaticism with rigorist demands. He goes his way calmly, is full of humour, has an extraordinary sense of adaptation, but also a mysterious shyness. In everything he undertakes he is animated by an incredible gentleness, and an all-embracing sense of responsibility.

Respect for life! Respect for all that breathes! In this idea Schweitzer sees the real solution of the question of the relationship of man to the world. He is the missionary who has understood the true object of missionary endeavour—to bring light to those who sit in darkness, and to redeem oneself by expiating the sins of Christendom.[1]

This comes nearer the truth. Africa, for Schweitzer, is not an escape from life, nor is it even the goal of his life; it is the symbol of his life. His departure from Europe was not actuated by any intention to set an example, it was not a "gesture"; it was inspired by the motive of an inner compulsion to satisfy his own personal sense of what life demands from him, and of how he ought to live it. "He went away silently." If his example should result in inducing any others to take a similar step—a thing greatly to be desired indeed, for the need is great—that were a great gain, but their affair, not his. His own decision was made in response to the demand which allegiance to the command of Jesus upon His true disciples involves, as being but one among the many tasks which He sets us to fulfil for our time. It was also a sane and reasonable decision to make because it is the repayment of a debt, which is a debt of honour. In his eyes, there is nothing at all heroic about it; it is a simple matter of duty, and so a matter of course. And having been made deliberately it must never be relinquished. It is like a marriage bond. That is why Schweitzer has steadfastly resisted suggestions that have since been made to him from other quarters, as—that he should return to Europe to help in arresting the decay which he foresaw, as soon as it became apparent to everyone else; or exercise his talents in the same way in the Far East: no, he has given his life to Africa; there is his task, and there at his self-appointed post he must remain. Without irony but in sober earnest it may be said, that so far from turning his back on civilization he has gone into the wilderness to find it.

[1] Pierre van Paassen on Albert Schweitzer in *That Day Alone*, pp. 223-227.

Africa is the symbol of his life. All art is symbolism; it is "a kind of speaking in parables"; it points to a meaning beyond itself. Africa is the symbol; the meaning is Reverence for Life. An artist in every-thing, Schweitzer is *par excellence* an artist of living. Just as each one of the scholarly treatises that he has written is itself a work of art, so is the hospital which he founded and built and which is the sym-bolic representation of his whole soul, the work of an artist too. For it is the ideal of an artist to bring all his work to the fullest possible perfection. So it is the ideal of the ethical man who, in an honest and good heart, has received the word of life, to bring forth fruit to perfection, with patience.

What is the nature of the sacrifice involved for him? It is not the deprivation of "civilized amenities" nor of cultural interests, nor of the stimulus of social intercourse nor of friendly fellowship, nor of the exchange of ideas with kindred minds, nor of all access to libraries or to organs,—it is none of these things that he himself counts as loss. It is something quite different, and almost startling in its simplicity.

Not to preach any more, not to lecture any more, was for me a great sacrifice, and till I left for Africa I avoided, as far as pos-sible, going past either St. Nicholas' or the University, because the very sight of the places where I had carried on work which I could never resume was too painful for me. Even today I cannot bear to look at the windows of the second lecture-room to the east of the entrance of the great University building, because it was there that I most often lectured.[1]

Often since then, he tells us that as a man of individual action he has been approached by people wishing to embark on a similar venture, but has only rarely felt justified in giving them immediate encouragement. Too often he has had to recognize that the impulse "to do something special" was born of a restless (perhaps one might add—a romantic) spirit; that is, of a spirit that does not appreciate the worth-whileness of its own immediate duty. With memorable words he sums up his conclusions on this point.

Only a person who can find a value in every sort of activity and devote himself to each one with full consciousness of duty, has the inward right to take as his object some extraordinary activity instead of that which falls naturally to his lot. Only a

[1] *My Life and Thought*, p. 134.

person who feels his preference to be a matter of course, not something out of the ordinary, and who has no thought of heroism, but just recognizes a duty undertaken with sober enthusiasm, is capable of becoming a spiritual adventurer such as the world needs. There are no heroes of action: only heroes of renunciation and suffering. Of such there are plenty. But few of them are known, and even these not to the crowd, but to the few.[1]

Of those who would prove fitted both by character and capacity to devote their lives to independent personal activity, he is obliged to recognize that the majority are compelled by circumstances to forego it. It may be that they have a responsibility to dependents, or are constitutionally unfitted for the physical strain, or in the stress of modern economic conditions must labour to get their own living. His own case he regards with thankfulness as one that falls to the lot only of the privileged few, and adds, "Those who are so favoured as to be able to embark on a course of free personal activity should accept this good fortune in a spirit of humility."

Of all the will for the ideal which exists in mankind only a small part can be manifested in action. All the rest is destined to realize itself in unseen effects, which represent, however, a value exceeding a thousandfold and more the effects of the activity which attract the notice of the world. . . .

Yet no one finds himself in the position of having no possible opportunity of giving himself to others as a human being. . . . Anyone can rescue his human life, in spite of his professional life, who seizes every opportunity of being a man by personal action, however unpretending, for the good of fellow-men who need the help of a fellow-man. Such a man enlists in the service of the spiritual and good. . . .

Judging by what I have learnt of men and women, I am convinced that there is far more in them of idealist will-power than ever comes to the surface of the world. Just as the water of the streams we see is small in proportion to that which flows underground, so the idealism which becomes visible is small in proportion to what men and women bear locked in their hearts, unreleased or scarcely released. To unbind what is bound, to bring the underground waters to the surface; mankind is waiting and longing for such as can do that.[2]

---

[1] *My Life and Thought*, pp. 110-111.   [2] *Ibid.* pp. 112-114.

CHAPTER V

LAMBARÉNÉ: FIRST PERIOD

". . . To become a spiritual adventurer such as the world needs."—
It is the characteristic of every true explorer, whether in the sphere
of geographical discovery, or of science or art, or of spiritual experience, that he is driven by the Spirit into the wilderness of the
unknown. Those who wonder why such men should deliberately
prefer discomfort to security, and hardships to the comforts of a
home, cannot understand—and therefore will hardly realize—ideals.
They say, it is not common sense. But there are higher things than
common sense. Nothing great has ever been achieved merely by
common sense: this has always required the exercise of a sense which
is uncommon. And that uncommon sense is motivated by what is
called inspiration, the quest of an ideal, the sense of the supremacy of
spiritual over material values.

The stimulus which drove Schweitzer out of the cool, sequestered
vale of life into the heat and dust of the arena, which impelled him to
abandon further prospects of a brilliant career in science and music
and letters in order, as he put it to himself, "to try and live in the
spirit of Jesus," may well strike the reader as a strange one; yet it
demonstrates how deeply the recorded sayings—even the "hard
sayings"—of the historical Jesus had woven themselves in the very
fibres of his being. It is the parable of Dives and Lazarus. He saw
himself—as one among a myriad heirs of all the ages, representative
of centuries of civilization and culture—as Dives; he saw his brother-
man, the primitive negro—victim of want and woe, diseased and
neglected, too often exploited and oppressed—as the poor man at
his gate. Among so many ills in the world that call for curing, so
many wrongs that call for redressing, he saw herein the need for a
simple and immediate duty: as a white man to atone, if only in an
infinitesimal degree, for all the wrongs that white men have inflicted
on the black.

I had read about the physical miseries of the natives in the virgin
forests; I had heard about them from missionaries; and the more I

thought about it the stranger it seemed to me that we Europeans trouble ourselves so little about the great humanitarian task that offers itself to us in far-off lands. The parable of Dives and Lazarus seemed to me to have been spoken directly of us! We are Dives, for, through the advances of medical science, we now know a great deal about disease and pain, and have innumerable means of fighting them: yet we take as a matter of course the incalculable advantages which this new wealth gives us! Out there in the colonies, however, sits wretched Lazarus, the coloured folk, who suffers from illness and pain just as much as we do, nay, much more, and has absolutely no means of fighting them. And just as Dives sinned against the poor man at his gate, because for want of thought he never put himself in his place and let his heart and conscience tell him what he ought to do, so do we sin against the poor man at our gate.[1]

Not far distant from his native Günsbach, in the Champ de Mars at Colmar, stands the great sculptor Bartholdi's [2] statue of Admiral Bruat. At the foot of the statue rests the figure of an African negro, whose wistful expression embodies the very soul of the perpetual suffering of his race. It is this look of haunted sadness that first startled Schweitzer as a boy, and which has never ceased to haunt his mind. On every visit to his homeland, fresh from the scene of his life's work for the African, he goes again to Colmar and gazes at it.

In moving words in the conclusion of his book *On the Edge of the Primeval Forest*, he exclaims against the long series of injustices and cruelties that the coloured races of mankind have suffered at the hands of Europeans—the "primitive" at the hands of the "civilized"—and concludes:

Ever since the world's far-off lands were discovered, what has been the conduct of the white peoples to the coloured ones? What is the meaning of the simple fact that this and that people has died out, that others are dying out, and that the condition of others is getting worse and worse as a result of their discovery by men who professed to be followers of Jesus? Who can describe the injustice and the cruelties that in the course of centuries they have suffered at the hands of Europeans? Who can measure the misery produced among them by the fiery drinks and the hideous diseases that we have taken to them? If a record could be compiled of all that has

---

[1] *On the Edge of the Primeval Forest*, pp. 1-2.
[2] Designer of the Statue of Liberty in New York Harbour.

THE HOSPITAL AT LAMBARÉNÉ, 1913

IN THE SURGICAL WARD, LAMBARÉNÉ

happened between the white and the coloured races, it would make
a book containing numbers of pages, referring to recent as well as
to early times, which the reader would have to turn over unread,
because their contents would be too horrible. We and our civilization are burdened, really, with a great debt. We are not free to
confer benefits on these men, or not, as we please; it is our duty.
Anything we give them is not benevolence but atonement. For
every one who scattered injury someone ought to go out to take
help, and when we have done all that is in our power, we shall not
have atoned for the thousandth part of our guilt.[1]

Schweitzer and his wife left Günsbach on the Good Friday of 1913;
broke journey at Paris to keep Easter Day and to listen to Widor's
organ music in St. Sulpice's Church; and on March 26th embarked at
Bordeaux. The political atmosphere of Europe was showing ominous
signs of sultriness even then, and Schweitzer sensed the brewing of a
thunderstorm. In France and Germany gold was being withdrawn
from currency, and foreseeing the probability of an embargo on
bank credits later on, he had taken the precaution to possess himself
of gold instead of paper money. On April 14th they anchored in the
roadstead of Port Gentil at the mouth of the Ogowe and trans-
shipped on to the river-boat for Lambaréné. From this point the tale
of their African travel-journey begins.

His first sight of the scene of his future labours is thus vividly
described.

River and forest!—Who can really describe the first impression
that they make? We seemed to be dreaming! Pictures of antediluvian scenery which elsewhere had seemed to be merely the
creation of fancy are now seen in real life. It is impossible to say
where the river ends and the land begins, for a mighty network of
roots, clothed with bright-flowering creepers, projects right into
the water. Clumps of palms and palm-trees, ordinary trees spreading out widely with green boughs and huge leaves, single trees of
the pine family shooting up to a towering height in between them,
wide fields of papyrus clumps as tall as a man, with big fan-like
leaves, and amid all this luxuriant greenery the rotting stems of
dead giants shooting up to heaven.—In every gap in the forest a
water mirror meets the eye; at every bend in the river a new
tributary shows itself. . . .

So it goes on hour by hour. Each new corner, each new bend, is
like the last. Always the same forest and the same yellow water.

[1] *Ibid.* pp. 171-172.

The impression which nature makes on us is immeasurably deepened by the constant and monotonous repetition. You shut your
eyes for an hour, and when you open them you see exactly what
you saw before. . . .[1]

On the Edge of the Primeval Forest is mainly a publication of the
half-yearly reports which Schweitzer wrote as circular letters to his
friends until the war banned them; thereafter they are supplemented
by memoranda which he made for his own use. As his publisher has
truly said: "It has become a classic of its kind because of its burning
sincerity, its understanding of the primitive mind, its humour, the
triumphs and tragedies of the adventure, and above all because the
personality of one of the most remarkable figures of modern times
is reflected so vividly in his writing."—Withal it is a simple homely
record, unadorned with picturesque phrases or any striving for effect;
its opening chapters telling of the journey, the founding of the hospital, and first impressions of African life; then, of many poignant
incidents as evidence of the extreme urgency of the work,—the plea
for more help, more medicines, more money; then, of the native
industries, especially of the timber trade, with shrewd observations
upon the economic problems, problems of colonization, and the
relations between white and black; of the equal need with medical
work for purely missionary enterprise, and of the "terrible prose" of
African life; and finally a very outcry from the heart, the more
intensely moving because of its restraint, the cry of the Fellowship of
those who bear the Mark of Pain.

Even more informative, because the product of fuller experience,
are his two books published eighteen and twenty-five years later,
More from the Primeval Forest and *From My African Notebook*. In the
latter he has much to say of his predecessors in this region, of De
Brazza and Du Chaillu, and most notably of that born adventurer
and lover of the wilds, "Trader Horn." There is one singular omission from among the names of these pioneers, however; namely,
Mary Kingsley. In a letter to the writer Dr. Schweitzer explains the
omission as due to the fact that he was limited to a short book and
devoted several pages to Trader Horn because the latter made Lambaréné his permanent headquarters. But readers of the *Travels* of this
gallant and noble-hearted Englishwoman or of her biography by
Stephen Gwynn will have been made as familiar with the Ogowe

---

[1] *On the Edge of the Primeval Forest*, pp. 22-23

River and its hinterland, with a glimpse of the Mission Station at Lambaréné as it existed fifty years ago, as if they saw with their eyes the vast ceaseless flow of the brown water, and the rapids far above; the papyrus reed-beds; the cliff-like wall of towering tree-stems with their interlacing crests; the shadowed gloom; the apparently current-less dark waters making a mirror of the forest floor; the twisted medley of bush-ropes; the little villages clinging to their island mounds; the life-in-death of vegetation; the steamy suffocating heat; the ghostly, swirling river-mists; the hippopotamuses and crocodiles; the birds and fish, reptiles and insects. Nevertheless, although the free march of her idiomatic style would be impossible to render into any other language, it seems a pity that Schweitzer has not remarked upon her first-hand observations of native life among the cannibal tribes, since in so many respects they confirm, and in one respect conflict with, his own.[1]

A disappointment awaited Schweitzer on his arrival at the Mission Station. The promised building for his hospital was not in evidence: it had not been possible to recruit the labour. Not to be outdone by any frustration, and anxious only to begin work without delay, he utilized a windowless broken-roofed fowl-house for his surgery, his bungalow for his dispensary, and the open sun-smitten courtyard for the treatment of his patients till the regular evening shower drove them for cover to his verandah. (It was necessary to secure his own living-quarters from the risk of infection as far as was humanly possible.) From the very first he was besieged with patients who came to him upstream and downstream from distances of anything upwards of a hundred miles, even up to two hundred. These conditions caused him needless fatigue and acute anxiety, since they involved the loss of much precious time; but to his intense relief a rain-proof building roofed with palm leaves by the riverside became available in the autumn, the premises of which were gradually extended by the erection of several bamboo huts.

[1] Although the present writer yields to no one in his admiration for Charles Kingsley's niece—as a traveller, a descriptive writer, a champion of justice, and (more than all) as a human being—he would have thought that the evils of the drink trade among native races were too apparent to be a matter for argument. No doubt in the exuberance of her zest for life, out of sheer high spirits she said some things in fun provocatively; and other things with vehemence, in defence of righteous principles; yet in this particular matter there is no doubt that she was serious, and her gay retort to opponents, "I've seen worse in Whitechapel!" does not dispose of it, since she brings well-considered reasons to support her contention.

From the very first he was working against time. In his first nine months he treated nearly two thousand patients. Malaria, leprosy, sleeping sickness, dysentery, tropical ulcers, elephantiasis,—these were the commonest plagues; but hernia, pneumonia, and heart disease were also common; and during this period he found every European disease represented, with the exception of cancer and appendicitis. Worst of all were the various unmentionable diseases, "each one more loathsome than the last, which have been brought to these children of nature by Europeans, at which I can only hint. . . . Thus I had during the very first weeks full opportunity for establishing the fact that physical misery among the natives is not less but even greater than I had supposed. How glad I was that in defiance of all objections I had carried out my plan of going out there as a doctor!"

At once he issued verbally his list of Doctor's Standing Orders— which he called his "Six Commandments." They may be briefly summarized as follows: (1) Don't spit. (2) Don't talk loudly. (3) Bring enough food for the day. (4) Don't stay the night without leave. (5) Return tins and bottles. (6) Bring only urgent cases in the middle of the month.

The last commandment was rendered necessary by the arrival of the mail-boat and the fact that the Doctor was then busy "sending home for more of his valuable medicines." The fifth was the most difficult to keep. Paper and cardboard packings soon disintegrate in the humid air of the river; and the supply of tins and bottles soon diminish by the fact that natives are apt to treasure them more than their contents. Ointments for treatment of the skin are frequently eaten, and powders intended to be swallowed are frequently used by them for application to their skins!

These commandments were daily proclaimed in stentorian tones by Joseph, one of his first patients, who was soon promoted to the rank of interpreter, cook, and surgical assistant. His French was excellent, but since he had acquired his knowledge of anatomy from the practice of the culinary art, his use of terms in reporting cases for treatment was peculiar: "This man's right leg-of-mutton hurts him," or "This woman has a pain in her upper-left-cutlet!"

Schweitzer gives each patient an identification disk for the record of his name, complaint and previous treatment, and for reference to his own register. These they wear round their necks on a fibre string and regard as a fetich. He disapproves on principle of the maxim "something for nothing," and from the first impressed upon his patients a sense of their obligation to show some tangible evidence of their gratitude, however little, pointing out to them that with a few bananas or eggs or poultry he could feed those others whose provisions had given out. He found that the exaction of a gift has an educational value (though a quite different conception of a gift prevailed among the most primitive. On leaving the hospital cured, they would demand one from him, because he had "now become their friend"!). In this way his hospital is very largely run on lines of mutual self-help, and the gratitude of his patients or their kinsfolk is often expressed spontaneously in terms of services rendered.—"An uncle of the boy with foot-sores put in fourteen days' work for me making cupboards out of old boxes."—"A black trader offered me labour to roof my house in good time before the rains."—"Another came to see and thank me for having come out here to help the natives, and presented me with 20 francs for the medicine chest."

When he first came out to the country he was often exasperated by the natives' unreliability, dilatoriness, and laziness. But in his second year he wrote: "I can no longer talk ingenuously of the laziness of the negro after seeing fifteen of them spend some thirty-six hours in almost uninterrupted rowing in order to bring up the river to me a white man who was seriously ill. The negro, then, under certain circumstances works well, but—only so long as circumstances require it. The child of nature—here is an answer to the puzzle—is always a casual worker."

Again and again we read in these letter-diaries: "The need out here is terrible"; again and again the words: "Their pain is dreadful." The burden of their universal suffering is borne out by the testimony of the natives who come to him. One says: "Here among us everyone is ill"; and another (an old chief), "Our country devours its children." Despite the patience and serenity to which this man of iron will has schooled himself, his sensitivity for the suffering of others is such that it wrings him to the heart, so that he can never get used to it.

The actual work, heavy as it was, I found lighter than the care and responsibility which came with it. I belong unfortunately to the number of those medical men who have not the robust temperament which is desirable in that calling, and so are consumed with unceasing anxiety about the condition of their severe cases and of those on whom they have operated. In vain have I tried to

train myself to that equanimity which makes it possible for a
doctor, in spite of all his sympathy with the sufferings of his
patients, to husband, as is desirable, his. spiritual and nervous
energy.[1]

One of the most terrible afflictions with which he has to deal is
strangulated hernia.

There are few negroes who have not as boys seen some man
rolling in the sand of his hut and howling with agony till death
came to release him. . . . How can I describe my feelings when a
poor fellow is brought to me in this condition? I am the only
person within hundreds of miles who can help him. . . . This does
not mean merely that I can save his life. We must all die. But that
I can save him from days of turture, that is what I feel as my great
and ever new privilege. Pain is a more terrible lord of mankind
than even death himself.[2]

The brain of the man who a few years earlier had astonished
philosophers with his insight into the mind of Kant, and the world
of music by his brilliant interpretation of the soul of Bach, and had
startled the world of biblical scholarship by the radical result of his
quest for the historical Jesus,—behold him now, in a shed by a riverside in Equatorial Africa, holding, with a comrade's grip, the hand
of a primitive negro whom his surgical skill has just rescued from an
agonizing death.

When the poor moaning creature comes, I lay my hand on his
forehead and say to him, "Don't be afraid. In an hour's time you
shall be put to sleep, and when you awake you won't feel any more
pain." Very soon he is given an injection of omnipon; the doctor's
wife is called to the hospital, and with the help of Joseph, my negro
servant, she makes everything ready for the operation. When this
is to begin she administers the anaesthetic, and Joseph, in a pair of
long rubber gloves, acts as assistant.

The operation is finished, and in the hardly lighted dormitory
I watch for the man's awaking. Scarcely has he recovered consciousness when he stares about him and ejaculates again and
again, "I've no more pain! I've no more pain!" His hand feels for
mine and will not let it go. Then I begin to tell him and the others

[1] *My Life and Thought*, p. 166.
[2] *On the Edge of the Primeval Forest*, pp. 92-93.

in the room that it is the Lord Jesus who has told the doctor and
his wife to come to the Ogowe, and that white people in Europe
give them money to live here and cure the sick negroes. The
African sun is shining through the coffee bushes into the dark shed;
but we, black and white, sit side by side and feel that we know by
experience the meaning of the words, "And all ye are brethren." [1]

Another of the afflictions which he has to contend with are cases
of mental disorder. In these cases, the custom is for relatives to tie
the afflicted person hand and foot, and, if these measures do not
suffice to allay his screams and struggles, to cast him bound into
the river.

My first contact with a mentally-diseased native happened at
night. I was knocked up and taken to a palm-tree to which an
elderly woman was bound. Around the fire in front of her sat the
whole of her family, and behind them was the black forest wall.
It was a glorious African night and the shimmering glow of the
starry sky lighted up the scene. I ordered them to set her free,
which they did, but with timidity and hesitation. The woman was
no sooner free than she sprang at me in order to seize my lamp and
throw it away. The natives fled with shrieks in every direction and
would not come any nearer, even when the woman, whose hand
I had seized, sank quietly to the ground as I told her, and offered
me her arm for an injection of morphia and scopolamin. A few
moments later she followed me to a hut where, in a short time,
she went to sleep. [2]

It is natural that a man who is possessed of a more than usual fund
of sanity himself, and for whom self-consciousness is lost in his
concern for the welfare of others, should be devoid of fear: "because
fear hath torment, but perfect love casteth out fear." It is the same
with the dangerous beasts and reptiles that infest the river and its
banks, since, in a different though not less real sense, he loves them
too. The prospect of imminent capsize in a canoe from the behaviour
of a pair of angry hippopotamuses, for instance, would appear (for
all his confession of feeling somewhat "uncomfortable") to have
been for him a matter of curiosity and pleased excitement.

But the people among whom he lives are the slaves of perpetual
fear.

[1] *Ibid.* pp. 92–93.   [2] *Ibid.* pp. 46–47.

Only those who have seen this misery at close quarters will understand that it is a simple human duty to bring to these primitive peoples a new view of the world which can free them from these torturing superstitions. In this matter the greatest sceptic, did he find himself out here, would prove a real helper of mission work.[1]

It is not surprising that he is known all over the province of Gabôn as Oganga—"Medicine-Man"—or that the natives ascribe to him magical powers far beyond their own witch-doctors. That he is able to "stitch up their bellies with string" is matter enough for marvel, but what impresses them most is the fact that he has the power to put them to sleep ("make them die"), and wake them up again. As a little girl put it in a letter to one of her Sunday School correspondents in Alsace: "Since Oganga came here wonderful things have happened. First of all he kills the sick people; then he cures them; and after that he wakes them up again." He does not trade on their superstitions however; he regards it as part of his mission to put an end to fetichism, and to educate the native mind to a rational view of life.

From the first his relations with his fellow-missionaries were friendly, and became increasingly so upon improved acquaintance. His first meeting with them was on the occasion of a conference held at Samkita, several miles up the river, whither he went by canoe to put his case for the establishment of a new hospital on a better site.

> With the conference, which sat for a whole week, I was strongly impressed. I felt it inspiring to be working with men who for years had practised such renunciation in order to devote themselves to the service of the natives, and I enjoyed thoroughly the refreshing atmosphere of love and good-will. My proposal had a most friendly reception: it was decided that the iron shed and the other hospital buildings should be erected on the place I had in view, and the mission gave me £80 (4000 fr.) towards the cost.[2]

Elsewhere he records as another matter for thankfulness that, contrary to what he had been led to expect by the committee in Paris, questions of doctrine formed practically no part in the teaching of the missionaries on the spot.

---

[1] *On the Edge of the Primeval Forest*, p. 50.   [2] *Ibid.* p. 43.

If they wanted to be understood by their hearers they could do nothing beyond preaching the simple Gospel of becoming freed from the world by the spirit of Jesus. . . . That in matters of belief some of them thought more strictly than others played no part in the missionary work, which they carried on in common. As I did not make the smallest attempt to fóist any theological views upon them, they soon laid aside all mistrust of me and rejoiced, as did I also on my side, that we were united in the piety of obedience to Jesus, and in the will to simple Christian activity. . . .

I was also invited to attend as a visitor the sittings of the Synod, when the missionaries and the native preachers sat in council together. And one day, when at the request of the missionaries I had expressed my opinion on a certain point, one of the native preachers suggested that the matter was outside the Doctor's province "because he is not a theologian as we are." (!) [1]

There is an unpublished story connected with one of these conferences. The question under discussion was polygamy after conversion. The decision was nearly unanimous that monogamy must be strictly enjoined upon every baptized negro. Schweitzer, who had made himself thoroughly conversant with native law and custom and was well aware of the disastrous consequences of enforced monogamy to the whole structure of tribal life, interposed with a gentle remonstrance. Would it not be more Christian," he asked, "to allow a chief to keep all his wives than send them into the forest where they would be quite helpless?" Subsequent investigation into this complicated problem confirmed this judgment, and prompted him to discuss it in greater detail in his studies entitled *From My African Notebook*.

The sole means of recreation which he allowed himself during these four and a half years of arduous labours (and how arduous only his wife, and his fellow-helpers later, can tell) was to play on the piano with pedal attachment—the parting gift of the Paris Bach Society—in the lunch hour and on Sunday afternoons. Then from his little bungalow, hundreds of miles from civilization, can be heard those strains of music which tell that he is "doing honour to the shade of J. S. Bach." It was an anxious moment for him when, standing on the river-bank, he watched the precious and magnificent instrument which had been specially built for the tropics and encased in a zinc lining, borne precariously up the river in a huge canoe

[1] *My Life and Thought*, pp. 168-169.

hollowed out of a single tree. It was his one link with the culture he
had left behind.

At first, however, I had not the heart to practise. I had accustomed myself to think that this activity in Africa meant the end
of my life as an artist, and that the renunciation would be easier if
I allowed fingers and feet to get rusty with disuse. One evening,
however, as in melancholy mood I was playing one of Bach's
organ fugues, the idea came suddenly upon me that I might after
all use my free hours in Africa for the very purpose of perfecting
and deepening my technique. I immediately formed a plan to take,
one after another, compositions by Bach, Mendelssohn, Widor,
César Franck, and Max Reger, study them carefully down to the
smallest detail, and learn them by heart, even if I had to spend
weeks or months on any particular piece.[1]

None but a musician can appreciate the enormous concentration
required for such a task, even under favourable conditions. How
much more so, then, in the sweltering heat of the tropics which
so deleteriously affects both energy and memory! But Schweitzer
adds: "How much I enjoyed being able to practise at leisure and in
quiet, without the slavery of keeping dates for concerts, even though
I could not find more than a bare half-hour in the day for the
purpose!"

His work was proceeding harmoniously and with increasing success when, in August 1914, it received an unwelcome interruption.
As one of those who for years had laboured for a better understanding
between Germany and France, the news of the war came with the
shock of a personal sorrow. This was accentuated by the fact that he
and his wife, as German subjects, were immediately interned in their
bungalow under orders to refrain from any converse either with
Europeans or with natives and "to obey unconditionally the regulations of the native soldiers who were assigned to us as guards." The
unfortunate guards came in for a torrent of abuse from the neighbouring villagers, thanks to whose protests the prisoners were released by the end of November, and "thanks too to Widor's
exertions," as they afterwards learnt.

On Christmas Day, 1914, Schweitzer lit the candles on the little
palm tree that served them for a Christmas tree, and when they had
burnt to half their length he blew them out to save them for the next
Christmas.

[1] *My Life and Thought*, p. 170.

We are all of us conscious that many natives are puzzling over the question how it can be possible that the white men, who brought them the Gospel of Love, are now murdering each other, and throwing to the winds the commands of the Lord Jesus. When they put the question to us we are helpless. . . . I make no attempt to explain or to extenuate. . . . I fear that the damage done will be very considerable. . . . In my own house I take care that the natives learn as little as possible of the horrors of war. I must not leave illustrated papers about, lest the boys who can read should absorb both text and pictures, and retail them to others.

Meanwhile the medical work goes on as usual. Every morning when I go down to the hospital I feel it as an inexpressible mercy that, whilst so many men find it their duty to inflict suffering and death on others, I can be doing good and helping to save human life. This feeling supports me in all my weariness.[1]

The interest of the natives was pathetic in its lack of comprehension. They asked him if it was true that many people were being killed. "Yes," he answered sadly.—"More than ten?"—"Yes, many, many more."—"What!" exclaimed an old Pahouin (a cannibal tribe). "More than ten! Why don't they have a palaver and stop it? How can they pay for all the dead?" (In native warfare compensation is made for the slain both by victors and vanquished.) "They must be killing each other for cruelty, since they do not eat their dead!"

His brief period of internment, however, proved to be a blessing in disguise. It gave him a respite to employ his ever-busy mind on a theme which had occupied it from youth, and which now drove him along the path towards a new discovery. This was nothing more nor less than to find a clue to the ultimate meaning and purpose of existence. It is the deepest problem possible to thought, and one which the outbreak of the war now brought to "a live issue." For years he had detected, and with apprehension, a growing tendency on the part of governments to accept what he calls "inhumane courses of action," and for nations to condone them.

As early as my first years at the University I had begun to feel misgivings about the opinion that mankind is constantly developing in the direction of progress. My impression was that the fire of its ideals was burning low without anyone noticing it or troubling about it. . . . From a number of signs I had to infer the growth

[1] *On the Edge of the Primeval Forest,* p. 138.

of a peculiar intellectual and spiritual fatigue in this generation which is so proud of what it has accomplished.[1]

Realpolitik, the slogan originating in Germany, had become the slogan for all countries, but it meant "the approbation of short-sighted nationalisms." (*Realism*, he might have added, was soon to become the catchword of superficial philosophies.)

On the second day of his internment, accordingly, Schweitzer set to work on his Philosophy of Civilization, and, when his medical work was resumed, sat up night after night "covering sheet after sheet, as I thought with emotion of the men who were lying in the trenches." Mental work of some kind, he tells us, is necessary if one is to keep one's moral health in Africa; otherwise, "the terrible prose" of African life will drag a man to ruin.

Strange indeed are the surroundings amid which I study; my table stands inside the lattice-door which leads on to the verandah, so that I may snatch as much as possible of the light evening breeze. The palms rustle an *obbligato* to the loud music of the crickets and the toads, and from the forest come harsh and terrifying sounds of all sorts. Caramba, my faithful dog, growls gently on the verandah, to let me know that he is there; and at my feet, under the table, lies a small dwarf antelope. In this solitude I try to set in order thoughts which have been stirring in me since 1900, in the hope of giving some little help to the restoration of civilization. Solitude of the primaeval forest, how can I ever thank you enough for what you have been to me! . . .[2]

There is an unrecorded story connected with the little antelope. It consumes paper with the same voracity as a goat. When Schweitzer found that it was behaving as a live waste-paper basket for the sheets of manuscript which he discarded after revision from his *Decay and the Restoration of Civilization*, he carefully kept all his papers hung high up out of its reach. But the depredations of the little pet antelope were far less serious than some of the senseless thefts committed by his human charges.

There disappeared one day from my bookshelf the piano edition of Wagner's *Meistersinger* and the copy of Bach's Passion Music (St. Matthew), into which I had written the organ accompani-

---

[1] *My Life and Thought*, p. 173.
[2] *On the Edge of the Primeval Forest*, pp. 148-149.

ment, which I had worked out very carefully! This feeling of
never being safe from the stupidest piece of theft brings one almost
to despair, and to have to keep everything locked up and turn
oneself into a walking bunch of keys adds a terrible burden to life.[1]

In the summer of 1915, he says, "I awoke from a sort of stupor."
Why only criticism of civilization? Why not something constructive?
The collapse of civilization was due to the collapse of a philosophical
world-view. That he clearly saw, and could trace the collapse of both
historically. But what is civilization? and what constitutes a stable
world-view? "The will to civilization is the universal will to progress
which is conscious of the ethical as the highest value both for the
individual and for society."—But on what kind of world-view are
they based and also linked with each other? "It consists in an ethical
affirmation of the world and of life." But, concretely and precisely,
what is this affirmation? This was the question that he set himself to
solve, ransacking the wisdom of the ages without finding the solution, till the autumn of that year. He had been staying for a few
days with his wife at Cape Lopez for the sake of her health, when
he was summoned to visit the ailing wife of another missionary at
N'gomo, 160 miles upstream. What followed must be told in his
own words.

Slowly we crept upstream, laboriously feeling—it was the dry
season—for the channels between the sandbanks. Lost in thought
I sat on the deck of the barge, struggling to find the elemental and
universal conception of the ethical which I had not discovered in
any philosophy. Sheet after sheet I covered with disconnected
sentences, merely to keep myself concentrated on the problem.
Late on the third day, at the very moment when, at sunset, we
were making our way through a herd of hippopotamuses, there
flashed upon my mind, unforeseen and unsought, the phrase,
Reverence for Life.
   The iron door had yielded: the path in the thicket had become
visible. Now I had found my way to the idea in which world- and
life-affirmation and ethics are contained side by side! Now I knew
that the world-view of ethical world- and life-affirmation, together
with its ideals of civilization, is founded in thought.[2]

It was to develop the implications of this discovery, and to show

[1] *Ibid.* p. 64.   *My Life and Thought*, pp. 185-186.

it to be a necessity for thought, that he devoted the next seven years, laying aside in the meanwhile his work on the interpretation of the thought of St. Paul. For several weeks after this discovery he lived, he tells us, in a condition of perpetual excitement; but soberly and without haste he began to commit to paper, as time and opportunity allowed, rough drafts of a major treatise. "Now there stood out clearly before my mind the plan of the whole Philosophy of Civilization." A critical admirer of all his work, who rightly regards this chievement as his greatest, has written well:

> As with a surgical needle he probes to find the vital artery of the African arm, that intravenous injection may cure the patient who would otherwise die of sleeping sickness, so he searches for the artery of European faith, that he may inject into the dying civilization a life-giving inspiration. The probing may be painful.[1]

The strain of the life was telling seriously on the health of his wife and truest comrade, and for the last year of their work together Schweitzer was obliged to leave her at a friend's house on the coast. He recalls entering some huts near by, once used as quarters for the natives passing through, but now half ruined, and finding them vacant except the last, in which was a negro "with his head almost buried in the sand and ants running all over him." He was a victim of sleeping sickness, and though past all help still breathed.

> While I was busied with him I could see through the door of the hut the bright blue waters of the bay in their frame of green woods, a scene of almost magic beauty, looking still more enchanting in the flood of golden light poured over it by the setting sun. To be shown in single glance such a paradise and such helpless hopeless misery was overwhelming, but—it was a symbol of the condition of Africa.[2]

He was at N'gomo again to witness the embarkation of conscripted native carriers for service in the Cameroons, and to hear the wailing of their women-folk as the vessel started down the river.

The crowd had dispersed, but on the stone of the river-bank an old woman, whose son had been taken, sat weeping silently. I took

---

[1] Magnus Ratter, *Albert Schweitzer*, p. 203.
[2] *On the Edge of the Primeval Forest*, p. 169.

her hand and tried to comfort her, but she went on crying as if she did not hear me. Suddenly I felt that I was crying too, silently as she was, towards the setting sun.[1]

At the same time he says that he was reading an article which maintained the necessity of wars, "because a noble thirst for glory is an ineradicable element in the heart of man." These champions of militarism would reconsider their verdict, he thought, if they would spend a single day in the virgin forest between lines of corpses of unwilling and innocent native carriers who had sunk under their load and found a solitary death by the roadside.

The reaper Death was soon to take its toll of him. "My mother," he writes (with what Miss Royden has called "a dreadful brevity"), "was knocked down and killed in 1916 by cavalry horses on the road." It is his sole reference to the event: a fact that must be recorded, but without comment or complaint. It struck too deep for that.

It is not that Schweitzer would call himself a pacifist, any more than he would label himself by any other trite catchword. Life as it is lived is too complex a business for that. Both as a historian and a natural scientist he would recognize that wars, hideous as they are alike in the human and the natural order, are sometimes less evil than their alternatives might be. It is one thing to be, as he is, actively a peace-maker; another thing to be merely a peace-lover, that is, to acquiesce in a condition of things that renders wars sooner or later inevitable.

What is the Fellowship of those who bear the Mark of Pain, and who are its members? They are an unknown company of men and women who, inspired by Schweitzer's example, have banded themselves to carry out his work of redemptive succour to the oppressed and afflicted—human and creaturely alike—wherever they may find them. By unobtrusive deeds of mercy they bear witness, as he does, to the patent truth that what the world needs, if it is ever to become truly Christian, is not less humanitarianism but more.

Those, who have learnt by experience what physical pain and anguish mean, belong together all the world over; they are united by a secret bond. . . . They bring to others the deliverance which they themselves have found. . . .

[1] *Ibid.* p. 170.

But—Europe is ruined and full of wretchedness. With all the misery that we have to alleviate even under our very eyes, how can we think of far-off lands?

Truth has no special time of its own. Its hour is now—always, and indeed then most truly when it seems most unsuitable to actual circumstances. Care for distress at home and care for distress elsewhere do but help each other if, working together, they wake men in sufficient numbers from their thoughtlessness, and call into life a new spirit of humanity. . . .

The work indeed, as I began it, has been ruined by the war. The friends from two nations who joined in supporting us have been, alas, deeply divided by what has happened, and of those who might have helped us farther, many have been reduced to poverty. . . .

Nevertheless, I have not lost courage. The misery I have seen gives me strength, and faith in my fellow-men supports my confidence in the future. . . . I do hope that among the doctors of the world there will soon be several besides myself who will be sent out, here or there in the world, by the "Fellowship of those who bear the Mark of Pain." [1]

NOTE

It cannot fail to strike the attentive reader of this terse chronicle that, remarkable as it is for what it tells, it is equally so for what it leaves untold. There is no lack of particularization in describing the special problems that confronted the Lambaréné venture, though indeed, even there, the sober matter-of-factness of the telling leaves much to the reader's imagination. But of the more general problems that confront a medical pioneer in the untamed wilderness—more especially of the contrast between starting from nothing under such conditions and the practice of medicine and surgery in civilization with all the scientific appliances and amenities of the profession ready to hand—all this seems to be taken for granted by the narrator as a matter of course. So, at all events, it struck the reader who has here attempted no more than a bare bald summary of Schweitzer's narrative; so much so that he requested another medical pioneer to supplement this apparent lack from his own experience in dealing with these problems in another part of Africa.

Dr. C. C. Chesterman, O.B.E., writes: "As one among many who have since tried to do the sort of thing Dr. Schweitzer has done, I

[1] *On the Edge of the Primeval Forest*, pp. 173-176

gladly respond; and hope that it may be of some little value in showing the magnitude of the task which he has accomplished." He adds to the following notes the hope that Schweitzer's example may stimulate other young medical men to follow in his steps.

Divers Difficulties Disadvantages, and Drawbacks in Bush Doctoring

Bush doctoring is not a dark, drear, and dismal business. It is alluring, agreeable, and adventurous. But it is difficult.

The African Bush is a paradise for parasites, but a desert for the doctor. The parasites find everything they want, warmth, water, and warm-blooded animals, all naked and accessible, and myriads of mosquitoes and biting flies all ready to carry them from one human host to another. But the doctor feels that he has to spend so much time beating about the bush in order to get down to his real job that he risks being dead beat before he starts.

PRELIMINARY PROBLEMS

The Hospital Site: selection—native rights over—Government permission for—clearing—stumping—levelling ant-hills.

Labour: recruitment—housing—feeding—training—supervision—palavers —quarrels and fights.

Water: collection—storage—pumping—leading in.

Drainage: pits—bore-hole latrines—septic tanks.

Light: palm-oil drips—hurricane lanterns—petrol pressure lamps and eventually installation of an electric generating plant.

Timber: find—fell—cut—transport, season, and dress.

Bricks: discover suitable clay—hand mould or machine press—dry and burn in kilns.

Roofing: leaves—thatch—tiles—or tin sheets.

Furniture: to be made or improvised.

Fittings: import glass, hardware, and theatre equipment and hospital beds.

Transport: canoes or bicycles and later provision and care of motor-boat and car.

Food: arrangement of markets—employment of gardeners, fishermen, and hunters.

SUNDRY SNAGS

White ants: consume paper, books, curtains, cloth, and floor coverings.

Black and brown ants: of varying dimensions, get into everything.

Mosquitoes: are a menace demanding constant counter-measures.

Biting flies: of many sorts, keep alive as many diseases.

Jiggers: live by making dug-outs in the skin of your feet.

Rats: eat patients' food and nibble their feet at night. Their fleas carry plague.

Leopards: slay one's goats and sheep.

Bush cats: kill one's poultry.

Elephants: trample down the gardens.

Baboons: uproot the crops.

Storms: blow down trees—blow off roofs. Lightning often strikes trees and buildings.

Humidity: makes everything mouldy.

POPULAR RESISTANCE MOVEMENT

Ignorance of the reasons underlying care of hygiene.

Apathy born of familiarity with epidemics.

Superstition, preventing rational thinking and acting.

Belief in witchcraft which seeks who and not what causes disease.

Witch smelling which seeks to isolate "carriers" who have nothing to do with disease.

Poison ordeals which often kill a victim for each death from natural causes.

Suspicion of natives, born of any of the above or of vested interests.

But neither these nor any other creation can separate us from the Love of God in Christ Jesus, and this love and purpose is best revealed *by* us in the way it was revealed *to* us, by Jesus the Good Physician, who went about doing good and healing.

CHAPTER VI

VISITS TO SWEDEN AND ELSEWHERE

SCHWEITZER spent the rainy season of 1917 with his wife for her recuperation again on the coast, and they had barely returned to Lambaréné to resume work when they were ordered to embark at once in a ship just due to sail for a prisoners' camp somewhere in Europe. "Fortunately," he says, and it is another instance of characteristic understatement, "the ship was a few days late, so that we had time, with the help of the missionaries and a few natives, to pack our belongings in cases, the drugs and instruments as well, and to stow them all into a small building of corrugated iron."

But he dared not take with him his precious manuscripts on the Philosophy of Civilization for fear of confiscation. He therefore entrusted them to the care of an American missionary friend who, though he loathed philosophy and would have preferred to consign the heavy package to the river, "promised, of his Christian charity, to keep it and to send it to me at the end of the war." Still, to avoid all possible mischance, Schweitzer spent two whole nights in making a summary of it in French, with chapter-headings suitable to a history of the Renaissance: "I did in fact thus secure its escape from the confiscation which on several occasions threatened it."

His last duty was to operate in haste, amid packed and half-packed cases, on a strangulated hernia. The most touching of their farewells came from the Father Superior of the Roman Catholic Mission.

> just as we had been taken on board the river steamer and the natives were shouting an affectionate farewell to us from the bank, he came on board, waved aside with an authoritative gesture the native soldiers who tried to prevent his approach, and shook hands with us: "You shall not leave this country," he said, "without my thanking you both for all the good that you have done it." We were never to see each other again. Shortly after the war he lost his life on board the *Afrique*, the ship which was taking us to Europe, when she was wrecked in the Bay of Biscay.[1]

[1] *My Life and Thought*, p. 194.

The ship's steward treated them with a kindness rarely shown to prisoners, explaining that a few months previously a French gentleman, who had been one of Schweitzer's patients at Lambaréné and afterwards a passenger on the same ship, had said to him, "Gaillard, it may happen that before long you will be taking the Lambaréné doctor to Europe as a prisoner. If he ever does travel on your ship, and should you be able to help him in any way, do so for my sake." —Since writing on the ship was not allowed, Schweitzer set himself to learn by heart some of Bach's fugues, and one of Widor's symphonies.

At Bordeaux they were lodged in the Temporary Barracks, where Schweitzer at once developed dysentery—his first illness. He fought it off with emetine, but continued to suffer from its effects. Next they were taken to the great Internment Camp at Garaison in the Pyrenees. The Governor was a retired colonial official, and a theosophist. Here another prisoner introduced himself as one who was in his debt, Schweitzer having been the means, though indirectly, of curing his wife of an illness—and asked what he could do to serve him now. Schweitzer desired nothing so much as a table. His fellow-prisoner at once contrived one from some loose wood in the loft. "Now I could write, and—play the organ. For before we left the boat I had begun some organ practice by using a table as manual and the floor as pedals, as I used to do when a boy."—Once again: only a musician can appreciate the concentration required for this mute playing.

Though he was the only medical man among the interned, he was at first forbidden to attend the sick. But later he was allowed the same privileges as the dentists, and the Governor placed a room at his disposal. "Thus I was once more a doctor. What leisure time I had left I gave to the Philosophy of Civilization (I was then drafting the chapters on the Civilized State), and practising the organ on table and floor."—There is a world of irony in that innocent parenthesis.

In this capacity he got a glimpse into the manifold misery that prevailed among those who were either psychically or physically unfit for internment; and a valuable insight also into the lives of those who were stronger, and whose number comprised a wide range of professions and of nationalities. The varieties which he lists are indeed astonishing, and occupy the best part of a page.

To improve one's education one needed no books in the camp. For everything he could want to learn there were men with specialized knowledge at his disposal, and of this unique opportunity for learning I made liberal use. About banking, architecture, factory building and equipment, cereal growing, furnace building, and many other things, I picked up information which I should probably never have acquired elsewhere.[1]

With the spring of 1918 came an order for their removal to another camp at S. Rémy de Provence, though they and the Governor (who had now become their friend) both begged for their retention at Garaison. Here, among other Alsatians whom he knew, Schweitzer met a young pastor who had been one of his pupils: "he had permission to hold services on Sundays and, as his curate, I got a good many opportunities for preaching." On entering the large day-room on the ground floor, it struck him "in its unadorned and bare ugliness" as being strangely familiar.

> Where had I seen that iron stove, and the flue-pipe crossing the room from end to end? The mystery was solved at last: I knew them from a drawing of Van Gogh's. The building in which we were housed, once a monastery in a walled-in garden, had till recently been occupied by sufferers from nervous or mental disease. Among them at one time was Van Gogh, who immortalized with his pencil the desolate room in which today we in our turn were sitting about. Like us, he had suffered from the cold stone floor when the mistral blew! Like us, he had walked round and round between the high garden walls![2]

Here, as at Garaison, Schweitzer was at first relieved of medical duties since one of the interned was a doctor, and so was able to work all day on his outline of the Civilized State; but later when his colleague was exchanged for repatriation, he took his place. His wife's health suffered from the bleak winds of Provence, and he too tried in vain to master the continually increasing languor which results from dysentery. Neither of them could take the walking exercise permitted to prisoners. It was therefore with all the greater cause for thankfulness that he heard that their own turn for exchange was due about the middle of July. When the time came for departure, and the convoy had started through the gate, he ran back to say good-bye to the Governor. "I found him sitting, sorrowful, in his office. He felt the departure of his prisoners very much. We

---

[1] *My Life and Thought*, p. 202.   [2] *Ibid.* p. 205.

still write to each other, and he addresses me as 'mon cher pensionnaire.' "

On arrival at Tarascon, heavily laden with baggage, they found themselves scarcely able to cross the railway lines for weariness.

> Thereupon a poor cripple whom I had treated in the camp came forward to help us. He had no baggage because he possessed nothing, and I was much moved by his offer, which I accepted. While we walked along side by side in the scorching sun, I vowed to myself that in memory of him I would in future always keep a look-out at stations for heavily laden people, and help them. And this vow I have always kept.[1]

Early on July 15th they arrived at Zürich and to their astonishment were greeted by Dr. Arnold Meyer, Professor of the New Testament; Robert Kaufmann the singer; and other friends who had been aware for weeks of their coming. From the windows of the train to Constance they feasted their eyes on the well-tilled fields and clean houses, hardly able to grasp the fact that they were in a land untouched by war. Very different was the scene in Constance, where none but weary, pale, emaciated people stood about the streets; and again in Strasburg, which they reached at night, where not a light was burning in the streets, or glimmer from a house.

Here he left his wife to the care of her parents, pending permission for her to re-join him in Günsbach, and himself with difficulty journeyed on to Colmar, to find that all trains had ceased to run from there to the Vosges; so made his way to Günsbach, a distance of twelve miles, on foot to seek his father. Reticent as always about his deepest personal feelings he has nothing to say about his homecoming but much about his native village.

> So this was the peaceful valley to which I had bidden farewell on Good Friday 1913! There were dull roars from guns on the mountains. On the roads one walked between lines of wire-netting packed with straw, as between high walls. . . . Everywhere there were brick emplacements for machine guns! Houses were ruined by gun-fire! Hills which I remembered covered with woods now stood bare. . . . In the villages were posters ordering that everyone must always carry a gas-mask about with him.[2]

[1] *My Life and Thought*, p. 208.   [2] *Ibid.* pp. 210-211.

The little village itself owed its preservation to its position of concealment in the hills, but the harvest was ruined by scarcity of labour and by a severe drought. His father told him that he could no longer imagine a time when his manse was not occupied with soldiers.

Schweitzer had hoped that his native air would dissipate his increasing languor, but at the end of August "high fever and torturing pains" convinced him that an operation was necessary. Accompanied by his wife he dragged himself along the road nearly half-way to Colmar before they got a lift, and almost as soon as he got to Strasburg underwent the operation. When on his feet again he gladly accepted the offer of a position on the staff of the Municipal Hospital there, "for I really did not know how I was going to live." At the same time he was again appointed curate at his beloved St. Nicholas', and an empty parsonage was provided for both his wife and himself to live in. A daughter, Rhena, was born to them on January 14th—his own birthday—1919.

Before leaving Alsace for Africa he had, at the request of an American publisher, collaborated with Widor in editing the works of Bach, and five volumes—containing the Sonatas, Concertos, Preludes, and Fugues—were already completed. The three other volumes—containing the Choral Preludes—he had undertaken to complete at Lambaréné, and had done so, but had been obliged to leave them there together with his other manuscripts. In expectation of their arrival he now began to prepare for their publication, but still the parcel did not come; and so he laid the work aside. "Several circumstances have conspired to prevent me, ever since, from bringing the work to completion."

Instead, he continued for a while with his work on the Philosophy of Civilization, but finding this equally impossible to bring to a conclusion without his manuscripts, he occupied himself with a study of the great world-religions and the world-views they implied, examining them, as he had examined the great philosophical systems, against the background of ethical world- and life-affirmation.

Only very rarely during this time, the year 1919, did he break from his seclusion at Strasburg, feeling, as he says, "rather like a coin that has rolled under a piece of furniture and remained there lost. . . . In learned circles I could have believed myself entirely forgotten, but for the affection and kindness shown to me by the theological faculties at Zürich and Berne." The one occasion when he broke bounds was when "having with much trouble secured permission to travel, I scraped up every shilling I could and went to Barcelona to let my friends of the Orféo Català once more hear me play the organ. This first emergence into the world let me see that as an artist I was still of some value."

For two years after the Armistice, Schweitzer was a well-known figure at the Customs Office on the Rhine Bridge at Kehl, laden with a rucksack of provisions for his starving friends in Germany.

It was in the spring of this year that, as he happened to be passing the Strasburg-Neudorf station, he saw among a crowd of waiting German passengers whom the French authorities were expelling from Alsace his old instructor in Pharmacology, Professor Schmiedeberg. In reply to a question whether he could help him save his furniture, "the dear old man showed me a parcel wrapped in a newspaper, which he had under his arm. It was his last work on Digitalis." He was afraid that he might not be allowed to take it with him. "I therefore took it from him and sent it later on, when a safe opportunity offered, to Baden-Baden, where he found a refuge with friends. He died not long after the appearance of his work in print."

In the summer he found it necessary to undergo a second operation from which, though it proved ultimately beneficial, it took him a long time to recover.

On December 23, 1919, he received an entirely unexpected invitation, through the Archbishop of Canterbury, from Archbishop Soderblöm of Sweden, to deliver the Olaus-Petri lectures at the University of Upsala in the following spring. He chose as his subject the theme with which he was then so much engrossed, "The Ethical Foundations of Civilization." He arrived on April 20th, and at once began his lectures. "I came to Sweden," he says, "a tired, depressed and still ailing man.—In the magnificent air of Upsala, and the kindly atmosphere of the Archbishop's house, in which my wife and I were guests, I recovered my health and once more found enjoyment in my work." There can be little doubt that this re-invigoration was due also to the opportunity for giving expression to the thoughts that had been kindling in his mind for five years.

But this visit to Sweden was to prove productive of good in other unforeseen ways, with far-reaching consequences. Schweitzer felt that he was still under financial obligation to the Paris Missionary Society, and to his Parisian friends, for their help in making possible the continuance of the hospital in Lambaréné during the war; but now, so many sources of funds were lacking because so many countries were impoverished. He confided this anxiety to the Archbishop, "in a walk in which we shared an umbrella in a mild spring rain-shower," who advised the experiment of giving organ recitals and lectures in Sweden, one of the few countries which had actually profited by the war. Acting upon this advice immediately, with the assistance of his good host's introductions, he found himself able within the course of a few weeks to defray what he considered to be the most pressing of these debts.

Several years later, in 1933, Schweitzer was moved to write from Lambaréné his memories of Nathan Soderblöm, in admiration of him as a scholar, a musician, a creative artist, a great leader of the Church, and even more in gratitude to him as a friend who, he felt, had intervened at a critical period in his own life to rescue it from oblivion. Hitherto Schweitzer, unaware of Soderblöm's elevation to the archbishopric of Sweden, had known him only through his works and especially through the important contribution that he had made to the comparative study of religions; now he found himself able to measure his worth as a distinguished personality and more than all as a human being. Among the delightful incidents of his visits which he records is one which occurred on the second day of his lecture tour when he was joined by the Archbishop at Bergsjö where the latter was due to officiate at the institution of a clergyman to his benefice. It happened that the upper part of the crozier by some mischance had been left behind, and there was some discussion in the vestry as to whether the assembled congregation should be kept any longer to await its arrival, when a young clergyman was inspired with the happy thought of cutting a flowering branch from the vicarage garden, and inserting it "like Aaron's rod" into the lower end of the crozier, which he then handed to the Archbishop, who accepted it with a beaming smile and forthwith proceeded with it up the aisle. Delighted as Schweitzer was by this manifestation of the Archbishop's urbanity and humour, he was still more so by an incident the same night. His bedroom was next to his host's, and he had retired early but could not sleep on account of the incessant conversation issuing from the next room. At length, at midnight, piqued with curiosity, he rose, dressed, and knocked at the door. To a welcoming call "Come in!" he entered to find several clergy on the sofa, others on the Archbishop's bed, and himself with the newly-instituted cleric seated together on a trunk. A nocturnal conference was in progress, which he was cordially invited to join. On all his subsequent visits to Upsala he was the Archbishop's guest, and when he heard of his death in 1931 he held a memorial service in Lambaréné, and wrote: "Among all the many people whom he helped, I doubt if anyone owes him as much gratitude as I do."

Before delivering his lectures he rehearsed them carefully with his interpreter "in short, simple and clearly constructed sentences," and this is the method which he adopts when lecturing to any foreign audience. In this way the interpreter finds no difficulty in, as he says, "catching each sentence like a ball which he throws on at once to the listeners." In his view it is a much better way than for the speaker to "inflict torture on himself and his audience by attempting to speak in a language of which he is not fully master."[1] As for the old Swedish organs: "though not large, their admirable resonance pleased me greatly. They were admirably adapted to my method of rendering Bach's music."

Returning to Strasburg in the summer of 1920, having worked himself to the last ounce of physical energy, he wrote his first book on the "Primaeval Forest," which was translated into Swedish by Baroness Lagerfelt in the same year; soon afterwards into English by C. T. Campion; then into French, Danish, and Finnish. There also now, to his great relief, came to hand the long-expected manuscripts from Lambaréné. In this year he received the honorary degree of Doctor of Divinity from the University of Zürich.

In April 1921 he resigned both his posts in Strasburg, medical and pastoral, determining to depend for a living upon the organ and his pen; and removed with his wife and little daughter to his father's home in Günsbach for the necessary quiet to devote to his work on the Philosophy of Civilization. But by this time he had emerged, almost unwittingly, from obscurity into general recognition once again not only as a scholar and writer and musician, but as a personality of international repute, and was in much demand for lectures.

In the autumn of 1921 he was in Switzerland, and in the winter

[1] It was before an English audience several years later that Schweitzer first explained in public whence he had originally learnt this method. He opened his Hibbert Lectures at Oxford in 1934 with the following little apologia: "I first learned that it was possible to talk to others whose language I could not speak when, many years ago, I heard your General Booth speak through an interpreter at Strasburg. This gift I had from him I now return to the country that gave it."

again in Sweden. At the end of January 1922 he made his first visit
to England and in the course of six weeks had—besides giving many
organ recitals—delivered the Dale Memorial Lectures at Oxford on
The Decay and the Restoration of Civilization; and other lectures—at the
Selly Oak College in Birmingham on *Christianity and the Religions
of the World*; at Cambridge on *The Significance of Eschatology*; and in
London to the Society for the Study of the Science of Religion on
The Pauline Problem. Of these the first two were afterwards published
in German, in which they were delivered, and have since been
translated: the Dale Memorial Lectures into English, Swedish,
Danish, and Dutch; the Selly Oak Lectures into the same languages
as well as into Japanese.

In March of this year he returned to Sweden for more concerts
and lectures, and then to Switzerland again for the same purpose.
In the summer he worked undisturbed at his Philosophy of Civilization. In the autumn he went again to Switzerland, and then to
Denmark for lectures on Ethics at Copenhagen University, and
for lectures and recitals in various other towns in Denmark.

In January 1923 he was in Prague at the invitation of Dr. Oscar
Kraus, Professor of Philosophy at the university there, "travelling
third-class from Kehl in a winter overcoat of Bavarian homespun
worn over his somewhat shabby suit." Kraus, who knew him only
through his books, was keenly desirous of making his personal
acquaintance. Profoundly differing from each other as they did in
philosophical outlook, they recognized in each other kindred spirits
and formed a lifelong friendship. It was on Kraus' introductions that
Schweitzer undertook several lecture and concert tours in Czechoslovakia, Moravia, and Bohemia.[1]

Kraus' short biographical study of Schweitzer[2] is remarkable in its
combination of his unqualified admiration of Schweitzer as a man
with his strong disapproval of Schweitzer as a thinker. He writes:
"I do not think I exaggerate when I maintain that the cultural world
of today has produced no one who could equal Albert Schweitzer

[1] Kraus suffered for his faith in a concentration camp in 1939 and employed
this period of physical misery in focussing his mind on an attempt to render flaw-
less Brentano's proof of the existence of God, which was the object of his own lifelong philosophic search. He was eventually released on the intervention of the
British Ambassador, with 10s. in his possession, having sacrificed everything else.
He delivered the Gifford Lectures at Edinburgh in 1940–41, but died at Oxford in
September 1942.

[2] *Albert Schweitzer: His Work and his Philosophy*, trans. by E. G. McCalman
(1944).

in originality, in many-sidedness, and in the intensity of his intellectual, his artistic, and above all in his ethical qualities." At the same
time he rejects Schweitzer's philosophy as "a mystic speculative phase
of modern thought."

This little book, on its translation into English, has met with a
mixed reception. It was adversely criticized by the Master of Balliol,
in all too slight a preface, in which he records his own dissent from
"the queerness" of its author's presuppositions, but pays him this
high personal tribute: "When you met the man there was a single-
heartedness and simplicity that shone from him, a wonderful example
of scholarly devotion carried to a pitch of saintliness." A closer and
more careful analysis of its defects was made by Professor J. M.
Thompson of Magdalen in *The Oxford Magazine* for January 1945.
In it he shows that Kraus' ineffectual attempt to classify so strongly-
marked an individuality as Schweitzer's into any of the specimen
character groups arranged by genetic psychology is "preposterous,"
and that Kraus himself is seriously disturbed by his inability to do so.

Whilst in full agreement with these strictures, and with others
which blame the book because it is ill-arranged and a medley of its
author's deterministic presuppositions with his presentation of biographical material,—the present writer feels it fair to say that Kraus
should nevertheless be assigned the credit of having pointed out at
least one apparent inconsistency in Schweitzer's thought (which will
be referred to in its place);[1] as well as of having, in his tribute to
what he calls Schweitzer's "unparalleled greatness," made the following important observations.—Many idealists have entertained the
thought of embracing a life of activity in circumstances of privation
and hardship, but few have carried it into effect. And of those few,
how many have sacrificed so much as Schweitzer? Again: Many—
and these are commonly reckoned as among the saints—have been
upborne by the inner support of a kind of psychic mysticism which
is subject to blissful states of consciousness, raptures, visions, and the
like. But not only is Schweitzer lacking in the encouragement of
any such spiritualistic aid: he is also utterly devoid even of that
sanguine confidence implicit in naïve philosophical theism with its
trust in a divine providence which overrules events to the eventual
advantage of the believer. Nor has he any belief in the divinity of
Jesus in the doctrinal sense.[2] His mysticism is wholly ethical (even

---

[1] pp. 305 ff.
[2] But there is a truer sense in which he does believe it. (See Chap. XIII, end.)

though to Kraus it appears as "a peculiar mixture of agnosticism and animistic pantheism"!), and is the outcome of "a special type of soul, whose will reacts with exceptional intensity to feelings of compassion and is unusually alive to the impression which the personality of Jesus evokes." Among the many tributes to his friend which Kraus makes, none perhaps is more to the point than this: "Schweitzer *lives* his philosophy of compassion, it is compassion in action; he only feels pity for others, never for himself."

In the spring of 1923 his first two volumes on the Philosophy of Civilization were completed, with the titles *The Decay and the Restoration of Civilization* and *Civilization and Ethics*. In the same summer, travelling again across Switzerland and having two hours to wait for a train at Zürich, he sought an interval for rest and refreshment with his friend Oscar Pfister, a well-known Swiss psycho-analyst, "who made me stretch and rest my weary body, and at the same time relate to him incidents of my childhood just as they came into my mind." The incident was responsible for Schweitzer's publication subsequently of his *Memoirs of Childhood and Youth*.

Pfister has since confessed the inability of psycho-analysis to explain the personality of Schweitzer:

In spite of all we know of Schweitzer's inner life and development, the actual problem of his personality as a whole remains unsolved. Even if we were to possess far more material for analysis than that with which Schweitzer actually provides us, even if such analysis could be undertaken in ideal circumstances, and even if it were to penetrate to the depths of the unconscious and furnish us with the key to many important data, it would nevertheless remain patchwork. In the last instance it is bound to stop short somewhere in deference to those creative powers which spring from the realm of the Eternal Logos, from Eternal Freedom.[1]

Such, in bald summary, is an outline of his activities during these years which were only an interlude in his real life's labours.

How wonderful were the experiences vouchsafed to me during these years! When I first went to Africa I prepared to make three sacrifices: to abandon the organ, to renounce academic teaching activities, to which I had given my heart, and to lose my financial independence, relying for the rest of my life on the help of friends. —These three sacrifices I had begun to make, and only my intimate friends knew what they cost me.[2]

[1] Quoted by Kraus, *op. cit.* p. 68.   [2] *My Life and Thought*, p. 230.

But now, and in a manner exceeding abundant above all that he had asked or thought, he found that he was to be spared these sacrifices, and that the talents he had surrendered were given back to him with the express purpose of furthering the work to which he had dedicated his life. His health was mercifully restored, and he could now devote the proceeds of his organ recitals, his lectures, and his books, to the maintenance of his Mission in Lambaréné.

During the many quiet hours which I was able to spend with Bach in my four and a half years of loneliness in the jungle I had penetrated deeper into the spirit of his works. I returned to Europe, therefore, not as an artist who had become an amateur, but in full possession of my technique, and privileged to find that as an artist I was esteemed more than before.

For the renunciation of my teaching activities in Strasburg University I found compensation in opportunities of lecturing in very many others.

And if I did for a time lose my financial independence, I was able now to win it again by means of organ and pen.[1]

The overcoming of the difficulties which the aftermath of the war had brought upon him, and, he adds, upon so many others, "had buoyed me up, and made me ready for every effort and every renunciation."

"Effort and Renunciation."—The words would appear to have been chosen advisedly, since for him they signify (and none better) the outer and the inner, the active and the passive, aspects of his own philosophy: the discipline of self-devotion and of self-perfection, that is, of "life- and world-affirmation in which self-denial is present."

Something must be said of the books that were published as a result of his lectures.—*Christianity and the Religions of the World* is elementary, and does justice neither to the subjects which it too cursorily surveys nor to the future author of *Indian Thought and its Development*. As Schweitzer says himself: "Unfortunately I was obliged to confine within too small a compass this epitome of my examination of these religions, since I had to publish it in the form of those lectures." This being so, it seems a pity—despite its popularization and many translations—that it was ever published at all. Its

[1] *My Life and Thought*, p. 231.

value lies in the differentiation which Schweitzer makes between Christianity and the others, as being the sole and ultimate law of life, ethically and spiritually; the only faith which provides a real answer to the question: How ought I to live ?—His knowledge of the other religions of the world, and his insight into the philosophies of life that underlie them, are both profound; and they are not to be judged by this little book. His treatise on Indian thought, however, is a real contribution to the subject; but he has never yet found time to write a similar book on the thought of China, with which his own thought—on account of its ethically optimistic character—is much more in tune; as it is also with the thought of Persia. With Mohammedanism he has never had much sympathy, a fact which makes the following comment (taken from his book *My Life and Thought*) the more interesting.

Islam can be called a world-religion only in virtue of its wide extension. Spiritually it could not develop to be such because it never produced any thinking about the world and mankind which penetrated to the depths. If ever any such thought stirred within it, it was suppressed in order to maintain the authority of traditional views. Nevertheless the Islam of today carries within it stronger tendencies to mysticism and to greater ethical depth than appearances would lead one to suppose.[1]

The title of *The Decay and the Restoration of Civilization* was chosen by way of counterblast to Spengler's *Decline and Fall of the West*. Slighter in substance and more diffuse in style than its sequel *Civilization and Ethics*, it is intended as no more than a general introduction to his whole Philosophy of Civilization, of which these two are the only volumes yet published. Of *Civilization and Ethics* it must suffice to say, in this place, that it is the coping-stone of all his work, his supreme achievement. Every paragraph, and every sentence of every paragraph, is packed with thought; the book is written with the strictest economy of phrasing; indeed it is the most condensed of all his works.[2]

During his visit to Oxford he asked a young journalist, Hubert

[1] *Ibid.* p. 216. He refers no doubt to some modern developments in the teaching of the Sufis, and to certain elements in the doctrine of al-Ghazali.

[2] The present writer has attempted a summary of it in another book, *Albert Schweitzer: Christian Revolutionary*. But a much better exposition of its contents, because the result of a more careful and discerning study, will be found in Ratter's *Albert Schweitzer*, pp. 181-232.

W. Peet (now editor of *The Friend*),[1] who had come to Mansfield College to interview him, to act as his guide in London.

..The characteristic that impressed me most about him [writes Mr. Peet] was that genuine humility which is the hallmark of greatness, and which expresses itself in his case in an extreme modesty and consideration for the feelings of others. (By way of an amusing example, he could not be sufficiently apologetic when, deceived by my youthful appearance, he afterwards discovered that I was already the father of four children!)—It was a strenuous time, conveying the burly black-cloaked figure from theologian to theologian, and from organ to organ. There was a memorable tea at Baron von Hügel's,[2] but as the conversation was in German I could follow little of it. (My French is not much better, when it comes to conversation; I found, however, that the Doctor could understand my English, and I could follow his French.) Another notable meeting was with C. F. Andrews[3] on the platform of Charing Cross Station. They had long been correspondents, but this was one of the rare occasions when they were able to meet.

The Doctor is indefatigable when rehearsing for a recital. He will spend most of the previous day experimenting with the organ, and eats practically nothing till it is all over. He sometimes forgets that other people are not quite so tireless as himself, and I've sometimes been quite sorry for dear Madame Schweitzer! When travelling he carries linen bags about with him for his correspondence, which is of course enormous. In one he keeps the

[1] Also author of the penny biography *Schweitzer of the African Forest* in the Religious Tract Society's series.

[2] In his *Eternal Life* Baron von Hügel wrote: "It is surely very interesting to note how that brilliant German-French teacher and writer, Albert Schweitzer, who insists more exclusively than Professor Loisy, upon one single element, the eschatological and apocalyptic, in our Lord's life and teaching, has found even the picture of Christ so deeply fascinating for his own soul, that he has abandoned his high posts and brilliant prospects in Europe, and has gone as a simple medical missionary . . . to win the heathen to this purely ascetical and transcendental Messiah-Christ and Saviour."

To correct what might appear to be a misunderstanding on the part of this great mystic-theologian, it must be said that Schweitzer would not claim himself to be a "transcendentalist" any more than he would claim to be an "immanentist." For him, the truth which is *latent* in every human soul becomes *patent* in the awakened spiritual consciousness as, simply, "Jesus risen in the hearts of men." To the natives of West Africa he speaks of Him as "The King of our hearts."

[3] This gentle mystic and spiritual adventurer in his book *What I Owe to Christ* explains how Schweitzer's *Quest* first came to him as a veritable gift from God which changed his whole life's outlook, and then how Schweitzer's example and personal friendship compelled him to explore afresh the ultimate meaning and purpose of his own life. The chapter entitled "Albert Schweitzer" and the one

letters waiting answer; when the answer is written he transfers it
to the other.

We afterwards repaired for a quiet meal to Gatti's in the Strand.
I had my wife and daughter with me and we were expecting a
party of half a dozen. But it seemed a little cavalcade which finally
entered the restaurant, and developed into a long row of tables
for about two dozen people. He got little to eat himself, for he
insisted on going along the table and spending a few minutes
with every new-comer, saying that perhaps it would be his only
chance of doing so—even with my little girl; he would leave no
one out. And I remember similar scenes at restaurants in Victoria
Street and Piccadilly, after his recitals. He would never think of
himself, but always of others.

By the end of 1923 he had again (according to his friends' account,
not his own) worked himself to physical exhaustion. In spite of this
he exerted himself to undertake an additional course in obstetrics
and in dentistry at Strasburg, and also to attend lectures at the
Institute for Tropical Hygiene at Hamburg. At the same time he
was planning and supervising all the details of equipment, packing,
and transport for his second expedition to Lambaréné; in addition to
which he designed and helped to construct a collapsible ward of
corrugated iron. Though far from well, he booked his passage from
Bordeaux at the earliest possible date after the New Year.

As Dr. Maude Royden has said:

The student of Albert Schweitzer's life and work is conscious
of a continual sense of paradox in it. His greatness is of the kind

which follows it testify to the profound impression made by Schweitzer's thought
and work on a mind of childlike simplicity and candour.—"In the last chapter [of
The Quest], which had moved me most of all, he carried on his own argument and
interpretation of Christ, not any longer with the logic of the scholar, but with the
passion of a saint. . . . In one further respect, he gave me the greatest help of all.
This was by the example of his own life. For he had decided unflinchingly to live
out in action what he had written, and to continue the quest for the historical
Jesus, not in word only, but in deed. . . . For Christ, he feels, is not merely a
past character in history whose record may be found in ancient documents by
scholarly research. He lives on in the hearts of men. To be fully known and
loved with devotion, He has to be sought afresh in every age by heroic souls; and
in every country there are those fearless lovers who have thus found and known
Him. . . . Later on in my life, it was my rare privilege to stay with Albert
Schweitzer for a time when I was in Europe. . . . He has remained, all through
his career, simple as a little child; his character has been fashioned, line upon line,
by the living Christ whom he worships."

that escapes definition and defies all ordinary rules. It has . . . the quality of unexpectedness and inevitability. That is to say, one could never predict beforehand what he would do, and yet one would say afterwards that what he did was in fact exactly what one ought to have known that he must do.

But that his wife should accompany him again was out of the question; her own health was not equal to the strain; besides, she had the care of their infant daughter. "For the fact that she had so far sacrificed herself as to acquiesce under these circumstances in my resumption of work at Lambaréné, I have never ceased to be grateful to her." So he wrote in *My Life and Thought*; and on the voyage out, as the well-remembered places came into view, "Unceasingly I thank her in my heart."

CHAPTER VII

LAMBARÉNÉ: SECOND PERIOD

ACCOMPANIED by a young Oxford medical student, Noel Gillespie, Schweitzer embarked on February 21, 1924, on his second journey in a cargo boat; partly in order to familiarize himself with several West African ports and especially with Dalua, inland from which was an abandoned Mission—a possible future offshoot from Lambaréné; and also for the sake of leisure to make up his arrears of correspondence. Not the customary linen bags, but four potato sacks stuffed full of unanswered letters, came under the vigilant but bewildered scrutiny of the Customs officer at Bordeaux. "He had never encountered a passenger with so many letters"; and as the transfer of French money abroad was at that time prohibited, he could not help suspecting that some of these letters must contain banknotes. "He therefore spent an hour and a half examining them, one by one, till, on getting to the bottom of the second sack, he shook his head and gave it up as useless."—Perhaps if Schweitzer's many well-wishers and supporters were aware of his enormous correspondence, and of his conscientiousness in replying personally to every letter he receives, and of the heavy drain upon his time involved thereby—to say nothing of postal and excise officials'— they would be more considerate.

The only other passenger was a lady bound for the Cameroons. "When off Cotonou this passenger takes advantage of the presence of a Doctor in the ship to bring into the world a baby which was not expected till she should be at Dalua. As there is no other woman on board the care of her falls on me, and the care of the baby on Noel, who now learns what the temperature of a ship's galley is in the tropics. Eight times a day he has to visit the galley to prepare the milk for the feeding bottle." (He does not add that on arrival at Dalua he would allow no one but himself to carry the young mother down the swaying companion-ladder and deposit her safely in the launch.)

He arrived at Cape Lopez on the Monday of Passion Week, to

be greeted by the vociferously jubilant welcomes of the many natives
who recognized him; to them he was now the "old Doctor."
And so it came to pass that on the Good Friday of this year he was
steaming once again between the tree-walled banks of the Ogowe
River, "past the same antediluvian landscape, the same papyrus
swamps, the same decaying villages, and the same ragged negroes,"
and reached Lambaréné on the following day—to find his hospital
a skeleton: with only the shell of its solid structure standing, con-
sulting room, operation room, and pharmacy; roofs rotted, all the
native-made buildings collapsed, the paths so overgrown as to be
barely traceable, and native labour unprocurable on account of the
prosperity of that very timber trade which so disastrously affects
their own.

Saddened but by no means disconcerted by this spectacle, and
allowing himself time only for a meal and exchange of news with
three of his missionary friends, Schweitzer set off with his young
companion in a canoe to search for "leaf-tiles" for roofing (raffia
leaves stitched over bamboo). An old negro in a distant village gave
them twenty; with perseverance and persuasion they acquired sixty-
four; and returned with this treasure as darkness fell, in drenching
rain.

"I can keep Easter with a quiet mind, for the worst holes can now
be mended." Within a fortnight, by dint of further journeys, he had
secured two hundred leaf-tiles, but even these were too few: it was
the rainy season.

> But the flattery and the presents I had to distribute in order to
> be able to take these leaf-tiles away with me is something I should
> like to forget! I even go so far as to threaten that if the people
> will not meet my requests I will never treat any sick person from
> that village. But such threats, coming from "our Doctor," were
> only greeted with laughter. Even my moral principles are deterior-
> ating. Just as when a boy I asked every aunt who came to visit
> us whether she had brought along a present for me, so now I am
> asking for leaf-tiles from everyone with whom I have anything
> to do.[1]

But his struggles with recalcitrant circumstances were only beginning: his work for the next eighteen months was literally a race with
time, to rescue from death the multitudes of seriously ill natives who

[1] *More from the Primeval Forest*, p. 11.

flocked to him for treatment, and to construct for them some shelter and accommodation whilst doing it. "My life during these months was lived," he says, "as a doctor in the mornings, and as a master builder in the afternoons." His work on *The Mysticism of Paul the Apostle*, which for a second time he had brought out to Africa for revision and to which he had intended to devote his evenings, had for a second time to be abandoned; for when darkness fell with sunset, he was far too exhausted.

With no possibility of recruiting native labour, and no assistance save that of the half-reluctant and listless attendants who brought patients, with no materials for building at hand and no canoe of his own to transport them from distant places—he struggled on, not grimly but with gallantry, upheld by his faith in God and in his fellow-men and in the supreme worth-whileness of his vocation, and also by his unfailing ability to see the amusing side of a situation, however bleak.

For lack of adequate shelter, several of his patients died; and he was torn between his constant anxiety for them and the urgency of getting leaf-tiles. Once he even wrote, "I am quite in despair." Sometimes he let fall a remark which, though it may be read ironic-ally, is nevertheless intended as no more than a statement of simple fact, as thus: "For the possession of places from which bamboos, raffia, and corded bark can be easily brought away, the tribes used in former days to wage war on each other, just as white nations do for the sake of deposits of metal or coal."

As one reads between the lines of his letter-diaries, afterwards published as *More from the Primeval Forest*, one feels that he is fight-ing continually—fighting against disease and death, fighting the pests of the jungle swamps, fighting his own exasperation with native superstitions, apathy, and indolence, fighting his own weariness. But he is too busy in the day-time to notice this last, or to worry about "several slight sun-strokes" caused by flaws in the leafy roof as he bends over his ailing patients. It is all part of the "terrible prose" of life in Africa.

Death was an unpleasantly frequent visitor in the open hospital wards, performing his grim office before the eyes of the sufferers who yet lived. To add to his gruesome harvest many incurables were brought to Lambaréné, with whom the witch-doctors would have nothing to do, for—"With the medicine-men, my native colleagues, it never happens that a patient dies. They reject hopeless cases at once, acting in this respect like some doctors in European hospitals, who do not want to have their statistics spoilt." But Schweitzer was careless of his reputation in this respect. "If I cannot save them from death I can at least show them love, and perhaps make their end easier."

Burial was even more of a problem, since the negro shares the belief of other primitive peoples that there is uncleanness attaching to a corpse. "If there is a death, every man who can use a spade has disappeared, ostensibly to fish." Schweitzer was reduced to devising artifices to get graves dug, but with little success, and he and his volunteers who were being trained as orderlies generally had to do it themselves.

But by the middle of the year, with the arrival of a young Swiss missionary,[1] and seventy-three packing-cases from Strasburg containing linen, and surgical and medical and kitchen apparatus; and with the arrival a month later of a nurse, Mlle. Kottmann, from Strasburg —he can write with a thankful heart, "Now the clouds are beginning to lift."

In August Noel Gillespie's time was up, and his departure was another cause for sadness.—"I do not know how to thank this good comrade sufficiently for all the help he gave me. . . . But he himself, amid his lectures at Oxford, will remember as if it were a dream, how once he was in Africa doctor's assistant, carpenter, foreman, sexton, and other things besides."

But Gillespie's help, valuable as it was, and the help of a nurse to relieve him of the routine work in the wards, and the spiritual help of his fellow-missionaries,—none of these could relieve him of the main weight of his responsibility, the purely medical. Only a reader with imaginative insight can even begin to appreciate the severity of the strain to which he subjected himself, in body and mind, during this period. His chronicle is too sober, too matter-of-fact; the incidents that he relates are chiefly the amusing ones, and even to some of the many tragedies he gives, if he can, a turn that converts the tear to a smile. Only a man with such qualities as he possessed—a rugged frame and an iron will, a brain of ice and a heart of fire— could have stood such a strain without a respite during these first

---

[1] Monsieur Abrezol was drowned a month after his arrival while bathing in a lake at N'gomo. A strong swimmer, paralysis from the sting of electric fishes was assumed as the cause of this fatality.—"He was a lovable and extraordinarily good all-round man and had won all hearts."

A GROUP OF CHILDREN BORN AT THE HOSPITAL

With the Doctor outside his workroom and study

THE OLD HOSPITAL REBUILT, 1924

months. It came at last in October and, on his own confession, none too soon, yet earlier than he had ventured to hope—"the fulfilment of my dream of having another doctor to help me." And the doctor, Victor Nessmann, was young and vigorous; and a fellow-country-man, even an erstwhile fellow-student of medicine in Strasburg!

And his help came in the very nick of time. Not for a day longer could I have supported the double burden of builder and doctor. How I had suffered from being unable to make my examinations of patients as thorough as they should have been, because in spite of all my efforts I could not summon sufficient energy for the task! And how it had disquieted me that with the strong and risky remedies which so many tropical diseases demand, I could not give sufficient time to each patient! How often ought microscope and test-tube to have been called upon for guidance and were not. In surgery too, only the necessary minimum was undertaken.

So the hoot of the river steamer, which is bringing my country-man, means my release from the distress of medical work which, in spite of the best of good will, has had to be too superficial.[1]

How thankfully and yet how questioningly this man of much experience and many travails must have scanned the deck that was bearing his young untested comrade, "who does not yet know what fatigue is," to Lambaréné. The canoes are quickly manned, and soon lay-to beside the steamer. There is the cheerful greeting, "Now you shall rest and I will take over all the work"; and the quiet rejoinder, with the infectious smile (it is with his eyes that Schweitzer smiles), "Good, then begin at once, and look to the lading of the canoes with your baggage."—Youth's happy untried confidence, and man-hood's stern experience of the harsh realities! How will he shape, this young adventurer? Will he weather the stress? First impressions are favourable: "he proves to be a skilful stevedore." Schweitzer is overcome with emotion. "I can hardly get a word out, so overcome do I feel by the fact that I now have a professional colleague. It is blissful to be able to confess to myself how tired I am."

The first impressions are confirmed as time goes on: the new doctor seems to have been made for Africa! "He is of a practical turn of mind, has the gift of organization, and knows how to tackle the natives. Moreover, he has a sense of humour, without which no one can get on properly out here."

[1] *More from the Primeval Forest*, p. 40.

Schweitzer has now more time to devote to his arduous building operations, and time is now more than ever the factor to be reckoned with. He is now turned carpenter, for the need is for more and more beds. Beds and bed-frames; but he has no planks. Wood in the round must be fetched from a distance of twenty-five miles, and beams from a distance of sixty; then cut on the spot to the required sizes. Phenomenal floods have made navigation difficult. Yet soon forty beds are ready, with frames detachable from the posts for cleaning in the sun. Next, a hut for the storage of tools, with lock and key; and another for bananas and rice; and a large chest with partitions for various tins and bottles. Then another ward must be built to accommodate thirty beds, and yet another for the separate treatment of surgical cases. Then a house on piles for the new doctor, and for the white patients. All this is done with people who have no knowledge of figures or measurements or geometry.

The number of patients increases alarmingly; there has been a migration to the Ogowe district of even more primitive tribes from the interior. This raises many problems, social, industrial, and economic. Schweitzer's discussion of these problems and their most practicable solution occupies a long and highly important section of his book. But the incursion of these foreigners renders linguistic difficulties more knotty than ever. Formerly a knowledge of two, the Galloa and Pahouin, sufficed to render the daily proclamation of his "Six Commandments" intelligible; now this must be abandoned, since "today there are some ten languages spoken in our wards." The arrival of these undisciplined strangers excites in him "a complex feeling of sympathy and despair." Nothing in the hospital is safe from their depredations, and yet their condition is pitiable in the extreme.

Schweitzer shows himself as much a master of all the intricacies of native law and custom, fetich and taboo, as he does of economic problems that are beyond their ken, and of tropical diseases beyond their power to cure. Some of the most informative chapters of his book are devoted to these; and as in philosophical and theological discussion he avoids the use of abstruse terms, so here, avoiding technical phraseology as far as possible, he writes in a language that the uninstructed layman can understand.

Since his first residence, a notable advance had been made in the cure for sleeping sickness by the introduction from the Rockefeller Institute in America of the drug called Tryparsamide; and from

Leverkusen (near Cologne) of "Bayer 205."[1] Schweitzer is now able to record with heartfelt thankfulness numbers of cures effected in cases which would formerly have been given up as hopeless. Of the afflictions inflicted by the natives on each other, one can but note in passing his treatment of homicidal maniacs, of victims of witchcraft, and diagnosis of poisoning. "For investigation of the poisons used," he says, "I have never had time," but the remedies he employs have proved remarkably effective none the less.

But it is impossible in a brief chapter to do justice—even the faintest justice—either to the wealth of interest or the inspiration of this book, or to measure the immensity of the "toils and conflicts" against the magnitude of the achievement. As was well remarked by a reviewer in *The Times Literary Supplement*, it has, "in spite of the absence of any appeal to the emotions, all the zest excited by a well-told story of adventure." But here, says the reviewer—

> "The syringe replaces the rifle; the microbe the big game; and there is a parallel for the thicket to which the man-eater is tracked: [and he quotes Schweitzer]—'In many cases scratches and cutaneous eruptions have turned our patients' skins into coats of mail through which the most practised finger can no longer find any blood-vessel.'"

Once, at the end of a particularly bad day of struggles with theft and shiftlessness, and complete disregard of the elementary sanitary precautions on which the well-being of the whole hospital depends, and the nervous exhaustion all this entails upon himself and his colleagues,—Schewitzer adds the dry comment: "We are learning the full meaning of the interesting fact that we are allowed to spend our life among savages."

Through it all he was oppressed by the thought that pressure of work to secure their physical welfare prevented him from showing himself to the natives "as a man to men."

> I daresay we should have fewer difficulties with our *sauvages*, if we could occasionally sit round the fire with them and show

[1] By a coincidence, one of the first white men in Africa (actually the first in Rhodesia) to be treated by this means was a friend of the writer's with whom he often camped in 1921 in the fly-infested belts of the Loangwa valley, and who was stricken with the disease, to which he succumbed at the end of that year. His case is fully recorded in *Transactions of the Royal Society of Tropical Medicine and Hygiene*, vol. xvi, No. 7, pp. 374 ff., by Sir Philip Manson-Bahr, D.S.O., M.D., whose patient he became, and to whom the writer is indebted for the reference.

ourselves to them as men, and not merely as medicine-men and custodians of law and order. All three of us, we two doctors and Nurse Kottmann, are really so overwhelmed with work that the humanity within us cannot come out properly. But we cannot help it. For the present we are condemned to the trying task of carrying on the struggle with sickness and pain, and to that everything else must give way.[1]

It was not long before Schweitzer was himself a patient. Footsores contracted during his first residence, though long since healed over, had broken out again and developed into ulcers, aggravated by repeated injuries whilst building. Unable to walk he insisted on being carried, against all remonstrances, to the hospital each day to continue his medical work and his carpentry. Before Christmas six white patients (among them a lady and child) arrived at once (he already had on his hands a Canadian with a multiple abscess), and a few days later came another, an Italian who had been mauled by a leopard; "so that at Christmas we had eight white patients to provide for." But he had just got one room ready to accommodate four, and made shift somehow for the remainder.

On Christmas Eve there is a general feeling of depression. The lady, who is lodged in our house, feels very miserable, and while we others sing carols round a decorated palm-tree, Nurse Kottmann sits on the edge of her bed and tries to stop her tears. On the hillside below there is a light burning far into the night, for the Canadian is celebrating his recovery with his roommates. He can even walk about again and help me with the building. . . .

We begin the new year badly, for all three of us are unwell. The new doctor is in bed with boils; Mlle. Kottmann feels miserably out of sorts; and I am suffering more than ever from the ulcers on my feet, which are spreading. I cannot get a shoe on, so I drag myself about in wooden ones. We get through the work after a fashion, but that is all.[2]

But now there comes a piece of news which puts fresh heart into them all. Another surgeon, Mark Lauterburg of Berne, is coming; and of course he must be bringing with him another nurse, perhaps even two! This compels Schweitzer to think about more building.

---

[1] *More from the Primeval Forest*, p. 62.   [2] *Ibid.* pp. 65-67.

Rooms too for reserves of linen, bedding, foodstuffs, bandages, drugs, all which are at present stored in makeshift chests and cases. And so he sets to work, much helped by the convalescent Canadian, to build another house on piles, with a corrugated-iron roof, to contain ten rooms. All went well till the Canadian succumbed to a sunstroke, persistent fever, and so an outburst of new abscesses. Meanwhile Schweitzer and Nurse Kottmann are nearly drowned in a canoe, owing to the thoughtlessness of their crew.

But once again fresh hope is born. The day following this adventure there arrives from Sweden the long and eagerly awaited hospital motor-boat. "Completely covered by a canvas awning, it will protect us both from sun and rain, if the latter is not too heavy." The gift of friends in Sweden, it bears the name "*Tack sa Mycket*" (Many Thanks).—And ten weeks later Dr. Lauterburg appears (though without nurses). And a little later still another young Swiss volunteers his services as a builder for several months. And not long afterwards there arrives another motor-launch, the *Raarup*, the gift of friends in Jutland.

But now the work on the ten-roomed house threatens to come to a standstill for lack of labour. Thirty splendid beams of hardwood— the gift of a grateful timber merchant—are lying on the ground, but there is no one but himself and the Swiss builder to cut them, a task involving precious weeks. "If I wanted five and twenty native clerks, I should have fifty applying tomorrow. But sawyers? No." And here Schweitzer unburdens himself of a protest against the "educated" native which anyone who has had any practical dealings with them will heartily endorse.[1]

How true it is, after all, that civilization does not begin with reading and writing, but with manual labour. Because we have no manual workers here, real progress is impossible. The natives learn to read and write without at the same time learning to use their hands. With these accomplishments they obtain posts as salesmen and clerks, and sit about in white suits. But manual work is despised.

Had I any say in the matter, no native would be allowed to read and write without being apprenticed to some trade. No training of the intellect without simultaneous training of the

[1] The same protest is of course equally valid in the case of the average "educated" British child. For a further expansion of Schweitzer's views on the subject as it affects the native, and especially in relation to agriculture, see Appendix I.

hands! Only so can there be a sound basis for further advance. How ridiculous it seems to me to read that Africa is being opened up to civilization because a railway has been built to this place, a motor-car has got through to that, and an air service is being established between two other localities. That does not mean any real gain. "How far are the natives becoming efficient men?" That is the one thing that matters, and efficient men they can become only through religious and moral teaching combined with manual work. All other things have meaning only when this foundation has been well and truly laid.

And of all handicrafts that of the sawyer is, once more, the most important, for he turns tree-trunks into beams and planks with which we can build houses to live in. Before there were any saw-mills, our ancestors sawed them by hand, and if the natives do not advance by the same road they remain just savages, even if one or another of them, as a commercial or a Civil Service clerk, earns money enough to get his wife silk stockings and high-heeled shoes from Europe. Both they and their descendents will continue, in that case, to live in bamboo huts.[1]

The immediate difficulty was, however, overcome "by an inflamed throat," from which the wife of another timber merchant was suffering. Schweitzer cured her throat, and her grateful husband sent him experienced sawyers for kind services rendered. "A few days see the job finished, and I now have 120 small beams. The new house can now have its roof put on."

At the beginning of May came news of something which, little though he guessed it at the time, was to cause a complete change in his own plans and in the establishment of his hospital. This was an outbreak of dysentery on a timber site far away to the north of Lake Azingo. So on the third of the month he set off in the motor-launch with Dr. Nessmann on a journey of forty-four miles across the lake, and thence by canoe for another fifteen upstream against a strong current, plagued with tsetse-flies. They spent a day examining the workers, giving advice for treatment of the less serious cases, and taking the worst back with them to hospital the next day.—There follows this brief entry in Schweitzer's letter-diary: "On this journey I write my last letter to my father, but it never reaches him, for death called him home that very day, May 5th."

Within a few weeks the dysentery epidemic—of both kinds,

[1] *More from the Primeval Forest*, pp. 81-82.

amoebic and bacillary—had spread to an alarming extent and the hospital was crowded with patients suffering from this painful and very infectious disease. The danger of infection was acute; there were no wards for the isolation of the patients, who polluted everything they touched—the beds, the ground, the food, and worst of all the water; and scarcely a sound native could be persuaded to help. "To such disgusting work there is no bringing them. If there ever *is* a black man who will help, he is loaded with presents and smothered with praise."

This was the very nadir of Schweitzer's misfortunes. Once, in despair at the utter imbecility and incorrigible disobedience of his patients, he threw himself into a chair in his consulting-room and groaned aloud: "What a blockhead I was to come out here to doctor savages like these!" Whereupon Joseph—the faithful Joseph, who had deserted him long since for the timber trade but had now returned more faithful than ever—quietly remarked: "Yes, Doctor, here on earth you are a great blockhead, but not in heaven." But the compliment was lost on the Doctor, whose comment is: "He likes giving utterance to sententious remarks like that. I wish he would support us better in our efforts to check the spread of dysentery!"

On top of the dysentery came news of famine, a disaster which could have been prevented had the natural resources of the country been developed instead of supplanted by unnatural industry. Instead of cultivating maize, plantains (bananas), and manioc (cassava) root, their proper diet, natives had too long been accustomed to depend on the export from Europe and India of polished rice (removal of the inner husk from which has already deprived it of most of its nutritive value and essential vitamin[1]); and now as a result of phenomenal rains in the dry season, this rice could not be transported into the interior. Districts whose people had been provident enough to plant maize were therefore raided by those who had not.

Schweitzer could do nothing to alleviate the famine, at least for the present; he could only continue to fight dysentery and sleeping sickness, build more wards, and repair roofs. And now comes his report of a little difference which he had with an "educated" native, which has been often quoted, but not too often, for it does but make one marvel at the patience of the man.

[1] As is true also of the "white flour" of wheat on which the English public has allowed itself to be nourished for a century.

In the middle of September we get the first rains, and the cry is to bring all the building timber under cover. As we have in the hospital hardly a man capable of work, I begin, assisted by two loyal helpers, to haul beams and planks about myself. Suddenly I catch sight of a negro in a white suit sitting by a patient whom he has come to visit. "Hullo! friend," I call out, "won't you lend us a hand?"—"I am 'an intellectual' and don't drag wood about," came the answer.—"You're lucky," I reply; "I too wanted to become 'an intellectual,' but I didn't succeed."[1]

Surely this deserves to be counted among the classic instances of the "retort courteous"! (It was whilst actually engaged in these exertions that Schweitzer received news that he had been elected honorary Doctor of Philosophy in the University of Prague.)

With the autumn of 1925 the famine had reached Lambaréné. Schweitzer, foreseeing its approach from the early summer, had (like Joseph of old) laid in an emergency store of rice, and was thus able to supply at need the Mission at Samkita, two friendly merchants, and an English factory. Without the aid of the motor-launch, both to fetch and to carry, there would have been provision for none.

In the autumn he was joined by another friend from Alsace, Mlle. Haussknecht, who came as second nurse, a great relief to Mlle. Kottmann, especially in the oversight of the dysentery patients. But the dysentery epidemic was fast going from bad to worse, and a resolution was taking shape in Schweitzer's mind which for the present, however, he kept to himself.

He had long felt that the area of the present hospital was too small, that its site was not the best that could have been chosen, that even the new isolation wards were inadequate, that the space for his mentally afflicted patients was too cramped. He had been obliged to send away so many of these last in bonds to their villages, there to suffer torment till death released them, whereas under his care so many might have been cured. "What I suffer at heart in such cases I have never let even my helpers know." He could not isolate the dying, nor even the dead. He could not house his workers properly. There were many other considerations which, as he turned them over in his mind, seemed to make the undertaking of building a new hospital imperative. He reproached himself with lack of courage in not having done so at the outset, instead of rebuilding

---

[1] *More from the Primeval Forest*, p. 103.

Schweitzer setting piles

Painting the main building

BUILDING THE NEW HOSPITAL, 1926

THE MAIN HOSPITAL BUILDING COMPLETED, 1926

the old one; but then reflected that without labour or canoes or materials this would have been impossible at the time. But now he had the materials and he had two motor-launches; and, with regard to labour, the famine, dreadful as it was, had put an unexpected weapon into his hand. "If a man will not work, neither shall he eat." The attendants who accompany their patients and who have to be fed in any case, why should they sit about all the day idle? Similarly, the light patients and the convalescents. Even as things were, the inmates no longer sought to evade work, but were even volunteering for it, because they got an extra ration if they did. Further, the famine convinced Schweitzer that his hospital could never be established on a satisfactorily sound basis until it could, in a measure at least, maintain itself with the necessities of subsistence.

Pondering on such thoughts during "these dismal weeks," Schweitzer made solitary journeys to a site nearly two miles upstream which had attracted his attention, for several reasons, during his first residence at Lambaréné. Next he interviewed the District Commissioner, with satisfactory results. Not till all negotiations were completed did he broach the matter to the doctors and nurses. (It may be said at this point that in their minds, and in the minds of anyone who has since worked with Schweitzer at Lambaréné, there has never existed a doubt as to who was the natural leader, the most able administrator, the hardest worker, the most competent doctor and surgeon, and in every respect the most practically-minded of them all.)

At first they were dumb with astonishment; then they break out into shouts of joy. There is no need to convince them of the necessity of the move.... The natives stare at us with astonishment; to such gesticulation and such a din of conversation among us they are quite unaccustomed![1]

To concur with and applaud a proposal, however, is one thing; to execute it and assume full responsibility for it is another. There was only one man who could plan the design, only one who could superintend the building, for his was the only authority which the natives would recognize without question. And this, working the old hospital concurrently, would take a year. Schweitzer says nothing of what this meant to him, but only of the sacrifice it entailed for

[1] *Ibid.* p. 114.

his wife and daughter, who were expecting him home at the end of
the winter of 1925–1926.

The first thing to be done was to peg out the area, and to
clear it.

> Compass in hand, we work our way into the forest and cut
> tracks which make measurements possible. If we come upon a
> swamp, we have to content ourselves with driving long poles
> into the soft ground at intervals of 20 metres. If we stumble on a
> thicket inhabited by the formidable red ants, white men and black
> all try who can retreat the quickest. These ants establish themselves
> on the branches, and drop in clusters on invaders of their preserve.[1]

In addition to their full ration, Schweitzer gives his helpers
presents. If asked to choose, one and all would ask for tobacco or
alcohol. He gives them only useful things, such as spoons or sleeping-
mats. Each day of tree-felling passes "like the movement of a
symphony": *lento, moderato, adagio, scherzo,*—picturesquely and
amusingly Schweitzer describes each one. Then comes the grand
finale:

> All are jolly now. The wicked forest, on account of which
> they have to stand here instead of sitting comfortably in the
> hospital, shall have a bad time of it. Wild imprecations are hurled
> at it. Howling and yelling they attack it, axes and bush-knives vie
> with each other in battering it. But—no bird must fly up, no
> squirrel show itself, no question must be asked, no command
> given. With the very slightest distraction the spell would be
> broken. . . .[2]

But the watchful eyes of the superintendent, so anxious to get the
utmost possible amount of work out of his charges, are equally
vigilant of the weather. They must not be allowed to get wet, they
must not be surprised by a rainstorm on the river. This would induce
malaria. One day, when Dr. Nessmann was in charge, their canoes
on their return were overtaken by a violent thunderstorm, and
Schweitzer awaited their arrival for an hour and a half on the river-
bank "in dreadful anxiety." At last they came in.

> One after another the canoes return in pitch darkness and under
> a deluge of rain. They had just time to reach the bank somewhere

---

[1] *More from the Primeval Forest*, p. 115.   [2] *Ibid.* p. 118

or other, and no one was drowned. I mount to the doctor's house, almost dizzy with joy.[1]

Meanwhile the condition of his patients in the old hospital, both black and white, is causing him ever-increasing solicitude. He spends his second Christmas Eve by the deathbed of a dying Swiss. "We bring him a little tree decked with candles and sing carols at his bedside. He has a clear moment or two and understands what it means, a happy smile lighting up his thin, yellow face."

The new hospital must be built on piles; and it must be built of durable materials. Brick or stone are unobtainable, but hardwood and sheet-iron can be had in plenty. "So," says Schweitzer, "I shall be a modern prehistoric man, and build my hospital like a lake-dweller's village, but roofed with corrugated iron."—He is careful to char the ends of his piles, which have to be ferried by canoe from sixteen miles up-river, and to wet the glowing ends in order to secure the maximum hardness; to sink them on a foundation of stones; to make certain that they are true to perpendicular, and that their tops are exactly level. He sets and fixes each pile himself. He works out with mathematical precision the most suitable measurements for their width and height; also their numbers and distances apart. So too the measurements for each ward, by a calculation based upon the positions, numbers, and requirements of each bed. He arranges for the accommodation of 200 patients and their attendants. Gradually the new hospital takes shape and begins to grow before his eyes, till three long, narrow, parallel lines of buildings have arisen, aligned to the course of the sun, and so arranged as to take the utmost advantage of any breeze. Utilizing his expert knowledge of the principles employed in the craft of organ-building, he devised a novel method of double-roofing for air-space between the timber and the iron, which makes for coolness and ventilation: it is a method which has since been copied elsewhere in Africa. Other details which he does not mention, but to which attention is drawn by his translator, C. T. Campion, are these: the laundry is opposite the ward where the patients receive treatment, so that the nurses can supervise the dressers and washerwomen without leaving the premises; the fowl-house is close to the nurses' bungalow, so that their clucking can be heard if wild animals, driver-ants, or thieves attack them. But indeed a scrutiny of the ground-plan of the hospital as shown on

[1] *Ibid.* p. 119.

the first page of his book, and then of the photographs of the finished product at the end of it, is sufficient evidence of the extraordinary care and thoroughness with which it was designed and completed.

By the end of April a young Swiss carpenter arrives—"and now I can breathe freely, though not quite." The great question is whether he will get on with the natives. What are the essential prerequisites for this? "Ability to combine in right measure firmness and kindness, to avoid unnecessary talk, and to find a jocular remark at the right moment."—With him too comes another nurse, a sister of Dr. Lauterburg; and a little later Dr. Nessmann[1] (recalled for his military training) is replaced by Dr. Trensz. The latter had been in the country but a few months before he made an important discovery into the cause of the so-called bacillary dysentery (published in Strasburg in 1928).

Other things now demand Schweitzer's time; in addition to fixing piles and preparing sites, collecting and distributing materials, economizing time and labour for all, he can give his mind to the digging of a well, the cultivation of a garden for vegetables, preparing colour-wash for buildings as they are completed, and attending the serious cases, which are many and various, in the old hospital.

At the beginning of 1927 the new hospital was completed sufficiently to allow for the removal from the old one to begin.

In the evening [of January 21st] I make the final journey and bring up the last patients, the mental ones among them, and the latter behave excellently. They have been told that in the new hospital they will live in cells with wooden floors, so they imagine they are moving into a palace. In the old cells the floor was the damp earth.

I shall never forget the first evening in the new hospital. From every fireside and from every mosquito-net they call out to me: "This is a good hut, doctor, a good hut!"

For the first time since I came to Africa my patients are housed as human beings should be. How I have suffered during these years from having to pen them together in stifling, dark rooms! Full of gratitude I look up to God who has allowed me to experience such a joy. With deep emotion, too, I think of friends in Europe, in reliance upon whose help I could venture to move the hospital, and replace the bamboo huts with corrugated-iron wards.[2]

[1] Dr. Nessmann suffered and perished for his faith in a Nazi concentration camp during the war.

[2] More from the Primeval Forest, p. 162.

Towards the end of March, Dr. Trensz, whose full year's term of invaluable help is over, is replaced by Dr. Ernest M. Mündler from Switzerland, who brings with him an English lady volunteer, Mrs. C. E. B. Russell. She supervises the timber-felling and the laying-out of a plantation, and is presently assisted by another Swiss volunteer, Karl Sutter, formerly in the timber trade.

Schweitzer is impressed with the command which the new English lady at once assumes over the natives. "Since then it has been my experience on the whole that the authority of a white woman is more readily recognized by our primitive negroes than that of us men."[1] The value of Mrs. Russell's services to the cause did not end with her outdoor labours, however; a good German scholar, she was afterwards responsible for the translation of Schweitzer's *From My African Notebook* into English, as well as of his *Indian Thought and its Development*, and of several of his lectures; acted as interpreter on his tours in Great Britain; and has given many lantern and cinema lectures on behalf of the Hospital not only here but also in British Columbia and New York. She also visited Lambaréné on three subsequent occasions as a volunteer on the staff. *The Path to Reconstruction* from her pen is an important introduction to Schweitzer's Philosophy of Civilization, and her charming little book *My Monkey Friends*, which is largely reminiscent of Lambaréné, she dedicates to "Dr. Albert Schweitzer, who teaches reverence for life, and who has saved many a little orphan, human and sub-human, from misery and destruction." To her also the present writer is indebted for a translation of one of Schweitzer's sermons to the natives which will appear in its place,[2] as well as for much valuable help and information in collecting and compiling the materials for this book, and for several of the illustrations.

His last act (while building the boat-house) was to set the piles for another house to contain five rooms: "it is for the doctors to

---

[1] This was also on the whole the experience of the present writer during five years' close contact with other tribes of the Bantu race in Northern Rhodesia. He attributes it to the fact that the mentality of the child-races of the world is still very literally that of children; and would venture the opinion that, although inter-tribal wars and other causes have in the main rendered government by chiefs and headmen a necessity, the natural form of government is matriarchal. In fact, primogeniture is still most often through the female line.

In Mrs. Russell's case the faculty of command was inherited, and was also due to close experience with natives in many parts of the world as well as to an innate sympathy with them.

[2] pp. 119 ff.

live in some day." All the main buildings were now complete; he could safely leave the internal arrangements to his colleagues. By the middle of July 1927 he was ready to start for home. One would have thought that the prospect would have afforded him unmixed joy, like the prospect of release from prison. But such was not the case. Of the many farewells that he had to take—of his colleagues, of his Mission friends, of his native helpers, and of many others— perhaps the one that touched him most was his parting with a murderer.

The report that I am going to Europe has reached a mental patient, N'tschambi by name, who is now allowed to go about in freedom. He had been brought to us some months before in chains, having in his mental darkness killed a woman. With tears in his eyes he comes to me and says: "Doctor, have you given orders that no one can send me away while you are in Europe?" —"Certainly, N'tschambi. No one can send you away without first having a great palaver with me." Deeply relieved, he presses my hands, and the tears stream down his cheeks. . . . How glad I am that I can offer to him and to others in the same misery a refuge for a long period![1]

As the ship steamed away from port at Cape Lopez, Schweitzer stood a long while on deck watching the receding coast till it was no longer visible.

All the needs and all the work of the past three years sweep through my memory, and with deep emotion I think of the helpers of both sexes who have shared them with me, as well as of the friends and associations as whose deputy I was allowed to start this work of mercy. Joy at the success of it is not what I feel; rather I feel myself humbled, and ask myself how I earned the privilege of carrying on such a work, and in such a work attaining to success. And there breaks through, time and again, a feeling of pain that I must leave it for a time, and tear myself loose from Africa, which has become for me a second home.[2]

[1] *More from the Primeval Forest*, p. 166.   [2] *Ibid.* p. 168.

CHAPTER VIII

VISITS TO LONDON AND PRAGUE

WHEN Schweitzer returned to Europe for the second time, he was for the second time at the limit of his strength. Nevertheless, for the first six weeks after his return he spent only three nights in his own home; "rushing" (says a friend) "from one city to another, often by night, always without comfort, and always third class if no fourth class was available." From November 1927 to February 1928 he was again on tour in Sweden and Denmark, and wrote to Mr. Peet from Amsterdam: "I am under doctor's orders to take a rest, though I have broken them to come to Holland to perform the marriage ceremony for the son of an old friend. If I am guilty of breaking them again by going this week-end to England, now I am so near, it is because I want to show Miss Maude Royden of the Guildhouse, before she goes on her world tour, my appreciation of all that she and her friends have done in raising money to provide a special section of my hospital for the mental cases. But I cannot give any organ recitals till I am thoroughly rested. Please tell my English friends that this visit is almost 'incognito,' but I shall be returning to England in the spring to carry out many lecturing and organ engagements."

He returned from Sweden early in March 1928, stopping at Paris and Strasburg for organ recitals on the way; and after six weeks' "rest" for writing at Königsfeld, arrived in London early in May. Here he gave two recitals each in the churches of St. Martin's and All Hallows, and for the Bach Cantata Club at the Royal College of Music, and took part in the Bach Choir Concert in the same hall. Thence to Birmingham University, and the West Midlands, for similar recitals and for lectures on his work in Africa.

Among his first and truest friends in London were two whose admiration for his life's work and thought found immediate expression in practical aid to his hospital. Their names, already distinguished equally in the furtherance of sound learning and in the cause of social service, were destined—indirectly as a result of their friendship with him—to be linked sixteen years later in the bond of a closer fellow-ship. The Rev. G. W. Hudson Shaw, Fellow of Balliol, was then Rector of St. Botolph's, Bishopsgate, and chief among the promoters of education and social welfare in Bethnal Green; whilst Miss Maude Royden, D.D., in pursuance of her activities as an Oxford University Extension Lecturer, had resigned her position as assistant preacher at the City Temple in order to administer her Guildhouse for Fellowship Services in Kensington.

So moved was Mr. Hudson Shaw by an address on Lambaréné given by the Doctor to a meeting of which he was chairman that, without a thought, he cast his gold watch into the collection. Remembering later that the watch, precious though it was to him, was of old-fashioned make and probably worth not more than the value of its gold, he offered to "ransom" it for a much larger sum. Somewhat to his surprise, Dr. Schweitzer asked if he might keep the watch for a few days longer. It was soon returned, but this time with an inscription: "Rev. Hudson Shaw et Dr. Albert Schweitzer —fratres. 21/5/28." The considerate thoughtfulness of this gesture was noted by Miss Royden as characteristic of the "quality of per-fection—and I should add, of exquisite care—that gives a grace and fitness to all he says and does—trifles in themselves perhaps—but not trifles to those to whom beauty is as precious as strength."

The same quality of artistic perfection was remarked in his sermons. These, delivered with the utmost simplicity of phrasing and direct-ness, were in much request at the Guildhouse, packed as it always was almost to suffocation on these occasions by a spell-bound audience. "He never gave us a long sermon, but we always wished he had. . . ." Miss Royden volunteered to interpret for him, but with some trepidation when she found that she was required to translate sentence by sentence. "It seemed impossible that, by such a method, the speaker would ever really get into his stride or seize his audience. But I soon realized my mistake. The address was com-posed with such a perfect understanding of the difficulties, and so great a mastery of the construction needed for each sentence by itself and in its relation to the whole, as to leave one convinced that it was the *only* right way of speaking through an interpreter at all." Of the many sermons that he has preached at the Guildhouse, perhaps the best remembered is one on the subject of Forgiveness. This affords one of the most striking examples of Schweitzer's faculty of adapting his treatment of the same subject to accord with his hearers' understanding; for he has preached on Forgiveness in a very different manner to his negroes in Lambaréné, and has written upon it in his *Civilization and Ethics* in a manner suitable to the comprehension of philosophers and psychologists alike.

Even more striking was the "terrific impact" of his presence within doors—a veritable tornado—with a riot of people surging round him; secretaries with their typewriters relegated to the bathroom and the stairs; important and importunate callers, with whom he had light-heartedly made appointments and had forgotten all about, demanding interviews,—their indignation melting, when admitted eventually, "like wax in the sun." And when before his departure, itself an uproarious occasion, Miss Royden tried to express in halting French their gratitude for his visit and the "honour" that she and her household felt in entertaining him as their guest, the Doctor, gravely shocked, drew her aside and besought her never to use such a word as that, "*parce que ce n'est pas convenable parmi les chrétiens.*"

One of his sincerest admirers was Mr. Ambrose Pomeroy-Crag, who acted as treasurer to the Guildhouse. This gentleman had made it a regular practice, when London was in darkness during the war, of meeting the night trains at Victoria Station and guiding the troops on leave to their destinations. This he did for a thousand nights. After his death in 1931 the Guildhouse resolved to perpetuate his memory by linking his name with a gift to the Hospital at Lambaréné, and wrote to ask the Doctor what form of memorial would be most acceptable. He replied that there was dire need of a ward for the mental patients, many of whom were too violent to be safely housed in a bamboo hut. When the ward was erected he wrote that he had inscribed and affixed to the wall a plaque to commemorate the gift,[1] and proposed to send an exact replica of it in teak to the Guildhouse. The inscription on the original read as follows:

En Europe, pendant la Guerre, il guida les soldats dans les ténèbres de Londres. En Afrique, dans la forêt vierge, dans la case Pomeroy-Crag, à l'hôpital de Lambaréné, il sera l'hôte de ceux dont l'esprit est dans les ténèbres.

Que sa mémoire soit bénie et que son esprit vive en nous.

At the request of the Guildhouse he sent a translation for the replica:

[1] A graphic description of the ceremony of unveiling the tablet at Lambaréné was contributed by Mrs. Russell to the *Torch* for May 1931.

In Europe, during the Great War, he guided the soldiers on leave through the darkness of London. Today in Africa, in the depths of the primaeval forest, at the Lambaréné hospital, in his name we receive and shelter those whose minds wander in darkness. Blest be his memory and may his spirit live ever in us.

Another of his friends was Miss Dorothy Mannering, honorary secretary to the Guildhouse. When some years later she, too, died, the Doctor was again consulted. This time he replied that the most pressing need in Lambaréné was for a well. It was sunk, with this inscription cut into the cement:

In memory of Dorothy Mannering, this well of pure water so precious to all who benefit by it.

Again, when at the Rector's instance the Church of St. Botolph's presented and endowed a lamp to be placed on the quay of the riverside where patients to the hospital were often landed in the darkness of the tropical night, he received a letter of thanks "in words as full of light as the lamp itself."

Schweitzer's first care on his arrival home was to find doctors and nurses to replace his colleagues at Lambaréné who for reasons of health, or from family necessities, were obliged to return to Europe sooner than was expected. His new volunteers were Drs. Mündler, Hediger, Stalder, and Mlle. Dr. Schnabel—all from Switzerland. To his sorrow a fifth, Dr. Eric Dölken, died of heart failure *en route* to Lambaréné.

His second care, and one which occupied all his spare time during this two years' interlude, was to complete his work on *The Mysticism of Paul the Apostle*. "I did not wish to take the manuscript with me to Africa a third time, and I soon found myself once more at home in the subject-matter. Chapter after chapter came slowly into existence." This last sentence might well be called a euphemism. For the truth of the matter is (though he does not confess it) that he would often work all through the night, enjoying the absolute peace and freedom from interruption, until six o'clock in the morning when he would retire to rest for four hours.

But his spare time might be described as sparse, for in the spring and early summer he and his wife were again in Holland and England, and in the autumn and winter in Switzerland, Germany, and Czechoslovakia; and in 1929 he undertook several organ recitals in Germany. "When not travelling, I lived with my wife and child at the mountain health resort of Königsfeld in the Black Forest, or at Strasburg." The fact that he had not completed his monumental work on St. Paul before the end of this "furlough" is not surprising; the miracle is that he succeeded in doing so before reaching Lambaréné. The last chapter was written on shipboard between Bordeaux and Cape Lopez, and the Preface on the river steamer from Cape Lopez to Lambaréné.

On August 28, 1928, Schweitzer delivered an address on Goethe at Frankfort, on his receiving from the city the Goethe Prize, which is awarded in recognition of "Service to Humanity." Like all his utterances it is distinguished by its own high literary quality. It was translated by his friend, C. T. Campion, and published in the *Hibbert Journal* the same year.

In his studies both of St. Paul the missionary and of Bach the musician, several aspects of Schweitzer's own personality are mirrored, whether consciously or unconsciously, to himself: it is the nature of the great to reflect greatness. But in his study of Goethe the humanist they spring to light, and with the candour of grateful affection and admiration he acknowledges them. And in the honour which the citizens of Frankfort accorded him they testified their own recognition of the fact that the mantle of "this Frankfort child" had descended on the pupil-teacher of Strasburg, who, in the many-sided genius and lofty character of Goethe, had himself found a supreme example of the union of creative with practical serviceable activity. Hence his explanation of the personal debt which he owes to this "giant among the intellectuals,"—who was no "Olympian" after all, but one whose spirit, though it dwelt among the heights, deemed no task too lowly that could be of service to his fellows.

In November 1928 Schweitzer was in Cologne and Barmen for lectures and recitals, and early in December again in Prague to receive his honorary degree of Doctor of Philosophy. Here he lectured on "The Hellenization of Christianity"; on Bach; and on his work in Africa. After lunching with President Masaryk—one of the most active sympathizers with Schweitzer's thought and life-work—he went directly to the Smetana Saal to try the organ, where he remained till 7.30 P.M. at which time another concert was due. He sat through the performance till it was ended, refreshed with a few sandwiches, and then continued his practice at the organ till nearly midnight, when he went off to supper with friends and remained till 2 A.M. Having given his recital the following afternoon, he spent the same evening in trying the organ at the Evangelical Church, again till nearly midnight, when the police intervened to inform him that he was breaking the law, by disturbing the slumbers of good citizens. His sense of the comedy of the situation so diverted the police that they departed in great good-humour, while he adjourned with his friends for another nocturnal supper.

Accompanied by his wife and also by Mrs. Russell, he left for Germany in the first week in December.

Here, from the diary of their companion, is an account of a day in Germany about this time.

> Writing till 2.30 A.M. After a roll and coffee at 10 he began to prepare for a recital on an unknown organ. He went on without a break till 3, when he was carried off to see and try a bad new organ. At 4 his midday dinner, his first refreshment since 10. At 5 an unknown artist begged to draw him, was accorded ten minutes, and took twenty. Then he had twenty minutes' rest on his bed. At 6 by motor-car fifty minutes to another town. Meeting strangers and preparations for a lantern-lecture. Fifteen minutes' rest lying across two chairs. Lecture from 8 to 10. Then to a restaurant so that all who wished might have an opportunity of meeting him while he tried to snatch some supper. Back to the other town at midnight. Bed at 1.30 A.M.—The money he earned in Germany was not given to Lambaréné, but to German charities as there was much distress.

Leaving his wife at their holiday home in Königsfeld, Schweitzer continued the journey to Alsace to fulfil other engagements in western Europe, having Mrs. Russell's company as far as Strasburg whence she was bound for her second visit to Lambaréné.

> I think [she writes] if he had been nothing else, he might have been a great composer. There is a marked individuality about what he improvises, though not infrequently it is dance-music. But he never writes it down, and it is never the same twice over. Before I said farewell to him, just before my second visit to Lambaréné, he took me to St. Nicholas Church in Strasburg and offered to play me anything I asked. I chose the Prelude and Fugue in E. Moll, and he said, "What next?" I said I should like it again, and got it again and yet again. Then the Prelude and Fugue in C. Dur, twice. Then he switched off the light and said, "Now I'll

play something for 'Canada' " (my little monkey, left at Lambaréné), and proceeded to improvise more beautifully than I have
ever heard before or since. It was all full of the magic of the African
forest, the moonlight in the jungle and on the river, the merry
gambols of the little monkeys in the trees when the sun is shining.—
I think this organ-recital, which lasted nearly two hours, was the
loveliest of all I heard. Then we had supper at the station, and he
saw me off by a late train.

At the end of 1929 Schweitzer was again in Lambaréné, and
returned to Europe at the beginning of 1932.

It was during this period that there appeared the first noteworthy
study of Schweitzer in English, by Professor J. D. Regester of
Washington in 1931, a book that is worthy of its subject. Though its
author had but few materials wherewith to make his portrait at
that date, it is a remarkably life-like portrait none the less. Its
features are revealed in such passages as these:

> Almost boundless energy and activity, directed by a peculiarly
> sensitive sympathy with all human experience and a remarkably
> intensive concern for the spiritual and physical fortunes of
> mankind, are the features which appear most prominently in
> Schweitzer's character. When confronted at any place by human
> misfortune, pain, or difficulty, his helping response is spontaneous
> and unrestrained. . . .
>
> His intellectual frankness and vigorous self-expression make their
> appearance only through victory over a native reserve. A pro-
> tective reticence concealed his feelings in boyhood, but has yielded
> to the earnestness of his later intellectual life and the vigour of
> his convictions. . . . Each feature in the intellectual history of
> Schweitzer has its essential place in this development; and, taken
> together, his studies and their results led to his humanitarian
> activity as inevitably as the premises of a syllogism to their
> conclusion.

During this period also Schweitzer wrote *My Life and Thought*,
translated by his friend C. T. Campion into English and published
in 1933. Among the many appreciations which it received, perhaps
the most discerning was a review contributed to the *New Statesman
and Nation* by Lyn Ll. Irvine. Referring to Schweitzer's remark
in the memoirs of his childhood that "the great secret of success is
to go through life as a man who never gets used up," the writer
continues:

Schweitzer has never got used up, neither in his early prodigality, when as a student in Paris he studied philosophy straight through the night until it was time for his morning lesson on the organ with Widor; nor in his later years facing the demands of an overcrowded and under-staffed tropical hospital. Part of the secret of his inexhaustibility must be physical, but the greater part is the sense of proportion that made the curate stop speaking, and made the theologian of European fame content and amused to be set aside by an African preacher.

But as this rather bare, entirely unemotional book shows, Schweitzer has never taken any sort of egotistical satisfaction in the fine organization of his life. It is the most objective of autobiographies. He does not trouble to underestimate his own achievements any more than he would wish to underestimate those of another man; and nowhere does he make any suggestion that he was providentially gifted to play a special part in a mission to humanity. He examines the failure of the nineteenth and twentieth centuries, and expounds his doctrine of reverence for life as a scientist putting forth the results of many years of research. . . .

There is so much forethought and there are so few loose ends in his life that the whole book is in danger of floating away from us. But just at the end, with uncanny fitness, the Blakean worm lifts its head and speaks. "Only at quite rare moments," says the philosopher of world- and life-affirmation, "have I felt really glad to be alive." It is the last thing we expect him to say; it sweeps us in a moment from daylight almost too clear to be true into the twilight of the mystery of existence: and yet by it—coming so strangely at the end of this record of achievement, success, and service to mankind—our belief in Schweitzer's greatness is established.

D.D., HONORIS CAUSA, OXFORD, 1932
With his English translator, the late C. T. Campion

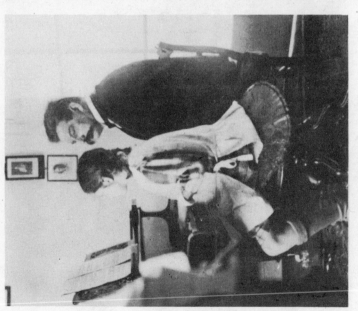

WITH HIS DAUGHTER RHENA, 1930

A STREET IN THE HOSPITAL, 1932

CHAPTER IX

LAMBARÉNÉ: THIRD PERIOD

As anyone who has lived in any of the French or British dependencies in Africa will know, there are on a rough classification three influences, for good or ill, at work in the life of the negro: political; industrial or commercial; and missionary. In the case of the first, obedience to the white man is unquestioned because, whether civil or military, it is backed by the whole weight of law, and the native knows that the law is supported by force if need be. In the case of the second there is more room for freedom, because (although the native is generally bound by contract to his employer, whether planter or miner or trader) he knows that he has redress for injustice in the civil courts. In the case of the third there is absolute freedom, since the authority of the missionary must depend entirely on the exercise of moral suasion, not of coercion in any form. On the whole it may be said that the civil servant is there to protect; the industrialist to exploit; the missionary to educate.

Fluency in the native dialect is an obvious asset to any kind of settler, and ignorance of it an equally obvious disadvantage. It is a curious deficiency in Schweitzer that—though he has cultivated a remarkably retentive ear-memory, speaks French, German, and his native Alsatian with equal fluency, and has a scholar's close knowledge of three dead languages besides—he has never yet acquired a facility in speaking to the negroes in any of their very much simpler languages, although he can follow them to some extent when they speak to him; but in expressing himself to them he has still to depend on an interpreter. It is all the greater tribute to his personality that, despite this, he is able to exercise an authority over them almost as great as the impersonal authority of a District Commissioner. To such an extent is this so that they have got into the habit of taking their domestic feuds to him for arbitration or judgment, as if to a self-appointed court. From the first he gained the reputation among them of "something of a military character," and his young colleague was at once known as "lieutenant"; since then, the title of "Captain" has become for him a variant appellation for his other affectionate soubriquets, "the old Doctor," and "the big Doctor" ("big" in respect of physical size).

Social morality is so much a matter of social custom and depends upon conditions peculiar to the collective life of the community, that it must needs differ widely between the white and black races. This is especially so in the case of marriage. The whole economic life of the black races is regulated by the property valuation of their wives. Wives are so expensive that a negro is obliged to marry on the hire-purchase system, and premiums for his future wife are paid on his behalf by his parents till he is in a position to pay them himself. Often even after marriage the unfortunate husband is still in arrears with his payments, and if these are not forthcoming on demand, his wife's family are liable to remove her without warning. This custom used to cause Schweitzer grave concern till he realized that it, like polygamy, is part of the whole structure of native life and will take generations of education to eradicate. Drastic abolition of this custom, as of many others, would be a worse evil than their present retention. If some of the customs and even the laws which prevail among ourselves were sanely and rationally examined they might possibly be found to be just as anomalous. Meanwhile, both here and there, one has to make the best of them.

How excited I was in my early days in Africa when on entering the Hospital one morning I was told that a man had had his wife stolen in the night! I instituted a thorough investigation, heard what the husband had to say, sought out witnesses, and tried to learn who might be suspected, why he had carried off the woman and whither he was likely to have taken her. But it seemed to me that the natives were taking the affair less tragically than I did, and were not particularly anxious about the fate of the poor stolen woman.

Since then many women have been stolen from the Hospital. But I make no investigation; I am content to express to the husband a friendly regret that he must now take the trouble to find the money.

Truth demands that I should here observe that if the wife's family did not proceed in this way, in the majority of cases they would not get their due.[1]

[1] From *My African Notebook*, pp. 52-53.

Here is an amusing instance of the summary way in which the Doctor sometimes deals with his litigants.

Very early one morning the noise of an altercation at the Hospital was wafted up to our dwelling-house. In the night a patient had taken another man's canoe and gone out fishing by moonlight. The owner of the boat surprised him as he returned at dawn and demanded for the use of the canoe a large monetary compensation as well as all the fish he had caught. By the laws current among the natives, this was his actual right.

The case was brought before me and, as often before, I had to act as judge. First I made known that on my land not native law, but the law of reason of the white man is in force and is proclaimed by my lips. Then I proceeded to examine the legal position.

I established the fact that both men were at the same time right and wrong. "You are right," I said to the owner of the canoe, "because the other man ought to have asked for permission to use your boat. But you are wrong because you are careless and lazy. You were careless because you merely twisted the chain of your canoe round a palm-tree instead of fastening it with a padlock as you ought to do here. By your carelessness you led this other man into temptation to make use of your canoe. Of laziness you are guilty because you were asleep in your hut on this moonlight night instead of making use of the good opportunity for fishing."

"But you," I said, turning to the other, "were in the wrong when you took the boat without asking the owner's permission. You were in the right because you were not so lazy as he was and you did not want to let the moonlight night go by without making some use of it."

In view of the established legal usage, I then gave sentence that the man who went fishing must give a third of the fish to the owner as compensation, and might keep one-third for himself because he had taken the trouble to catch the fish. The remaining third I claimed for the Hospital, because the affair took place here and I had to waste my time adjusting the palaver.[1]

When, as happens not seldom at Lambaréné, members of mutually hostile tribes arrive simultaneously for treatment, Schweitzer refuses them admission until they have composed their differences. He tells them that the hospital belongs, not to him, but to Jesus who has

[1] *Ibid.* pp. 101-102.

given a commandment, "Love one another," obedience to which is the condition of their admission for treatment. In this way, he tells us, he has been the witness of several poignant scenes of reconciliation!

It is against the background of this wholesome respect of the natives for their Doctor as a disciplinarian that his own description of "A Sunday in Lambaréné" should be read.

Even during the years of his most arduous labours, Schweitzer has never relinquished his right and his privilege to preach to the natives of West Africa the simple gospel of Jesus. To their minds the subtleties of "sound doctrine" would in any case be manifestly something incomprehensible. By orthodox theologians, whatever their particular shibboleth, the Christian faith is uniformly represented as "not easy," but as "difficult." And so indeed it is if viewed through the fog of their confused and variable interpretations. But until it can be disengaged from these webs of fine-spun sophistries, and shown to be the most elementally simple truth of which the mind is capable, and therefore also the most profound—not an intellectual puzzle to be wrestled with, but the impact of Life upon life, and therefore self-evident to the most childlike intelligence—it can never claim to be authoritative, absolute, and universal.

In 1916, towards the close of his first three years' sojourn with the Africans, Schweitzer was already in a position to rebut the doctrinaire view of Christianity—that it is intellectually difficult.

> What does the forest dweller understand of Christianity, and how does he understand—or misunderstand—it? In Europe I met the objection again and again that Christianity is something too high for primitive man, and it used to disturb me; now, as a result of my experience, I can boldly declare, "No, it is not."[1]

So he wrote in 1916. Many years later, in the early 1930's, he allowed his friends in England a glimpse into his methods as an evangelist. His aim is to present the Christian faith as a "way"—a following, an allegiance; not to substitute one form of superstition for another. It does not consist in correct postures or attitudes or the vain repetition of prescribed prayers, but in an inner attitude of heart and will. Therefore he chooses for his themes passages from the first three Gospels chiefly, as well upon what he describes as

[1] *On the Edge of the Primeval Forest*, p. 153.

"the finest sayings" of St. Paul. But even here:

> How careful one must be in preaching not to speak of things of which the Africans can have no notion! There are a number of the parables of Jesus one either cannot use or must re-write because the natives of the Ogowe region do not know what a vine or a cornfield is.[1]

The subject of this sermon is "Forgiveness." (It is very instructive to compare his simple explication of its meaning to these untutored children of nature with his treatment of the same subject as he explains it to philosophers.[2])

A Sunday in Lambaréné

The old Hospital was at the Mission station. So the sick and those who came with them had the opportunity of attending Divine Service. The new Hospital lies two miles up-stream from the Mission. There is no path along the river-bank, and it is impossible to make one because of the numerous swamps. Anyone then who wants to go from the Hospital to the Service at the Mission must go in a boat. But most patients have neither boat nor rowers. It is true they come in a boat. But the people who brought them have paddled off home again, leaving them there alone, or with an attendant, to be fetched away later.

If, therefore, the inmates of the Hospital are to get to know the Gospel, a Service must be held for them here. So I preach every Sunday morning in the Hospital.

Among my sick people there are many who know nothing whatever of Christianity, and have scarcely had an opportunity of hearing a missionary. They are young men who do not belong to this district, but only live here for a time. Coming from hundreds of miles away in the interior, they have let themselves be recruited for two or for three years as timber-workers, and they live far in the forest amid swamps at lumber-camps never reached by the missionaries, when making visits to the indigenous population in the villages. After two or three years these natives return home with their earnings, if these have not been given in pledge for the purchase of a wife. If they hear the news of the Gospel in the Hospital, they carry it back first to the lumber-camp and later to their distant homes, where as yet there are no missionaries. So to preach to my patients and those who accompany them is to sow seed which may be re-sown far away.

From *My African Notebook*, p. 112.　　　[2] *Civilization and Ethics*, p. 252.

On Sunday morning at 9 o'clock a hospital orderly with a bell goes round the separate wards to call the people together for "Prayers," as he calls the Service. Slowly they make their way to the place between the two wards on the side of the hill and sit down under the wide roofs in order to be in the shade.

A good half-hour goes by before they are all together. Mrs. Russell's gramophone plays a record of solemn music, and as soon as it is finished the sermon begins. My parishioners cannot sing hymns, for they are almost exclusively heathens, and what is more, they speak six different languages. To begin with prayer is also impossible, because the many new people who every Sunday are at the Service for the first time would not know what it meant and would cause a disturbance. So they must be prepared for prayer by means of the address.

During the address I have two interpreters at my side, one on the right and one on the left, who repeat each of my sentences. The one on my right translates them into the Pahouin language, the other on my left into that of the Bendjabis, which most people from the interior understand more or less. The interpreter on the right is either the hospital tailor, Sombunaga, who is a Christian, or the hospital orderly, Mendoume, who is not yet one. On the left the orderlies Boulingui and Dominique, who are both in the same position as Mendoume, take it in turns to act as interpreter.

I cannot demand of my hearers that they should sit as stiff as the faithful in an Alsatian church. I overlook the fact that those who have their fireplaces between these two wards cook their dinners while they are listening, that a mother washes and combs her baby's hair, that a man mends his fishing-net, which he has hung up under the roof of the ward, and that many similar things take place. Even when a savage makes use of the time to lay his head on a comrade's lap and let him go on a sporting expedition through his hair, I do not stop it. For there are always new people there, and if I were continually to keep on admonishing them during the Service, its solemnity would be much more disturbed; so I leave things alone. Nor do I take any notice of the sheep and goats who come and go among my congregation, or of the numerous weaver-birds which have nests in the trees near by and make a noise that forces me to raise my voice.

Not even Mrs. Russell's two monkeys are regarded as a disturbance. They are allowed to run about free on Sundays, and during the Service they either practise gymnastics in the branches of the nearest palm tree, or jump about on the corrugated-iron roofs, and finally, when their energy is spent, settle down on their mistress's shoulder.

In spite of all this movement, the Service in the open air has an impressive solemnity from the fact that the Word of God here comes to men and women who hear it for the first time.

While preaching I must take pains to be as simple as possible. I must assume nothing. My listeners know nothing of Adam and Eve, of the Patriarchs, of the People of Israel, of Moses and the Prophets, of the Law, of the Pharisees, of the Messiah, of the Apostles. And as my congregation is in a constant state of renewal, I cannot think of attempting to teach even the most elementary of those historical ideas with which we have been familiar from infancy. I must let the Word of God speak to them almost without reference to Time. Since I must avoid so much while I am speaking, I feel as if I were playing the piano without being allowed to touch the black keys.

If I utter the word "Messiah," I explain it at once as "the King of our hearts, who was sent by God."

Once having accustomed oneself to preaching on this assumption that nothing is known already, the task is comparatively simple. The difficulties that have to be overcome are more than compensated for by the permission of writing the words of Scripture on the hearts of men to whom they are sometimes entirely new. Every Sunday this is to me a fresh and a beautiful experience which "almost passeth understanding."

As text I choose a saying to which I add some Scripture story or one or two parables which explain it. At the end I repeat this saying several times, until I think that my hearers have got it by heart and will remember it. If anybody after a stay at the Hospital takes away with him even three or four such sayings, which give him something to think about, it is already a great thing for all his life.

As much as possible I try to resist the temptation, to which everyone who addresses heathens is exposed, of "preaching the Law" (one's first thought, of course, is to keep on holding up the Ten Commandments to people who take lying, stealing, and immorality for granted) and in this way to try and prepare them for the Gospel. Naturally, too, I often preach about some one commandment or another. But in addition to that I try to awake in their hearts the longing for peace with God. When I speak of the difference between the heart that knows no peace and the heart that is full of peace, the most savage of *mes sauvages* know what I mean. And when I describe Jesus as He who brings peace

with God into the hearts of men and women, they understand
Him.

Thus my sermon endeavours in a quite elementary way to be
concerned with what the hearers have already themselves experienced, and with what they may experience if they have the will
to let Jesus have power in their hearts. Whatever I make my
starting-point, I always lead on to the innermost fact involved in
becoming a Christian, namely the being led captive by Christ,
so that even the man who is only present at one Service can get
an inkling of what it really is to be a Christian.

In order to be understood, I must diligently endeavour to speak
as much as possible to the point. Thus, for example, I must not
leave Peter's question to Jesus whether it is enough to forgive
one's brother seven times, as a general proposition, but with
examples from real life must show my natives what it may mean
for one of them, as it did for Peter, to forgive seven times in one
day. In one of my last addresses I described this to them in the
following way:

"Scarcely are you up in the morning and standing in front of
your hut, when somebody whom all know to be a bad man comes
and insults you. Because the Lord Jesus says that one ought to
forgive, you keep silent instead of beginning a palaver.

"Later on your neighbour's goat eats the bananas you were
relying on for your dinner. Instead of starting a quarrel with the
neighbour, you merely tell him that it was his goat, and that it
would be the right thing if he would make it up to you in bananas.
But when he contradicts you and maintains that the goat was not
his, you quietly go off and reflect that God causes so many bananas
to grow in your plantation that there is no need for you to begin
a quarrel on this account.

"A little later comes the man to whom you gave ten bunches of
bananas in order that he might sell them for you at the market
along with his own. He brings the money for only nine. You
say, 'That's too little.' But he retorts, 'You made a mistake in
counting, and only gave me nine bunches.' You are about to
shout in his face that he is a liar. But then you can't help thinking
about many lies, of which you alone know, for which God must
forgive you, and you go quietly into your hut.

"When you want to light your fire, you discover that somebody
has carried off the wood that you fetched out of the forest yester-
day, intending it to serve you for a week's cooking. Yet again
you compel your heart to forgive, and refrain from making a
search round all your neighbours' huts to see who can possibly

have taken your wood so that you may bring an accusation against the thief before the headman.

"In the afternoon, when you are about to go and work in your plantation, you discover that somebody has taken away your good bush-knife and left you in its place his old one, which has a jagged edge. You know who it is, for you recognize the bush-knife. But then you consider that you have forgiven four times and that you may want to forgive even a fifth time. Although it is a day on which you have experienced much unpleasantness, you feel as jolly as if it had been one of your happiest. Why? Because your heart is happy in having obeyed the will of the Lord Jesus.

"In the evening you want to go out fishing. You put out your hand to take the torch which ought to be standing in the corner of your hut. But it isn't there. Then you are overcome by anger, and you think that you have forgiven enough for today, and that now you will lie in wait for the man who has gone fishing with your torch. But yet once more the Lord Jesus becomes master of your heart. You go down to the shore with a torch borrowed from a neighbour.

"There you discover that your boat is missing. Another man has gone fishing in it. Angrily you hide behind a tree in order to wait for him who has done you this wrong, and when he comes back you mean to take all his fish away from him, and accuse him before the District Officer, so that he will have to pay you just compensation. But while you are waiting, your heart begins to speak. It keeps on repeating the saying of Jesus that God cannot forgive us our sins if we do not forgive each other. You have to wait so long that the Lord Jesus yet again gains the mastery over you. Instead of going for the other fellow with your fists, when at last in the grey of the morning he returns and tumbles down in a fright as you step out from behind the tree, you tell him that the Lord Jesus compels you to forgive him, and you let him go in peace. You don't even ask him to give up the fish, when he does not leave them to you of his own accord. But I believe he does give them to you from sheer amazement that you don't start a quarrel with him.

"Now you go home, happy and proud that you have succeeded in making yourself forgive seven times. But if the Lord Jesus were to come into your village on that day, and you were to step in front of him and think he would praise you for it before all the people, then he would say to you, as to Peter, that seven times is not enough, but that you must forgive yet seven times, and yet again, and yet again, and yet many more times before God can forgive you your many sins. . . ."

So far as is possible, in every sermon I find an opportunity of speaking of the nothingness of idols and fetiches, and then at the same time I attack the mad delusion that there are evil spirits, and that fetichists and magicians are in possession of supernatural powers. All my savages live with these ideas. It is possible that the words he has heard in a single sermon at the Hospital may bring liberation to a man who is under the spell of these horrible ideas. In the course of our medical work, how much do we learn of ill-treatment and murder as the result of the pronouncement of a fetichist carried out against people to whose magic he refers as illness or death! Again and again I get a shock when I see this misery of superstition.

I need not complain of any want of attentiveness among my hearers. One can see in their faces how their minds are occupied with what they have heard. I often break off in order to ask them whether their heart and their thoughts agree that what they have heard of the Word of God is right, or whether anyone has anything to say to the contrary. Then in a loud chorus they reply that what I have said is true.

A black evangelist who, as a patient, attended the Hospital Services, related at the Mission station that the Doctor preaches just as if he had studied theology like a missionary.

At the end of the sermon I give a short explanation of what prayer is. Then I tell them all to fold their hands. Those who don't yet know how, learn by looking at the others. When at last all the hands are folded, I say very slowly an extempore prayer in five or six sentences, and it is repeated equally slowly by the interpreters in both languages. After the Amen, heads are bent long over the hands. Only when the soft music of the gramophone begins do they raise them. All sit motionless until the last note has faded away. Then after I have said "thank you" to the two interpreters and have taken my leave, my listeners begin to rise.

The sceptic who would be disposed to doubt the power of such methods of evangelism to effect a permanent change of direction in the life of primitive man would be well advised to read the story of "Oyembo the Forest Schoolmaster" in *From My African Notebook*. But precept and exhortation, however good, are less telling than example; and it is even more by the unconscious influence of a life dedicated and consecrated to the service of Christ than by anything he says, that Schweitzer delivers the primitive negro from darkness

A SUNDAY SERVICE AT LAMBARÉNÉ, 1931

ABOVE THE RIVER OGOWE, 1927
Overlooking proposed site of the New Hospital

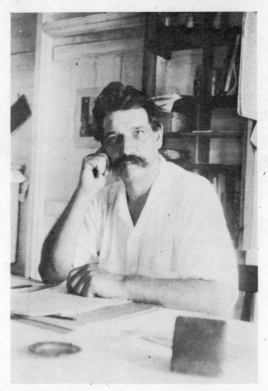

AT WORK ON THE GOETHE ORATION, LAMBARÉNÉ, 1932

to light, from discord to love, from the death of sin to the life of righteousness, and guides his feet out of the tangle of superstitious fears into the way of peace.

For Schweitzer's activities during this third period of his African labours we have nothing from his own pen. For lack of funds and of further medical help he has so far been unable to realize his next great ambition,—to build a small additional hospital above the rapids on a tributary of the Ogowe for the treatment of operation cases; and his next after that, to teach the natives practical agriculture. In this latter scheme he is balked by the fact that the population is floating (in two senses of the word): work is sought in widely separated areas where timber merchants require tree-felling. He also envisages the possibilities of pressing further into the interior to continue the fight against sleeping sickness. "I have not been able to carry out any original research work," he writes in a letter, "but we have made good progress in treatment, especially of long-standing cases. Given the personnel, all that Africa needs to be freed from sleeping sickness is money and medicine."

At the end of 1931 he was joined by a volunteer from England in Miss Margaret Deneke, Honorary Fellow and Choirmaster of Lady Margaret Hall in Oxford, who had been so impressed by his Dale Memorial Lectures in the University nine years before, that she determined to work for his cause when opportunity allowed, and meanwhile arranged concerts on its behalf. (On his next visit to Oxford he came to her home to thank her, and there met Sir Donald Tovey, whose piano rendering of his completed *Kunst der Fuge* of Bach delighted him and which its author dedicated to him. Miss Deneke recalls the Doctor's visible pleasure and his muttered "*Vollständig Stylgemäss!*" when the piece was ended.)

Her memories of Lambaréné, which she has kindly contributed in a letter, cover the period of a two-and-a-half months' visit at the end of 1931 and may be said to reflect the lighter side of life there.

My jobs there were varied; I did a few hospital rounds with Dr. Schweitzer and took my turn in doling out rations to patients and their friends, and settled down to a lengthy piece of work as the foreman of a gang of about thirty negroes, who built a garden on the banks of the Ogowe River, and dug a road in the plantation. A strange company we were: Dr. Schweitzer said we looked like the prisoners' chorus from *Fidelio*, mixed tribes, friendly, lazy, hot-tempered at times, a criminal and a homicidal maniac among us.

Now and again I had to have recourse to the Doctor for control of squabbles. But rapidly soothing as these authoritative interferences were, I soon took pride in trying to manage my job myself. Singing nursery rhymes and methods of cajolery not unlike kindergarten work, proved reasonably efficacious in getting things done and in keeping tempers happy. At six o'clock tools were locked up and we went to our rooms for rest.

The first night I heard Dr. Schweitzer play Bach's *Ach wie nichtig* and *Christe Du Lamm Gottes*, in the bureau next to my bedroom. Hearing music became the most reviving tonic after the monotony of day labour, and I was always disappointed when the vast correspondence, that was kept in large laundry bags, crowded out our half an hour with Bach. Now and again Dr. Schweitzer most generously entrusted the fragile piano to me, allowing my gang to shift alone whilst I spent a refreshing hour playing in the bureau. Once, some of the hospital staff and Dr. Schweitzer, with the small portable harmonium, performed a chorale outside my bedroom before breakfast. It was a Lambaréné birthday tradition; so was the speech at dinner before the toast of pineapple juice. I wish I could remember the masterly little speeches Dr. Schweitzer made on these occasions; the wit, the wording, all showed the care he bestowed on the detail of everything he did.

My gang cleared the churchyard of elephant grass for Christmas, and I helped to inscribe the name of De Brazza's cook on a tomb of fast hardening cement. Most of the graves were marked with plain wooden crosses on which a crippled negro carved a name.

When my road was completed Dr. Schweitzer allowed me to pencil "Oxford Street" on a piece of wood. With that duly carved, he and I went with two workmen to put up the board. Miss Haussknecht reported later there had been whispering among our natives that the Doctor and Mademoiselle Miss (my nickname) had conducted a funeral without a corpse! In a recent letter Dr. Schweitzer says: "*On a prononcé ton nom en voyant l'indicateur d'Oxford Street.*" So it is still up.

On one occasion an army of ants on tour came across a path. My excited gang clamoured for a bonfire to destroy them. I asked Dr. Schweitzer, but he forbade it, outraged at the cruelty of the suggestion.[1] On the other hand, when danger threatened, he

---

[1] Cf. the 112th commandment for the monks of Monastic Taoism in China: "Thou shalt not pour hot water on the ground for the purpose of destroying insects and ants." (Quoted in *Indian Thought and its Development*, p. 143.)

had no scruple in killing a snake which met me outside.

The four nurses who travelled home with Dr. Schweitzer in January 1932 were in high spirits. The building of the huts, the paths, the new landing stage, had all been achieved according to schedule, and now we were enjoying sea-air, leisured meals, and books. Even these days were planned. Every evening I went into the ship's dining-room before dinner to read and clip together the pages of the Goethe Discourse[1] that Dr. Schweitzer was writing for Frankfurt. And most evenings after dinner I gave him English lessons, reading light articles or advertisements from *Home and Country*. The energy of the day had been devoted to the lecture; the lessons were little more than a game, but a very amusing one.

One evening he challenged me to make up a tune for his improvisation, on the piano in the dining saloon. I produced something and he started but broke off and asked for a rhythmical figure. Then starting again he built up a fine shapely structure of sound out of this fragment.

At Bordeaux he gave us nurses an organ recital in one of the largest churches in the town on a wonderful old organ, playing Bach's *Passacaglia* and the *Little E Minor Prelude* and *Fugue* by heart. We were in the organ loft with him and could witness his own delight in having a real organ once more at his command.

In spite of all the burdensome claims on his time he insisted on choosing my train to Calais and escorting me to the station with the other nurses. He thanked me *au grand sérieux* for all I had done for the hospital. I demurred somewhat at this. With quick intuition he characteristically modulated to a lighter mood: "But your gang were very fond of you. They came as a deputation to protest against what they supposed to be your dismissal. You must let me agree with your negroes that you are a good white woman."

Dr. Ernest Walker and I have often combined in lectures on Dr. Schweitzer, showing my film and playing Dr. Walker's West African Piano Duet based on Lambaréné tunes. Year by year we have made Dr. Schweitzer's work known to first-year students of Lady Margaret Hall in this way, and on one occasion Dr. Schweitzer was present himself; he was delighted to meet so many temporary nieces, as he called them, and his obvious enjoyment and personal magnetism infected everyone.

[1] *i.e.* the Memorial Oration, delivered that year.

CHAPTER X

THE GUEST-HOUSE AT GÜNSBACH

WHEN Schweitzer came home for the second time in 1927, so many people from all over Europe wanted to come and see him that, since there was no accommodation for visitors in the little village of Günsbach, he said: "I will build a house for them."

It was the proceeds of the Goethe Prize, presented by the City of Frankfort, which enabled him to put this project into effect. He was himself responsible for the general architectural plan, and entrusted the execution of technical details to his friend F. Walter, an architect of Colmar. The building grew gradually between the years 1928 and 1929. Designed as a rendezvous for his colleagues from Lambaréné as well as for friends and chance-comers, it was completed for habitation in 1930, and from then on, whether its host was present or absent, it was generally thronged with guests. The site in Günsbach was determined upon with deliberation, so as to be out of "harm's way."

I have a specially happy memory [writes Mrs. Corbett-Ashby] of a visit to their lovely home at Günsbach: the deference and affection shown him as he pointed out to us the beauties of Strasburg Cathedral; his immense pride in the prosperous tiny villages and rich comfortable homesteads of his native country. Glancing up at the hills above his house, he said in a matter-of-fact tone, "I built it here because it will be under the hillside where the guns of the next war will not reach it." I was appalled that he should take the thought of another war so calmly and inevitably, though this was only 1934. And so I begged him to remain in Europe where he could do so much to check the rising tide of Fascism; but he felt that others could do that, and that his special work in Africa was not yet ended.

Simple in design and construction, the house is practical through and through. The staircase is lined with photographs of famous old Dutch organs on which he has played. No corner in it is without

THE GUEST-HOUSE, GÜNSBACH

a purpose: work-room, study, music-room, office—each has its appropriate fittings and place in the structural economy. Simplicity, homeliness, and peace, these are the qualities of its atmosphere. Should guests volunteer to help in the kitchen, the garden, or at the typewriter, these offers are accepted with gratitude. In one of the rooms is a piano with organ-pedal on which he plays with unfailing regularity whenever he is at home.

The front door opens directly on to the village street. A suggestion that he should build the house back in the garden was declined: the "house by the side of the road" is symbolical of his wish to be "a friend to man." Schweitzer will not fence himself off from his kind, and this in spite of the fact that light or general conversation is often a strain to him. To those who have known him only as a genial host at late supper parties after an organ recital, when his animated and often jocular conversation has made him the life and soul of the company, this may seem surprising. But a temporary elation of spirits is natural to an artist when his task is performed: it is by no means indicative of his deeper disposition. The fact is that Schweitzer is not naturally gregarious and, keen and sympathetic as his human interests are, the world of superficial intercourse is still an alien world to him. Intimate personal fellowship with individuals, whether in hard work shared together or in the close exchange of deeply felt ideas, mean much more to him than social gatherings or chance-made acquaintances. It is therefore characteristic of his selflessness and inner discipline that he should give himself unreservedly to all comers, and that he should regard this as an important duty, never to be shirked. While engrossed with work in his study, he will leave it to oblige the most casual stranger who desires an interview. But, kind and considerate as he is for the comfort of every member of his household, he discourages discussion about trifles. An artist of life no less than of music, *Nur das Wesentliche* (only the essential) may appear in the composition.

At first he occupied the large front room as his study, a fine sunny room with a view of the distant hills, and he would often pause in his work to gaze at them with delight. Later, however, he relinquished this room for the use of his guests, and retired with his books to his bedroom, ostensibly because he could work there without disturbance. His bedroom is the least attractive in the house, with a somewhat gloomy aspect to the north and looking immediately on to the street below; it was for this reason that he chose it.

Sometimes after supper he will take his guests across to the village church, and there he will open his soul to the floodtides of Bach's music. Of this, and of his effect as a preacher in the same little church, let one of his oldest friends, Mr. Emil Mettler, tell.

We go to the little village church. Darkness has fallen when the last note of the chorales dies away. Putting out all the lights, the Doctor improvises on a simple church tune in order to show the singing quality of his beloved instrument. At the close we all go out silently, as under a spell, into the star-lit night.

The next morning is Missionary Sunday in the village, a rare coincidence. He is asked to speak in the church of his native village, which is crowded to its utmost capacity. The people flock from distant places to hear him. They consist mainly of peasants and labourers, young and old; but how simply the learned Doctor imparts his thoughts to them!

He says there are people who do not believe in missionary work among primitives, on the ground that they are far happier left alone. But are they happy, he asks? No, for they are the slaves of terrible superstitions. They have become the children of Fear. They live in constant fear of spirits, departed spirits, evil spirits; and in fear, too, of the fetich-men who are supposed to control the supernatural powers and perform all kinds of ceremonies to keep them away.

Sudden death is a thing unintelligible to them. They seek for the "culprit." And who is the culprit? They have their secret societies to find out. So much has to be paid to the fetich-man who is sent to find out. And woe to the person to whom the finger of the fetich-man points! The most horrible methods of torture are employed to kill him.

"Now will you understand what the Gospel means," says the Doctor. It means release to the people from the fear which cripples them and shackles their lives. Henceforth they know that the destiny of all of us is in the hands of the same loving Father. And once this has been made clear to them the door is opened for the Good News. "Some people think that the Gospel is too difficult to understand. No, it is exceedingly simple, as all the profound things in life are simple. And the Gospel of Love can be understood in every language. In fact it is latent in every human heart."

Mr. Hubert Peet's visit took place in 1931, when the Doctor was away in Lambaréné, and his account is valuable for its impressions of the power of a personality that even in absence can make its presence felt.

When we arrived in company with the Doctor's brother and nephew who had brought us a glorious, if wet journey through the Vosges from their home in Lorraine, we were greeted by a former nurse at the Lambaréné Hospital, who makes the Doctor's house the headquarters of his work in Europe. We knew that he himself would not be there, for he cannot leave Africa until next year, but he likes to know that even in his absence his friends from England, America, Holland, Switzerland, Germany, Scandinavia, or the Far East—representatives of all these lands have stayed at Günsbach this year—should be guests in the house he has built.

He had bought from the Commune the little promontory of rocks, the Rochers de Kanzenrain, jutting out from the vineyards above the village, where as a lad he would sit and meditate as he sat and looked up the valley to Münster and the heights of the Vosges. Whenever he returns home this is still the first spot he visits.

The Doctor's house is on the outskirts of the village, and here he loves to entertain his friends. He himself may be absent in body, but you feel his spirit and influence are all around you. The building consists of two flats on the Continental plan, the lower being occupied by guests and the upper being used as the European headquarters of his work where some of his devoted helpers live and carry on the office work for Lambaréné. How great this is one realizes by a sight of the extensive mail each morning, and the continual tinkling of the telephone bell upstairs by which communication is kept with the warehouse in Strasburg and a hundred and one persons and businesses which the work of a hospital entails.

But upstairs, too, we go for our meals, where we are a delightfully international group, representing England, France, Germany, Switzerland, and Holland, making a happy best of the barriers of language. And in the evening, too, we gather together in the Doctor's study to talk of the work at Lambaréné.

Tolerance is a lesson to be learned early at Günsbach. The church with the slender spire has been renovated since the war. Happily it did not have to be practically rebuilt as was the case with the war-shattered churches at Münster half an hour distant. As in the days of Dr. Schweitzer's boyhood, it is still the scene of Protestant and Roman Catholic services, a custom in a number of churches in Alsace. At eight on Sunday morning, its bell rings for the Catholics, about a third of the whole population of the

two villages, to come to mass. At ten, it summons the Protestants
to the same building. As we sit and follow the young successor
of Pastor Louis Schweitzer, leading the service from below the
high pulpit, we catch glimpses through the wooden chancel
screen of the decorated altar before which earlier worshippers of
another communion have knelt that morning. For both, however,
is the beautiful crucifix on the wall and its inscription "*Er ist unser
Friede*" (He is our Peace), and there is harmony and love in the
atmosphere rather than any sense of clash. The service is in German,
for though French is now the official language, many of the older
folk only know the former, whereas the children are bilingual.
Men and women sit separately, and to the men is given the precedence in rising for the prayers. Half an hour's sermon closes
with "Our Father," during the saying of which the sexton
vigorously rings the bell, a custom distracting to the newcomer,
but a message to those outside the Church of the offering of a
common petition to Our Heavenly Father.

Not often in a country church is to be found as fine an organ
as that at Günsbach. It, too, is being renovated, and no longer is
it necessary for there to be a mirror by its side in which the player
can see whether the pastor has entered or left the pulpit. I regret
that mirror, for you may remember that it was in it that little
Albert thought he used to see the Devil, whose face dimly came
and went during the service. It was not for long that he realized
it was only the reflection of Daddy Iltis, schoolmaster and organist,
who now rests peacefully in the village cemetery. His successor
sits before his three manuals in the front of the gallery, facing the
pastor, and can follow his movements without reflection's aid.

For all the inhabitants of Günsbach Schweitzer is still their
fellow-villager. Grey-haired men tell you how they used to go to
the village school with him. To them he is "Albert" still. The
cheerful old *sabot* maker whose house and workshop are just
across the road from the Doctor's house, regularly makes presents
of his "wooden shoon" for the hospital workers in Africa, whose
feet they keep dry during the rainy season. The maker and repairer
of implements for farm and vineyard is one of his greatest friends.
Another old gentleman will tell you smilingly that he and Albert
are both scholars—one a scholar of books, the other of the
soil.

In the Doctor's house, there are of course many reminders of
his work in Africa. Among them is a little stuffed dwarf gazelle,
of which he makes pets in Africa. I believe this is the one which
once ate up a great sheet of postage stamps which the Doctor had

carelessly left on his table. In the study upstairs are African instruments and a great snake-skin from Lambaréné. On the book-
shelves are copies of the Doctor's books on music, theology, and
philosophy, not only in French and German, but in many other
tongues as well.

One visit beyond the Günsbach Valley, I had to pay. That was
to the town of Colmar about twelve miles away towards the
Rhine. Here at the foot of the statue in the park in the centre of
the town to Admiral Bruat, is the figure of a Negro. It is the work
of Bartholdi, the sculptor who designed America's Statue of
Liberty. It was the pensive yearning gaze of this black figure which
first drew the attention of the young Schweitzer to the needs of
Africa. Each time he returns to Europe, he goes again and gazes
at it. What a joy it must be to feel that he listened to that appeal,
God's voice speaking to him even through the stone, and that
through his hospital in the African forest he is doing something
to heal the physical and spiritual troubles of the black man.

When, nearly ten years ago, I asked Albert Schweitzer for a
message to children, to include in a story of his work I had been
asked to write, he said, "Tell them that the truths they feel deep
down in their hearts are the real truths. God's love speaks to us in our
hearts and tries to work through us in the world. We must listen
to that voice; we must listen to it as to a pure and distant melody
that comes to us across the noise of the world's doings. . . ."

I keep this message in my notebook, and its words came to me
with new meaning and force as I read it again at Günsbach amid
the sights and sounds and the people that were familiar to him
as he learnt to listen. It was here in this valley, among these hills,
these folk, that he listened and learned.

Lady Pauline Kirkpatrick's memories are culled from diaries of
her visits in 1934, and in the spring and autumn of 1936. They
reflect the homelier, tenderer aspects of life in that peaceful
valley.

A visit to Dr. Schweitzer's dearly loved Alsatian home is an
experience never to be forgotten. From Colmar the train journeys
through a smiling valley where villages nestle in orchards and
green wooded hills rise beyond the vineyards.

Günsbach! On the platform Dr. Schweitzer is waiting and there
may be other guests or a member of his hospital staff. A warm
greeting. The luggage is piled into a little handcart which the
Doctor trundles through the village, past the Parsonage where he

spent such happy days in his childhood and youth, past the church with the slender spire, on whose organ he first learnt to play.

He takes his guest up to the room at the top of the house, the house he planned and is so proud of, built with the money of the Goethe Prize, but not till he had given twelve concerts in Germany and handed over the proceeds to charitable funds for children.

At supper a cheerful band gathers round the table, members of the Doctor's family, Lambaréné nurses, old friends, new ones from different parts of the world, a harmonious company in the happy Günsbach atmosphere. When his mind is free he is full of fun and tells story after story to the delight of all.

How strenuous his days are, even when he is at home! On one specially lovely Sunday in summer a choir of boys' voices is heard in the street. At the door stands the Doctor, listening to a group from a Roman Catholic school in the Rhineland who had been spending some time with French boys. As the Doctor could not accept their invitation to visit *them*, they have made a detour on their homeward way, and are singing a morning greeting to him. He signs a lot of picture postcards for them and goes as far as the church, inviting the Chaplain to come and visit him. Later all the household goes with the Doctor to morning service. He is in the black gown and Geneva bands worn by his father and carries the "toque" (cap) which belonged to his grandfather. That day he is taking the service and preaching, and the organist plays a prelude by Bach carefully practised for this occasion, for Dr. Schweitzer does not often preach. The sermon on the Parable of the Tares among the Wheat is full of the power of the love of God, a power that will burn up all that is wrong and sinful as the sun burns up the weeds. A children's service follows and he begins by asking each child his or her name, making a friendly remark when he recognizes the descendant of an old comrade.

Sunday dinner is a cheery meal followed by coffee in the sitting-room when the Doctor allows himself a few moments of relaxation. And then the traditional Sunday walk when he himself leads the cavalcade, and the same tour is made that his father used to take with his five children every Sunday. Dr. Schweitzer passes from one to the other, walking beside them for a little way and no one feels left out. They meander up a side valley to the path where the family party always turned back to return through the woods and vineyards. A shooting match is going on and several of Albert's old school comrades are among the competitors. A halt is made on a flowery rock and the Doctor and his sister exchange reminiscences. A niece is gently rebuked for picking a little bunch of wild flowers. "Leave the flowers, they have as much right to live as you have." A group of marksmen goes by and one lifts a jug he has won to show us. It is George, with whom the Doctor went to school; then comes Charles, and they chat, the Doctor reminding him of how Charles had corrected an exercise for him when Albert *would* write "*der* Butter" instead of "*die* Butter." All this in the Alsatian patois. The evening service is held in the village of Griesbach on the other side of the valley, in the village hall, because Griesbach has no church. It is filled with villagers, men, women, and children. One of them plays a voluntary on the little harmonium and the Doctor reads the Lesson and preaches with admirable clearness, directness, and simplicity. He makes a moving plea for a return to the old-fashioned way of keeping Sunday, reminding his hearers how their parents kept it; how many could remember them finding a quiet hour for the reading of the Bible to themselves. "When *you* join them in the churchyard yonder, what will *your* children remember about *your* way of keeping Sunday? How can we abide in Christ if we never try to cultivate the gardens of our souls and feed them and give them the chance of growing?" Home in the starlight and the Doctor speaks of the time when the road was black with people walking to Günsbach church.

One evening all go to hear him play on the organ which has been rebuilt from his own instructions in the village church. The guest of honour sits beside him on the organ bench. Sometimes he plays by heart and the church is in darkness. Behind the closed screen is the Sanctuary. One can see dimly the crucifix on the altar. Now there is a light on his hands and for an hour and a half he plays César Franck and Bach as he alone can play them. It is a glorious experience and our hearts are full as we stroll back through the village. As usual he goes back to his study to deal with his vast correspondence and often works on far into the night.

On another day a joyous caravan of his family friends and guests starts at six o'clock for a picnic-supper in memory of his mother whom he loved so tenderly. The Doctor likes to have these picnics, for as children their mother would take them all out on to the hill at the other side of the valley, and he is very particular that the ménu should always be the same as in those days. The guests learn much of his home life as they chat with members of his family and old friends. They trail through Günsbach, climb the hillside and stop at the edge of the wood. What a happy company!

The Doctor tells us that he often thinks of these evenings when he is away in the jungle and fancies himself looking over his beloved valley, the sun setting behind the rounded hills, Günsbach with its Renaissance houses nestling around the Church and well protected from the guns which in 1914–1918 destroyed the old factory and farms nearer the river. Over the flat green fields the blue mist rises to meet the wood-smoke floating from the chimneys. All is so lovely and peaceful. The Doctor is in his happiest, mood and tells many anecdotes and stories as the merry supper proceeds. When the moon rises behind the pinewoods the baskets are packed and we saunter homewards.

But these are rare interludes in very busy days. Dr. Schweitzer begins work directly after breakfast. His room is on the village street and through its uncurtained window his village friends and other passers-by can see him hour after hour at his plain deal table sitting on a hard bentwood chair, writing, writing, writing. They often leave offerings on the window-sill, a basket of wild raspberries, or yellow mushrooms, delicate "morilles" from the woods, or eggs or fresh vegetables. After dinner a short siesta, or none if he is very pressed, then more work till supper-time. If he has guests he has a short break for a cup of tea, and his helpers are glad of these moments for him. Sometimes a passing visitor asks to see him. Once it was a priest sent by his friend the organist at Bordeaux; he is warmly greeted, offered tea, invited to supper, shown his collection of photographs of fine organs, taken to see the church. Interruptions never seem to trouble Albert Schweitzer's serenity. Back to work after supper, though he sometimes joins his friends in the sitting-room, various refreshing "tisanes" are handed round, made of orange-flowers or cinnamon leaves from Lambaréné or lime-flowers from the local trees. The Doctor abounds in stories to the delight of his hearers, stories of Lambaréné and his patients, stories of his adventures among old organs and how he saved them from destruction or restoration which would have ruined their soft, mellow tone, organs on which alone can Bach's works be heard at their best. On modern machine-made instruments, he says, it is impossible to hear the various melodies in all their beauty. Then back to his room to deal with his huge correspondence from all over the world. He who, as he tells in his childhood memories, will never let a godchild write to thank him for a present, will never allow one of his helpers to send a letter of thanks without putting in a short message of gratitude himself. And so the hours go by, each quarter struck at the village church and echoed by churches in neighbouring villages, and often the night is very nearly spent when he puts out his light and goes to bed.

His guests are made to feel thoroughly at home because they can help in pleasant ways. Some can write letters for him in English to friends in America and Great Britain, and what peaceful mornings are spent in the orchard under the golden plum trees preparing the mushrooms, shelling peas, or doing some little job in the cheerful kitchen which opens out of the dining-room. Opposite is the house where his sisters live, and here are family portraits and heirlooms, and the friends of their brother are made welcome and love to hear more about his life from them. His home is a resting-place not only for himself and his family when he is in Europe, but also for his Nurses and for the entertainment of the friends of Lambaréné that they may learn to know more of his work in his jungle Hospital.

When the Doctor is preparing a concert tour he goes to the church every evening to practise. On the tour he will have to practise on each new organ, pencilling the stops on his music and altering them every time. He will have to climb up and down the steep stairs to the organ loft many times to satisfy himself that he has chosen the right stops for each passage. A friend plays while he listens below. After each concert there will be numberless people to see him, and he never refuses to see anyone who wishes to speak to him even if he can only give them five minutes. He knows how many precious friendships he has made in these ways. He works at César Franck's Chorales, at Bach's Preludes and Fugues, and at Widor's compositions. In the solitude of Lambaréné he feels that he can penetrate deeply into this music; there is always something new to learn in it.

On the occasion of a visit to Strasburg to hear him play, the opportunity occurs of seeing how the work for Lambaréné is organized in the old house in the Rue des Greniers. The offices are of a Spartan simplicity. Two little rooms with a few deal tables and chairs, bookcases, and cupboards. On the walls water-colour sketches and photographs of Lambaréné. Above is the store-room and packing-room where are the wooden cases in nests designed by the Doctor and made by a devoted carpenter-helper. On the shelves are rows of medicines, old linen, knitted bandages, etc. It seems impossible that hundreds of cases can be packed and labelled in such cramped quarters. Here, too, the vast list of remedies is checked and the goods packed. Interruptions occur all the time.

In the office are some charming drawings in coloured chalks, done by children of a school in Basle, mostly of scenes in Dr.

Schweitzer's life, and on the back of each one is a message written, "Welcome to our school, dear Albert Schweitzer," "Come soon to our school," and the name of the child. A school in America has written a play founded on his life; they have acted it and sent him the money they collected. Many are the touching ways in which quite poor people help him. One woman in Switzerland dries all the vegetables they need and sends a little at a time, collecting the vegetables from her neighbours. Another has found a way of making a dried paste of tomatoes. An old market woman was seen sitting by the roadside with her basket, reading the latest news from Lambaréné. She gives up a great part of her earnings for the work. Another puts aside a few pence from all her egg money. The caretaker at the Rue des Greniers cooks all the food for the office helpers and washes up, and she does it all for love. The shining look on the faces of all these helpers, men and women, is wonderful to see. Dr. Schweitzer never takes any help as a matter of course. His humility and gratitude are most touching, and his sense of humour a continual joy.

These are memories of visits before 1937. What has happened to "The House below the Rock" now? Where are the books, the possessions, the precious MSS.? How many friends are left? What has become of the nurses and helpers who were not in Lambaréné when war broke out? Shall we ever see that dear valley again and stay in that happy household where peace and love reign? Shall we ever worship again in the Günsbach Church and hear Albert Schweitzer play on its organ?

The writer of these tender memories died but a few months after they were written, in February 1946. But happily, beforehand, a reassuring answer to her anxious questions could be given her. Despite the offensives and counter-offensives that passed back and forth across this region early in 1945, the village of Günsbach survived without scathe and the Guest-House still stands. When on February 2nd the Germans' line of retreat towards Colmar and Neu Brisach was cut off, they essayed, but with scant success, to retire across the Vosges in the neighbourhood of Cernay and thence to fall back on the Rhine, as Ariovistus (so Schweitzer the historian remembers) had done in his campaign against Caesar.

CHAPTER XI

LATER VISITS TO GREAT BRITAIN

SCHWEITZER's first engagement on returning from his third "furlough" in 1932 was to deliver on March 22nd the Goethe Memorial Oration at Frankfort at the hour of the day of the poet's death a century before, when, writes Mrs. Russell in *The Path to Reconstruction*, his gravity held the packed audience in the Opernhaus spellbound for sixty-five minutes, as he proclaimed that a gigantic repetition of the Faust drama was even then being enacted on the world-stage. To attempt a summary of this oration, or to quote extracts from it, would be to mar the perfect symmetry of the whole. Happily a complete English translation of it has now been made by Mrs. Russell.

Schweitzer spent the greater part of April and May of this year on tour on the Continent, mostly in Holland; and on June 7th arrived in London.

If the pace of his going on these occasions seems fast and furious, it is necessary to say that this is only what is usual with him on every tour he undertakes; and that they are only items among a host of others undertaken in other countries of which we have no record.

All that he accomplishes on these journeys is done by sheer concentration of purpose, and nothing will induce him to deviate from his course. On his travels abroad he will allow himself to see nothing of a city but its organs. Even of an ancient cathedral he has no time to admire the architectural features or historical interest. "For him (says a friend) all is but framework for the organ. And yet there are moments when one suspects that he is seeing and feeling much more than he admits, and is only afraid of provoking irrelevant conversation if he makes any remark." To newspaper reporters who enquire his opinion of the great buildings of their cities, their art galleries and musuems and guild-halls, he rejoins with a laugh: "I shall not begin sight-seeing till I'm 75!"

His immense reserves of energy are such that he can afford the minimum both of food and sleep. To the remonstrance of a friend—

shocked by his frequent habit of working till 4 A.M. and rising be-times for more work still—that "you cannot burn the candle at both ends," he replied laconically, "Oh yes, you can—if the candle is long enough." To familiarize himself thoroughly with the indi-viduality of an untried organ, nothing less than eight hours' solid practice will satisfy him before undertaking a recital; for he will never give his audience less than his very best. To accompany him on a tour is an exhausting experience for his companion, unless blessed with a strong constitution. Yet he regards the principle of conservation of energy as a serious duty and never exceeds the limits of his own powers. Fortunately for himself he can sleep anywhere and at any time: even on three hard chairs for a quarter of an hour before a lecture or a recital. He regards afternoon tea as a totally superfluous meal and an unwarrantable interruption of work; and will eat nothing after his midday meal until the evening's task is over. Then he will go off, bohemian-wise, with a party of friends to a café, but hungry and weary as he is, he will give no thought to his own needs till he has exchanged a few words with everyone at the table individually. He frequently surprises the night-watchman at a hotel by his habit of going out for a stroll with a companion at midnight and returning in the small hours of the morning.

Perusal of his companion's journal on this particular tour is sufficient in itself to leave the reader almost breathless. Two full days' organ practice at St. Margaret's Westminster and at St. Paul's with Mr. Ashby's assistance at the stops, before evening recitals at each on the 9th and 10th of June respectively. By five o'clock on the second day his devoted helper, starving and exhausted, went out to get some tea; "but the Doctor was immovable."—The long and lovely recital itself being ended, he was begged to visit the Choir School. Accepting instantly, he entranced the boys with stories of his work in Africa. The hour being late, and having made no plans for a night's rest, he accepted Mrs. Ashby's offer of an impromptu supper and beds for himself and his companion at her home in Putney, which was to be his "home from home" on many subsequent visits to London. "He was the easiest of visitors to entertain" (writes Mrs. Ashby), "but a tyrant to work with; indefatigable himself he would work others to exhaustion; and I remember his good-tempered but dismayed surprise when I told him so!"

But it was not till 4.30 A.M. that he and his companion retired to rest that night; and having breakfasted at eight he repaired to St.

Botolph's Bishopsgate to practise on the organ for a recital there the next day, a Sunday, where he also preached, and addressed a gathering at the Guildhouse in Kensington the same evening. Leaving London for Oxford that night in order to receive his honorary Doctorate of Divinity there the next morning, he delivered the Philip Maurice Deneke Lecture at Lady Margaret Hall the same day on "*Goethe als Denker und Mensche.*" Miss Deneke, whose guest he was, writes: "With his recent Frankfort Oration in mind he had prepared a long discourse on aspects which he had omitted then. A few minutes before mounting the platform he was told that a lecture of one hour was expected. He then performed the amazing intellectual feat of extemporizing for exactly 60 minutes without gaps, distortion, or hesitation."

After practising all day on the New College organ for an evening recital on June 15th, he spent the next three days unintermittently in making up arrears of correspondence which he completed at 1 A.M. on the 18th, and at eight the same morning proceeded to Cambridge for a lecture. On the 20th he gave a recital in Manchester Cathedral, and the same evening addressed a meeting at the Houldsworth Hall on Lambaréné. The next day he delivered an address to the University on "The Philosophical Development of Goethe," when Professor C. H. Dodd acted as his interpreter. The interest of this lecture, which was well reported in the Manchester press, lies less in Schweitzer's lucid exposition of the poet's thought in combining, as it did harmoniously, elements of the philosophies both of Kant and of Spinoza, than in its conclusion:

> Thus Goethe introduced ethical mysticism within the framework of pantheistic mysticism, and this was a great achievement.
>
> He fully realized that in the realm of the finite there are everywhere limits to investigation. His aim was to understand that which is conceivable; all that is inconceivable he reverenced as a mystery. He repudiated the idea that anyone could construct a notion of Pure Being; he remained satisfied with the belief that the spiritual reveals itself in the natural.
>
> We now know that he devoted himself to the service of his fellow-men. With him thought and conduct were one, and that is the best thing that one can say of any thinker.

No statement of Schweitzer's own practical philosophy could be more succinct or apposite than that.

No sooner had he delivered this lecture than he was off again, this time to Edinburgh, where he arrived on June 22nd, as the guest of Dr. and Mrs. Barbour Simpson. The same evening he began practising on the St. Giles' Cathedral organ, continuing till midnight, and most of the next day before his recital; after which he attended the annual reception of the College of Physicians, and lectured on his work at Lambaréné in the Music Hall.

This was Schweitzer's first visit to Scotland, and to him it was a most happy experience for more than one reason. He took an almost childish delight in the privilege of spending midsummer in so northerly a country, with its long light evenings which, after the punctual regularity of the tropical nights where he had spent so many summers, were a welcome relief; and he also felt a satisfaction in feeling that his visit to Scotland was in part-fulfilment of his mother's wish.

On the 25th he went to Glasgow and spent most of three days in testing the qualities of its cathedral organ, with intervals for addresses at Woodlands Church and Camphill Church; returning to Edinburgh by the last train on the 27th. The visit to Glasgow deserves special mention in that it drew from an anonymous correspondent to a London newspaper the following excellent description of Schweitzer.

One would know instinctively, I think, that he was no ordinary man, but it would not be altogether from his appearance—medium height and heavily built; a square, strongly marked, sallowy tanned face with rather weary eyes; thick moustache and shock of black hair tinged with grey; capable, alert hands, broad and muscular, which he lays now on your sleeve, now on your shoulder.

One would gather something from that face, and something from that cadenced baritone voice, listening to which one realized that the German language has a melody of its own. But one would gather more from the kindness and warmth of humanity which his personality radiates, an entirely masculine sweetness.

I had asked him what particularly interested him in Scotland. He leant back and closed his eyes. His face softened, and he murmured in short cadenced sentences, while Mrs. Russell softly translated.

"My mother from childhood had a great longing to see Scotland because of Sir Walter Scott. . . . I always hoped I would be able to earn enough money to bring her to Scotland and show it

to her . . . it was really the only country she had a great longing
to see . . . she travelled very little. . . ." There was a pause, and he
smiled rather sadly. "She was killed during the war . . . knocked
down by cavalry in a village street in Alsace . . . and so she never
saw Scotland at all. . . . I have been much moved to see Scotland. . . ." It is rarely an interview comes to such a perfect
close.

Leaving Edinburgh by the earliest train on the 27th, he reached
St. Andrews in time for the conferring of another honorary degree,
the LL.D., amid immense applause from the students. Among other
notable recipients of honours was Sir James Frazer, author of that
monumental tome *The Golden Bough*. Later Schweitzer was asked
to stand for the Rectorship of St. Andrews in succession to General
Smuts, and was told that his election was certain if he would. But
he declined the honour on the ground of the insufficiency of his
English.

The next day, feeling that his tasks in Scotland for the time being
were nearly ended, he allowed himself the relaxation of a walk over
the famous links, rejoicing in the long vista of smooth green turf,
the grand outline of the coast, the sea, the gulls; and interesting himself in the ground plan of the old Cathedral destroyed by John Knox;
till it was time to get back to Edinburgh to be ready next day to
receive the honorary degrees which that University had conferred
upon him *in absentia* the year before, of Doctor of Divinity and
Doctor of Music. This was his first appearance there and he was
accorded a great ovation. He left Edinburgh the same afternoon for
the south, and worked in the train solidly with his companion at
the translation of one of his books till Peterborough was reached
at 1.15 A.M., where they broke journey for the night, and reached
Norwich the following day, July 1st. He was joined by two friends
for the night, Mr. Ashby and Father C. F. Andrews, and with two
or three other friends spent the evening in the Close discussing
philosophy. The next day he made a visit to his friend Sir Donald
Tovey, who was ill at his country house several miles away. Leaving
Norwich by the first train the next morning for Harwich, he was
joined there by his wife from London, and together they returned
home to the Continent. Thus concluded a memorable visit to these
shores.

On March 16, 1933, Schweitzer arrived at Bordeaux to embark on
his fourth journey to Lambaréné, looking, says Mrs. Russell who

accompanied him, "weary and aged." "He was *very* tired after his 'rest' in Europe," says his companion, "and was constantly falling asleep on deck."

South of Teneriffe one of the twin-screws of the good ship *Brazza* went out of action when its shaft snapped. Had this occurred off the coast of Portugal with a west wind the results would have been disastrous, for the other screw proved also to be frail. As it was, a strong north-east wind carried the vessel to Dakar, whence she had to return under escort without cargo or passengers. A week of enforced inactivity on board beside the quay, and another week in a good hotel amid delightful surroundings in a glorious climate, proved an effectual restorative to the Doctor's health. He reached Lambaréné on April 22nd, and continued .there till the beginning of 1934.

His next visit to this country was in October 1934 to deliver his Hibbert Lectures at Oxford on "The Religious Factor in Modern Civilization." This he did in four days between the 16th and 25th of that month, and repeated the lectures before the University of London on alternate days in the same period. He made Oxford his headquarters, where he was the guest of Miss Deneke, who recalls that he would sit up till the small hours of the morning simultaneously preparing his Gifford Lectures.

Although Schweitzer spends many hours in marshalling his thoughts before a lecture, and even in committing them to paper, yet he delivers them entirely without notes and never in the same form as that in which he prepared them. If his listeners express surprise at this apparent feat of memory, he playfully reminds them that he has a good exemplar in Cicero, whose orations were not written out until after he had delivered them.

A summary of the Gifford Lectures from Schweitzer's own pen was contributed to *The Christian Century* (New York) in November 1934.[1] An attempt must here be made to indicate the main points of his Hibbert Lectures. (As will be seen, these two courses of lectures overlap each other to some extent, and together represent a summary in homiletic form of the theme he had already developed in his Philosophy of Civilization: a type of lecturing to which academic circles, as was remarked at the time, "are not generally accustomed.")

[1] See Appendix III.

The past century (from about the year 1820) has witnessed the decline of idealism in thought and, as an inevitable consequence therefrom, the loss of ideals in conduct. Idealism is a free, constructive habit of thought proceeding, like all true growth, from within outwards, which seeks to shape events and transform circumstance into harmony with spiritual and ethical values. The movement of thought which in English moral philosophy began with Locke (in his *Reasonableness of Christianity*) and culminated in Shaftesbury, was essentially a movement in the right direction: it was animated by ideals. But it has been displaced by a spurious doctrine of "realism." This latter is the unfortunate legacy of the philosophies of Hegel and Spengler, and has resulted in a habit of mind which adjusts thought and action alike to "the march of events"—to "happenings"—and leads inevitably to the abandonment of ethics in favour of motives of expediency. [It is a distorted habit of mind which identifies the real with the actual. In any philosophy worthy of the name, the real is always the ideal, the actual merely the apparent. In genuine philosophy the word ideal signifies what ought to be realized, and is realizable. The perversion of modern thought consists in this, that it understands "realism" to signify what *is* in the sense of what *occurs*; that is, it confounds the real with the actual and so with the apparent. It would perhaps be unfair to charge the founder of Absolute Idealism with such an egregious perversion of thought; nevertheless, it is true that his philosophy has led to this deplorable result, and thus to the virtual abandonment of ethical ideals. As Schweitzer writes elsewhere: "Hegel's ethic is, in truth, only a species of law"; and this is precisely what the modern mind would have it be.]

"Realism" looks to externals for the determination of conduct, and in religious thought it represents an objectivization of Infinite Being. Its trend is away from freedom towards determinism: to the idea of man's impotence as a moral agent, and to the conception of God—the sole arbiter of human destiny—as the "Wholly Other." [This exteriorization of the Ground and Source of our being—as an Object, like other objects in the natural world, "over against" man and alien to his natural consciousness—has led, in modern theology, to disastrous results: in thought, to antinomies; in worship, to the adoration of concepts about God rather than to spiritual communion with Him; in conduct, to the sacrifice of ethical ideals for ceremonial "acts of devotion."]

The spirit of the age loves dissonance; that shows how far it is from genuine thought, for right thinking is a harmony within us. [To such an extent, it may be added, has modern thought since then run riot in its love of dissonance, that when its thinking is confronted with a plain logical dilemma, it dignifies this by the euphemism of "dialectic" which it defines as "opposites held in tension,"—an account of the matter which would have surprised the originator of the theory of thesis and antithesis resolving themselves in an ever new synthesis.]

The loss of ideals results in the loss of a sense of personal responsibility, and a lack of self-reliance. Modern man dares not face the world alone; he shrinks from freedom and from duty; he prefers to accept the domination of an impersonal arbiter— the State—which is the custodian both of his conscience and of his reason. But this is to de-personalize himself. It is the logical outcome of the application of "Realism" to the political sphere. The trend in this direction was already apparent in the theory of state-craft expounded by Marx, who did not awaken ideals to ameliorate the lot of his workers; the spirit of realism obliged him simply to await the progress of events. And in the world today there still prevails a contempt of life, a lack of reverence for it. No people knows whether or not another people will attack it tomorrow. Every nation is in a state of fear, because all are ruled by that terrible want of sense which is the unreasonableness of irreverence for life. [This world-weariness and moral apathy on the part of modern man is the cause of his retrogression to the gregarious instincts of the herd or group, miscalled "team spirit" or "community sense" or " nationalism." Politically, its refuge is the totalitarian state; religiously, an authoritarian church. We are now living in the situation that Schweitzer foresaw.]

Reporters in Oxford and London had much to say of the impression of Schweitzer's personality on the platform, at the organ, and in conversation; and also of the skill of his interpreter, Mrs. C. E. B. Russell.

Schweitzer is a large man, physically as well as spiritually. With his great frame, commanding presence, shaggy head of hair, prominent muscles, penetrating eyes, and directness of manner, he impresses one as a champion of humanity who is as fit to wrestle with nature or with the problems of the intellect, as with the forces of evil. . . .

Devotion to truth is for him the highest manifestation of the will to live, since it forces men to choose between the products of life, and does so with a rigidity which brooks no denial. Everything about him shows the power of this idea. When you hear him play Bach it is no longer Schweitzer who plays, and no longer Bach as an individual who is being interpreted. You stand rather in the presence of the eternal forms of beauty, and listen to their direct appeal. . . .

Energetic and robust, and without a grey hair, he has well withstood the battle of life. He seems to possess two qualifications to explain this happy condition; equanimity of temperament, and a deep interest in the best things of life. He spoke without notes, placidly, and with a sense that he seemed pleased to be in our midst.

Unlike some romantic figures, Dr. Schweitzer does not disappoint those who see and hear him. He suggests massive power, and Nature has fashioned him for arduous labours. In his pronunciation there is a touch of his native Alsace, but this is too slight to hinder understanding. A more serious obstacle to an English listener is the way in which final words of sentences are spoken on high thin tones. His language is free from philosophical jargon. . . .

The short crisp sentences, vivid gestures, and play of epigram were all characteristic of the speaker. . . . The lectures are translated into English sentence by sentence. Dr. Schweitzer and the lady who interprets are perfectly attuned. Not a fraction of a second is lost between the delivery and the translation. . . . Interpreters are often automatic in style and fail to convey emotional values. This one modulates her voice to the lecturer's mood and borrows from him a thrill in the voice. While speaker and interpreter are so well attuned mentally, they differ greatly in pose and demeanour. The translator's statuesque attitude is a foil to Dr. Schweitzer's constant liveliness. It is a marvel how they keep in unison. In such a performance concentration achieves a triumph. . . . The listener soon forgets that he is hearing a lecture in two tongues.

Even as they smiled and laughed with him his hearers felt the piercing truth of his message.

The following is an extract from a letter from Sir Michael Sadler to a mutual friend, the Rev. Hudson Shaw:

When Dr. Schweitzer was in Oxford, I went to hear him and was deeply impressed. . . . And his interpreter, reproducing his German in terse English, was an ideal accompanist. I shall never forget those two—playing a duet, as it were, on the low dais of Arlosh Hall—every word listened to with rapt attention by a crowded audience. The interpreter made herself Schweitzer's instrument, and reproduced his short sentences with precision and suppressed emotion—subordinating herself wholly to him and yet herself transfigured.

On October 28th he went to stay with his friends in Putney, and preached at the Guildhouse in the evening on the subject of "Forgiveness." The last days of the month were taken up with a "reception" at Friends' House; a Bach Cantata Concert at St. Margaret's Westminster; an "at home" to visitors; a Lambaréné lantern lecture; and a visit to Basil de Selincourt, then very ill.

He found time on his last day in London to visit an old friend of Lambaréné in Regent's Park. This was "Thekla," the Red River Hog. "She used to wander about the Hospital grounds like a dog," he wrote, "and got so fond of eating our chickens that I had to choose between killing her and sending her to a Zoo. I found her so sleek and glossy that I hardly recognized her, but when I patted her she gave me a grunt of recognition. 'Ah, Thekla,' I said to her, 'you have become a great lady of the world, but I'm not so sure you wouldn't rather still be eating our chickens!' "[1]

On November 3rd he went to Edinburgh for his Gifford Lectures which were delivered three times a week, in a series of ten, on "The Problem of Natural Philosophy and Natural Ethics." Here he was the guest of Sir Donald Tovey. Sir Wilfred Grenfell happened to be home from Labrador at the same time and to be staying in Edinburgh. Their mutual friend Dr. Barbour Simpson arranged a meeting between them, and both arrived on his doorstep at the same time.

"We began at once," says Schweitzer, "to question each other about the problems connected with the management of our hospitals. His chief trouble was the disappearance of reindeer for their periodic migrations; mine the loss of goats, from theft and snake-bites. Then we burst out laughing: we were talking not as doctors concerned with patients, but as farmers concerned with livestock!" Grenfell was much interested in the latest cinema films of Lambaréné and referred to Dr. Schweitzer's hospital in his next lectures. When they left the house they were asked to sign the visitors' book. Grenfell signed first, and Schweitzer, seized with sudden mirth at the thought of his own bulk and swarthy appearance contrasted with the smaller

[1] The life-story of "Thekla" is charmingly told by Mrs. Russell in the *Animal Pictorial* for March 1940.

frame of his spruce white-haired companion, and the appropriateness of their respective habitats, taking the pen inscribed beneath his own name the words: "*L'Hippopotame est heureux de rencontrer l'Ours Blanc.*"

And so back to London, with a lantern lecture at Harrogate on the way and an address to the boys at Ashville College, to stay with Miss Christian at Haverstock Hill, and to receive several visitations. After a farewell luncheon with Sir Wilfred and Lady Grenfell at their flat on the 30th, he left London for Paris.

On January 14, 1935, the city of Strasburg, to commemorate his sixtieth birthday, honoured him by giving his name to one of its beautiful parks. At the end of February he was again in Lambaréné, but this time for a period of only seven months.

Schweitzer's last visit to this country was at the end of October 1935. Having given organ recitals at St. Margaret's Westminster and for the Bach Cantata Club, and lectured to the Royal African Society at the Imperial Institute, he arrived in Edinburgh on November 2nd for the second course of his Gifford Lectures. He delivered them in French, in a series of twelve, in the Rainy Hall at New College as before. On the 17th he lectured to students in the Music Room at the University. On the 19th he gave a lecture in German to the Glasgow University Philosophical Society on the subject of "Ethics in Present-Day German Philosophy." Having spent the week-end at Mrs. Russell's home in Strone on Holy Loch, his only glimpse of the Highlands, and preached in Strone Church on the Saturday night, he left on December 2nd to lecture before the Newcastle Theological Society at Armstrong College, and to give a lantern lecture in the City Hall the same evening. Arrived at York at 1 A.M., he spent the same morning in the Cathedral at the organ, reaching Leeds in the early afternoon in order to speak at Silcoates School on "The Importance of Ideals in Life," and on his work at Lambaréné in the Brunswick Methodist Church in the evening, and again at the Leeds Modern School early the next morning. At Leeds he was the guest of the Rev. Leslie Weatherhead, who writes: "I think we were a little apprehensive of his arrival at our modest manse. But as soon as he came into the room he put us all at our ease at once. He brought with him an atmosphere of goodwill and happiness. He was amongst us not as one wanting to be served, but as a member of the fellowship, as ready at any point to serve others as to be served. I can see him now with my little daughter of seven on his knee, playing tunes for her on the piano and guiding her little fingers over the keys."

Thence he proceeded to Peterborough for another Lambaréné lecture. The Dean, Dr. J. G. Simpson, retains as the most vivid memory of his short visit "the tireless energy of a guest who in the space of a few hours could keep an appointment with a dentist, practise on the Cathedral organ, and work off a considerable correspondence; and of a lecturer who, aided by the remarkable skill of his interpreter, could not only hold an audience spell-bound, creating the illusion that we heard him speak in our own tongue, but also avoid the snare which besets the lantern lecturer of allowing his talk to become a disjointed explanation of the pictures rather than the pictures an unobtrusive illustration of the lecture."

Arrived in London on December 5th, he went at once to All Hallows Church to try the organ in preparation for recording for the Columbia Broadcasting System of America. Then on to Winchester the same day for a talk on Lambaréné in the Cathedral. When this was ended he went at once to the organ, and could only with difficulty be dragged from it in time to be present at a reception and dinner-party, which included the Bishops of Winchester and Southampton, and the Headmaster. The next day he left by an early train for Plymouth to lecture on Lambaréné in Abbey Hall, when more than a thousand people were denied admittance. This over, he tried the organ in St. Andrew's Church. The next day he journeyed to Aberystwyth for lectures to the College students in the afternoon, and in the Municipal Hall in the evening. Here he was the guest of the Principal of the University College of Wales, Mr. Ifor L. Evans, whose enthusiasm for the music of Bach and whose extensive first-hand acquaintance with tropical Africa provided themes for much animated talk, but who realized beyond this that Schweitzer was a mortal with qualities difficult to assess by ordinary standards.

Perhaps the strongest abiding impression is one of tireless energy devoted to a single all-embracing purpose. He rested little and never spared himself. As a corollary to this, he wanted to do everything possible for himself—carrying heavy bags from the station and even posting his letters with his own hand. I imagine that his unwillingness to cause trouble to others, coupled with his own great and apparently unlimited store of energy, might make it difficult for him to devolve functions, and thus, in certain circumstances, limit his sphere of administrative action. But this single-mindedness of his somehow enhanced and unified the many-sidedness of his interests and achievements and made one feel, in some mysterious way, that one was in the presence of a very great man. But above all Dr. Schweitzer remains, for me, as a striking manifestation of the life force which he himself respects so profoundly, rather than as a person in the ordinary meaning of the word.

On the 9th he was in Sheffield for another lecture in the City Hall; and on the 10th joined his wife in Manchester again, for a lantern lecture to a packed audience, in the Albert Hall. His host and chairman, the Earl of Stamford, recalls the horrifying realism of the lecturer's slides depicting tropical ulcers and cases of sleeping sickness and leprosy in their most gruesome stages; the force with which he impressed upon his hearers their obligations as Christian people to relieve distress, with phrases that were unforgettable, as *"le jeune homme qui ne savait pas ses responsabilités"*; and how, the lecture ended, he went to the Lads' Club named after him in the slums of Salford to entertain its members with an informal talk, "and made them rock with laughter."

Thence to Birmingham for another lecture on Lambaréné in the Central Hall, to be again the guest of Dame Elizabeth Cadbury and to delight her and her friends with a recitation of the fugues of Bach. Here he improvised on her organ, and transposed to paper a prelude which was published later.

On the 12th he was in Cambridge to visit Mrs. Burkitt, the widow of his old friend and translator, and to try the new organ in the King's College Chapel. The next day to London to repeat his practices on the organ at All Hallows, and to Canterbury the same day for a talk in the Deanery on his Hospital.

Of course [writes the Dean, Dr. Hewlett Johnson], the visit of Dr. Schweitzer was an outstanding event. He addressed some 150 or 200 people in my large drawing-room in December 1935, and his robust personality illuminated all he had to say through his interpreter, Mrs. Russell. It had been proposed that he and Dr. Grenfell and I, together with the Japanese Christian, Kagawa, should go on a mission of help to China at the time of the great flood in the previous year. Arrangements for that quarter, however, fell through, and I alone went, and Dr. Schweitzer wrote to me to say how gladly he would have come, but that he was tied to his work in Africa, at which he would continue, for his strength allowed him to go on running in the same old pair of shafts, but like an old cart-horse he might not run equally well in fresh shafts.

An amusing incident occurred on his third voyage to West Africa in December 1929, when he was engaged in writing his last chapter on *The Mysticism of Paul the Apostle*. It was too rough for him to write at his desk, or on his bed, and the only way he could keep himself steady was to kneel down at the bedside with the writing pad on his bed, and his feet wedged against the wall. His steward coming in and seeing him in this devotional posture said at once, "Oh, it's not quite as bad as that *yet*, sir!"

It was the mingling of these many lighter touches with the general optimism, vitality, and buoyancy of the man that helped to build up in one's mind a figure of massive proportions, such as I have seldom met elsewhere. In a sense he and Grenfell were counterparts, but Schweitzer had the additional quality of deep scholarship and extensive learning which, however, he carried lightly and easily. The humanity of the man predominated over all other elements. He was a man one would like to live with, however hard the physical surroundings might be.

For the next week Schweitzer was almost incessantly at the All Hallows Church organ, though he found time at intervals for a lecture at St. Botolph's Bishopsgate, and another at the Royal Institute of International Affairs on "The Ethical Problem in World Philosophy and World Religion,"—and for interviews. These were many and varied. As on similar occasions, it was noticed as a somewhat disconcerting feature of his reception of visitors that his friendly interest and attention were given first and longest to simple and unlearned folk, whilst several literary celebrities had perforce to wait their turn, concealing their impatience as best they might. On the 19th, having gone to bed at 2 A.M., he was up betimes to catch the 9 o'clock Continental Express.

WITH HIS ELDER SISTER AT GÜNSBACH, 1936

ALBERT SCHWEITZER, 1936

CHAPTER XII

LAMBARÉNÉ: FOURTH PERIOD

SCHWEITZER'S sense of gratitude for all the kindness that he had received from friends in this country was profound, and towards the end of another term of work in Lambaréné he wrote for the *Spectator* a few notes about it which he thought might interest them. The article appeared on September 6, 1935.

A grateful white patient had presented the hospital with a large petroleum lamp, a tremendous boon in the operating room at night when the need for urgent operations was frequent. [Surgeons accustomed to electric light—to say nothing of all the many other amenities of science—may well take note of this.] The risk of fire of course precluded the use of ether as an anaesthetic at such times, but a local anaesthetic was generally used in any case—in special cases an injection of Novocain solution into the spine—and "how grateful we colonial surgeons should be to Charles Louis Schleich for his discovery in 1892 which so enormously simplifies surgical work!"

The cemented floors of the wards are sprinkled with fresh ashes every morning as a precaution against the incursion of ants. But if the ashes become damp in the night air, and so of firmer consistency, these insect armies can find a foothold on their surface and march over the barrage. When this occurs in the ward for mentally deranged patients, who are always noisy and excitable, there is no alternative but to remove them and flush the whole ward out from floor to ceiling with a solution of Lysol. "Even the excited patients keep comparatively quiet when this situation arises, as if they realize the danger from which it is necessary to deliver them."

During this period the hospital had been filled to capacity, chiefly with natives suffering from an influenza epidemic complicated by pneumonia, but generally brought too late to benefit by the new early treatment which had been employed with good results in Europe. It was also filled beyond capacity—with more than thirty patients waiting their turn for operation. "Recently when Dr. Goldschmid, following the usual praiseworthy custom of surgeons, began a friendly conversation with a woman who lay on the operation table receiving the injections for local anaesthesia, in order to divert her attention and cheer her, he received the answer: 'This is no time for gossip; get on with the cutting!' "

Seldom indeed was the operating theatre not in use. In the year 1934, 622 major operations had been performed, and the following year saw no diminution. As example: "On March 28th, between 1 and 1.30 P.M., there arrived from different directions three patients with strangulated hernia on whom operations had to be performed forthwith, after the whole morning had been devoted to similar work." There were also many cases of severe wounds caused by the wild beasts of the jungle. But of accidents, by far the most common were those that occurred in the lumber camps. "Many have been injured while felling trees; others, and they are in the majority, have been run over by one of the light railway wagons by which the logs are conveyed from the camp to the nearest stream. These primitive people lack understanding of the danger threatened by the engine. A timber-cutter told me that one of his newly-recruited labourers remained standing on the rails without any misgiving as a wagon was coming down a steep hill, and had to be snatched aside at the last moment. He believed that he could have stopped it with his hand, simply because he had never seen a heavy mass in motion. And it happens again and again that new men jump off a wagon at full speed without realizing they will be violently thrown off their feet. They have no experience of speed."

Schweitzer is able to record the promise of satisfactory results in the treatment of elephantiasis of the feet, adopted by his colleague, Dr. Goldschmid. This is the intravenous injection every fourth day of Lugol's solution (gm. 1 of Iodine and gm. 2 of Potassium Iodide in 300 gm. distilled water). He combined this with the old method of cutting wedge-shaped strips out of the thickened tissue. "Of the twelve feet treated in this way up to now, all have shown a fairly rapid and considerable improvement. People who could hardly drag themselves along on heavy misshapen feet have again become capable of work. It still remains to prove whether the improvement is lasting."

The hospital staff had suffered one loss which was a cause for general regret. "At the beginning of April, Boulinghi, one of my earliest native assistants, returned to his home some 200 miles to the south. He was in my service for ten years. For years he supervised the ward for operated patients, and he helped to save many a human life by conscientiously observing the pulse, breathing, and general appearance of those in his care by day or by night, and immediately reporting to us any suspicious change in their condition. He has been ailing for three years and only occupied with light work, and now he has no longer been able to resist the longing to see his native village once more. Sorrowfully we gazed after the boat which bore away our faithful old helper."

During the spring of 1936 Schweitzer was giving lectures and recitals throughout his beloved Switzerland; and for the rest of the year working at his desk and preparing for another two years' tour at Lambaréné. At the end of January 1937 he started away again for Africa in very rough weather.

It was in this year that he made the discovery of a perennial spring near the Hospital, which he inscribed to the memory of Dorothy Mannering, and wrote to Dr. Maude Royden:

I had the great good luck to come upon a spring of water which never runs dry. To prevent the walls from falling in, I had to line them with 750 big concrete blocks which Mlle. Haussknecht and I made. The well has an excellent pump, which pumps the water from a depth of six and a half metres. It is some weeks now since the pump started to work, and it is a joy to see the happiness of the natives who come to fetch water all day. The pump does not rest for five minutes and is very precious to the Hospital. It will be used for five months of the year during the dry season; during the rainy season the inmates of the Hospital get water from the big reservoirs made of cement and built into the hill, which collect all the rainwater from our roofs.

An inscription will be cut in cement on the wall, saying that it was in memory of Dorothy Mannering, and so her name will be visibly associated with this well of pure water in Equatorial Africa so precious to all who benefit by it.

In 1938, to commemorate the 25th anniversary of the Hospital's existence, the European settlers in the Ogowe region made him a gift of 90,000 francs to install Röntgen Rays apparatus. With their approval, however, he used this money for the purchase of a large supply of the most necessary drugs; a wise provision as the event proved.

He had made plans for another furlough of several months early in 1939 in order to work continuously and without interruption on the third volume of his Philosophy of Civilization and bring it to completion. Leaving West Africa on January 12th he arrived in Europe at the beginning of February. But while in the Bay of Biscay he heard Hitler's provocative speech on the ship's wireless, and this convinced him that war was imminent. Feeling that he alone could make the arrangements for ordering his hospital on a war-time basis, he therefore decided to return by the same ship, without even unpacking his luggage, and await the course of events. The ship left Bordeaux again on February 12th: he had only ten days in Alsace in which to make provision for his wife and family, and to procure supplies necessary for the hospital. On March 4th he was again in Lambaréné, "much to the astonishment of everyone." The two fortnights that he spent at sea proved to be the sole recuperation he has had from unremitting labour since 1937.

With the outbreak of war in September 1939 communication between Lambaréné and the outside world was completely severed. Not till November 1940, when the Gabôn Province declared for the French Provisional Government in London, were the Doctor's friends in Britain and America in a position to hear of his welfare.

His own letters, being many, are for the most part brief: he is wont to say that the stamps on the envelopes (which are certainly an ornament to philately) are the most interesting part of them. It is, however, to his kindness in troubling to write long letters late at night that the writer is indebted for this sketch of his activities during the past nine years.

When the war broke out he was obliged to reduce his native staff because of the difficulty of finding enough food for the sick. Happily he had laid in a large provision of rice which no one else would take because it was infested with weevils; happily, too, he had built enough sheds in which to store it. This rice proved of incalculable value. Thanks to this nutritious grain, supplemented by native produce of bananas, cassava, maize, and salt, and to the abundance of fruit trees in the plantation, "there has always been enough to eat." The plantation covers an area of 90 hectares, and besides the indispensable nuts of 2000 palm-oil trees, it grows oranges, mandarines, grape-fruit, guavas, mangoes, and avocado pears. All this fruit is common property and can be gathered freely by patients and their companions, but it is strictly forbidden to gather fruit for sale. All the European settlers round about receive a regular supply of fruit from the hospital free of charge, since in the forest timber yards

SINGLE-ROOM WARDS BESIDE THE OGOWE

ABOVE THE RIVER OGOWE, 1945

Overlooking the New Hospital (compare with the photograph facing page 125)

they cannot grow their own. By way of acknowledgment they make gifts to the hospital from time to time, thus helping to feed the sick. But the harvesting of the fruit for the requirements of such a large community as the hospital now supports is in itself a sufficient labour: a dozen daily workmen are employed under two native foremen to tend to the trees, besides four gardeners to gather the fruit and bring it in. The trees must constantly be cleared of the growth of stifling creepers which cling to their trunks and branches. Twice a year it is necessary to clear the whole plantation and root up the stumps of ancient forest trees. "Hard work—always re-beginning. The virgin forest is tenacious of its life!" One man, helped by several women, prepares the oil from the palm trees in a great press. Another man, superintending half a dozen voluntary female workers who have accompanied their sick, is occupied daily in the laundry. Several other such women are employed, under the permanent native nurse in charge, to do the dressmaking and mending.

There are beds for 400 native patients. Taking into account the companions who come with them as escort, many of whom have travelled long distances, "there is a small army to feed!" For those who are not subject to a special diet a daily ration is provided of bananas, cassava, palm oil, and salt (the last being a physical necessity to the negro). Their companions eat with them and receive the same rations, in return for which they are obliged to do a fair share of work.

In addition to this, there are beds for twenty European patients, of whom those who are well enough eat with the hospital staff. Often as many as from twenty to twenty-five people sit round the same table. "You will see," writes the Doctor, "that our establishment is organized patriarchally. I am of the opinion that a patriarchal establishment is in every way the best one to adopt in the colonies."

The many difficulties of the war years have afforded him abundant proof of the growing sympathy which is felt for his hospital work by natives and Europeans alike in the colony. He has been much encouraged by the comprehension of its value to the colony by the chiefs of the French Medical Staff, and notably by General Sicé and his successors.

The hospital, which is separated from Lambaréné itself by a tributary of the Ogowe 500 feet in width, was untouched by the battles for occupation of that site between the Vichy and the de Gaullist

Governments in October and November of 1940. Since 1942, when communication with the hospital was resumed, it has been possible to send supplies not only from this country and from America, but also from Sweden by the aid of the British Red Cross. This boon came in the nick of time, for the resources of the hospital were exhausted. "I had no idea where to find the necessities of life either for ourselves or our patients."

When in May 1942 the shelves of his pharmacy were nearly empty, a large supply of drugs arrived from America, sent by the care of the Christian Medical Council for Overseas Work under the auspices of Dr. Hume. In 1944 he received a precious supply from England; and in April of 1945 yet another from America. "Every day I think with deep gratitude of those whose devotion has made possible the continued existence of my hospital and of so many lives in this vast territory." The representatives of the committees concerned with the welfare of the hospital at Lambaréné are: in America, Professor Everett Skillings of Middlebury College, Vermont; in Sweden, Baroness Greta Lagerfelt of Gammalkil; in Switzerland, Mr. Fritz Dinner of Basel; in England, Mr. T. D. Williams, Treasurer of the British Council for his hospital in London, successor to Miss O. Bronner, who for many years had undertaken this work most faithfully. The Principal of the Headquarters of his hospital in Günsbach is Mme. Emmy Martin who acts as the Doctor's representative when he is abroad. For the dispatch of correspondence and supplies she is helped by his nurses Mathilde Kottmann and Emma Haussknecht whenever they are on furlough. (And indeed, the provision of necessities for his hospital, financial and other, would fare but poorly if he were his own agent. Such is his horror of any sort of self-advertisement that he concludes his lectures not with an appeal for Lambaréné in particular, but with an earnest reminder to his hearers that it is but one out of many hundreds of medical missions equally deserving help, all over the world. And such is his gratitude for any donation, however small, that he insists that lists of the donors be sent to him that he may acknowledge each one personally.)

Soon after the outbreak of the war the services of his nurses began to be requisitioned, one after the other, by the Government for care of the injured in the timber yards, until from a peace-time staff of nine only four remained to the hospital, dividing between them the duties of the wards and of the household. But in 1944 two of them fell sick, and only Mlle. Emma Haussknecht (who had

A SUNDAY SERVICE AT THE HOSPITAL, 1946

OFF THE LANDING-STAGE, LAMBARÉNÉ, 1947

THE DOCTOR WITH ONE OF HIS ANTELOPES AND SOME OF THE HOSPITAL'S MANY DOGS

served the hospital since 1925) and Mlle. Gertrude Koch (since 1929) were left to him, both of them sorely in need of rest.

Of fully qualified colleagues he has had the valuable assistance of Dr. Ladislas Goldschmid and of a lady doctor, Mlle. Anna Wildikann. But when in 1943 Dr. Goldschmid was away in the Belgian Congo for five months—"this meant a great strain for me. It reminded me of my early days here." The surgical cases alone are far too many for one doctor to deal with. The most common ailments requiring surgical treatment are hernia, elephantiasis, and abdominal tumours. Early in 1944 Dr. Goldschmid was called upon to replace a Government medical officer wrestling with sleeping sickness four kilometres distant across the river, but by agreement with the Governor his services were given to the hospital during the afternoons: "an enormous relief to me, especially in the sleeping sickness cases."

In August 1941 a blessing, the more thankworthy because wholly unexpected, fell to his lot: "as if by a miracle, my wife arrived from Europe."

During the invasion of France in 1940 Madame Schweitzer had gone to join her daughter and son-in-law in Lausanne, but after its collapse in the summer she moved to the south of France and eventually succeeded in booking a passage to Lisbon and thence to Angola in Portuguese East Africa. In reply to a question from the writer as to how in the world she contrived to accomplish this journey at such a time, she writes in a letter dated March 24, 1945:

I am glad to answer your enquiry, especially since it gives me the opportunity of paying a tribute of gratitude to your country, from which such efficient help came to my undertaking; and next to it, the most kind and active assistance from the Red Cross Society in Geneva.

Knowing that a British visa was necessary, I asked the Red Cross to supply me with the address of the office in London to which to apply, stating as my reason the fact that I was the oldest of the nurses at Lambaréné, and might be of some use since no young nurses were available. They replied that their delegate was on the point of leaving for London and would present my application, but that the reply might take a long time. It took a very long time. But then I had a wonderful surprise: a telegram, followed by a letter, informed me—not of the address I had asked for, but—that I was at liberty to proceed at once! Moreover, the competent authorities in London had given instructions that my journey should be facilitated as much as possible!

The next step was to ask for permission to leave France. When this question had been discussed before, I had been told that if only I could obtain the authority to prove admission to the colony, there would be little or no difficulty in procuring a permit. But when—contrary to all expectation—I had received this authority, it took seven weeks to collect the necessary papers and permits to proceed from Bordeaux; and later on, four weeks longer, to continue my journey from Lisbon; in fact, I received my last permit just half an hour before the ship was due to leave that port!

My journey on the neutral (Portuguese) steamer was without accident, in broad daylight and brilliantly lit by night, and my reception in Angola quite in accord with the kind suggestions made by the competent authorities in London. I was relieved also of another trouble. I had prepared myself, with some apprehension, for a long and lonely journey of 3 months through the bush in unfamiliar territory, but found to my great relief that this was reduced to a week's drive by car on new roads, and finally to a cruise along the well-known river to the Hospital which I reached on August 2, 1941.

On my arrival I found that I was the first person—and so far as I know the only one hitherto—who has succeeded legally in coming here from France since 1940. Once again and with deep gratitude I would acknowledge my debt to that miraculous help which I have so often received in my life, and to so much undeserved kindness, to a large extent from strangers, which has made it easier to stand what would otherwise have been sad and difficult.

It should be remarked that there is no mention in this letter of the anxiety and fatigue that must have accompanied the delays and frustrations at the outset of this courageous undertaking, nor of the hazards of the voyage itself. The letter continues (after a message from her husband to its recipient):

It is now forty-three years since we became friends and started to work together. We met with a mutual feeling of responsibility for all the good that we had received in our lives, and a sense of our duty to pay for it by helping others. It has been the joy and the pride of my life to follow and assist him in all his activities, and my one regret that failing strength prevented me from keeping pace with him. But even he, strong and still fairly robust as he is, in spite of his hard and uninterrupted work, needs a thorough rest—now in his ninth year out here without one. May the end of this catastrophical war be near, and allow for the dawn of more humane and worthier conditions for all mankind!

Since 1943 their own happiness has been increased by the marriage of their daughter, Rhena, to a friend of old standing, Monsieur T. A. Eckert, and by the birth of a grandchild. Monsieur Eckert is the director of an old-established firm of organ-builders, the house of Kuhn in Switzerland. Here he has followed the lines of the craft laid down by Cavaillé-Col whose principles he studied for many years in Paris.

Schweitzer's own letters are almost as full of solicitude about the welfare of his friends as they are about his own concerns: as thus— "How intensely I have been thinking about my friends in London when I learned that you have been bombed again! But I do hope this is going to be finished now, once and for all."

From them we learn, in addition to the particulars mentioned above, that the pace of the work in the hospital—Sundays and week-days alike—is as strenuous as ever, and that the Doctor is on his feet all day long. "I surprise myself by the way I am able to carry on my work, week in and week out, without a break. . . . If I went on holiday I would soon find out how tired I am. I prefer to work from day to day. . . . I shall remain here till the end of the war. I can stand it."—"My wife stands the strain of the exacting climate far better than I had hoped. She also is at work all day, and her help in the household is most precious."

His daily routine is as follows. Day commences at 6.45, when he sets the workmen to their various tasks which he feels obliged to supervise in every detail. Breakfast from 7.30 to 8, when the workmen are called again and instructions given for the day, and the materials for gardening, building, forestry, and road repair are issued; and,—"I run from right to left, what with pumps to repair, missing keys to find, tools to mend, the refrigerators to set going, wood to fetch for the kitchen and laundry; bananas, cassava, and maize to buy from the natives who bring it in—*et que sais-je encore*." This goes on until 10 o'clock. From 10 to 12.45, medical work. The midday meal at 12.45; after which a siesta for all until 2. Again he supervises and participates in the outdoor work before returning to the hospital for his afternoon's pharmacy. If time permits he *runs* back to the plantation before 5 o'clock to check up on the day's work, and returns to the hospital to be busy with the sick until 6.30. Then he climbs up to his bungalow, if possible for an hour's practice on his piano-organ until supper in order to keep up his technique. "But often I am too tired, especially after a run to the plantation, and so I am obliged to rest until supper and play the piano afterwards." After supper, if nothing prevents, "I belong to myself." Then he attends to correspondence, or works at his book on Philosophy. "Happily I have always had the faculty, while busy with other work, of concentrating my mind on the chapter in hand." About 11.30 he goes down to the hospital again with his petrol lamp for a last look at the patients, and to give medicine or injections for the night to insure a sound sleep for those who are in pain. If not too tired himself, he works on until midnight or later.

But a life of activity without leisure, expenditure without recuperation, must—even if it cannot break the will—induce at times in the giver an involuntary heart-weariness. A recent letter to the present writer, outlining the routine of a working day and indited in the small hours of the morning, ends thus:

My capacity for sound sleep enables me to carry on like this and keep going without a day's rest. But oh! for one free day when I could at last sleep enough to get rid of the fatigue which more and more invades me; to concentrate entirely on finishing my book, to study my music and play the organ at leisure; to walk, to dream, to read for pure refreshment's sake. When will that day come? Will it ever come?—But meanwhile I give thanks to God who has given me the health and strength to carry on this existence, in so difficult a climate, and in continual pre-occupations of all kinds. I am upheld by the privilege of being allowed to give myself to those in pain, and by the generosity of friends which enables me to continue my work.

The British Council for Dr. Schweitzer's hospital published a special Bulletin in commemoration of his seventieth birthday in January 1945. At the same time the British public was reminded both by its press and its Broadcasting Corporation of the continued existence of this pioneer of civilization in the jungle swamps of West Africa, and of the debt which—even in the midst of its own life-and-death struggle—humanity still owes to him. An extract from the leading article of a London newspaper on January 14th is typical:

WITH HIS BABY ANTELOPE, LÉONIE, 1947

THE DOCTOR AND HIS CARPENTER, 1947

Basile, the carpenter, has helped Dr Schweitzer for a quarter of a century

If sainthood consists in making the good life attractive, Albert Schweitzer is a saint of our century. Yet his example does not belittle our own lives. He ennobles us, who are made of the same human clay. His story is a living sermon on the brotherhood of man. It gives perspective to the sufferings of our time.

For the rest, perhaps the most thoughtful tribute, because the fruit of a deep and genuine undertaking of Schweitzer's faith in human nature, comes from the pen of Frank Kendon in an article entitled "Truth Out in Africa" contributed to *John O' London's Weekly* in January 1945. Too long, unfortunately, to quote in full, the following extracts must suffice to indicate the author's very well considered point of view.

. . . One day when Schweitzer was a boy of twelve or so, a companion invited him out to shoot at birds with catapults. The boy wished to refuse, but he found it hard to do so. Puzzled by this conflict, and looking for the truth of it, as his habit was even then, he found that he was unwilling to appear kind-hearted because he felt that others would despise him for it. The fault in this motive was not so much that it was weak or cowardly, as that it was ill-found and untrue. An act of kindness is never despised. The boy need never stone birds after that glimpse of the truth.

In the same spirit of questioning, of finding and bearing only the truth of a matter, Schweitzer has tried to order his life and thought ever since. He diagnosed the onsetting sickness of civilization, not as a philosopher above it, but as one who, loving men, was one of them, and wished them well. He was himself a man of large mental gifts, and he might have determined to devote his knowledge and wisdom and persuasive powers to warn us away from the road we were taking. Instead he determined to work and learn, to equip himself, till he was thirty, and thereafter to act. In this, as in everything, he obeyed the truth that he had found. . . .

His decision was that he must himself begin to live out that attitude to life, and above all to human life, which he concluded was vital for the health of civilization. Like the rich young ruler in the gospel, he had great possessions. Unlike him he did not turn away sorrowful, but acknowledged the truth and, at thirty, resigned them all.

Whatever consolation in theology or philosophy did not obviously stand on verifiable fact, Schweitzer courageously left on one side. Of all that we say we know, only one fact is certain, that we are consciously alive. We desire in our living also to be good men, and when we are kind our reward is to be satisfied that we have done good. All life alike has this quality of the will-to-live; but man's life has in addition the quality of sympathy. These experienced facts depend upon no supposition, theory, revelation, or magic. On these Schweitzer bases a rule for action—Reverence for Life—which is honest, applicable to great or small actions, powerful to do good and do no harm. Let no one shallowly object that this is too simple for life as we know it. Simple is no condemnation; simple goes deepest. Within five minutes of your reading this, some decision which affects some other living creature, great or minute, must probably be taken; it will be the better decision (the more humane) if consciously made by the light of this simplicity. For another unmistakable fact with which honesty confronted this troubled thinker on our behalf was that life lives and must live at the expense of other life. That is an old, dark, mysterious, troublesome thought; but it cannot be gainsaid.

Schweitzer reads it illuminatingly (he does not—as who can?—explain it). He reads it as a *debt* to life which we must repay in part, if we can; a debt at least for those creatures capable (as men are) of responsibility. . . . The worst of us would, anyhow, save a friend in difficulty: it is but an extension of this inborn virtue to help a bird from a trap or a frog from the main road.

How does this save civilization? The answer is that it *is* civilization; for civilization means continuing forbearance for the sake of more than ourselves, without which community is impossible. The only bricks of the house of mankind are the forbearing hearts of innumerable separate persons. All life is one, and we are men.

There then is Schweitzer, seventy years old, doctoring with science and kindness the inhabitants of French Equatorial Africa, a great and honest thinker who has practised his conclusions for forty years, self-devoted, self-supported, living out his golden sermon. . . .

PART II

HIS THOUGHT

CHAPTER XIII

THE QUEST OF THE HISTORICAL JESUS

ANYONE who approaches the Gospels without preconceptions, reading them as if for the first time, must find himself in great perplexity. This is due not only to the many obvious discrepancies and disconnections in the narrative, not only to many apparent inconsistencies in the teaching, but also to a fact at first sight not so easily discernible, namely that the evangelists are often (though not always) projecting backwards into their records of the life of Jesus, conceptions of His personality which they formed only after that life was ended, so that historical elements, prospective and retrospective, are inextricably intermixed. It is the task of scientific historical investigation to endeavour to unravel these tangles, and to separate as far as may be these strands that are intertwined, so as to present the clearest possible account of His life in chronological order and thus to discover the essential *motive* that underlay His words and deeds. It is as Jesus that the historical investigator must seek to present Him, not as the Christ either of mystical experience or of rationalistic theology. For this reason he must exclude from the scope of his enquiry all that is non-historical, namely the fourth Gospel, the infancy narratives, the resurrection appearances; for these pertain to the realm of mysticism or of theology, and there are obviously no historical canons by which the purely factual truth of them can be assessed. The field of historical enquiry is thus limited to a consideration of the contents of the synoptic Gospels from the Baptism to the Crucifixion, that is from the beginning to the end of the public ministry of Jesus. It provides, as Burkitt said, "the greatest historical problem in the history of our race," and one "which the best-equipped intellects in the modern world have set themselves to solve"; and as Schweitzer says:

> The history of the critical study of the life of Jesus is of higher intrinsic value than the history of the study of ancient dogma or of attempts to create a new one. It has to describe the most tremendous thing which the religious consciousness has ever dared or

done. . . . That He continues to reign as the alone Great and the alone True in a world of which He denied the continuance, is the prime example of that antithesis between spiritual and natural truth which underlies all life and all events, and in Him emerges into the field of history.[1]

The task then is not so much one of historical research (for the materials are before us) as of historical investigation; and the method (like that of any other scientific enquiry) must be conducted *ex hypothesi*, proceeding from experiment to test, from test to verification, till that one is discovered which is in closest accord with all the incidents narrated, and makes a total reconstruction possible based upon their necessary inner connection. The mind best equipped for the task must combine keen observation of detail with the capacity to grasp the subject comprehensively; but he must also possess that imaginative insight which is the gift of genius.

Schweitzer's *From Reimarus to Wrede* appeared in the German original in 1906,[2] and in its English translation by Montgomery as *The Quest of the Historical Jesus* in 1910. It was regarded, even by those scholars who dissented from its radical conclusions, as the most conscientious and exhaustive history of the critical study of the life of Jesus that had ever been undertaken. To every one of his predecessors (no less than sixty-seven in number) Schweitzer pays worthy tribute, even when obliged to differ from them fundamentally; and of their achievements in general he had this to say: "It is impossible to over-estimate the value of what German research upon the Life of Jesus has accomplished. It is a uniquely great expression of sincerity, one of the most significant events in the whole mental and spiritual life of humanity." And in the scale of these pioneers for truth Wrede, in Schweitzer's estimation, stands very high, even though his investigations led him to a sceptical conclusion,—the conclusion, namely, that the Messianic consciousness of Jesus, as we find it in the Gospels, is a product of early Christian theology correcting history to suit its own conceptions; and that in consequence the general picture offered by the Gospels cannot be considered as a genuine historical representation of the Life of Jesus. Schweitzer devotes the last chapter of *The Quest* to a searching

[1] *The Quest*, p. 2.
[2] Revised and re-edited in 1913 with the title *History of Research into the Life of Jesus*—expanded from 418 to 642 pages. Unfortunately no English translation of this edition has yet appeared.

examination of Wrede's view and follows it with an exposition of his own, proving the negative conclusion of the former to be untenable and claiming for his own positive conclusion that it alone answers the problems which Wrede's inevitably leaves unsolved. His trenchant criticism of Wrede's view in no way detracted from his admiration for his rival's intellectual integrity, to which he pays high tribute in *The Quest*: a recognition felt by the latter as a welcome solace for the hostility provoked by "his fearless labour in the cause of truth." Deeply moved to hear from Wrede of the cardiac affliction which interrupted his pursuit of these labours in the high tide of a brilliant scholastic career, whilst he himself was blessed with such robust good health as enabled him to continue his own work without intermission, Schweitzer maintained a friendly and sympathetic correspondence with him to the end.

Not the least part of the charm of *The Quest* is its high literary quality (to which no English translation can do justice); and the wealth of its metaphors, as apposite as they are unexpected. They seem to spring to the mind of the writer effortlessly, and impress the mind of the reader with an effect that gives finality to every point they illustrate.

Scientifically considered, *The Quest* is the most creative reconstruction of the life of Jesus that ever has been or, in all probability, that ever can be made from the records available; it establishes the authenticity of many passages which, because unintelligible in their context to Schweitzer's predecessors, had been held by them to be unhistorical.

It puts an end to all need to doubt the credibility of the Gospels of Mark and Matthew. It shows that their reports of the public activity and the death of Jesus follow a faithful tradition which is reliable even in details. If some things in this tradition are obscure or confused, the explanation is to be found chiefly in the fact that in a number of instances the disciples themselves did not understand the sayings and actions of their Master.[1]

The result is destructive of that abstract theology which has borrowed its weapons from the armoury of metaphysics and masquerades as dogma.

Those who are fond of talking about negative theology can

[1] *My Life and Thought*, p. 62.

find their account here. There is nothing more negative than the result of the critical study of the Life of Jesus. . . .

It is nothing less than a misfortune for modern theology that it mixes history with everything, and ends by being proud of the skill with which it finds its own thoughts—even to its beggarly pseudo-metaphysic with which it has banished genuine speculative metaphysic from the sphere of religion—in Jesus, and represents Him as expressing them. . . . History will force it to find a way to transcend history, and to fight for the lordship and the rule of Jesus over this world with weapons tempered in a different forge.[1]

Schweitzer's earlier work entitled *The Secret of the Messiahship and Passion: A Sketch of the Life of Jesus* had appeared in 1901.[2] It is now less known than *The Quest*, but for the general reader it is the easier of the two to read. By a curious coincidence it appeared in Germany on the same day as Wrede's work *The Messianic Secret in the Gospels*, "with titles almost identical," and agreement in their strictures of accepted methods of approach to the subject "extending sometimes to the very phraseology." Yet, written as they were from different standpoints of criticism—the one literary, the other historical—they reached very different conclusions.

The Mystery and *The Quest* supplement each other in several points, and supplementing both there is a much shorter book, *The Problem of the Last Supper*, published in 1901 (as the first part of the full treatise *The Mystery*) and reprinted in 1929, but as yet untranslated into English.[3] Lastly, in the earlier chapters of his brief autobiography *My Life and Thought* there are to be found several passages which admirably summarize his conclusions, and are even more valuable for the light they throw on the religious implications involved by them for his life. Concise presentation of the subject is difficult not only on account of the extreme complexity of the material, but also because Schweitzer's own arrangement of it, made as it was in different works at different times, suffers from a certain lack of systematization. It must be remembered that his many-sided genius was finding other outlets for his tremendous intellectual and artistic

---

[1] *The Quest*, pp. 396-399.

[2] Translated by Lowrie in 1915, and entitled *The Mystery of the Kingdom of God*.

[3] This work, already delivered in lectures, Schweitzer had intended to have developed into a volume as a companion study to another on Baptism, but pressure of work precluded publication. A great part of the substance of both studies is, however, incorporated in his *Mysticism of Paul the Apostle*.

energies at the same time that he was engaged on these studies and between whiles.

It is possible here to touch only the fringe of a vast continent of scientific exploration. For the sake of clarity it is thought best to group the following attempted summary of the subject under separate headings, though a certain amount of overlapping is unavoidable, and a multitude of *minutiae* which go to support the argument are necessarily omitted. Where comments corroborating it are introduced by the present writer they are inserted in square brackets.

The Messianic Expectation

The religious atmosphere of Palestine in the time of Our Lord was tense with expectation of the appearance of the long-promised Messiah. This expectation was derived from rabbinical interpretations of the great prophets of Israel, notably the last chapters of Isaiah, as well as from the much later prophecy of Daniel (165 B.C.), and even more explicitly from those books (not till later regarded as apocryphal), known as the Book of Enoch and the Psalms of Solomon, written within the previous century, almost within living memory. As prelude to His coming would occur two events signalizing the imminence of the Times of the End. One would be the appearance of his Forerunner in the person of Elijah and the working by him of mighty signs and wonders. The other would be a period of Great Tribulation ($\pi\epsilon\iota\rho\alpha\sigma\mu\acute{o}s$) which would overtake the elect, as had been foretold by Daniel. Thereafter, the advent of the Messiah Himself, designated as "the Son of Man coming in the Clouds of Glory," would signalize the re-establishment of the Throne of David, [and the end of that long waiting for the Consolation of Israel for which just men and devout, like the aged Simeon in the Temple, had yearned (Lk. ii, 25)]. He would inaugurate the heavenly Kingdom of God and establish it upon earth, an event to be commemorated by the celebration of a Sacramental Meal which he, the divine host, would share with his elect. His coming (in the minds of some) would coincide with the End of the World: that is, it would terminate the natural order. Then also (in the minds of some) would occur the final Day of Judgment, as a result of which some would enter "in the resurrection of the just" into that heavenly Messianic kingdom, and others pass to the "resurrection of condemnation." The dominating note of Old Testament prophecy had been in its

stress on the essential prerequisite for entry into the Messianic kingdom of glory. This was Repentance—that is, "a moral renovation
and renewal, a recovery standing in retrospective relation to the
sinful condition of the past, in prospect of the accomplishment of
universal perfection in the future," to be ratified (though the origin
of the rite is unknown to us) by a Sacramental Baptism. The warning
note had fallen upon deaf ears; but it was now re-awakened with
sudden and dramatic urgency by the clarion call of John the Baptist:
"Repent! for the Kingdom of Heaven is at hand" (Mt. iii, 2).

The Messianic Consciousness

Such was the background of religious consciousness and national
aspiration into which Our Lord was born. The question is to what
extent, and with what qualifications, did He share it?

Reimarus (1694–1768) had first propounded the hypothesis that
Jesus shared the "eschatological" expectation of His day (the expectation, namely, that the End of the World was at hand); his data of
observation were correct, but his conclusion—that the Messiahship
was viewed by Jesus in a political sense—mistaken. His whole perspective, though rightly chosen, is distorted by this false view.—Not
till Johannes Weiss (1892) was the eschatological hypothesis revived.
He rightly realized that Messiahship is to be viewed, not in a political
but in a supernatural sense, but was mistaken in supposing that Jesus
agreed with His contemporaries in adopting a passive rôle with
regard to its advent. This conclusion again leaves many factors in
the total situation, especially the actions of Jesus, unexplained.—The
argument of Weiss was criticized adversely by Wrede (1901) who
denied that Jesus regarded Himself as the Messiah, and asserted that
the idea that He was so existed only in the imagination of His
disciples after His death.

According to Schweitzer, who followed the hypothesis of
"thoroughgoing" eschatology to its conclusion, Jesus from the
time of His Baptism, when the heavens were opened and a Voice
proclaimed Him Son of God, knew Himself to be the destined
Messiah who would be revealed as such in God's time, but kept it
a profound secret till it was disclosed to the disciples by the confession of St. Peter which was supernaturally revealed. "And He
strictly charged them that they should not make it known." The
secret was betrayed by Judas Iscariot to the Sanhedrin, and was made
he final point of the accusation by Caiaphas.

Jesus did not (as both liberal and catholic expositors have too easily supposed) idealize the current Messianic expectation by projecting it into a distant and indeterminate future vaguely denominated as "spiritual"; He regarded it as imminent and likely to occur at any moment; certainly within His own lifetime; and whereas the older prophets had conceived of it as a divine intervention within the *course* of human history, for Jesus it was to come as a final cosmic catastrophe which would *terminate* human history and would be brought about, in accordance with the apocalyptic prophecy of Daniel, by the "Son of Man" coming on the clouds of heaven. But more than that. "Whereas for His contemporaries it was a question of waiting for the Kingdom, of excogitating and depicting every incident of the great catastrophe ; for Jesus it was a question of *bringing to pass* the expected event through the moral renovation." [1] Hence He begins His evangel by re-echoing the Baptist's cry: "Repent! for the Kingdom of Heaven is at hand" (Mt. iv, 17).

"Our minds refuse at first to grasp that a religiousness and an ethic so deep and spiritual can be combined with other views of such naïve realism. But the combination is a fact." [2]

Period of the Ministry

Since only one Passover is recorded, and mention would certainly have been made of another had it occurred during the period, the public ministry of Our Lord cannot have exceeded one year. Schweitzer estimates its upper limit as eleven months and its lower limit as five or six. It was in the early part of the year or in the springtime that He began His Ministry; it was when the fields were "white unto the harvest" that He sent forth His disciples on their mission; it was in the early winter that He was crucified. The records of His Life and Teaching therefore, as contained in the synoptic Gospels—so far from being scanty—are extraordinarily detailed for the period they cover. [3]

It is unnecessary to suppose two contrasted periods in the life of Jesus,—the first a happy period of success in Galilee, the second a period of growing opposition encountered in Jerusalem; the interval between them punctuated by a "flight" to the north of Palestine. Such a conception is in fact at variance with a correct interpretation of the sequence of events recorded in the synoptic Gospels. The

---

[1] *The Mystery*, p. 115.   [2] *My Life and Thought*, p. 50.
[3] Cf. *The Quest*, p. 350.

supposed "flight" was as much a voluntary retirement from the
throngs who acclaimed Him as was His departure across the lake
o the country of the Gadarenes. The controversy with the Pharisees
on the subject of ceremonial purification (Mk. vii, 1-23), which is
assumed to mark the turning-point of their animosity against Him,
was slight in comparison with His earlier conflict with the Scribes
concerning the sin against the Holy Ghost (iii, 22-30). It was only
in the second period, however, when His popularity as a prophet
and healer was at its height, that Jesus disclosed to His disciples the
secret of His impending Passion: a fact which has caused expositors
to read "an unwarranted historical postulate into an inferred psychological situation." In estimating the contrast between these two
periods it is actually the second rather than the first which must be
regarded as successful,

> For wherever Jesus appears in public after the return of the
> disciples He is accompanied by a devoted multitude—in Galilee,
> from the Jordan to Jerusalem, and in the capital itself. . . . If this
> Galilean populace supported Him now by their acclaim and
> enabled Him to terrorize the magistrates in the capital for several
> days—for His purification of the Temple was nothing else than
> that—and to expose the scribes with His dry irony, is it possible
> that they did it for the man who a few weeks before had to yield
> to these theologians in His own land? [1]

Commission of the Disciples

To take now the first of the crucial events of His ministry: His
commission to His disciples to go forth and proclaim the imminence
of the Kingdom.

There can indeed be no question but that Our Lord did expect,
and led His disciples to expect, the dawn of the Messianic Kingdom
within the lifetime of His hearers. His utterance to them on the eve
of His Transfiguration is emphatic and is recorded by each of the
three evangelists: "Verily I say unto you, There be some standing here,
which shall not taste of death, till they see the Son of Man coming in
his Kingdom," or "—the Kingdom of God come with power" (Mt.
xvi, 28; Mk. ix, 1; Lk. ix, 27). Furthermore, He expected it to supervene while the disciples were actually engaged in proclaiming it:
"Verily, I say unto you, ye shall not have gone over the cities of

---

[1] *The Mystery*, p. 68.

Israel, till the Son of Man be come" (Mt. x, 23).[1]

[When the disciples returned with their mission fulfilled, their report of its success did indeed elicit from Him the triumphant ejaculation, "I beheld Satan as lightning fall from heaven" (Lk. x, 18). But together with this there is an evident note of frustration upon the non-appearance of the expected event in words which may be taken as a soliloquy, and which may surely be taken from their context to refer to this: "I am come to send fire upon the earth, and O that it were already kindled!—I have a baptism to be baptized with, and how am I straitened till it be accomplished!" (Lk. xii, 49, 50).]

Not only was the Messianic expectation unfulfilled, but so also was the expected prelude of the great Tribulation. The disciples returned without having suffered any persecution whatever; on the contrary, their mission was crowned with overwhelming success: "Even the devils are subject to thy Name."

> When, in accordance with His commission, by sending forth the disciples with their message, He hurled the fire-brand which should kindle the fiery trials of the Last Time, the flame went out. He had not succeeded in sending the sword on earth and stirring up the conflict. And until the time of Trial had come, the coming of the Kingdom and His own manifestation as Son of Man were impossible.[2]

The Mystery of the Passion

But meanwhile an event of a positive character had occurred. John the Baptist, unaware that he was the Forerunner, had suffered violent death.

The coincidence of these two unforeseen events drove Jesus again into solitude, to meditate on their significance. His Messianic consciousness had never been without the thought of the Passion. It was inseparable from His thought of the Kingdom. The theme of affliction, persecution, tribulation, to be endured unto the end by those destined to share His Kingdom, had been present in His teaching from the first, and it has reference solely to the travails out of

---

[1] The objection raised by Streeter on grounds of textual criticism (and subsequently followed by many N.T. critics), based on the conjecture that this verse, and indeed the entire chapter, is a "later conflation" and therefore not to be regarded as authentic,—is already met by Schweitzer's comment on Holtzmann's attempt, on grounds of higher criticism, to discredit it (see p. 15).

[2] The Quest, p. 387.

which the Messianic Kingdom was to be born. To interpret them
as predictions of martyrdom after His death is to place a false construction on the historical setting: on the contrary, it was to be after
His death and subsequent resurrection that the dawn of the Kingdom
would appear. Thus, in the first period of His ministry, prior to
Caesarea Philippi, He spoke of it much more frequently and freely
than in the second. And yet together with this thought He had also
always counted upon the possibility that God in His omnipotent
mercy would shorten the days and spare the elect, and had bidden
them to pray that they should not enter into the Great Tribulation
but would be delivered from the Evil One, that is from Satan, the
representative of the God-opposing forces.

But now in His solitude there was borne in upon His consciousness
the perception that the Kingdom could only come when He, the
Messiah-to-be, had by His own self-chosen suffering and death made
atonement for the elect and thereby saved them from the Great
Tribulation: it must be "brought about" in order that the Kingdom
might come. [Cf. the saying about the corn of wheat, John xii, 24.]
And so at Caesarea Philippi He imparts to them the secret that He
alone is to suffer. By means of this vicarious voluntary sacrifice the
perfect atonement will be made. His followers are spared the anguish.
[Cf. His words to the officers at His arrest, John xviii, 8.] He suffers
in their stead, *and gives His life a ransom for many* (Mk. x, 45; Mt.
xx, 28). This is the saying which, related by the two oldest Gospels
alone, gives the clue to the whole motive of His life and the meaning
of the *purpose* of His Passion. Significantly it occurs after Our Lord's
reply to the request of the sons of Zebedee for a place of pre-eminence
in His Kingdom. That they and Peter, His three most intimate
disciples, should share His sufferings was a possibility present to His
mind: it is shown to have been so not only on this occasion, but also
in Gethsemane. But whether so or not, it was He who must die to
make atonement, and rise again and so enter into His glory.

The Mystery of the Passion is therefore the fulfilment of the
prophecy of the last chapters of Isaiah, and it is complete in every
detail (Is. xl, xlix, lii, liii, liv-lxvi): "One must grasp the dramatic
unity in these chapters in order to enter into sympathy with One
who sought here mysterious intimation about the things of the last
time."

He must suffer for the sins of those who are ordained for His

Kingdom. In order to carry this out He journeys up to Jerusalem, that there He may be put to death by the secular authority, just as Elijah who went before Him suffered at the hand of Herod. That is the secret of the Passion. Jesus did actually die for the sins of men, even though it was in another sense than that which Anselm's theory assumes. . . .[1]

This is the secret between Himself and God. The others cannot and need not understand it. . . . The secret is intelligible only retrospectively, from the point of view of the glory that shall be revealed.[2]

The thought of Christendom has interpreted the meaning of the Death in another sense; it has taken it out of its historical and eschatological setting, and placed upon it a theoretical and theological signification; it has deified His Person, but in doing so it has lost the indwelling power of His Spirit.

[The experience of the soul's redemption, which is a spiritual reality, has been identified by theologians with an undefined theory of the Atonement. As is well known, the theory of Anselm is but one of four such "schemes," not one of which, however, has proved acceptable to the mind of the Christian Church. The doctrine has therefore remained an unverified and unverifiable theory, and the Church has been content to leave it so. Yet it is the very doctrine upon which the whole complex edifice of Christology has been based. It may be urged that until the Church has decided *how* the redemption came to pass, the question *who* the Redeemer is can be but speculation. The nature of the Work of Christ is the question that precedes the question as to His Person. Schweitzer's answer is contained in his study of *The Mysticism of Paul the Apostle*, but it is already implicit in the sentence with which he concludes *The Quest*: "To those who obey Him, whether they be wise or simple, He will reveal Himself in the toils, the conflicts, the sufferings which they shall pass through in His fellowship, till as an ineffable mystery they shall learn in their own experience *Who He is*."]

The Transfiguration

The Gospel records as they stand place the Transfiguration after Caesarea Philippi. Read in that order, the Transfiguration is "an obscure episode devoid of historical significance." But transpose the sequence of these two events, and assume the scene to have been

---

[1] *The Mystery*, pp. 235-236.   [2] *Ibid.* pp. 238-239.

enacted on the mountain by the lake-shore near Bethsaida, and the Transfiguration then becomes "a Galilean occurrence of far-reaching historical importance" which at one stroke explains how, a few weeks later, St. Peter came to be possessed of the secret of Jesus' Messiahship. Like the feeding of the multitude "it bears evident marks of intense eschatological excitement. It repeats in some sort the experience of Jesus at His Baptism": again there is the Voice sounding out of the Cloud the divine witness "This is my beloved Son."

In both cases a condition of ecstasy accompanies the revelation of the secret of Jesus' person. The first time the revelation was for Him alone; here the three disciples also share it. It is not clear to what extent they themselves were transported by the experience. So much is sure, that in a dazed condition, out of which they awake only at the end of the scene, the figure of Jesus appears to them illuminated by a supernatural light and glory, and a voice intimates that He is the Son of God.[1]

This revelation explains the confidence with which Peter answers the question of Our Lord at Caesarea Philippi (Mk. viii, 29), and also the significance of Our Lord's rejoinder.

That Jesus was Himself the Messiah-to-be was the stupendous fact that had been revealed to Peter and his two fellow-disciples on the Mount, and was a secret which they possessed in common until the confession at Caesarea; but that He was also to be identified with the Suffering Servant was something upon which, till then, Peter had not reckoned. Hence his agitation, and the fact also that Jesus, aware that the other disciples are curious, "with passionate abruptness enjoins silence."

Meanwhile the attitude of all the disciples towards Jesus undergoes little change, except that they now manifest towards Him "a certain awe" and that "they dare not interrogate Him when they fail to understand His words." But otherwise their relationship remains as it was. "For *not yet* was He the Messiah." It is true that the revelation of Jesus' future Messiahship gave rise to speculations among His disciples as to what manner of persons they should be in the coming age, and to rivalry as to which should be greatest in the Kingdom. "But meanwhile they remain what they are, and Jesus remains for them what He is." Even when two of those among them who had

[1] *The Mystery*, pp. 181-182.

witnessed His Transfiguration request the seats of honour in His
future Kingdom, it is with the familiar title of "Master" that they
address Him (Mk. x, 35). Significantly their request is met by another
prophecy of His passion and the challenging question whether they
can share it.

The Son of Man

Why did Jesus enjoin upon His disciples so strict a secrecy concerning His Messiahship? Because by its very nature it was a secret—it
was futuristic—He was *not yet* the Messiah. Only with the dawn-
break of the Kingdom would He, now the Messiah-to-be, appear
then supernaturally as the Messiah and simultaneously with it. Till
then, "it was a conception which could be fully formulated only in
His own consciousness." Till then it was His mission, both by word
and signs, to point men to the nearness of the Kingdom. Hence
whenever He uses the title Son of Man, He uses it in the third person.
Whenever we find it used by Him in the first person, *prior to the
Transfiguration or to the Confession of St. Peter*, this must be regarded
as an unhistorical literary interpolation, due to the Evangelists'
thinking back into their records the thought that *only afterwards* began
to dominate the minds of the disciples. The perspective had shifted.

> The Messiah in his earthly estate must live and labour un-
> recognized, he must teach, and through deed and suffering he
> must be made perfect in righteousness. Not till then shall the
> Messianic Age dawn with the Last Judgment and the establish-
> ment of the Kingdom.[1]

Did Jesus *require* of His disciples belief that He was Himself the
Messiah? No: for the faith which He required of them had nothing
to do with His Person, but only with the immediacy of the coming
Kingdom of God. "It was the fourth Evangelist who first presented
the history of Jesus as if its chief concern were with His Person."
It is true that there is a secondary literary stratum in the synoptists
"which depict his life as in harmony with the presumption that He
not only knew Himself to be the Messiah, but that others also had
this impression of Him." But all such references identifying Him
with the Messiah, prior to St. Peter's confession, must be read *ex
eventu* "as the casual and unreflecting introduction of a new mode

[1] *Ibid.* p. 188.

of conception." By the time the Gospels came to be written the historical perspective was necessarily shifted: the Evangelists knew *then* that He was the Messiah. "But so long as He lived Jesus required of no man faith in Himself as the Messiah."

What was it then that He did require of them? He required of them that allegiance to Himself which obedience to His absolute ethic of love involved, which would in itself guarantee their membership in the Kingdom when it should be revealed, and when simultaneously with it—though this (till His Transfiguration) was hid from them—He should be Himself revealed as the Messiah.

The popular Jewish expectation of the Messiah was of One appearing in the Clouds of Glory directly out of heaven. They had no conception that He would first appear as a man among men on earth, before His celestial manifestation. The Scribes and Pharisees, however, taught by Isaiah's prophecy, spoke of Him as the Son of David, that is, of royal lineage and human ancestry. Jesus therefore, as He taught in the Temple, "was prompted to touch upon the Messianic dogma of the Scribes, as though He would call attention to the secret that lurks behind it."—The Messiah is David's son; but David calls Him his Lord. How is He then his son? (Mk. xii, 35-37).

> The Messiah is David's Son—that is, subordinate to him—since in this era he is born of human parentage and lives and labours in obscurity. David's Lord, because at the dawn of the coming era he will be revealed as Christ in glory. Jesus has no notion of impeaching the pharisaic dogma. It is correct, Scripture so teaches. Only, the Pharisees themselves cannot properly interpret their dogma, and so cannot explain how the Messiah can be in one instance David's Son, and in another David's Lord.[1]

But the title "Son of Man" was that which Jesus Himself chose in preference to any other to designate the Messiah, and therewith to veil His own identity: "every other Messianic designation that is applied to him He corrects and interprets by Son of Man."

> Withal, he and the Son of Man remain for the people and for the Disciples two entirely distinct personalities. The one is a terrestrial, the other a celestial figure; the one belongs to the age that now is, the other to the Messianic period. Between the two there exists solidarity, inasmuch as the Son of Man will intervene

[1] *The Mystery*, p. 189.

in behalf of such as have ranged themselves on the side of Jesus, the herald of His coming. . . .[1]

The problem about the Son of Man is herewith elucidated. It was not an expression which Jesus commonly used to describe himself, but a solemn title which he adopted when in the great moments of his life he spoke about himself to the initiated as the future Messiah, while before the others he spoke of the Son of Man as a personality distinct from himself. In all cases, however, the context shows that he is speaking of one who is yet to come, for in all these passages mention is made either of the Resurrection or of the appearing upon the clouds of heaven.[2]

But a later period of Gospel composition made this title appear as if it were Our Lord's habitual self-designation. The writers of this period took it for granted that on earth Jesus was already the Messiah, "and appropriated this emphatic term without suspecting that it was appropriate only in certain sayings and in definite situations, employing it indifferently in any passage where Jesus spoke of Himself—and thereby created philosophical and historical impossibilities."

For these reasons also the title disappears from the language of the primitive Church. It only once occurs in the "Acts" (vii, 56). For once again the perspective had shifted. "Son of Man was the Messianic expression for a clearly defined episode of the Messianic drama —the moment of His manifestation upon the clouds of heaven."

To the mind of the primitive Church, Jesus, now exalted in heaven at the right hand of God, was *already* the Messiah, and His manifestation as Son of Man coming in the Clouds of Heaven was no longer thought of as the necessary sign of His Messiahship.

The Forerunner

We are thus brought to the second of those crucial problems requiring elucidation: the reply of Jesus to the question of John the Baptist from prison, "Art Thou the Coming One?"

Herod was persuaded, and with alarm, that Jesus was John the Baptist whom he had beheaded, risen from the dead, and that therefore these mighty works did show forth themselves in Him (Mk. vi, 14). Mighty works were the expected "signs and wonders" which would authenticate the message of the Forerunner and confirm the

[1] *Ibid.* pp. 191-192.   [2] *Ibid.* p. 193.

near approach of the Messianic Kingdom; yet John the Baptist had himself in his lifetime performed none. The general impression prevailed therefore that John was a prophet, and Jesus the Forerunner. For Jesus did perform these mighty works; and Jesus Himself held it against His countrymen in Galilee that they believed not nor repented, despite them. His power over the works of Satan in those who were devil-possessed presented an even more compelling proof of the signs of the times, but even this was regarded with blasphemous scepticism by the orthodox (Mk. iii, 22-30).

But to understand the confusion that had existed in the mind even of the Baptist concerning himself and Jesus, and which still persisted in the popular mind after his death, it is necessary to go back again to his question from prison to Jesus, "Art Thou the Coming One?"

It is the same question which the Pharisees had put to the Baptist himself and which he had expressly denied. "The historical Baptist says: I am not the Forerunner, for he is incomparably greater and mightier than I." But in the fourth Gospel the historical perspective is changed: it is the Messiah and no longer the Forerunner who occupies the foreground, so that the people, having received the Baptist's disclaimer that he was the Forerunner, could even conjecture that he was the Messiah (John i, 20).

The question which the Baptist now puts to Jesus is posed "at the moment when Jesus' confidence that the Kingdom is immediately to dawn was at its highest pitch."

In the light of our knowledge of the identity of the Baptist with the Forerunner, and of Jesus with the Messiah, and assuming a similar contemporaneous knowledge of his own identity in the mind of the Baptist, we take it for granted that his question to Jesus means: "Art Thou the Messiah?" Quite otherwise is the case. It means: "Art Thou the Forerunner of the Messiah? Art Thou Elijah risen from the dead?" The Baptist died unaware of the fact either that he was himself the Forerunner, or that Jesus was Himself the Messiah. The reason of Our Lord's evasive reply to this direct question is explained by the fact that He was not yet ready to make public whom He believed Himself to be.

The fact was, the Baptist had put Him in an extremely difficult position. He could not answer that He was Elijah if He held Himself to be the Messiah; on the other hand He could not, and would not, disclose to him, and still less to the messengers and the listening multitude, the secret of His Messiahship. Therefore He sends this obscure message, which only contains a confirmation of the facts which John had already heard, and closes with a warning, come what may, not to be offended in Him. Of this the Baptist was to make what he could.

It mattered, in fact, little how John understood the message. The time was much more advanced than he supposed; the hammer of the world's clock had risen to strike its last hour.[1]

On the other hand He did let fall "a mysterious hint" to the people concerning John: "If ye can receive it, he is himself Elijah, the Coming One" (Mt. xi, 14), and again to His disciples after the Transfiguration: "Elijah is indeed come, and they have done unto him whatsoever they listed" (Mk. ix, 13),—thereby preparing their minds for the fuller revelation concerning Himself. The occasion and opportunity for this occurred after the death of John the Baptist, when, having elicited from St. Peter the spontaneous confession, supernaturally revealed, that He was Himself none other than the Messiah, He confirmed it, at the same time enjoining upon His disciples the strictest secrecy, and leaving no cause for doubt in their minds as to the connection of His Messiahship with His Passion. The secret was still His and theirs alone when He went up with the festival caravan of Galileans to the Passover in Jerusalem. The enthusiastic acclaim of the multitude at His entry was not at all for the Messiah, but for the Coming One, and for "the coming Kingdom of our father David" (Mk. xi, 9, 10). The acclaim as recorded by the first evangelist erroneously connects the Coming One with the Son of David. Coming One means the Forerunner: Son of David means the Messiah. The entry into Jerusalem therefore was an ovation not to the Messiah but to the Forerunner, the great prophet of Nazareth in Galilee. And even the confused cry of the blind Bartimaeus for help to the Son of David does not invalidate the fact, since, when brought to Him, he addressed Him simply as "Rabbi."

The Teaching

Our Lord's teaching was an *interim-ethic*, that is to say it was conditioned by His conviction of the nearness of the supernatural Kingdom, and was therefore designed for so fateful an *interval*, in

[1] *The Quest*, p. 373.

order to key the minds of His listeners up to the highest pitch of
moral and spiritual intensity, and awaken them to watch and pray
in hourly expectation of this stupendous event. There was to be no
thought of marriage, or disposal of property, or social reform; no
idea of the founding of a church to serve the world for its future
religious needs, for the world itself was about to pass away. In short,
there was in His teaching nothing which the dogmatic necessities of
after ages have sought to read into it. His thought is on the present
and on the immediate future. Hence the alternation of the "then
and now" in the Sermon on the Mount: the interval is so short that
those who would enter the Kingdom must take heed lest it come
upon them unawares. Indeed there are already some whose inward
state of preparedness is such as to proclaim them as its members; for
whom the future and the present are, spiritually regarded, as one
and the same. "Theirs is the Kingdom of Heaven" and "They shall
inherit the Earth" are two ways of expressing the same truth; they
are to be regarded not as promises to the poor in spirit and the
meek, but as statements of fact. In other words, the Beatitudes
define the disposition which justifies admission to the Kingdom. So
also the pronouncement "Thou art not far from the Kingdom of
God" is to be understood, not qualitatively in the sense of perfection
nearly, but not quite attained, but rather chronologically in the sense
of one whose membership in the Kingdom is by his inward disposition of heart and mind already secured, and will be consummated
within a short space of time.

It is this sense of miraculous transformation that the nature parables
are designed to illustrate. They are not intended as proofs of spiritual
evolution on the analogy of natural evolution in the vegetable world
(for the process of growth is apparent to every observer); but rather
to raise the question: "How can a result so marvellous proceed from
causes so tiny and insignificant, and withal so *secret*, as the sowing of
seed in the ground? What a transformation takes place! It is mysterious: no one can tell how it comes to pass. Such too is the Secret of
the Mystery of the Kingdom of God."

Small as is the circle which He gathers about Himself in comparison with the greatness of God's Kingdom, it is none the less
certain that the Kingdom will come as a consequence of this moral
renewal, restricted as it is in its scope. It is no less confidently to
be expected that the seed, which while He speaks is slumbering in
he ground, will bring forth a glorious harvest. Watch not only

for the harvest, but watch for the Kingdom of God!—so speaks the spiritual sower to Galileans at the season of the seed-sowing.[1]

In other words, the cosmic catastrophe will be hastened by the ethical condition. This is the secret of the Mystery of the Kingdom of God, and it is in direct correspondence with the fundamental thought of the Hebrew prophets. But for Jesus, there was also a causal connection in actual temporal sequence between the ethical renewal and the supernatural event. For the time of the Messiah's advent depended on the state of preparedness, the eager watchful anticipation, the moral and spiritual renewal, in a word on the Repentance, of the faithful. They were "the men of violence who would take the Kingdom by force" (Mt. xi, 12).

Nor is there any trace of development to be found in the general content of His teaching, due to an alteration in His own conception of the purpose of His ministry (as has been erroneously supposed): it is the same "from the first day of His public appearance to His latest utterances on the way to Jerusalem"; it is still the same "absolute ethic of love," humility of heart and mind in unselfconscious service to God and man.

Was the preaching of Jesus about the Kingdom universalistic? No: for His commission to His disciples is explicit—"Go not into the way of the Gentiles, and into any city of the Samaritans enter ye not; but go rather to the lost sheep of the house of Israel" (Mt. x, 5, 6: cf. xv, 24). Salvation is of the Jews.—Nevertheless, though the preaching was particularistic in its scope, being restricted to the borders of Israel, it was to be universalistic in its consummation; qualification for membership to the Kingdom was to be based not on biological, but on moral and spiritual, considerations. Salvation is not *for* the Jews only. Indeed, many of those to whom the proclamation was addressed, the self-styled Chosen People, would find themselves excluded. "Many shall come from the east and west, and shall sit down with Abraham and Isaac and Jacob in the Kingdom of Heaven, and you yourselves shall be thrust out" (Mt. viii, 11; Lk. xiii, 29). The men of Nineveh and the queen of the south would rise up against this generation and condemn it (Mt. xii, 41, 42).[2]

[So too, it may be added, would the widow of Zarepta and Naaman the Syrian (Lk. iv, 26, 27); and to come nearer home, so

---

[1] *The Mystery*, pp. 109-110. Cf. *The Quest*, pp. 352-356
[2] *The Mystery*, pp. 117-118.

too would the Roman centurion, the Canaanite woman, the Samaritan leper, the beggar Lazarus. Herein we catch an echo of the words of ancient prophecy: "Is it you only of all the families of the earth that I have known. . . . Are ye not as the Ethiopians are unto me, O Israel? Have I not brought you up out of Egypt, and the Philistines from Caphtor, and the Syrians from Kir?" (Amos iii, 2; ix, 7); and of John the Baptist: "Think not to say among yourselves, We have Abraham to our father: for I say unto you, that God is able of these stones to raise up children unto Abraham" (Lk. iii, 8). The whole theme of the Apology of Stephen is a similar indictment of national exclusiveness, and is intended to demonstrate that God is no respecter of persons and that by no prerogative of blood or race can men claim a special monopoly of the divine favour. Nothing can be clearer in those parables of Jesus concerning the Day of Judgment (which were addressed to the religious leaders of His day who would certainly consider themselves as among the elect)—in which the separation of the just from the unjust (which they themselves taught as sound doctrine) is figured as that of wheat from tares, or sheep from goats,—than that a total reversal of their complacent expectations will occur, and that heathen, publicans, and harlots would be found among the former class, and scribes and pharisees among the latter.]

The Lord's Prayer

This prayer [repeated through the centuries as if it were a talisman, or chanted as if it were an incantation] was in its origin a Messianic prayer for the consummation of the final state of blessedness; the hallowing of God's Holy Name, and the fulfilment of His Holy Will on earth as in heaven; the Coming of His Kingdom; the consecration of the Sacramental Meal;[1] the Forgiveness of sins without satisfaction as we forgive our debtors (that is, "remission pure and simple, without atonement"); deliverance from the Great Tribulation ($\pi\epsilon\iota\rho\alpha\sigma\mu\acute{o}s$); and from the power of the God-opposing forces; ending with a triumphal ascription to the Father's eternal Kingdom and Power and Glory.

The Feeding of the Five Thousand

We come now to the third of those crucial events noticed as a

---

[1] τὸν ἄρτον ἡμῶν τὸν ἐπιούσιον δὸς ἡμῖν σήμερον = "Our bread, *the coming bread*, give us this day." The word ἐπιούσιος occurs here and nowhere else in Greek. (Cf. *The Mysticism of Paul the Apostle*, pp. 239-240.)

necessary clue in pursuit of our quest: the way in which Jesus acted on the return of His disciples from their mission. "The connection between the various scenes is here extraordinarily broken. It seems almost as if the thread of the narrative were here completely lost. Only at the moment of departure for Jerusalem do the scenes begin to stand out again in a clear and natural relationship."

It is unnecessary in this account of Schweitzer's studies to follow him in the complexities that are here involved, but rather to concentrate on the theme which he selects as of first importance. To be alone with His disciples Jesus withdrew in a boat across the lake. "But the people saw them going, and many knew Him, and they ran there together on foot from all the cities and outwent them" (Mk. vi, 33).

It is now the hour for the customary evening meal, "the day being far spent." But the meal is invested with a solemn ritual. After Jesus had taken the loaves and broken them, consecrating the act by a thanksgiving, He gave them to His disciples to distribute to the multitude.

As one who knew himself to be the Messiah, and would be manifested to them as such at the imminent dawn of the Kingdom, he distributes, to those whom he expects soon to join him at the Messianic banquet, sacred food, as though he would give them therewith an earnest of their participation in that future solemnity. The time for earthly meals is passed: hence he celebrates with them a foretaste of the Messianic banquet. They, however, understood it not, for they could not guess that he who distributed to them such consecrated eucharistic food was conscious of being the Messiah and acted as such.[1]

The uncomprehending piety of a later period of Gospel composition overlaid the sacramental Messianic character of this Feeding of the Multitude with the miraculous. Though tradition preserved the memory of its solemnity, its real significance was forgotten, if indeed it had been fully understood by the partakers.

The Resurrection of the Dead

Our Lord's prophecies about His Resurrection are not (as has been supposed) editorial adaptations of general utterances about His future glory turned *ex.eventu* into specific predictions of that event.

[1] *The Mystery*, pp. 172-173. Cf. *The Quest*, pp. 377-378.

They *are* specific predictions; and they explain the disciples' bewilderment as to what it could mean. For they were unable to disassociate the thought of the resurrection of the Son of Man from the general resurrection at the Last Day. For them Resurrection signified the transformation of both quick and dead "into another and incomparably higher state of existence," which would supervene with the coming of the Kingdom. In 1 Cor. xv we have "not a specifically Pauline thought, but a primitive Christian conception to which Jesus had already given utterance."

> This expectation of the eschatological Resurrection of the Dead ruled the consciousness of Jesus and His contemporaries. He assumes it in His discourses at Jerusalem. Expectation of the Kingdom and belief in the approaching Resurrection of the Dead belong together. It is an error in perspective to represent Jesus' thought in regard to the coming Kingdom as directed toward the future, as if it had to do with subsequent generations. So the modern mind thinks. It was just the opposite with Jesus. The Kingdom had to do with the past generations. They rise up to meet the Judgment which inaugurates the Kingdom. The Resurrection of the Dead is the condition precedent to the establishment of the Kingdom. Through it all generations of the world are lifted out of their temporal sequence and placed before God's judgment as contemporaries.[1]

The Resurrection of the Dead is therefore the bridge from the "Now" to the "Then." It accounts for the duality of consciousness in the minds of the disciples, so that when Jesus spoke to them of His own resurrection they correlated it with the general resurrection. They looked forward to it not as an "Easter Event," but as the dawn of the Messianic Kingdom.

But after His death the futuristic character of His Messiahship became obscured, even in the Gospel records. The Messiah-to-be was risen indeed, but there had been no general Resurrection nor inauguration of His Kingdom. Hence Christian piety sought to fill the breach by assuming a sort of pre-Resurrection which coincided with the Resurrection of Jesus. "It lent to this the colouring of the Messianic Day. Mt. xxvii, 50-53, furnishes an example in legendary form of such a method of reconciling fact and theory. . . . ('The graves were opened; and many bodies of the saints which slept arose')." [Cf. John v, 25, 28.]

[1] *The Mystery*, p. 204.

Time, however, inexorably intervened and "thrust itself like a splitting wedge" between the Resurrection of Jesus and the General Resurrection which would usher in the expected Messianic Day. The Church lost sight of the fact that these two events were to have been connected causally and to have coincided temporally, and henceforth began to regard Gospel history from the point of view that Jesus, by His Resurrection, was already the Messiah, and the General Resurrection an indeterminate future event.

[Therefore when on the Mount of the Ascension a *cloud* once again received Him out of their sight, "and they feared as they entered into the cloud," the angel's promise that He would come again as they had seem Him go—in the Clouds of Heaven—gave them the hope of a new assurance in the ultimate dawning of the supernatural Messianic Day; and henceforth the piety of the Church looks forward to a "Second Coming."]

The Last Supper

This eucharistic ceremonial meal was intended as the last of such celebrations, in foretaste of the supernatural Sacramental Meal which the Messiah would shortly share with His elect. By its very nature it was final and unrepeatable. "I say unto you, that I will not henceforth drink of this fruit of the vine until I drink it new with you in my Father's Kingdom." In character it corresponds with the Feeding of the Multitude: there is the same solemn act of distribution, the same act of thanksgiving. But whereas on the former occasion the partakers comprised a mixed multitude and disciples who had no understanding of its meaning, on this occasion they are the disciples alone, to whom the secret of the Messiahship had been revealed. The solemnity of this last act is further intensified by its celebration on the eve of their Lord's Crucifixion, and by the significance of His added words concerning the bread and wine— "My Body—My Blood."

This last never-to-be-repeated act, anticipating an Event which would render its repetition nugatory, was, however, by reason of an inner necessity repeated by the disciples, in expectation of their Lord's reappearance as Messiah. It was held in the same upper room, and in the early morning of the day on which Jesus had risen from the dead. It was not a memorial, not a symbolical representation of His atoning death. It was a Eucharist pointing forward—"till He come." The words of institution were not said, but only the prayers of thanksgiving. It was the only form of divine service held by the primitive community of Christian believers.

But as time went on another and a new interpretation was given to the ceremony in the Catholic sacrifice of the Mass. The words of institution and the act of consecration of the elements became central to the act; the thought of the atoning death of Jesus, rather than of His resurrection and impending return, was the dominant note; the mind of the Church looked backwards rather than forwards.

The Betrayal by Judas

This did not consist in a betrayal of the place and the hour at which the authorities could find Jesus to arrest Him; or even if so, it could only be incidental. He did nothing to make His comings and goings secret; if necessary, any spy could have traced Him out of Jerusalem towards Bethany in the evening. Arrest was simple; what the Sanhedrin desired was to *convict* Him. They had tried to entangle Him in His talk, but without success. The people were loud in His praises. They had no incriminating charge to bring against Him. Even at His trial the preliminary evidence was conflicting and proved a failure. "Then Judas appeared before them and put the deadly weapon in their hand." Jesus had claimed to be the Messiah! But such a claim was blasphemy; even His popularity with the people would not be proof against that.

> But the difficulty was that Judas was the sole witness. Therefore the betrayal was useless so far as the actual trial was concerned, unless Jesus admitted the charge. So they first tried to secure His condemnation on other grounds, and only when these attempts broke down did the High Priest put, in the form of a question, the charge in support of which he could have brought no witnesses.[1] The perfidy of the charge lay in the High Priest's insinuation that Jesus held Himself then to be the Messiah, just as He stood there before them.[2]

This accusing question Jesus at first refused to answer. But on its repetition "He repudiated it with a proud word about His Coming as the Son of Man"—*hereafter*, in the Clouds of Heaven. He was thus condemned as if He had admitted that He were already the Messiah.

---

[1] *The Quest*, p. 394.   [2] *The Mystery*, p. 217.

The Eschatological Perspective

To understand the Personality of the historical Jesus, even if only partially (for historical investigation can pretend to no more than this), it is necessary thus to study Him against the background of His own day. This involves the frank recognition that He was subject to the limitations of knowledge incident to His day: a world-view, that is to say, in which ideas of impending catastrophe to the world-process itself were prevalent. That subsequent history has belied that expectation detracts no whit from His superhuman great-ness, or from the abiding power of His life, or from the eternal value of His words. In Him the eternal is clothed in the temporal, but it is necessary to distinguish the eternal from the temporal. Towards the close of *The Mystery* Schweitzer points the contrast by the employment of a fine simile.

The situation may be likened to the course of the sun. Its brightness breaks forth while it is still behind the mountains. The dark clouds take colour from its rays, and the conflict of light and darkness produces a play of fantastic imagery. The sun itself is not yet visible; it is there only in the sense that the light issues from it. As the sun behind the morning glow—so appeared the personality of Jesus of Nazareth to his contemporaries in the pre-Messianic age.

At the moment when the heaven glows with intensest colour-ing the sun itself rises above the horizon. But with this the wealth of colour begins gradually to diminish. The fantastic images pale and vanish because the sun itself dissolves the clouds upon which they are formed. As the rising sun above the horizon so appeared Jesus Christ to the primitive Church in its eschatological expecta-tion.

As the sun at midday—so he appears to us. We know nothing of morning and evening glow; we see only the white brilliance which pervades all. But the fact that the sun now shines for us in such a light does not justify us in conceiving the sunrise also as if it were a brilliant disk of midday brightness emerging above the horizon. Our modern view of Jesus' death is true, true in its inmost nature, because it reflects His ethical-religious personality in the thoughts of our time. But when we import this into the history of Jesus and of primitive Christianity we commit the same blunder as were we to paint the sunrise without the morning glow.[1]

[1] *Ibid.* pp. 248-250.

The Personality of the historical Jesus, which honest scrutiny of the Gospel records reveals, has nothing to do either with the Christ of metaphysical theology on the one hand, or with idealized portraits of Him which modern biographies have attempted on the other. He is not a subject either for theological or psychological analysis. The former derogates from His Personality by making of it an intellectual abstraction, a "Person" with a dual "Nature," a being different in kind from His brethren, impossible to take as their Example, and one whose commandment "Follow Me" remains forever meaningless. The latter by endeavouring to lift Him out of His historical background and set Him in the modern world has made Him an impossible fiction.

Historical criticism of the Gospels has performed one signal service to the cause of truth:

> It loosened the bands by which He had been riveted for centuries to the stony rocks of ecclesiastical doctrine, and rejoiced to see life and movement coming into the figure once more, and the historical Jesus advancing, as it seemed, to meet it. But He does not stay: He passes by our time and returns to His own . . . by the same inevitable necessity by which the liberated pendulum returns to its original position.[1]

For the Jesus of history is inseparable from His own historical environment and world-view, and must be seen against their background to be understood; but that environment and that world-view are not ours. It is in vain that we try to make them coincide: "the Jesus of history is for our time a stranger and an enigma." Our knowledge of Him, even were it a hundred times more detailed and accurate than it is, could never tell us all we want to know, for "historical knowledge can never call spiritual life into existence." Therefore it can never present us with a portrait of the historical Jesus; the best that it can do is delineate a sketch. Not thus is He truly known; for "in the very moment when we were coming nearer to the historical Jesus than men had ever come before, and were already stretching out our hands to draw Him into our own time" —it was only to find Him receding from our grasp, withdrawing again to His own, only to find ourselves confessing our failure and the tremendous truth that lies hid in St. Paul's great paradox, "Even if we had known Him incarnate, yet henceforth we know Him so no more."

[1] *The Quest*, p. 397.

For the truth is, it is not Jesus as historically known, but Jesus as spiritually arisen within men, who is significant for our time and can help it. Not the historical Jesus, but the spirit which goes forth from Him and in the spirits of men strives for new influence and rule, is that which overcomes the world. . . . The abiding and eternal in Jesus is absolutely independent of historical knowledge, and can only be understood by contact with His spirit. In proportion as we have the Spirit of Jesus we have the true knowledge of Jesus.[1]

The eschatological perspective is the temporally conditioned world-view in which the Life was manifested and the Truth that is eternal was incarnate among men. If historically it has proved illusory, nevertheless to the spiritually-awakened it speaks as no other world-view can. For the commandment of Jesus to follow Him is perennial.

In reality that which is eternal in the words of Jesus is due to the very fact that they are based on an eschatological world-view, and contain the expression of a mind for which the contemporary world with its historical and social circumstances no longer had any existence. They are appropriate, therefore, to any world, for in every world they raise up the man who dares to meet their challenge, and does not turn and twist them into meaninglessness, above his world and his time, making him inwardly free, so that he is fitted to be, in his own world and in his own time, a simple channel for the power of Jesus.[2]

The titles which men have ascribed to Him, or even those by which He designated himself, are no longer applicable for our time. Messiah or Son of Man—Logos or Son of God—these are not the expressions of what He was or is; they are but the temporally conditioned phrasing of the thought-forms which were appropriate to the age which shaped them. Metaphorical or metaphysical—late Jewish or late Greek—they are figures of speech peculiar to their own remote religious climate; but on our lips they are only archaisms, for we no longer think in those terms. The men of that age were right to use them since they expressed the loftiest conceptions of the Personality of Jesus that could be found, and He is in truth forever greater than our greatest thoughts of Him. The measure of His stature exceeds the reach of our finite understanding; and a frank

---

[1] *Ibid.* p. 399.   [2] *Ibid.* p. 400.

confession of our inability to comprehend it is more reverent and less presumptuous than dogmatic definitions of His "Person" or His "Nature."

It is to be noted that Schweitzer does not use the term "supernatural" to describe the Personality of Jesus. It is a term which the natural man uses to disguise his ignorance of "the things of the Spirit" which can only be discerned spiritually. Schweitzer refrains from it for the sufficient reason, as would appear, that its employment by rationalistic theology must lead in the last resort to a position which is philosophically untenable. The term which he uses instead is the term "superhuman," but this he uses to connote, not a difference in kind between the nature of Our Lord and the least of His brethren, but a difference of degree which is immeasurably great. The oft-quoted words with which he seeks to describe Our Lord's acceptance of the eschatological world-view and His destruction of it in His supreme act of acceptance—and therewith the vindication of His right to be called "the spiritual ruler of mankind" —are these:

> . . . There is silence all around. The Baptist appears, and cries: "Repent, for the Kingdom of Heaven is at hand!" Soon after that comes Jesus, and in the knowledge that He is the coming Son of Man lays hold of the wheel of the world to set it moving on that last revolution which is to bring all ordinary history to a close. It refuses to turn, and He throws Himself upon it. Then it does turn; and crushes Him. Instead of bringing in the eschatological conditions, He has destroyed them. The wheel rolls onward, and the mangled body of the one immeasurably great Man, who was strong enough to think of Himself as the spiritual ruler of mankind and to bend history to His purpose, is hanging upon it still. That is His victory and His reign.[1]

"We can find no designation which expresses what He is for us." Only as we keep His commandments, only as we seek to do His will, only as we enter in our infinitesimal degree into the fellowship of His sufferings—only thus shall we ever come to learn in our own experience, as an unutterable secret, Who He is.

> He comes to us as One unknown, without a name, as of old, by the lake-side, He came to those men who knew Him not. He

[1] *The Quest*, pp. 368-369.

speaks to us the same word: "Follow thou me!" and sets us to the tasks which He has to fulfil for our time. He commands. And to those who obey Him, whether they be wise or simple, He will reveal Himself in the toils, the conflicts, the sufferings which they shall pass through in His fellowship, and, as an ineffable mystery, they shall learn in their own experience Who He is.[1]

Its Implications for Personal Belief

It is perhaps a truism to remark, how many go to the Gospels to seek in them only what they want to find; how many strive to force the truth into their own preconceived ideas of what the truth should be. Somehow the world-renunciation which Our Lord enjoined as the necessary qualification for admission to His Kingdom, the sole means of entry into the Life which is eternal,—somehow this must be made to fit with our too premature, too facile optimistic acceptance of the world and affirmation of our own self-will. We forget that "the essence of His teaching is world-affirmation which has gone through the experience of world-negation." This is the sin that lies chiefly at the door of what passes for Christian "liberalism."

> Many of His greatest sayings are found lying in a corner like explosive shells from which the charges have been removed. No small portion of elemental religious power needs to be drawn off from His sayings to prevent them from conflicting with our system of religious world-acceptance. We have made Jesus hold another language for our time than that which He really held.[2]

Another preconception we are fain to cling to is that the mighty spiritual truth contained in His utterances should correspond in all respects with literal truth. Only the bold explorer, the dauntless delver into the deep mountains of the true, is prepared to accept all that he finds there, including what he does not want to find. The majority, when they find that the spiritual does not correspond with the literal in the Gospel records, are dismayed and are tempted to abandon the quest. Not so Schweitzer and his predecessors who quarried in that mine. "They wrought at their task not seeing" and not seeking "whereunto it might grow." To find that Jesus in His human consciousness was mistaken as to the issue of world events, this was a grievous shock to faith. It would have been more in

---

[1] *Ibid.* p. 401. [2] *Ibid.* p. 398.

harmony with their natural desires if the teaching of Jesus were altogether independent of His time and circumstance: "so that it could be taken over simply and easily by each succeeding generation of men." But such is not the case, and there is doubtless, as Schweitzer observes, a reason for it. While at work upon the Synoptic Problem, he was troubled, as he tells us in his book *My Life and Thought*, "by the painful consciousness that this new knowledge in the realm of history would mean unrest and difficulty for Christian piety." But he drew comfort from the saying of St. Paul: "We can do nothing against the truth, but for the truth."

Since the essential nature of the spiritual is truth, every new truth means ultimately something won. Truth is under all circumstances more valuable than non-truth, and this must apply to truth in the realm of history as to other kinds of truth. Even if it comes in a guise which piety finds strange and at first makes difficulties, the final result can never mean injury; it can only mean greater depth. Religion has therefore no reason to avoid coming to terms with historical truth.[1]

How much greater depth his acceptance of this at first sight unwelcome truth has imparted to his own thought as a philosopher and to his life as a man of action is apparent in his life's work. But, purely as a scientist and scholar with a passion for intellectual integrity he recoils with loathing from the ingenious and covert artifices of so-called Christian "apologetics," which are forever trying to make facts subserve their theories, and which so far from "allowing truth its right, have treated it, whenever it caused embarrassment, in various ways, conscious or unconscious, but always by either evading, or twisting, or suppressing it."

Because, while I was busied with the history of earlier Christianity, I had so often to deal with its sins against the truth of history, I have become a keen worker for honesty in our Christianity of today. . . .

I find it no light task to follow my vocation,—to put pressure on the Christian faith to reconcile itself in all sincerity with historical truth. But I have devoted myself to it with joy, because I am certain that truthfulness in all things belongs to the spirit of Jesus.[2]

[1] *My Life and Thought*, pp. 65-75.   [2] *Ibid.* pp. 65-75.

CHAPTER XIV

RECEPTION OF *THE QUEST* IN ENGLAND

The Mystery of the Kingdom of God was published in 1901. In Germany, where the eschatological debate had been of long standing, it created little stir; it was there greeted "with passive hostility"[1] by liberals and conservatives alike: "in fact," as Lowrie who translated it remarked, "it contained more than could be readily digested by either.—It was met by something like a conspiracy of silence." But the publication of *From Reimarus to Wrede* in 1906 was a literary and theological event of such outstanding importance that it could not be ignored. Among the German liberal theologians whose inter-pretation of the Gospels Schweitzer had subjected to drastic criticism, it drew from Wernle (whose sincerity he had also praised) a sigh of reluctant admiration. In a review contributed to the *Theologische Literaturzeitung* (1906, No. 18) he wrote: "The title ought to read *From Reimarus to Schweitzer*, for Wrede is also one of the many corpses on the vast Life-of-Jesus battlefield on which Schweitzer is the sole survivor." And from Jülicher, the most chagrined of his victims—whose famous work on the Parables was stigmatized by Schweitzer as too subjective an interpretation of Christ's teaching, despite the author's sincerity—came the embittered pamphlet *New Lines on the Criticism of the Gospel Tradition* (1906), qualified by the admission, however, that Schweitzer was "the best-read and most undaunted critic" of them all. But except for the serious considera-tion accorded to it by his old tutor, H. J. Holtzmann (to whom, despite their differing methods of approach, Schweitzer had dedi-cated *The Mystery*), in his brief but magisterial work entitled *The Messianic Consciousness of Jesus*,—the reception given to this young student's masterpiece was in Germany distinctly chilly. It shattered

---

[1] According to one of our own scholarly critics. But Schweitzer will not him-self allow the censure. "It is only," he says in a letter to the writer, "that theologians, both of the left and of the right, reviewed the difficulties of adopting the eschato-logical view-point. I have always fully understood this, and I have never allowed myself to become involved in controversy. I have never debated the question with my critics. I have simply exposed the problem."

too many cherished illusions of the older school of liberals.

But in England, where New Testament criticism had proceeded along more conservative lines, it at once produced a great sensation. It was warmly championed by the two foremost divinity scholars of the day—Sanday of Oxford, who made it the basis of his lectures published in 1907 with the title *The Life of Christ in Recent Research*; and Burkitt of Cambridge, who wrote the preface to his old pupil Montgomery's translation of the work in 1910. Although Sanday expressed himself even then as not prepared to endorse all Schweitzer's conclusions without qualification, what attracted him to Schweitzer's point of view was the "sturdy individuality" and "unflinching realism" of the author, whose "conspicuous merit is that from first to last he holds a single clue firmly in his hand." Himself a theologian, and concerned to safeguard the tenets of sound doctrine even under the microscope of scientific scrutiny, he singled out three points in Schweitzer's argument for special commendation:

The author is a thorough critic. And yet, in spite of this,
(1) He keeps much closer to the texts than most critics do; he expressly tells us that his investigations have helped to bring out the historical trustworthiness of the Gospels;
(2) He does not, like so many critics, seek to reduce the Person of Christ to the common measures of humanity, but leaves it at the transcendental height at which he finds it;
(3) By doing this, he is enabled to link on, in an easy and natural way, the eschatology and Christology of the Gospels to the eschatology and Christology of St. Paul and St. John.[1]

Sanday saw in Schweitzer's work a welcome antidote to the imaginative Lives of Jesus which the liberal Protestantism of the nineteenth century had produced, and a hoped-for bulwark to his own type of Catholicism. But its severely non-theological character made him timid, and he eventually withdrew his support.[2] By Schweitzer he is remembered with nothing but gratitude, however.

[1] The addition "and St. John" is a misunderstanding of Schweitzer's position. See *The Mysticism of Paul the Apostle*, ch. xiii.

[2] In an article contributed to the *Hibbert Journal* for October 1911, entitled "The Apocalyptic Element in the Gospels," he publicly retracted the views he had formerly expressed. He was influenced thereto partly by von Dobschütz' lectures against eschatology at Oxford in 1908, and partly by Streeter's *Studies in the Synoptic Problem* in 1911. The former were made a subject for debate at the Church Congress in that year when it was noted by *The Times*—"The shadow of Schweitzer has fallen across the Congress."

Burkitt proved a stauncher ally.[1] His preface to *The Quest* evinces not only the affinity of mind that one great scholar feels for another in pursuit of pure objective truth, but also a depth of genuine spiritual insight which is akin to Schweitzer's own.

> . . . We are not accustomed to be so ruthless in England. We sometimes tend to forget that the Gospel has moved the world, and we think our faith and devotion to it so tender and delicate a thing that it will break, if it be not handled with the utmost circumspection. So we become dominated by phrases and afraid of them. Dr. Schweitzer is not afraid of phrases, if only they have been beaten out by real contact with facts.
>
> . . . It may well be that absolute truth cannot be embodied in human thought and that its expression must always be clothed in symbols. It may be that we have yet to translate the hopes and fears of our spiritual ancestors into the language of our new world. We have to learn, as the Church in the second century had to learn, that the End is not yet, that the new Jerusalem like all other objects of sense is an image of truth rather than the truth itself.

And in 1931 we find Burkitt writing in similar terms in his preface to *The Mysticism of Paul the Apostle*.

Very different was the reception of *The Quest* by the rationalistic critic J. M. Robertson,[2] at that time the leading supporter of the "Christ-Myth" theory (the theory, that is, that Jesus as a historical person never existed) which was advocated by Drews, the English Professor of Philosophy at Karlsruhe. The point of his attack is that Schweitzer "remains at the ultimately uncritical point of view which accepts, for instance, the triumphal entry into Jerusalem as a historical fact. The oft-put challenge as to how the Roman authorities could have permitted such an episode he does not even notice. For him the question is solely as to whether or not Jesus planned the Messianic entry, and he confidently decides in the affirmative." Robertson goes on to ask how the entry can have been Messianic and planned by Jesus as such if it was not also Messianic for the people, ignoring Schweitzer's explanation of the people's acclaim as due to their acceptance of Him as the Forerunner of the Messiah; and he adds:

[1] The range of Burkitt's learning was almost comparable to Schweitzer's in its versatility. He was distinguished in the spheres of Semitic and Oriental languages, palaeography, textual and higher biblical criticism, ecclesiastical history, liturgiology, mathematics, and music. The last was a strong tie between them.

[2] Author of *Christianity and Mythology* (1900) and *Pagan Christs* (1903).

"It is unnecessary to discuss in detail a theorem which thus finally stands the pyramid upon its apex more determinedly than any of those with which it competes"; but he has the grace to praise the "manly and unsectarian spirit" of the author and his "notable generosity in praise of his antagonists."

On the Catholic side *The Quest* was received, as might be expected, with candid disfavour.[1] It was reviewed very briefly in *The Tablet* together with Sanday's *Christologies Ancient and Modern.*

> These two books before us are samples of many modern efforts on the Life of Christ. His seamless robe is examined thread by thread. It is pulled this way and that, till we are almost under the impression that it is a patchwork of tatters. Schweitzer's work gives the history of the rending. Then, on the other side, an attempt is made to unravel the manufactured tangle. But was not His robe woven from the top throughout? . . .

In reading the reviews that appeared in the many other religious periodicals of the time, one is struck both by their fair-mindedness and by the liveliness of apprehension which on the whole they display. One reviewer, it would appear, bethought him of the phrase "vigour and rigour" as the most apt to describe the author's handling of the theme, and many another repeated it. Even dissentients were generous in their praise of "the exhaustiveness of its research"; "the brilliance of its style"; "the confidence of its author"; "his boldness, sincerity, and originality"; "his vast erudition"; while sympathizers wrote of the work as "a magnificent and sustained scholarly enterprise"; "a notable performance which fills a place of its own"; "an exceptionally fine piece of first-class scholarship"; "the most considerable critical history of the subject that has so far appeared."

Its detractors find the work "ingenious but unconvincing"; these are the worst epithets they have to find, however, and even these are tempered with admiration for its style and learning.—One of the kindest reviews comes, strange to say, from Ireland (strange in view of the conservatism of that Church):

> We have read no book for a long time that fills us with such profound admiration. . . . No one who reads it will fail to be

---

[1] Except by George Tyrrell, whose book *Christianity at the Cross-Roads* owed its whole *motif* to *The Quest.*

impressed by the gentleness and consideration of the pastor, the method and self-restraint and truthfulness of the man of science, and the learning of the professed student of theology and philosophy.

One of the best informed as well as the most comprehensive of the reviews was that which appeared in *The Times Literary Supplement* for May 19, 1910. It is much too full to quote, but attention must be drawn to it. The main point of its criticism is that Schweitzer, in pursuing the eschatological hypothesis to its logical conclusion, has been no less eclectic than were his predecessors. It is written from the evident standpoint of theological orthodoxy, but also in a spirit which sets a high value on objective truth. It ends by quoting Schweitzer's words: "Jesus means something to our world because a mighty spiritual force streams forth from Him and flows through our time also," and adds the pertinent enquiry: "Whence came this force?" In so far as that question can be answered at all, it was answered several years later by Schweitzer in his *Mysticism of Paul the Apostle*.

The main point of the criticism made by those who recoiled from Schweitzer's radical conclusion at the time when his book appeared, and also of those who have since dissented from it, is that it is *too* thoroughgoing,—too "one-sided," an "over-emphasis." As a text to their strictures they generally expand upon Burkitt's warning in his preface to the book: "It does not pretend to be an impartial survey"; or else they convict Schweitzer out of his own mouth, quoting his dictum that "Progress always consists in taking one or other of two alternatives, in abandoning the attempt to combine them." The alternatives which he posits, and which he maintains cannot be conjoined, are—*either* the purely historical *or* the purely supernatural; *either* the Synoptic *or* the Johannine; *either* the eschatological *or* the non-eschatological; and he chooses the former in each case. But what these critics seem to fail to realize—and what in the interests of truth and fairness it is essential to bear constantly in mind—is that Schweitzer is dealing here with an antithesis between historical fact and an idealized interpretation of fact. The synoptic Gospels may be said to present a series of objective snapshots taken at close quarters—some of them admittedly out of focus, others out of order, others inadvisedly corrected—which nevertheless by careful scrutiny and patient manipulation can be pieced together to form at least the outline of an authentic photograph of their Subject. The fourth

Gospel may be likened to the inspired reproduction by a master artist of his own mental image or spiritual conception of the same Subject, depicted from a distance,—through which indeed shines the light of the "supernatural," which awes us by its splendour, which we gaze upon and marvel, in which we may even discern some fragments of historical fact, but which nevertheless—because it omits the most salient characteristic preserved by the camera—cannot be considered a genuine portrait.

Historical fact is one thing; theological interpretation is another. To attempt to make the facts fit the interpretation is inadmissible. Such a delineation as the fourth Gospel gives us is, however, legitimate—more, it is an inspiration—but only within the limits of its own particular interpretation. Judged by the historical facts presented by the other three, that interpretation is incomplete.

Could any scientist in any other field of enquiry proceed upon the assumption that facts are susceptible of supernatural explanation? Why then should the critical historian be expected to do so? He cannot do so without falsifying or distorting fact. If he is convinced of the historicity of the first three Gospels with their eschatological setting he cannot commit himself to accepting *as history* the supernatural non-eschatological record of the fourth. An illustration may help to elucidate this difference. The phenomenon of the Aurora can be scientifically explained as due to bombardments of minute electrical discharges from solar rays which, gathered into the magnetic field of the earth, impinge upon the upper levels of the earth's atmosphere and weave themselves into swaying curtains of indescribable beauty. But, were a scientist to explain this marvellous luminosity as due also to celestial intervention, he would be putting an idealized construction upon the scientific facts which the facts cannot sustain. This latter account of the phenomenon may be regarded as a symbolic representation of the facts, or even as an interpretation; but it can never be confused with the facts as scientifically explained.

Those objectors who were convinced against their will may be represented as upholders of the "Yes, but—" theology. They would say in effect: "Yes, no doubt all this is true and he has proved his case, but only as far as it goes; there must be more in it than that." Here again it must be emphasized that Schweitzer is concerned to state only what he conceives to be the plain objective facts, that is the *setting*, not the *substance*, of the Gospel. That substance is the "something more." Nevertheless it must be conceded that the substance which he finds hidden like a pearl of great price within the historic setting is not that which these objectors are seeking. For whereas what they desiderate is another aspect of the historical Jesus which would serve as the basis for a theology, Schweitzer would say that no other historical aspect is possible, but that the substance is there—a substance, however, which history does not create but can only corroborate—and that it is "that absolute ethic of love" which, passing beyond the theologians of every age, is rooted, not in dogma, but in mysticism.

In this connection some observations of Dr. Lowrie[1] in his Introduction to *The Mystery* are very just:

> Jesus' moral teaching was oriented towards the coming Kingdom. . . . But it was not of merely transitory importance. From the expectation of the approaching Kingdom it received a sharpness of emphasis which it could not otherwise have had,—and it was a *true* emphasis. It described the conduct appropriate to a man in this present world *so long as this world shall last.* . . . "Thoroughgoing eschatology" is surely not incompatible with the recognition of a deeper intuition in Jesus which is necessary to explain the intensity of this very eschatology itself. . . . Jesus' eschatology was an expression of His God-consciousness—the most eminent expression of it.

New Testament criticism has moved far and fast and in diverse directions since Schweitzer wrote his *Quest*.

In face of this diversity on the part of scholars who are not only experts in New Testament criticism, but also men of the highest intellectual integrity, we are driven to conclude that the Jesus of history is One whom, in the fullness of His stature, we can never know. If even those who were nearest Him, the disciples who heard the tones of His voice and marked His gestures as He spoke, could not understand His words, much less can we who read them fragmentarily and disconnectedly in the printed page. We feel ourselves driven to accept the verdict with which Lightfoot concludes his *History and Interpretation of the Gospels*: "For all the inestimable value of the gospels, they yield us little more than a whisper of His voice; we trace in them but the outskirts of His ways."

Within recent years there has been a revival in favour of a modified eschatology. There has been the school of thought which, accepting

[1] Dr. Lowrie is now better known as the translator of the works of Kierkegaard.

it as the only possible historical interpretation, invests it with a theological significance and gives it the name of "realized eschatology." According to this view, we are even now living in the Messianic Age, and the visible Church of Christendom is itself the living witness to the fact that the Kingdom of God has come. Apart from the anomaly that the Church continues to pray for the coming of the Kingdom as if still future, it is hard indeed to see—bearing in mind its history, composition, and whole ethos—how such a claim can be seriously maintained.

It is undeniable that there are inconsistencies in some of the details of Schweitzer's argument, and that he is guilty here and there of committing the same offences as those for which he blames his predecessors. It is true that his portrait of Jesus is austere, and to that extent an "over-simplification." But it must be remembered that his portrait is not only a critical study, as true to fact as he can make it; it is also in the nature of a polemic both against dogmatic and against liberal theology. The former, despite the "supernatural nimbus" with which it had surrounded Jesus, had for centuries "bound Him hand and foot with grave-clothes—the grave-clothes of the Dual Nature." The latter, having released Him from that remote and rocky tomb, had humanized Him beyond recognition "by translating Him into the terms of our modern psychology which are utterly inapplicable to Him": and so "one got a hybrid figure, half modern, half antique." But—"Jesus is a superhuman personality moulded in one piece."

Furthermore, it must be remembered that Schweitzer is a genius in more ways than one. He is not only in the first rank as a scholar; he is in the first rank also as a scientist and an artist. It is as a scientist that he seeks to adhere as closely as may be to cold objective fact; it is as an artist that he will leave no loose threads about his work. And The Quest, like all his other work, is architectonic. It is true that he has left much that is still unexplained about the words and deeds of Jesus; but he has explained on his own hypothesis far more than has been explained before or since, on it or on any other. Within the limits that he set himself—the only possible limits—the historical limits, that is, of the first two Gospels (for the third is virtually excluded as being little more than a supplement, though a most important and valuable supplement, to the other two)—his delineation is the clearest, most faithful and consistent, of any that have been produced.

It is the delineation of a figure, stark, august, tremendous—like the figure of Epstein's "Christ." And so he would have it left. He would not invest it with any theological nimbus to veil its heroic grandeur, he would not adorn it with any picturesque fancies to blur its sharp-edged outline. And having etched it thus he turns away, away from the historical Jesus who can never be other than the Jesus of His own age, to find Him as He is in ours,—not in the study or the cloister, but in the field of self-renouncing action in lowly service to the least of His brethren.

CHAPTER XV

THE MYSTICISM OF PAUL THE APOSTLE

"IMMEDIATELY after completing *The Quest of the Historical Jesus* I had gone on to study the teaching of St. Paul." This statement must be taken to explain the insertion at this point of an all too brief account of Schweitzer's studies on St. Paul, though they were not brought to a conclusion till several years later.

Theological as well as historical considerations attracted him to the task. Hitherto doctrinal interpretation of Paulinism had represented it as "something complicated and loaded with contradictions," —an account of it which had always seemed to Schweitzer as "irreconcilable with the originality and greatness of thought revealed in it." (For him, profundity of thought is very largely to be measured by its simplicity or "elemental" quality.) Another was the fact that "research into the history of the scientific exposition of the Pauline teaching was a task that had never yet been undertaken." He determined to apply to his own elucidation of the Pauline Problem the same hypothesis that he had applied to the Synoptic Problem, in order to discover whether here also eschatology might prove to be the solution. "When I began examining it with this possibility in view, I arrived with astonishing rapidity at the conclusion that that was the case."

His first book *Paul and his Interpreters* (1912, translated by Montgomery) deals chiefly with the history of Pauline criticism, and is valuable more for its negative than for its constructive argument. It is concerned to clear the ground for the development of his own positive exposition of the apostle's thought which is contained in his second book *The Mysticism of Paul the Apostle* (1931, same translator). These two books taken together were intended to form the second volume, with *The Quest* as the first, of a comprehensive History of the Early Church, of which the third would trace the development of the history Hellenization of Christian thought through the Johannine literature and the sub-apostolic age to the Fathers of the Church. There can be no question but that it, like the other two, would have proved a classic of its kind; but lack of time, not lack of will or capacity, was the obstacle; and this projected treatise, like his three-volume edition of Bach's Chorale Preludes, is among the uncompleted tasks that still lie locked in his mind.

Anyone who, without preconceptions, goes straight from the Gospels to the Epistles of St. Paul (even if he takes the Acts of the Apostles on the way) must feel himself at once in a totally different world of thought. The sober yet majestic utterances of Jesus, clothed as they are in simple concrete idiom, are replaced by the perfervid language of religious enthusiasm at white heat. But it is not only a difference of idiom; it is also a difference of ideas—or so it seems at first sight. The ideology of Jesus is purely Jewish; that of the apostle seems Graeco-Jewish. Schweitzer, however, will not admit this. In his view it is only the terminology of the epistles which is Hellenistic; there is not a trace of Hellenism in St. Paul's essential thought. The latter, like that of Jesus, is wholly Hebraic and eschatological—but with an important distinction. For whereas the eschatology of Jesus is informed by His own Messianic consciousness and the expectation of its imminent realization in the coming Kingdom, that of Paul is informed by the significance of an event which has supervened, namely the death and resurrection of Jesus, and his expectation of the Appearing ($\pi\alpha\rho o\nu\sigma i\alpha$) of the Lord in the immediate future. In other words, the Messianic period has, for Paul, already begun. It has been inaugurated by the death and resurrection of Jesus.

This then is "the great and undischarged task which confronts those engaged in the historical study of primitive Christianity": how did Pauline doctrine develop out of the teaching of Jesus? and further, how did the theology of the Christian Fathers of the Church, which is Greek, develop out of the doctrine of Paul?

Such questions are startling when frankly posed, and admit of no facile answer. It has been said that only one Christian thinker, the heretic Marcion, ever really understood Paul, and that even he misunderstood him. Does Schweitzer understand him?

The Question of Authorship

The field of learning which Schweitzer surveys in his work on St. Paul is vaster even than was the case in *The Quest*. In *Paul and his Interpreters* the substance of the work of more than a hundred critics, beginning with Grotius in 1641, is passed in review before the reader. and as in *The Quest* so here—the more drastic the criticism the more welcome to Schweitzer, if only it be scientifically and consistently maintained. "For hate as well as love can write a life of Jesus," so he had written in *The Quest* with reference to works of Reimarus and Strauss, "and their hate sharpened their historical insight." So here, when he comes to deal with the work of Baur, the most radical of Pauline critics, with whom (as with them) he disagrees profoundly, he can write: "Nevertheless, his book breathes the spirit of Paul, the prophet of freedom, more fully than almost any other book which has been devoted to him."

It has always been a vexed question how many of the epistles that bear the name of the great apostle can with certainty be ascribed to him. Baur rejected all but four: Galatians, first and second Corinthians, and Romans. Schweitzer accepts the genuineness of all except second Thessalonians, both epistles to Timothy, and Titus. In his second work on St. Paul he devotes a chapter to this problem, and also to the dates and occasions upon which these epistles were written. He finds, as do others, the genuineness of Ephesians and Colossians less easy to establish than the rest of the epistles, but feels that "the assumption of their spuriousness offers almost as many difficulties." As in the case of the Synoptic Problem his application of the test of eschatology had established the historicity of passages in the Gospels formerly regarded as dubious, so in the case of the Pauline Problem his application of the same test establishes the genuineness of those epistles which most other scholars accept on other grounds.

According to Schweitzer, it was the attribution to Paul of a Hellenizing influence that led Baur to imagine a Pauline versus a Petrine faction in the primitive Christian community from the very first; and led his successors, assuming a spurious authorship for the four main epistles, to post-date them to as late as the second century, in order to provide the necessary lapse of time to account for the resolution of this controversy, when both factions made common ground in defence against Christian gnosticism. But Schweitzer cuts the ground from under the feet of the upholders of the Tübingen theory by denying any Hellenistic influence at all.[1]

Christianity and the Mystery Cults

He is particularly severe with the theory that St. Paul's teaching on the Sacraments was affected by the Greek Mystery-cults[2] (con-

---

[1] *Paul and his Interpreters*, p. 85.
[2] Represented chiefly by Reitzenstein, Bousset, and Deissmann.

cerning which our actual knowledge is much more limited than comparative students of religion assume). Mystery-cults did indeed affect the Johannine teaching and it was the Johannine teaching, and not the Pauline, which determined the Sacramental doctrine of the early Church. The Johannine emphasis, like the Mystery-cults in the initiation ceremonies, was upon Re-birth; that of Paul upon Resurrection. These two conceptions are different. The former is uneschatological and "reckons upon the duration of a normal life-span"; the latter is eschatological: "it is a precursory phenomenon of the approaching end of the world."

Again, in seeking analogies for the celebration of the Lord's Supper in the Mystery-cults, comparative students of religion have drawn an illegitimate inference within their own domain. They have assumed without proof that these cults contained the idea of eating the flesh of the Redeemer-god in order to draw supernatural strength from it. This idea is certainly found in some primitive Nature-religions, but there is no evidence whatever that it came to life again in the higher Mystery-cults. And in any case, the parallel which St. Paul draws in 1 Cor. x is between the Christian Sacrament and the pagan sacrificial feasts, not between it and any Mystery-cult. Furthermore, there is no trace in his Sacramental doctrine, any more than there is in the higher Mystery-cults, of eating and drinking the body and blood of the Lord. To assume otherwise is to interpret St. Paul by a misunderstanding of St. John.[1]

It is certain, however, that neither he nor the primitive Christian community held that the body and blood of Christ was partaken of in the Supper. That is evident from the fact that the historic words of Jesus did not form part of the service, and this is the case down to a later date. No kind of consecration of the elements as the body and blood of the Lord occurred in the liturgy. . . .

The Church's celebration was not shaped by the "words of institution" at the historic Supper; it was the latter, on the contrary, which were explained in accordance with the significance of the celebration.[2]

But Sacramental doctrine is in any case not fundamental to the

---

[1] Those who think of Schweitzer as a biblical scholar primarily in connection with his work on the Synoptic Problem and on St. Paul would do well to mark the real contribution that he has also to make to Johannine literature and to the Logos doctrine, in *The Quest* and in both his works on St. Paul.

[2] *Paul and his Interpreters*, pp. 199-200.

apostle's doctrine of redemption. "He preaches sacraments but does not feel himself to be a mystagogue." For him the sacramental idea is derived from "the notion of marking out or sealing" which is congenial to apocalyptic thought, rather than to the metaphysical notion of *ex opere operato*.[1] He would appear to have found the Sacraments already established in the primitive Christian community and to have adapted the form of his own teaching to them. "If Baptism and the Lord's Supper are taken away his doctrine of redemption is not destroyed, but stands unmoved. It looks as though the weight of the building rested upon these two pillars, but in reality it does not totter if these supports are withdrawn." For the sacramental system is, in the last resort, "a question of externalization, not of intensification."

Another point that tells strongly against Hellenistic influence is the apostle's doctrine of "corporiety" (*naturhaft*). Greek philosophical mysticism teaches the ultimate separation of the purely spiritual from the corporeal nature of man, that is, the complete severance of the intelligible (or intellectual) from the sensible (or sensuous). But St. Paul's conception of *metamorphosis* is that "the whole spirit, soul, and body, be preserved unblemished till the day of His Appearing."

Space forbids further references to the text of *Paul and his Interpreters*, every page of which is packed with evidence of that massive learning and close thinking that makes Schweitzer's advocacy of any line of argument so weighty and impressive. Step by step the argument advances, consolidating its ground with every step, till the position reached seems impregnable. [Nevertheless—since it is no part of a biographer's duty to pretend agreement with his subject in every matter, even in a matter where he is far less qualified than his subject is to venture an opinion—the present writer must confess that, despite the extraordinary cogency of Schweitzer's arguments to the contrary (which are still further elaborated in his second work), he is still unconvinced that there is *no* trace of Greek influence in St. Paul. The arguments against it, as Schweitzer marshals them, are

[1] But in *The Mysticism of Paul the Apostle* Schweitzer would appear to correct this view: ". . . The rite effects what it represents. . . . That Paul should have regarded Baptism and the Lord's Supper as inherently efficacious acts, and redemption as being bound up with them, seems to us as inconsistent with the deep spirituality which is elsewhere the shining characteristic of his religion" (p. 18). This apparent confusion between the symbolic and the efficacious in St. Paul's view of the baptismal *rite* is, however, of quite secondary importance compared with his view of baptism, as such, as the mystical experience of dying and being buried with Christ, and rising again with Him into newness of life.

indeed very difficult to controvert, and yet the impression remains. It is the impression not of any analogy that can be drawn with the Mystery-cults, either on their sacramental or their soteriological side; but that of a distinctively Platonic influence which makes its presence felt—an intrusion as it were into the Jewish and Rabbinic stratum of the apostle's thought—and it is most noticeable in three of the epistles whose genuineness is least in dispute,[1] and it is much more than a question of similar terminology. This influence became part of the heritage of the Fathers of Alexandria, but it did not enter into the structure of that other Christian-Greek theology which became the orthodoxy of the Western Church.]

Still less easy is it to do justice to his second and much weightier volume on St. Paul, to which the first was originally intended only as a preface. It was to have followed immediately after the first, but illness and the work of revising the enlarged edition of *The Quest*, his work on Bach, his medical studies, the business of preparation for his first term of missionary work in Africa in 1913, and the war which prevented his return and access to libraries—all caused delay. Then when he returned for his first leave home in 1920 he was immersed in writing his two volumes on the Philosophy of Civilization. Not till the end of 1927 was he able to begin again to give his Pauline manuscripts their final shape, and it was a task to which he devoted two years. *The Mysticism of Paul the Apostle* was finally translated into English by Montgomery in 1930, whose sudden death left Burkitt with the responsibility of seeing it through the press. Altogether, the book is an example of a labour of love undertaken and accomplished with perseverance under difficulties.

The Meaning of Mysticism

In the first chapter we plunge *in medias res*. What is the meaning of mysticism essentially, and what is the character in particular of the mysticism of St. Paul?

We are always in the presence of mysticism when we find a human being looking upon the division between earthly and super-earthly, temporal and eternal, as transcended, and feeling himself, while still externally amid the earthly and temporal, to belong to the super-earthly and eternal.[2]

[1] Cf. Rom. i, 20; 1 Cor. xiii, 12; xv, 49; 2 Cor. iii, 18; iv, 18; **v**, 1.
[2] *The Mysticism of Paul the Apostle*, pp. 1-2.

But mysticism may be either primitive or developed. Primitive mysticism depends on the due performance of efficacious ceremonies in sacrificial feasts, whereby the participant is brought into union with the divinity and shares his supernatural mode of existence. In developed mysticism this union with the divinity is attained by means of initiation, whereby the neophyte is born again into an eternal and immortal state of being. But there is a higher type of mysticism than these.

> When the conception of the universal is reached and a man reflects upon his relation to the totality of being and to Being in itself, the conscious personality attains the power to distinguish between appearance and reality and is able to conceive the material as a mode of manifestation of the Spiritual. It has sight of the Eternal in the Transient. Recognizing the unity of all things in God, in Being as such, it passes beyond the unquiet flux of becoming and disintegration into the peace of timeless being, and is conscious of itself as being in God, and in every moment eternal.[1]

The great Indian, Platonic, Stoic, and Christian mystics are all types of this higher form of mysticism, and they display a unanimity in spiritual experience beyond the doctrinal or philosophical colour of their respective faiths.

The Mysticism of St. Paul

Of what precise kind then is the mysticism of St. Paul?—It is entirely peculiar to himself.

> It occupies a unique position between primitive and intellectual mysticism. The religious conceptions of the Apostle stand high above those of primitive mysticism. This being so, it might have been expected that this mysticism would have to do with the unity of man with God as the ultimate ground of being. But this is not the case. Paul never speaks of being one with God or being in God. He does indeed assert the divine sonship of believers. But, strangely enough, he does not conceive of sonship to God as an immediate mystical relation to God, but as meditated and effected by means of the mystical union with Christ.
>
> The fundamental thought of Pauline mysticism runs thus: I am in Christ; in Him I know myself as a being who is raised above this sensuous, sinful, and transient world and already belongs to

---

[1] *The Mysticism of Paul the Apostle*, pp. 1-2.

the transcendent; in Him I am assured of resurrection; in Him I
am a Child of God.

Another distinctive characteristic of this mysticism is that being
in Christ is conceived as a having died and risen again with Him,
in consequence of which the participant has been freed from sin
and from the Law, possesses the Spirit of Christ, and is assured of
resurrection.

This "being-in-Christ" is the prime enigma of the Pauline teaching: once grasped it gives the clue to the whole.[1]

In order to substantiate his view that the concept of being-in-God
is not Pauline, Schweitzer is obliged to reject the apostle's speech
at Athens, as reported in the "Acts," as a literary device. But he is
able to adduce other reasons, archaeological and patristic, for suspecting it as such. The whole speech, like the Stoic quotation which it
contains, is pantheistic in its tone. True, our own religious sense does
crave this God-mysticism, "this need to conceive of ourselves and
all nature with us as being in God," but the fact remains that the
world-view of St. Paul is "not one of an immanent but of a transcendent God."

Nor is St. Paul's view of salvation universalistic, as the Stoic is.

The possibility that man, as man and universally, stands in close
relation to God, lies outside his horizon. For him there is no
homogeneous humanity, but only various categories of men.

His thought is dominated by the idea of pre-destination. A
mighty cleavage cuts humanity asunder. Not man as such, but
only the man who is elected thereto, can enter into relation with
God. The glorious words of Rom. viii, 28: "We know that for
those who love God He makes all things work together for good,"
are followed by the dreadful limitation, "namely those who are
called according to His purpose."[2]

Nor again is his view of humanity egalitarian: "he assures a
hierarchic gradation"(1 Cor. xi, 3).

This difference in nearness to God is abrogated only by the
being-in-Christ. It is in Christ that the elect portion of mankind
first attains to homogeneity.[3]

---

[1] *Ibid.* p. 3. See Gal. ii, 19-20; iii, 26-28; iv, 6; v, 24-25; vi, 14; 2 Cor. v, 17;
Rom. vi, 10-11; vii, 4; viii, 1-2, 9-11; xii, 4-5; Phil. iii, 1-2. This distinctive Christ-
mysticism is the more remarkable in view of the fact that St. Paul equates the
Spirit of Christ with the Spirit of God (Rom. viii, 9; Gal. iv, 6).

[2] *Ibid.* p. 9.   [3] *Ibid.* p. 10.

Again, as a Jew, "he holds the world and God firmly apart": and in his own eschatological world-view he assumes that "so long as the natural world endures, even down to the Messianic period, angelic powers stand between God and man and render direct relations between the two impossible." It is solely on the ground of their election that the Elect in Christ, "who are called according to God's eternal purpose," enter upon a supernatural life which renders power-less this angelic interposition between themselves and God. "Hence-forth no accusing angels have any right to appear before God against them" (Rom. viii, 38-39).

Again, whereas the Stoic pantheistic world-view is conceived as static, St. Paul's world-view is a cosmic movement—*from, through, and unto God*—but never, until the final consummation, *in* God (Rom. xi, 36).

The consummation which St. Paul expects (1 Cor. xv, 24-28), "When GOD shall be ALL in ALL," is eschatological. That for which Christ prays in John xvii, 20-23, "I in them and THOU in Me," is uneschatological and Johannine theology is in line with it (cf. 1 John iv, 15). But for St. Paul it is only in the End of All Things that there will be a being-in-God. His God-mysticism is not, as St. John's is, contemporaneous and synonymous with Christ-mysticism. For him "it is impossible that they should co-exist, or that one should necessitate the other. They are chronologically successive."

But this Christ-mysticism of St. Paul, thus seen to be distinct from the Christ-mysticism and God-mysticism of St. John (as also from the God-mysticism of the Hermetic literature), possesses "an extra-ordinarily realistic character."

> The being-in-Christ is not conceived as a static partaking in the spiritual being of Christ, but as a real co-experiencing of His dying and rising again.[1]

Outside the Johannine and Petrine theology (cf. John iii, 5, and 1 Peter i, 23) it is only in the "deutero-Pauline" epistles that the conception of Baptism as the Bath of re-birth occurs; the classic text is in Titus iii, 5. But with St. Paul the conception is entirely dominated by the doctrine of dying, being buried, and rising again with Christ. St. Paul's conception in all its realism died with him; it was the doctrine of re-birth which prevailed and was carried on by the

---

[1] *The Mysticism of Paul the Apostle*, p. 13.

Fathers of the Church. "While in the Hellenistic mystery-religions the two mystical conceptions of resurrection and re-birth thus interpenetrate, Paul is a one-sided representative of resurrection-mysticism."[1]

Then, too, whereas in the former the ceremony of initiation is symbolical of the deification of the initiate in *union* with the divine, for St. Paul Baptism unto death is no mere imitative representation, but a real spiritual experience, not however of union, but of *fellowship* with Christ. Also, the Pauline doctrine of predeterminism marks off his mysticism as something utterly foreign to Hellenistic mysticism.

So realistic and withal so simple is St. Paul's view of the Sacraments that he can even regard the Crossing of the Red Sea as a Baptism and the partaking of the Manna and the Water from the Rock as a Communion; thus "raising to the rank of Sacraments experiences undergone by a whole nation which neither the participants, nor anyone else subsequently, had regarded as sacramental" (1 Cor. x, 1-6).

> For us modern men it goes against the grain to have to recognize this realistic sacramentalism in Paul. But reverence for truth must be placed above this distaste. We must let his sayings mean what they say, and not what we should like them to mean. . . .
>
> His Sacraments have their beginning in the death of Jesus—that is, in the immediate present—and continue until His return in glory —that is, into the immediate future. It is only for this span of time that they exist. Before, they were impossible; after, they will be unnecessary. They were created *ad hoc* for a particular class of men of a particular generation, the elect of that generation, "upon whom the ends of the world are come" (1 Cor. x, 11).
>
> As temporary *ad hoc* institutions they have their counterpart in the sacraments of the Israelites on their way from Egypt to Canaan; these also were valid for one generation and with reference to a benefit expected in the near future.[2]

"From his first letter to his last Paul's thought is always uniformly dominated by the expectation of the immediate return of Jesus, of the Judgment, and of the Messianic Glory."—Schweitzer substantiates this point with an imposing array of texts.

Lastly, the fact that the mysticism of St. Paul is unique and indi-

---

[1] *Ibid.* p. 14.　　　　　[2] *Ibid.* p. 22.

vidual to himself is shown by this peculiarity: "he is not wholly and solely a mystic." He allows non-mystical views of redemption an equal right to expression with views that are mystical.

There are in fact three different doctrines of redemption which for Paul go side by side: an eschatological, a juridical, and a mystical.

If the co-existence of such disparate views is in itself difficult enough to conceive, it becomes a complete enigma when we find it in a mystic. For when all is said and done, Pauline personal religion is in its fundamental character mystical. It can no doubt find expression for its thought in the eschatological and juridical doctrines of salvation, but its own essential life lies in the mystical.[1]

The Doctrine of Redemption

With this eschatological expectation is bound up St. Paul's view of Redemption, which is cosmologically conditioned. Jesus Christ by His resurrection from the dead has "made an end of the natural world and is bringing in the Messianic Kingdom. By it a man is transferred from the perishable world to the imperishable, because the whole world is transferred from one state to the other, and he with it. . . . The Redemption is a world-event in which he has a share."

The natural world, according to Jewish eschatological belief which St. Paul shared, is not only transient but is also as it were the battle-ground of opposing "powers of the air"—angels and demons: "in its simplest form the conception of Redemption is that the Messianic Kingdom puts an end to this condition. . . . As Messianic King, Jesus has the host of heavenly angels at His command, in order to over-throw finally all that is opposed to God."

It is necessary at this point to revert to the meaning of the death of Jesus as it was present to His own consciousness.—"To give His life a ransom for many." The "many" are the Elect who would share His Messianic Kingdom; the "ransom" was the atoning sacrifice for their sins, to save them from the great pre-Messianic Tribulation. For Him, the forgiveness of sins was identical with the deliverance.

How much more living and fruitful is this historically true version of Jesus' thought, growing naturally as it does out of the universal attribution of atoning value to suffering, than the host of

The Mysticism of Paul the Apostle, p. 25.

theological or untheological inventions which have been foisted upon Him![1]

But the conception of Redemption which the disciples and early believers held, after His death and resurrection, was of necessity not so simple.

Whereas for Jesus the forgiveness of sins is identical with "deliverance from the Trial," the Early Christians believed in forgiveness of sins because of the death of Jesus, and still expect the pre-Messianic Tribulation, interpreting the suffering and persecution which they undergo as a chastisement which is to precede the appearing of the Messiah.[2]

This is the teaching which St. Paul found and took over—"how that Christ died for our sins according to the scriptures," and which he then developed into his own doctrine of righteousness by faith alone.

The other traditional doctrine that Jesus, in virtue of His death and resurrection, is always the Messiah, now exalted in glory and soon to appear as such, also plays its part in his teaching (Rom. i, 4; Phil. ii, 8-11). And that, having been exalted above all angelic powers, the Elect are (by anticipation) no longer subject to their power, is clear from Rom. viii, 31-39.

The destruction of the dominion of the Angels will be completed by the Return of Jesus. His appearing will not be announced by preliminary signs (1 Thess. v, 1-4). Suddenly He is there. At His coming there will sound from heaven a voice of command; the voice of the Angel will be heard; the trumpet of God rings out. Those believers who have already "fallen asleep" will awaken, and those who are still alive will pass through a transformation into the mode of being which belongs to the resurrection. All together will be caught up into the clouds of heaven to meet the Lord in the air, and will thenceforth abide with Him for ever (1 Thess. iv, 16-17).

Then follows the Messianic judgment held by the Messiah. As in the post-Exilic and Danielic eschatology God Himself was to be the Judge, and only from the Book of Enoch onwards is the Messiah once more, as in the old prophetic eschatology, the Judge. The language of Paul, like that of Jesus Himself, varies from time

---

[1] *Ibid.* p. 62.　　　　[2] *Ibid.* p. 62.

to time; sometimes the judgment is called the judgment of God, sometimes the judgment of the Messiah.

The Kingdom he conceives, strangely enough, not as peaceful blessedness, but as a struggle with the angelic powers. One after another these powers will be overcome by Christ and His people, until at last Death also shall be robbed of his power (1 Cor. xv, 23–28).[1]

The Resurrection of the Dead

"With the overcoming of Death the Messianic Kingdom comes to an end." After the Resurrection of the Elect there ensues the General Resurrection of the Dead and the Last Judgment. St. Paul gives no description of the Times of the End; he takes it for granted as a thing well known. "What he is principally concerned about is to make clear that the Messiah, after subjugation of the angel-powers, will render up His authority to God, that God may be all in all. In that moment world history will have reached its consummation."[2]

The General Resurrection of the Dead is, however, a doctrine peculiar to himself. In a superb figure Schweitzer likens St. Paul's conception of the Resurrection of Christ, of the Elect, of Nature, and finally of all Mankind, to a series of volcanic upheavals.

Paul knows that the immortal world is about to rise by successive volcanic upheavals out of the ocean of the temporal. In the Resurrection of Jesus (the first-fruits of them that have fallen asleep) one island peak has already become visible. But this is only part of a larger island which, still beneath the waves, is actually in process of rising, and is only so far covered as to be just invisible. The larger island is the corporiety of the elect who are united with Christ. In their transformation and anticipatory resurrection the further portion of the immortal world will forthwith appear. Thereafter, in temporally separated upheavals, one portion of land after another will rise about this island. In this Messianic period all Nature will take on immortal being. And then, as the final event of the renewing of the world, at the end of the Messianic Kingdom, will come the general resurrection of the dead. With that the whole continent of the immortal world will have become visible. Then comes the end, when all things are eternal in God, and God is all in all.[3]

[1] The Mysticism of Paul the Apostle, pp. 65–66.
[2] Ibid. p. 68.   [3] Ibid. p. 112.

It is through the Resurrection of Jesus that the Elect are enabled to enter into their joyful resurrection with Him, even before the incidence of physical death. For they have already "died"; they have passed through the grave and gate of death by baptism; for to be "baptized into Christ" is to be baptized into His *death* (Rom. vi, 3-6); they are already incorporate into His mystical body, and though they continue to move about the world as natural men, they are already in process of being transformed into a supernatural mode of existence (2 Cor. iv, 16). They are already—beyond all outward seeming—risen with Christ, though they will not be made manifest as such till the Kingdom comes; and henceforth they live no longer after the flesh but after the spirit. The Resurrection power of Jesus will even quicken their mortal bodies (Rom. viii, 11).—"The original and central idea of the Pauline Mysticism is therefore that the Elect share with one another and with Christ a corporiety which is in a special way susceptible to the action of the powers of death and resurrection, and in consequence capable of acquiring the resurrection state of existence before the general resurrection of the dead takes place."[1]

The Mystical Body of Christ

It is precisely out of this conception of a preordained solidarity of the Elect with one another and with Christ—this corporiety—that St. Paul's conception of the mystical Body of Christ is to be understood. "The body of Christ is no longer thought of by him as an isolated entity, but as the point from which the dying and rising again, which began with Christ, passes over to the Elect who are united with Him; just as the Elect no longer carry on an independent existence, but are now the Body of Christ."[2] Membership in the Body of Christ is not mediated materially; it is predestined spiritually. It is as binding and indissoluble as a marriage bond (1 Cor. vi, 16-17). But it can be annulled by ungodly or unethical behaviour, and by three deadly sins in particular: namely, unchastity (1 Cor. vi, 13-19), circumcision after baptism (Rom. vii, 4-6; Gal. v, 4), and partaking in heathen sacrificial feasts (1 Cor. x, 14-21). So close is this fellowship that there is even a communicability of the mystical experience between believers: the living can by proxy be baptized for the dead (1 Cor. xv, 29); the suffering of one member of the Body is efficacious for the comfort in tribulation of another (2 Cor. i, 5-7); the

---

[1] *Ibid.* pp. 115-116.   [2] *Ibid.* p. 118.

reciprocity of relationship between the sufferings of Christ and of His Elect is so close that the latter can even be said to supplement the former (Col. i, 24).

Suffering is the hall-mark of those who have fellowship with Christ. It is a "daily dying"; so much so that for St. Paul the two terms are synonymous. "That I might know Him, and the power of His resurrection, and (*i.e.* through) the fellowship of His sufferings being made conformable to His death, if by any means I also might attain to the resurrection from the dead" (Phil. iii, 10-11)—"Heirs of God, and co-heirs with Christ, if so be that we suffer with Him, that we may also be glorified together with Him" (Rom. viii, 17). This is the burden of the apostle's heroic aspiration. Suffering as a mode of manifestation of dying with Christ is exemplified pre-eminently in his life.[1] It is the very core of his mysticism; for the secret of his being-in-Christ is his conscious experience of dying-and-rising-together-again-with-Christ.

Since Paul's ethic is, like that of Jesus, eschatological, it is also dominated as was His by the conceptions of judgment and reward. The truth of this doctrine receives its supreme and most august vindi-cation in the example of Christ Himself, whose voluntary renuncia-tion of His divine glory and acceptance of humiliation was rewarded by God's exalting Him to be ruler over all existence, "thus bestowing upon Him a rank which, divine as He was, He did not previously possess" (Phil. ii, 6-11).

Once the eschatological character of the Pauline doctrine of mystical union with Christ is grasped, the alternative which some theologians have posed—the teaching of Jesus *or* the teaching of Paul —becomes irrelevant. The truth is that St. Paul's teaching is the direct development of the teaching of Jesus.[2] As Jesus had taught His disciples that their devotion to Him and to each other would be the guarantee of their recognition as members of the Kingdom at the coming of the Messiah, with whom He knew Himself (though they did not) to be identified—in sharing His Cross, in drinking His cup, in being baptized into His baptism of death; so the Christ-mysticism of St. Paul is grounded on "the eschatological concept of the pre-destined solidarity of the Elect with one another and with the Messiah," but with this difference, that the death and resurrection of Jesus Himself had intervened, giving rise to another dispensation and

---

[1] *The Mysticism of Paul the Apostle*, pp. 147-159.
[2] Cf. *The Quest*, pp. 364-366.

another world-view than that which prevailed during His incarnation; for He was now already the Messiah, the Messianic age had already dawned, the dying and rising to life again with Him was no longer a future possibility, but a present fact.

Significance of the Resurrection of Jesus

The death and resurrection of Jesus is the supreme event which has changed the whole cosmic situation. Consequently there are elements in the teaching of the incarnate Jesus which, appropriate though they were to the pre-Messianic age, are appropriate no longer. This explains St. Paul's silence concerning the teaching of Our Lord, as well as the significance of his tremendous saying: "Though we had known Christ after the flesh, yet now no more." It explains also his attitude to the Law. For whereas Jesus—though He had indeed required of His disciples a righteousness exceeding that of the religious formalists of His day—had nevertheless insisted on the validity of the Law as such, no jot or tittle of which should pass away till all be fulfilled, for St. Paul the fulfilment had come. Jesus Himself had died and risen again, and the Law, which pertained to the natural world lying under the dominion of Angels (cf. Gal. iii, 19), was no longer of force for men in a supernatural state of existence (i.e. under "grace") who were dead-and-risen-again with Him. "Men in whom God Himself works irresistibly do not need a Law in order to fulfil His Will."[1] Only for those who were still as it were denizens of the natural world could the Law thenceforth possess validity.—They were yet in their sins (Rom. vii, 1; viii, 1 ff.; Gal. ii, 19-20; iii, 10; v, 2-5). "Paul thus affirms the co-existence of a validity and a non-validity of the Law corresponding to the difference of world-era within the sphere of the being-in-Christ and outside of it."

This explains, too, the supreme importance that he attached to proclaiming the message to the Gentiles, and, as being alone in apprehending the necessity for this, he is led to regard himself as preeminently their Apostle. His eschatological expectation of redemption is universalistic in the sense that the number of the Elect is not limited to Jews: there are also the "Elect among the Gentiles." That the Gospel must be preached to them is an urgent necessity, "for their election cannot become actual unless they receive the knowledge of Christ, and in consequence enter upon the being-in-Christ." His compelling motive is not to convert the Gentiles into Christian

[1] The Mysticism of Paul the Apostle, p. 192.

Jews in order that they might be assimilated to the believers from Judaism, but to fill up the number of those who were predestined, outside Judaism, to share in the membership of the Messianic Kingdom. "It is from these theological motives that he desires to penetrate even to Spain. . . . Before the return of Christ the Gospel must be preached throughout the whole world!"[1]

Justification by Faith

For St. Paul, observance of the Law is now replaced by faith in the redemptive power of Christ, and this is the original meaning of his doctrine of Righteousness (or Justification) by Faith, as briefly expounded in his epistle to the Galatians. Although the term has a futuristic reference—as "a claim to be pronounced righteous at the coming Judgment and consequently to be a partaker of the Messianic glory"—it is nevertheless an immediate attainment, as the effect of the mystical experience of being risen-with-Christ; it is a resurrection state of existence, just as Possession of the Spirit is a mode of manifestation of the same condition. For St. Paul, Righteousness by Faith is not a condition of passive receptivity, still less is it a proposition for academic debate; it is the mystical experience of being-in-Christ in action and in passion. Righteousness by Faith is thus nothing theoretical, nothing rationalistic; nothing theological; it is a living experience, an earnest of redemption. "Faith, in the abstract, has no effective significance"; it becomes operative and effective only through being-in-Christ. For purposes of linguistic and dialectic convenience, St. Paul abbreviates the complete expression "Righteousness, in consequence of faith, through the being-in-Christ" into Righteousness by Faith; just as he shortens "Fellowship in the corporiety of Christ" into Being-in-Christ.

But in the epistle to the Romans, where he develops his doctrine of Righteousness by Faith at length, he attempts to present it independently of his eschatological doctrine of redemption. Here his doctrine of Righteousness by Faith is made to depend upon a juridical doctrine of redemption: he gives to the death of Jesus the significance of the vicarious sin-offering of Leviticus as "satisfaction" to God, which obliterates sin and makes it possible for God to forgive. "He dispenses with the argument of Galatians which derives the sonship to Abraham of believers in virtue of their being-in-Christ, and which makes them Abraham's seed purely by their act of faith." In Romans,

---

[1] *The Mysticism of Paul the Apostle*, pp. 181 ff.

redemption is conceived of as an act of "intellectual appropriation" rather than as a mystical experience. The concept of Righteousness by Faith now becomes something "individualistic and uncosmic"; it is not linked with the cosmic concept of Corporiety. The argument proceeds on strictly logical lines, but lines which it must be confessed are also somewhat tortuous and ingenious. "That it is an unnatural construction of thought is clear from the fact that by means of it Paul arrives at the idea of a faith which rejects not only the works of the Law, but works in general. He thus closes the pathway to a theory of ethics. This is the price which he pays for finding the doctrine of freedom from the Law in the doctrine of the atoning death of Jesus." As it stands by itself, it is alien to his fundamental thought of redemption as mystical experience, in which ethics—no less than liberation from the bondage of the Law, the destruction of sin in the flesh, and the possession of the Spirit—are made the natural resultant phenomena of the dying-and-rising-again with Christ. And so in fact it does appear even in this epistle. For after the juridical explanation of Righteousness by Faith, advanced at length in an earlier section (Rom. iii, 1 to v, 21), "it is explained again, without any reference whatever to the previous exposition, as founded on the mystical dying-and-rising again with Christ (vi to viii)."

> To the presence of these two independent expositions of the same question is due the confusing impression which the Epistle to the Romans always makes upon the reader. . . . But it was this fragment of a doctrine of redemption which proved to be the most influential of all Paul's teaching. . . . Those who subsequently made this doctrine of Justification by Faith the centre of Christian belief, have had the tragic experience of finding that they were dealing with a conception of redemption from which no ethic could logically be derived.[1]

Mysticism and Ethics

But the apostle has an ethic, which in his epistle to the Romans must be considered as "among the most fundamental and impressive passages that have ever been written about ethics." And this ethic of his, though it has remarkable affinities with the Stoic and the Chinese,[2] is "in reality and in its essence comparable to no other than the ethic of Jesus." And this in spite of their difference of approach. Both have their roots in an eschatological world-view;

---

[1] *Ibid.* pp. 225 and 226.   [2] *Ibid.* pp. 308-309.

but whereas for Jesus (as also for the Baptist) ethics is the fruit of repentance, and the standard of perfection possible of attainment by man in virtue of "his natural constitution,"—for St. Paul ethics is the fruit of the Spirit of the risen Christ, and perfection possible only as the result of the "new creation" which emerges in the-dying-and-rising with Him. (His teaching in Romans ii about conscience as a natural instinct for goodness, which amongst the Gentiles has the force of an inner law, is only an expedient designed to demonstrate the fact of universal sinfulness.) But how then are those who have died-and-risen with Christ any longer capable of sin? In principle they are not, since they have entered upon the supernatural resurrection of existence. But in fact they are so, since this condition is still only in process of being realized: hence the necessity of ethics, even for them. "The believer, by his will, should progressively make into a reality his death to the flesh and to sin, and his being ruled in his thinking and acting by the new life-principle of the Spirit. He will show by his ethical conduct how far the dying and rising with Christ has proceeded in him."

Hence the solidity and withal the entire naturalness of St. Paul's ethical mysticism.

He is not unduly impressed with sensible manifestations of the spiritual, such for instance as "speaking with tongues." "How sure an instinct guided him in this can now be appreciated when it is recognized that ecstatic speech is merely a psycho-physical phenomenon." Schweitzer holds that St. Paul's decisive championship of the rational over the sensible manifestations of the spiritual (1 Cor. xiv) is a fact of tremendous importance and establishes him as a thinker who goes to the heart of things.

Nor is the apostle's mysticism in any sense "quietistic." It is, being ethical, an active practical mysticism.

The great danger for all mysticism is that of becoming supra-ethical, that is to say, of making the spirituality associated with the being-in-eternity an end in itself. . . . Even in Christian Mysticism, whether mediaeval or modern, it is often the semblance of ethics rather than ethics itself which is preserved. There is always the danger that the mystic will experience the eternal as absolute impassivity, and will consequently cease to regard the ethical existence as the highest manifestation of spirituality. . . .[1]

[1] The Mysticism of Paul the Apostle, p. 297.

In the Epistle to the Romans Paul develops his mysticism and his ethics side by side. And in this exposition the unity of active and passive ethics is admirably shown. For the only profound ethic is one which is able, on the basis of one and the same conception, to give an ethical interpretation to all that a man experiences and suffers as well as to all that he does. The great weakness of the utilitarian ethic at all times is that it can relate itself only to man's action and not to that which he undergoes, although for his full development both must be taken into account. It is only in so far as a man is purified and liberated from the world by that which he experiences and endures, that he becomes capable of truly ethical action. In the ethic of the dying and rising again with Christ, active and passive ethics are interwoven as in no other. . . . This constitutes the greatness and originality of Paul's ethics.[1]

The above quotations may well be taken as the text of Schweitzer's own ethical mysticism of "Reverence for Life" as expounded in *Civilization and Ethics*. Therein he shows that the two streams of ethical philosophy, represented as self-fulfilment and self-devotion, must merge in one if ever ethics is to become a reality for life. In the writings of the apostle the description of the attributes of this principle reaches its peak in the famous chapter (1 Cor. xiii) where Love is shown among spiritual gifts to be "the only pre-eternal," the highest manifestation of the being-in-Christ. "It is the only true knowledge, in which God and the believers are mutually known to each other."

If in so many Pauline passages it remains uncertain whether by "the love of God and the love of Christ" is meant the love felt by God and Christ or the love felt for them, this ambiguity is not a mere consequence of linguistic inadequacy; it belongs to Paul's thought. Love for him is not a ray which flashes from one point to another point, but which is constantly vibrating to and fro. Love to God and Christ is always at the same time love proceeding from God and Christ, which works effectually in the Elect who love.[2]

The Personality of St. Paul

"Seen in the light of his ethic, Paul is a figure to provoke admiration. For he is the embodiment of what he taught." Schweitzer's

[1] *Ibid.* p. 302.   [2] *Ibid.* p. 307.

chief aim in his book is to vindicate the consistency of thought in one of the greatest religious geniuses that the world has known, and his success in doing so—in showing how the various and apparently complex strands of thought in the epistles are in reality but parts of the whole texture of one uniform constructive system—is a monument of theological interpretation. But no less remarkable than the intellectual penetration required to discover and elucidate this synthesis—to unravel and re-knit these separated strands in the apostle's thought—is the depth of sympathetic insight with which he enters into his very heart and soul. These (though they cannot be quoted here) are the most eloquent and moving passages in his book.

Side by side with Paul's achievement as a thinker must be set his achievement as a man. Having a personality at once simple and profound, he avoids an abstract and unnatural ideal of perfection, and makes perfection consist in the complete adjustment of spiritual with natural reality. So long as the earthly world with all its circumstances still subsists, what we have to do is so to live in it in the spirit of unworldliness that truth and peace already make their influence felt in it. That is the ideal of Paul's ethic, to live with the eyes fixed upon eternity, while standing firmly on the solid ground of reality. . . .

He proves the truth of his ethic by his way of living it. Alike in suffering and in action he shows himself a human being, who by the Spirit of Christ has been purified and led up to a higher humanity. . . .

As one who truly thought, served, worked, and ruled in the Spirit of Christ he has earned the right to say to the men of all periods: "Be imitators of me, as I am of Christ." [1]

Hellenization of Judaism

Although St. Paul owed nothing to Hellenism, and although he did not Hellenize Christianity, his teaching was nevertheless cast in a form which made it "Hellenizable," and this, too, even before the eschatological expectation had waned. At first sight, there is nothing which seems at all compatible between Greek conceptions of immortality and Jewish conceptions of resurrection,[2] or between Greek

---

[1] *The Mysticism of Paul the Apostle*, p. 333.

[2] Belief in bodily resurrection is of course not indigenous to Judaism. Common both to Egypt and Babylon, it was adopted into Judaism after the Captivity. But St. Paul himself does not share it in its crude sense (1 Cor. xv, 50).

immanentism and Jewish transcendentalism, or between Greek ideas of a redeemer-god and the Jewish apocalyptic expectation of a super-earthly world-kingdom and its King. "Belief in the early coming of the kingdom, in the Messiahship of Jesus, in His atoning death and subsequent resurrection, in the saving effect of baptism as understood by the primitive Christian community, is not Hellenizable." But these objective and naïvely realistic conceptions of redemption which St. Paul took over from Judaism underwent, as they passed through the crucible of his mind, a transformation in the new emphasis which he placed upon redemption as a resurrection to actual participation in the Kingdom in the mystical fellowship of its believers with Christ. And this is Hellenizable. Belief in the redemption by Christ could thus maintain itself, long after the eschatological·expectation had died away, as belief in the resurrection through Christ. He explains the efficacy of the sacraments on the basis of the same concept, as the guarantees of the being-in-Christ.

This Hellenization of the primitive Christian belief, developed by the early Fathers of the Church in Asia Minor, received its loftiest and most lucid expression in "The Gospel according to St. John." The transition took place unobserved and without coming into con-flict with the eschatological expectation. The latter "surrounded it like an outer integument which was later to drop away." Schweitzer traces the transition with minuteness from Ignatius through Justin Martyr to the fourth Gospel, and so to the Fathers of the Alexandrian Church. For him it represents an impoverishment of the original Christ-mysticism of St. Paul. How shallow, in comparison with the original Pauline eschatological mysticism, were the theologies which subsequently derived themselves partially from fragments of his teaching, but without comprehending it as one consistent whole, is seen by the fact that none of them could produce a genuine Christian ethic. While Eastern theology was content to Hellenize the Pauline mysticism and abandon the connection of belief in redemption with belief in the Kingdom of God, Western theology —and after it the theology of the Protestant Reformers in a different sense—fell back upon a rationalization of the Pauline doctrine of Justification on the basis of the atoning death of Jesus as a sacrificial offering. "They all contain the gospel of Paul in a form which does not continue the Gospel of Jesus, but displaces it."[1]

[1] *Ibid.* pp. 334 ff.

Things Temporal and Things Eternal

Is the Christ-mysticism of St. Paul capable of being universalized? So far as its "outer integument" is concerned it is not, since the realistic eschatological world-view which it presupposed is not ours "who live in expectation, not of a catastrophic ending of the world, but of the world's continuance with its mixture of good and ill." But so far as its pure spiritual content is concerned—in its power to envisage things temporal in the light of their eternal issues, to actualize the future in the present, to experience redemption as mystical union with Christ and as membership in the Kingdom of God—it is valid for all time. "As a fugue of Bach belongs in form to the eighteenth century, but in its essence is pure musical truth, so does the Christ-mysticism of all times find itself in the Pauline in its primal form."

St. Paul is thus the champion of all thinkers who will have the courage to translate the thought-forms of primitive Christian belief into those which are proper to the world-view of their own times. For our times the eschatological world-view which he accepted is entirely obsolete; to attempt to force it into ours is an anachronism. So too is the attempt to designate Our Lord in terms of Greek metaphysics.

> By simply designating Jesus as "our Lord" Paul raises Him above all the temporally conditioned conceptions in which the mystery of His personality might be grasped, and sets Him forth as the spiritual Being who transcends all human definitions, to whom we have to surrender ourselves in order to experience in Him the true law of our existence and our being.[1]

> He who has fallen under the power of the conception of dying-and-rising-again-with-Christ advances into an ever deeper consciousness of sin, and attains in the struggle to die from sin a quiet certitude of the forgiveness of sin. This is what Paul promises to those who, like himself, are determined to make the being-redeemed-through-Christ not a matter of word only, but of deed.

> How penetratingly true is the lesson he teaches, that we cannot possess the Spirit of Christ as mere natural men, but only in so far as the dying-with-Christ has become a reality in us![1]

This forms the theme of the final chapter of his book, headed

[1] *The Mysticism of Paul the Apostle*, p. 378 and p. 388.

"Permanent Elements." Though impersonally and objectively set forth, it is the clearest and fullest expression of his own personal faith to be found in all his theological and philosophical writings, and must rank high among the noblest passages in the religious literature of the world. ("I wrote it," he tells us with characteristic brevity in his autobiography, "in December 1929 on board ship between Bordeaux and Cape Lopez.") He was on his way again to take up his self-sacrificing labours in West Africa and the example of the first and greatest missionary to the Gentiles must have been in the background and the forefront of his mind. In this chapter he vindicates St. Paul's claim to be called pre-eminently "the minister of Jesus Christ"; and he concludes it with these words:

> In the hearts in which Paul's mysticism of union with Christ is alive there is an unquenchable yearning for the Kingdom of God, but also consolation in the fact that we do not see its fulfilment.
> Three things make up the power of Paul's thought. There belong to it a depth and a reality which lay their spell upon us; the ardour of the early days of the Christian faith kindles our own; a direct experience of Christ as the Lord of the Kingdom of God speaks from it, exciting us to follow the same path.
> Paul leads us out upon that path of true redemption and hands us over, prisoners, to Christ.[1]

The Mysticism of Paul the Apostle is a greater work than The Quest of the Historical Jesus,—greater in scope, greater in depth, greater in erudition, and much greater in originality. The latter, great as it is, is the work of a young genius who has made a notable discovery in New Testament exegesis, but who is as yet untried in putting it to the test of Christian discipleship. But the former represents the fullness of Schweitzer's intellectual powers as a New Testament scholar at their maturity, co-extensive with his experience as a labourer in the vineyard of Christ; and the fact that his work upon it suffered from prolonged interruptions so that its completion was delayed over a period of several years gave to his thought upon the subject what he himself calls "an inner lucidity." This was very greatly enhanced by the opportunities afforded both for practical work and silent meditation in the solitudes of the African jungle. "Solitude of the

---

[1] Ibid. p. 396.

African wilderness," he exclaims in another book, "how much I have to thank you for!"

But in contrast with the reception accorded to *The Quest* on its appearance in English dress, the reviews of his *St. Paul* in the English periodicals, theological and literary, show a singular lack of comprehension. Few reviewers appear to have read the book as a whole. But even the dissentients cannot forbear to voice their admiration, as thus:

> He has studied the New Testament with unremitting care, and has an extraordinary power of holding innumerable facts in his mind and finding links between them. . . . Every sentence has hard thinking in it, and much learning behind it (*The Guardian*).
>
> He proclaims on almost every page a profound truth. . . . Our religion sorely needs a new spring-time. It is to this that Dr. Schweitzer would fain point us (*The New Chronicle*).

Other reviews speak of it as "monumental in its thoroughness" and "unique for Christian thought." But the best comes as before from *The Times Literary Supplement*, qualified in its appreciation by some (not very careful) censure.

> One may disagree profoundly with its conclusions, but it is a great book,—great in two ways. The first is that it is alive with the spirit of a modern man who has made a great renunciation. This theologian-doctor-musician-missionary, whose conception of Christ is different from that of nearly all his contemporary Christians, has more of the true Christian spirit than many who worship Christ as God, or who regard God's Kingdom as the progressive realization of social—and other—ideals. And secondly, this book is great by reason of the architecture of its thought. Here we have a massive scheme with great and vigorous lines—a weight of scholarship borne aloft on the logical fury of youth. And the author compels us too by his quiet indifference to acceptance or rejection of his thesis, so sure is he that it is true.

In the face of these comparatively lukewarm appraisals, the opinion may here with sober consideration be advanced that *The Mysticism of Paul the Apostle* is by far the greatest study of the apostle's thought that has ever been produced, or that in all likelihood ever can be.

CHAPTER XVI

MUSIC: AND THE MUSIC OF J. S. BACH

THE world of music owes what is still the classic work on Bach to the prompting of Schweitzer's old friend and instructor, Charles Marie Widor. Widor extracted a promise from his pupil that he would write an essay in French in the autumn vacation of 1902 on the nature of Bach's art for the Paris Conservatoire. The essay was to be also biographical. While engaged upon it Schweitzer realized that he could not get all he had to say on the subject into an essay, but that it must expand into a book. He was at this time simultaneously immersed in the writing of his *Quest of the Historical Jesus,* a sufficiently strenuous undertaking in itself. "With good courage," he says, "I resigned myself to my fate": and his work on these two masterpieces proceeded side by side.

"That I wrote the book in French at a time when I was also lecturing and preaching in German was an effort for me." His care in both languages was for the rhythmical construction of the sentence, and for simplicity in style. Care for rhythm is the more necessary in French, and as the work grew "it became clear to me what literary style corresponded to my nature."

The volume appeared in 1905, and was at once acclaimed not only in France, but also in Germany. The question of a translation was raised. So, in the summer of the following year, having finished his *Quest,* Schweitzer set to work to translate his French *Bach* into German. He soon abandoned the attempt, however, for a reason and with a result that must be told in his own words.

I soon became conscious that it was impossible for me to translate myself into another language, and that if I was to produce anything satisfactory, I must plunge anew into the original materials of my book. So I shut the French *Bach* with a bang, and resolved to make a new and better German one. Out of the book of 455 pages there sprang, to the dismay of the astonished publisher, one of 844. The first pages of the new work I wrote at Bayreuth in the Black Horse Inn after a wonderful performance of *Tristan*. For weeks I had been trying in vain to get to work. In the mood of exaltation from which I returned from the Festival Hill, I succeeded. While the babel of voices surged up from the *Bierhalle* below into my stuffy room, I began to write, and it was long after sunrise that I laid down my pen. From that time onwards I felt such joy in the work that I had it ready in two years, although my medical course, the preparation of my lectures, my preaching activities, and my concert tours prevented me from busying myself with it continuously. I often had to lay it aside for weeks.[1]

The German edition appeared early in 1908 and was translated into English in 1911 by Ernest Newman. At Schweitzer's request the text received yet further additions and alterations. "The English edition," says his translator, "is thus fuller and more correct even than the German." It must be confessed that Schweitzer has not always been equally happy in his English translators, though indeed the labours of all of them were labours of love: the rendering of German philosophical works into their corresponding English idiom is in any case notoriously difficult, and the balance and rhythm of Schweitzer's original phrasing has suffered considerably in those subjects, as in others, in its English reproduction. But in none of his translators has he been more fortunate—indeed, almost unbelievably so—than in the translator of his *Bach*. Even as a translation, it is an adornment to English literature.

Schweitzer's *Bach* brought him many friends. Among them was the conductor, Felix Mottl, who read it through without a break during a railway journey and in a hotel between Munich and Leipzig. Another was the Queen of Roumania, Carmen Sylva, "because I had made her beloved Bach still dearer to her." Though he could not accept her frequently repeated invitation to stay with her before he went to Africa—"with the single obligation of playing the organ to her for two hours daily,"—because during those years he had no time for a holiday, she corresponded with him frequently and at length; "and when I returned home she was no longer among the living."

As in his works on biblical criticism so here, Schweitzer provides his reader with the necessary background for an understanding of his subject by an exhaustive survey of the historical conditions that

---

[1] *My Life and Thought*, pp. 80-81.

led up to it. His sources for his study of Bach are on the same comprehensive scale as those for his studies of the historical Jesus and of St. Paul, and are to be considered—together with the biographical sections—as only incidental or introductory to the main subject of his work, which is both an explanation of the real nature of Bach's music and a discussion of the correct method of rendering it. "As a musician," he tells us in *My Life and Thought*, "I wanted to talk to other musicians about Bach's music."

Nevertheless it is impossible, even for the uninstructed layman, to read these opening chapters—which tell of the origins of the Chorale Texts and of the Chorale Melodies; of the use of the organ in congregational singing after the Reformation; of the liturgical and musical evolution of the Cantata; of the Chorale Prelude, and of the Cantata and the Passion music, before Bach's time,—without a kindling sense of the high enthusiasm for the whole range of the subject which so inspired its author, and without at the same time feeling at a loss which to admire most,—the mastery of the treatment, or the felicity and cadence of the phrasing. Whatever his theme may be,—whether it is the Mystery Plays with their cradle-songs whose rocking lilt "kept alive the bright Christmas enchantment"; or the evangelical musicians in Germany and notably Johann Krüger; or the hymn-writers, who, "in the hour of her bitterest need, created a religious poetry with which nothing in the world can compare and before which even the splendour of the Psalter fades"; or the salutary check upon subjectivity and over-subtilization which church-song received in the emergence of that "king of hymn-makers" Paul Gerhardt; or the old folk-tunes which Luther pre-served (one of which "caused even Calvin—for the only time in his life—to laugh"), some of them to become enshrined, touched by the magic of genius, in Bach's own works; or the introduction of the madrigal into German sacred music, effected in the person of the young Schutz whose art is primitive "but of such a kind that it cannot be surpassed by any later art, precisely because it is not form but spirit";—everywhere historical insight is blended with artistic discernment, the sure touch of the scholar with the musician's sensibility.

In discussing the work of Bach's predecessors, Schweitzer says that Bach alone, "almost before he had ceased to be their apprentice," realized that the true Chorale Prelude must bring out the poetry that gives the melody its name, and points out that Bach created no new forms, but that he took the three main formal types: the "motivistic" of Pachelbel; the "coloristic" of Bohm; the "melodic core" of Buxtehude's free fantasias,—and did what none of them could do, by making something more of them than form, and by infusing them with a spirit that "had the secret of making tones speak." He concludes:

The more we try to see into the development of things, in any field whatever, the more we become conscious that to each epoch there are set certain limits of knowledge, before which it has to come to a halt, and always at the very moment when it was apparently bound to advance to a higher and definitive knowledge that seemed just within its grasp. The real history of progress in physics, philosophy, and religion, and more especially in psychology, is the history of incomprehensible cessations, of conceptions that were unattainable by a given epoch, in spite of all that happened to lead it up to them,—of the thought it did not think, not because it could not, but because there was some mysterious command upon it not to. . . . Thus it is incomprehensible that the masters who created the types of the Chorale Prelude did not recognize that they were no more than forms, and felt no necessity to give life to the form by breathing into it the poetic spirit that was associated with the melody. . . .

In no other art does the perfect consign the imperfect to oblivion so thoroughly as it does in music. Early painting retains its own artistic charm for all time. It deals with nature, with reality, and renders it, no matter how awkwardly, with a primitive truth that makes so direct an appeal to the spectator of all epochs that he himself looks at the scene with the childlike eyes of those early artists. Music, however, does not depict the external universe, but is the image of an invisible world, which can only be expressed in eternal tones by those who see it in its whole perfection and can reproduce it as they have seen it. . . .

Thus the Chorale Preludes of the composers before Bach are finally, for the modern admirer who wishes to do them justice, and even more than justice, no more than what they are in themselves,—forms that they created for the greater master who was to come after them, so that he might find them when he needed them, and make living things of them.[1]

The passage is important, not only as explanatory of Schweitzer's view of the significance of history for the development of the forms

[1] *J. S. Bach*, vol. i, pp. 48-50.

of music and art, but also as expressing a characteristic feature of his whole philosophy of the history of thought.

The failure of Bach's predecessors in the Chorale Prelude then was just this, that they harmonized only the melody; they sought "pure music" without poetry. However admirable, however "interesting" their productions, they failed for this reason to give direct artistic satisfaction. Bach himself stands in this respect as in others, at the end of an epoch,—"an epoch of excessive scribbling, of superficial art." He was not the inaugurator of a new epoch (as was Beethoven); he transformed and transfigured his own.

> Whereas at other times and in other places the great artist has been only one star among others, whose light, if less brilliant than his, he nevertheless did not extinguish, Bach is surrounded by mere will-of-the-wisps, which his epoch—and he with it—mistook for stars. . . . There is no stronger testimony to the greatness of Bach than the fact that in an epoch of error, and sharing its errors, he nevertheless wrote imperishable works. We have finally, however the sad consciousness that he was only great enough to save himself, but not his epoch as well. . . .
>
> He was in fact not the beginning of a new epoch, but the end of an old one, in which the knowledge and the errors of successive centuries found expression for the last time, as if seeking salvation together by genius. Since Bach held his peace and, though inwardly opposed to this epoch, nevertheless went his way with it, it was inevitable that his works should be thrown into the general grave with those of his contemporaries, there to await their resurrection.
>
> If the talents succumb to the errors of their time, what matters? But when the men of genius are ensnared in them, centuries have to suffer for it. The very greatness of Aristotle held Greek philosophy back when it was already on the path that would have led it to the discoveries of Galileo and Copernicus. Bach, with an easy consciousness of his own strength, burdened himself with the Italian forms and formulas, and so retarded the progress of German religious music along the path that would have led it, even at that time, to an art such as Wagner was afterwards to realize in drama.[1]

"Bach is not a single but a universal personality." His artistic talent was inherited; his family, through three or four generations, produced a galaxy of musicians unique in genealogy.

---

[1] *Ibid.* pp. 95-96.

When we pursue the history of this family, which occupies so unique a position in Germany, we have the feeling that everything that is happening there must culminate in something consummate . . . that some day a Bach shall come in whom all those other Bachs shall find a posthumous existence, one in whom the fragment of German music that has been embodied in this family shall find its completion. Johann Sebastian Bach—to speak the language of Kant—is a historical postulate.[1]

Bach is thus, in every sense of the word, an inheritor. Wherein does his own superlative greatness consist?—His art is wholly objective: it represents "pure musical truth."

Whether it be true, as Plato held, that there exists an ideal and transcendent Beauty, absolute and objective, eternal in the heavens, of which all manifestations in the natural world, and art along with them, are the faint and partial images, reflecting the one pure unmanifested essence,[2]—it would at any rate seem certain that the less the personality of the artist intrudes itself into his composition, the more perfect is the resultant work of art. It is for this reason that Shakespeare is supreme; he is, as he would have his actors be, no more and no less than a mirror of the external world of human circumstance,—and the more colourless the medium, the more perfect the reflection. He is detached from the creations of his fancy; nowhere among them is it possible to detect even a glimpse of his own personality; the soul of Shakespeare remains an enigma. He, too, was a child of his age and worked with whatever instruments lay ready to his hand, but in such a fashion that we cannot see him. He is so absorbed in what he sees that he does not see himself. He is utterly unselfconscious.[3]

It is in this sense that Schweitzer would seem to interpret Bach, for all that he has to say of Bach in the opening paragraphs of his book might with equal truth be said of Shakespeare. Again: Shakespeare, like Bach, is "a terminal point. Nothing comes from him; everything merely leads up to him."

Some artists are subjective, some objective. The art of the former has its source in their personality; their work is almost independent

[1] *J. S. Bach*, vol. i, p. 2.

[2] Schweitzer himself rejects the Platonic Theory of Ideas. (*Civilization and Ethics*, pp. 40-41.)

[3] The writer's attention has since been drawn to an admirable article, where the same point is better made, by George Sampson, entitled "Bach and Shakespeare," in the *Quarterly Review*, April 1923.

of the epoch in which they live. A law unto themselves, they place themselves in opposition to their epoch and originate new forms for the expression of their ideas. Of this type was Richard Wagner.

Bach belongs to the order of objective artists. These are wholly of their own time, and work only with the forms and the ideas that their time proffers them. They exercise no criticism upon the media of artistic expression that they find lying ready to their hand, and feel no inner compulsion to open out new paths. Their art not coming solely from the stimulus of their outer experience, we need not seek the roots of their work in the fortunes of its creator. In them the artistic personality exists independently of the human, the latter remaining in the background as if it were something almost accidental. Bach's works would have been the same even if his existence had run quite another course. Did we know more of his life than is now the case, and were we in possession of all the letters he had ever written, we should still be no better informed as to the inward sources of his works than we are now.

The art of the objective artist is not impersonal, but supernatural. It is as if he felt only one impulse,—to express again what he already finds in existence, but to express it definitely, in unique perfection. It is not he that lives,—it is the spirit of the time that lives in him. All the artistic endeavours, desires, creations, aspirations, and errors, of his own and of previous generations, are concentrated and worked out to their conclusion in him.

In this respect the greatest German musician has his analogue only in the greatest of German philosophers. Kant's work has the same impersonal character. He is merely the brain in which the philosophical ideas and problems of his day come to fruition. Moreover he uses unconcernedly the scholastic forms and terminology of the time, just as Bach took up the musical forms offered to him by his epoch without examining them. . . .

Bach is thus a terminal point. Nothing comes from him; everything merely leads up to him. To give his true biography is to exhibit the nature and the unfolding of German art, that comes to completion in him and is exhausted in him,—to comprehend it in all its strivings and its failures. This genius was not an individual, but a collective soul. Centuries and generations have laboured at this work, before the grandeur of which we halt in veneration. To anyone who has gone through the history of this epoch and knows what the end of it was, it is the history of that culminating spirit, as it was before it objectivated itself in a single personality.[1]

[1] *J. S. Bach*, vol. i, pp. 1-4.

Even more strikingly is Schweitzer's perception of this dichotomy between the outer and the inner man revealed in the chapter in which he deals with Bach's personal appearance and character. After a most interesting description of his facial expression as depicted in the portraits that have been preserved, Schweitzer continues:

> In the last resort, the whole man is for the most part an enigma, for to our eyes the outer man differs so much from the inner that neither seems to have any part in the other. In the case of Bach, more than in that of any other genius, the man as he looked and behaved was only the opaque envelope destined to lodge the artistic soul within. In Beethoven, the inner man seizes upon the outer man, uproots him from his normal life, agitates and inflames him, until the inner light pierces through him and finally consumes him. Not so with Bach. His is rather a case of dualism; his artistic vicissitudes and creations go on side by side with the normal and almost commonplace tenor of his work-a-day existence, without mixing with or making any impression on this.
>
> Bach fought for his everyday life, but not for the recognition of his art and of his works. In this respect he is very different from Beethoven and Wagner, and in general from what we understand by an "artist."[1]

(Here, too, is another resemblance to Shakespeare, who appears to have been quite unconscious of his genius, and careless of his literary reputation.)

Bach was a deeply and sincerely religious man. But in what sense? He was sharply opposed both to the pietism on the one hand, and the orthodoxy on the other hand, of his day.[2] His music was the expression of his religious faith. "Music is an act of worship with Bach—it was an end in itself." It is true that "his works exhibit visible traces of pietism; the texts of the cantatas and Passions are strongly influenced by it, as indeed the whole of the religious poetry of the early eighteenth century is. Thus the opponent of pietism invested with his music poetry filled with the breath of pietism, and so made it immortal." But from the element of subjective sentimentalism that clings to pietism Bach is himself inwardly free.

[1] J. S. Bach, vol. i, pp. 164-165.
[2] Here surely is another link with Kant. In another book, Albert Schweitzer, Christian Revolutionary, the writer has expressed the view that Kant was fundamentally, though unconsciously, a mystic.

In the last resort, Bach's real religion was mysticism. . . . This robust man, who seems to be in the thick of life with his family and his work, and whose mouth seems to express something like comfortable joy in life, was inwardly dead to the world. His whole thought was transfigured by a wonderful, serene longing for death. . . . The Epiphany and certain bass cantatas are the revelation of his most intimate religious feelings. Sometimes it is a sorrowful and weary longing that the music expresses; at others, a glad serene desire, finding voice in one of those lulling cradle-songs that only he could write; then again a passionate ecstatic longing, that calls death to it jubilantly, and goes forth in rapture to meet it. . . . The existence that, considered from the outside, seems all conflict and struggle and bitterness, was in truth tranquil and serene.[1]

This judgment would seem to be borne out by the character of Bach's last composition, which he dictated from his death-bed. It was a Chorale Prelude (fortunately included entire in the first edition of the *Art of Fugue*).

In the dark chamber, with the shades of death already falling round him, the master made this work, that is unique even among his creations. The contrapuntal art that it reveals is so perfect that no description can give any idea of it. Each segment of the melody is treated in a fugue, in which the inversion of the subject figures each time as the counter-subject. Moreover the flow of the parts is so easy that after the second line we are no longer conscious of the art, but are wholly enthralled by the spirit that finds voice in these G major harmonies. The tumult of the world no longer penetrated through the curtained windows. The harmonies of the spheres were already echoing round the dying master. So there is no sorrow in the music; the tranquil quavers move along on the other side of all human passion; over the whole gleams the word "Transfiguration."[2]

Schweitzer, in commenting on the fact that Bach sought no recognition even for his greatest works, says: "His immense strength functioned without self-consciousness, like the forces of nature; and for this reason he is as cosmic and copious as these." But when he comes to discuss Bach's method of working, he says that "everything points to the fact that Bach did not invent easily, but slowly and with difficulty"; that his melodies, "quivering as they are with inner

[1] *J. S. Bach*, vol. i, pp. 169-170.   [2] *Ibid.* p. 224.

life," are not the result of "effortless invention"; and that the more deeply we penetrate into Bach, the stronger does this impression become. There is indeed "a certain aesthetic-mathematical necessity" about his work; his art was "essentially architectonic"—it is "music in the perfected Gothic"; the whole piece with all its developments is already implicit in the theme; but of the long and arduous mental work that presupposes the whole conception we can but form a faint idea.

Bach thus worked like the mathematician, who sees the whole of a problem at once, and has only to realize it in definite values. His way of working, as Spitta says, was consequently quite different from that of Beethoven. The latter experimented with his thoughts. In each case the explanation must be sought in the nature of the music itself. With Beethoven the work is developed by means of "episodes" that are independent of the theme. These do not occur in Bach; with him everything that "happens" is simply an emanation from the theme. . . .

In Bach's music, much more than in that of any other composer, the plastic outline of the whole is the result of the optical effect of the details; it requires, in order to become visible, a synthetic activity of the hearer's aesthetic imagination. Even to the best musician, at a first hearing, a Bach fugue seems chaos; while even to the ordinary musician this chaos becomes clear after repeated hearings, when the great lucid lines come out.[1]

Parenthetically it must be noted that Schweitzer has no invidious comparisons to draw between Bach and the other great composers, or between them and one another. Each speaks in his own language, and for the apprehension of each is required its own imaginative faculty. Whenever he has occasion to compare Bach's music with that of Beethoven, for example, as he often does in order to explain their points of difference, it is by no means to derogate from the latter. As one star differeth from another star in glory, so there is one glory of Beethoven and another glory of Bach.

Bach makes no effort to represent all the episodes and evolutions of the text. He expresses the essential elements in the idea, not in its vicissitudes. He underlines, indeed, every characteristic detail, brings out contrasts, employs the most powerful nuances;

[1] *J. S. Bach*, vol. i, pp. 211-213.

but the vicissitudes of the idea, its struggles, its combats, its despair, its entry into peace, all that Beethoven's music and that of the post-Beethoven epoch try to express—of this there is nothing in Bach. Nevertheless his emotional expression is not less perfect than Beethoven's. It is simply another kind of perfection. His emotional utterance has a power and an impressiveness such as we rarely meet with in other music. His capacity for characterizing the various nuances of an emotion is quite unique.[1]

The music of Bach's period, whose consummation he is, described itself as "expressive," that is, its aim was graphic representation. Musical aestheticists, in their revolt from Wagner, have preferred to ignore this, and to define Bach's music, as well as Mozart's, as "pure" or "absolute" music. "To give to beautiful lines of sound the most perfect existence possible"—this was their ideal of the highest musical excellence, and this they believed they found in Bach supremely.

As a contrast to the Bach of these Guardians of the Grail of Pure Music, I present the Bach who is a poet and painter in sound. All that lies in the text, the emotional and the pictorial, he strives to reproduce in the language of music with the utmost vitality and clearness. Before all else he aims at rendering the pictorial in lines of sound. He is even more tone-painter than tone-poet. His art is nearer to that of Berlioz than to that of Wagner. If the text speaks of drifting mists, of boisterous winds, of roaring rivers, of waves that ebb and flow, of leaves falling from the tree, of bells that ring for the dying, of the confident faith that walks with firm steps, or the weak faith that falters insecure, of the proud who will be abased and the humble who will be exalted, of Satan rising in rebellion, of angels poised on the clouds of heaven,—then one hears and sees all this in his music.

Bach has, in fact, at his disposal a language of sound. There are in his music constantly recurring rhythmical motives expressing peaceful blessedness, lively joy, intense pain, or pain sublimely borne.[2]

These motives are represented symbolically. Their appeal is not to feeling, but to the conceptual imagination, and as such it addresses itself to the eye as much as to the ear.

Now Schweitzer is perfectly willing to allow to the aestheticians the pure or absolute or classical quality of the music of Bach's Fugues

[1] *Ibid.* vol. ii, p. 40.   [2] *My Life and Thought*, p. 82.

and Preludes: and this is a concession which most of his critics appear
to overlook. He is also as stern as they are to condemn much modern
music which aspires to be expressive, as "pathological perversions of
pure music": and this is another concession which they appear to
overlook. But his whole contention in regard to Bach is this, that he
was *much more* than a purist; and that in his Chorales, Cantatas, and
Passions—which after all represent by far the greatest part of his
whole output as a musician—there is to be found a quality which in
the truest sense may be called pictorial. "Today it is still a reproach
to our aestheticians, even the best of them, that they know nothing
of the two hundred Bach cantatas and but a few of the organ chorales.
The extraordinarily expressive and pictorial conception of music that
these works reveal have exercised no influence whatever on the ordi-
narily accepted or debated theories of the nature of music." For Bach
was after all from first to last a church organist whose music was
necessarily associated with scriptural texts; and this is what the
"guardians of the grail of pure music" not only overlook, but refuse
to see even when it is pointed out to them. Bach is not only the
supreme grammarian of sound; his grammar is the articulation of a
language; his language is the product of a felt experience.

Bach's music then is, in the main, "not self-existent, but has sprung
from some strong external force, that will not obey the laws of
harmonious thematic structure."—In other words, Bach is a poet and
painter in sound, and more of a painter than poet. Nor is this unnatural or a thing to be wondered at: since, first, he was a child
of his age, though at the same time immeasurably beyond it; and,
secondly, every great creative artist is an artist in more than one
sense. It is in order to develop this latter point that Schweitzer wrote
the chapter entitled "Poetic Music and Pictorial Music,"—a masterpiece of profound artistic reflection, even though it is a rock of
stumbling and a cause of offence to musical aestheticians. They perhaps forget that its author is himself not only an experienced musician,
but one whose aptitude for music is paralleled with his appreciation
of poetry and painting; that he is a philosopher as well as an artist;
and not only these, but a scientist with a specialist's knowledge of
physiology and psychology.

"All utterances about art," says Schweitzer, "are a kind of speaking in parables." Its form of expression, that is to say, is symbolic of
a meaning which points beyond itself. The form of expression may
be audible (as in music), or visual (as in painting), or conceptual

(as in poetry). Each artist expresses himself in his own language. But the medium which the artist chooses is of secondary importance to his essential artistic creativity. The true artist "is not only a painter, or only a poet, or only a musician, but all in one. Various artists have their habitation in his soul. His work is the product of their co-operation; all have a part in each one of his ideas. . . ."

Schweitzer illustrates this thesis from the testimony of several of the world's great artists. To cite a few: Goethe, the poet of drama, was a self-confessed painter in words; the lyricist Heine also; Bocklin, the painter, was a poet in colour; Schiller, the poet, was a self-confessed musician; so too was Nietzsche, the thinker and master of prose; Wagner, the musician, was a poet of sound. . . .

He might well have adduced his own case as another example. A philosopher and musician, his academic works abound in pictorial metaphors,[1] and had he turned his artistic talent to painting, his pictures would have been drawn on a wide canvas. Readers of *The Quest*, for example, may forget his elaboration of the argument for eschatology derived from a multitude of minutiae in the sacred text; but they cannot forget his majestic image of the Man who lays hold of the Wheel of the World to set it moving to its final revolution, and then throws Himself upon it to be crushed.—Readers of his *Paul* may forget his detailed explanation of the apostle's sublime conception of the General Resurrection from the Dead; but they cannot forget his visualization of the rising of the immortal world from the ocean of the temporal in a series of volcanic upheavals, island upon island, till the whole is merged in one vast continent of the redeemed. —They may forget in their reading of his *Philosophy of Civilization* his analysis of the causes that led to the bankruptcy of the discursive reason in the history of rationalistic abstract thought; but they cannot forget his picture of the master-mariner, Hegel, on the bridge of his ocean liner, proudly explaining to passengers the marvels of its machinery and the mysteries of its log, whilst the fires in the boiler are burning out, and the vessel, no longer responsive to the helm, is becoming a plaything of storms.—In truth, as has been justly remarked,[2] what he says of Goethe might well be said of himself:

How beautiful are his metaphors! He does not invent imagery to fit a thought, but the pictures of what he has seen and experi-

[1] "There are few philosophical writers whose works contain such a wealth of apt metaphor as the works of Schweitzer" (Kraus).

[2] Mrs. Russell in her preface to *The Path to Reconstruction*.

enced, stored in his mind, wait within him ready for the thought which is destined to gain form from them.

But not only is there this blending of the arts in the creative imagination of the artist; there is the same blending in the critical appreciation of the percipient of their art. "Anyone who does not hear the bees in Didier-Pouget's picture of the flowery heath does not see it with the eye of the artist"; and the same is true of anyone who, in contemplating the most ordinary painting of a pine wood, does not hear "the infinite distant symphonies of the wind sweeping over the tree-tops." Similarly the effect of Palestrina's music upon a listener should be to transport him into the vast nave of a church and make him see "the sunlight streaming through the windows of the choir into the twilight of the building."

Every artistic feeling is itself an act. Artistic creation is only a special case of the artistic attitude towards the world. . . . The part of a work of art that is perceptible by the senses is in reality only the intermediator between two active efforts of the imagination. All art speaks in signs and symbols. No one can explain how it happens that the artist can waken to life in us the existence that he has seen and lived through. No artistic speech is the adequate expression of what it represents; its vital force comes from what is unspoken in it.[1]

Poetry is, perhaps, of all the arts the most readily intelligible, since words—the familiar currency of daily life—are the suggestive symbols. Painting is less so; "we cannot estimate how much the spectator must add of his own before a coloured canvas can become a landscape." And yet an etching—a mere symbolical delineation in black and white—is, for anyone who can interpret it, a more potent means of visual representation.

In this way there comes into painting, in place of the naïve "This is," the noteworthy "This signifies" of artistic speech. It will be learned and assimilated by familiarity. It even happens at times that the speech fails, the symbols not being clear to the spectator, and appearing merely as agglomerations of lines and colours,—either because the artist has put more into them than they can express, or because the spectator has not caught the secret of his speech.[2]

[1] *J. S. Bach*, vol. ii, pp. 15-16.   [2] *Ibid*. p. 16.

But music, being of all the arts the least adapted to depict concrete ideas, suffers violence at the hands of those who use it as a medium for poetic or pictorial ideas which are beyond its capacity to express. This is the reason why musical aestheticians, jealous for the fair fame of this the least tangible of all the arts, look with suspicion upon *all* poetic and pictorial tendencies in music, "and in times of danger adopt the motto of 'absolute music,' this being the banner of pure art they hoisted over the works of Bach and Beethoven,—erroneously and inappropriately as it happens."

> Certainly only the pure music lies before us. But this is only the hieroglyph, in which are recorded the emotional qualities of the vision of the concrete imagination. The hieroglyph appeals perpetually to the fancy of the hearer, requiring it to translate the drama of the emotions back again into concrete events, and to find a path along which he can see, as well as he can, the line that has been taken by the creative imagination of the composer. Notable musicians have confessed that they could not grasp the latest works of Beethoven. This derogates neither from them nor from Beethoven; it only implies that their imagination had no point of contact with his.[1]

In his zeal to vindicate the supremacy of tone-speech in music Schweitzer even goes so far as to assert:

> It is wrong to imagine that so-called pure music speaks a language that is not symbolical, and that it expresses something of which the meaning is unequivocal. It, too, appeals to the hearer's power of imagination, only that it is concerned more with abstract feeling and abstract beauty of line than with concrete expression. . . .
>
> As a rule we employ the criterion of immediate intelligibility, and, from the standpoint of absolute music, will allow only that art to be valid which appeals immediately to the unprepossessed and unprepared hearer. This would make perfect tone-speech an impossibility. It is like refusing to recognize a foreign language unless it is immediately intelligible to everyone at a first hearing. Every language subsists only by a convention, in virtue of which a certain sensation or idea is regarded as corresponding to a certain aggregation of sounds. It is the same in music. . . .[2]

[1] *Ibid.* p. 20.   [2] *Ibid.* p. 17

It is so pre-eminently in the case of Bach, who "before all else aims at rendering the pictorial in lines of sound." Of the many images which Schweitzer employs to illustrate this truth, perhaps the most felicitous is that in which he speaks of the text being reflected in Bach's music "as in clear running water." The structure of Bach's musical phrase is indissolubly wedded to the structure of the verbal phrase. Even if they were to fall apart, the musical phrase would run on of itself unbroken, "because it is only the verbal phrase re-cast in tone."

> His music is indeed not so much melodic as declamatory. . . . The melodic impression his phrases make on us is due to his clear and consummate sense of form. Though he thought declamatorily, he could not help writing melodically. A vocal theme of Bach's is a declamatorily conceived phrase, that by accident, as if by a marvel perpetually repeated, assumes melodic form, whether it be a recitative, an arioso, an aria, or a chorus.[1]

And this despite the fact that the biblical texts upon which he worked are not in themselves rhythmical. His music seems actually to confer a higher vital power on the words. And this marvel is so perpetually repeated in the cantatas and Passions, that the more we ponder upon it "the more we are filled with the ever-renewed and ever-increasing astonishment that the thoughtful soul feels in presence of those daily occurrences of nature that are at the same time the greatest marvels." Schweitzer cites, as one of the most remarkable examples of Bach's power of declamation, the arioso-like opening recitative of the cantata to Isaiah lv, 10 and 11, where—

> The nearly equal divisions of the original passage are gathered up by the music into one great unified phrase that resolves and obliterates, as if by magic, all the rigidities of the verbal passage, giving us the impression that the poetic thought has waited for centuries for this music in order to reveal itself in its true plastic outline.[2]

He adduces an imposing array of instances to illustrate still further Bach's power of tone-painting, and affirms that "hundreds of examples of the same kind could be given." Bach converts into

---

[1] *J. S. Bach*, vol. ii, p. 26. "Architecture" and "declamation"—these are the two words which Schweitzer whispers constantly to himself while playing Bach.
[2] *Ibid.* pp. 27-28.

tone not only the body but the soul of the verbal passage, and
his interpretation of a theme is not always the customary one,
but springs from "a profound and very personal emotion." For
example:

> The music he has given to the sacramental words of the Last
> Supper in the *St. Matthew Passion* is astounding. There is not a
> trace of grief. The music breathes peace and majesty; the nearer it
> draws to the end, the more stately becomes the quaver-movement
> in the basses. Bach sees Jesus standing before the disciples with
> radiant face, prophesying of the day when He will again drink
> from the cup at the heavenly supper with them in His Father's
> kingdom. Bach has thus emancipated himself from the conven-
> tional idea of the scene, and, by means of his artistic intuition,
> has attained a juster sense of it than theology has ever done.[1]

When Schweitzer says that "Bach's relation to his text is active,
not passive; it does not inspire him so much as he inspires it"—we
cannot fail to be reminded of another parallel with Kant for whom
the subject-self, by the act of his "transcendental unity of appercep-
tion," subsumes the outer world which he perceives, and re-creates
it, rendering it plastic to the power of thought.

It is of the essence of Bach's genius that he was able to communi-
cate his experience, by means of his musical art, with surpassing
clarity of expression; and in this "Bach is the greatest among the
great."

> His music is poetic and pictorial because its themes are born of
> poetical and pictorial ideas. Out of these themes the composition
> unfolds itself, a finished piece of architecture in lines of sound.
> What is in its essence poetic and pictorial music, displays itself as
> Gothic architecture transformed into sound. What is greatest in
> this art, so full of natural life, so wonderfully plastic, and unique
> in the perfection of its form, is the spirit that breathes out from it.
> A soul which out of the world's unrest longs for peace and has
> itself already tasted peace, allows in this music others to share its
> own experience.[2]

So much then by way of explanation of the real nature of Bach's
music. What now of the correct method of rendering it?—Schweitzer's directions in this important matter are exact and particular,

Ibid. p. 35.   [2] *My Life and Thought*, pp. 82-83.

and illustrated by very many representative examples culled from the whole field of the composer's works. As in the case of every other creative genius, so here: Bach must be studied against the historical background of his own time. He had no experience of the Venetian shutter swell, or of the cylinder swell, or of combination stops, or of adjustable combinations,—none of the apparatus in fact with which the modern organ is equipped. But we have lost the old tone of the organ that Bach wrote for, with those "delicate and beautiful reeds that just add a lustre to the diapasons without over-whelming them as ours do." We must therefore use diapasons, mixtures, and reeds with careful discretion in order to reproduce as nearly as may be the old quality of tone. We must never destroy the "dramatic majesty" of Bach's effects by an attempt to senti-mentalize his music. The essential prerequisite above all for a modern interpreter of Bach is a capacity to reproduce the "marvellous plasti-city" of his music. "Bach thinks as a violinist"; his phrasing "comes from the idea of the natural use of the somewhat slackened bow"; no composer "makes such play with light and shade." But he was unconscious of the need for frequent changes of register. He obtained variety and gradation, when he needed them, by transitions from one manual to another. A *mezzoforte* for example was unknown to Bach: he shaded the *piano* into *forte*. The ideal way of rendering Bach's music, therefore, is "to link the notes in such a way that they do not seem to be struck one after the other, but as if several bows were being simultaneously drawn over the strings."

But the correct phrasing can only be secured by attention to correct accentuation. "It is characteristic of the structure of his periods that as a rule they do not start from an accent but strive to reach one. They are conceived as beginning with an upward beat." And further, the tonic accents do not invariably coincide with the natural accents of the bars, but advance together with them, preserving their own freedom. It is from this tension between the accents of the line of sound and those of the bars that there is born "the extraordinarily rhythmical vitality of Bach's music."

But if the main thing for an interpreter of Bach to remember is the extreme and unique plasticity of his style, it is equally necessary for a conductor to do so. Bach's music should never be performed with huge orchestras and massed choirs: no more than from forty to fifty voices are needed, or from fifty to sixty instrumentalists. "Bach's orchestra does not accompany the choir, but is a partner

with equal rights, and there is no such thing as an orchestral equivalent to a choir of a hundred and fifty voices. . . . The wonderful
inter-weaving of the voice parts must stand out, clear and distinct."
And for the alto and soprano boys' voices are preferable to women's,
not only because Bach himself used boys' voices, but also because
"choirs of male voices form an homogeneous whole."

Bach is as a rule played much too fast. "Music which presupposes
a visual comprehension of lines of sound advancing side by side
becomes for the listener a chaos, if a too rapid tempo makes this
comprehension impossible." Organists who imagine that they play
Bach "interestingly" by playing him fast betray their incapacity to
play him plastically, and so obscure detail, and so sacrifice vitality.

The more we play Bach's organ works, the slower we take the
tempi. Every organist has this experience. The lines must stand
out in calm plasticity. There must be time also to bring out their
dovetailing and juxtaposition. . . . [But] it is quite a mistaken idea
that what Bach wants chiefly is a monotonous smoothness. He
certainly favoured the legato style. But his legato is not a mere
levelling; it is alive. It must be filled with a fine phrasing which
the hearer need not peceive as such, but of which he is conscious
as a captivating lucidity in the playing. Within the legato, the
separate tones must be grouped into living phrases. This intimate
style of phrasing breaks up the stiffness of the organ tone. The
effect should be as if what is impossible on the organ had become
possible,—that is to say, that some notes have a heavy and others
a light touch. That is the ideal to be aimed at.[1]

So much for the quality of Bach's music. What of his fingering
and touch? His music itself instructs us as to these, and compels us
in some measure to adopt them. "Strongly incurved and loose fingers
and loose wrists, with the fingers resting directly on the keys." His
fingering represents the transition from an old method to a new one:
of the old he retained the simple passing of one finger over another,
and of the new he adopted the passing of the thumb under the fifth.

He played with so slight and easy a motion of the fingers that
one could hardly notice it. Only the front joints of the fingers were
in motion; the hand preserved its rounded form even in the most
difficult passages; the fingers were only slightly raised above the
keys.

[1] *J. S. Bach*, vol. i, pp. 311-312.

His touch was very complex. He aimed chiefly at a singing tone. To this end he did not merely let the key, after pressing it down, come to rest and then ascend, but raised it by a gradual drawing back of the finger-tips towards the inner flat of the hand, so as to give the string the proper time to vibrate and die away. . . .[1]

Schweitzer goes on to show that in this respect Bach's touch was absolutely modern, in that it agrees with the latest theories of the "singing tone."

The question whether Bach's cantatas should be rendered only in a church service has been a subject for much unnecessary debate. We cannot put the clock back to reproduce the conditions under which his cantatas were played at Leipzig in the eighteenth century. Nor is this desirable. The independent position of music in the ritual of the church service is a thing of the past, and rightly so. "The evolution of things has led to a separation between the church service and art that is good for both of them,—we have the service on one side and on the other the sacred concert, or whatever name people may prefer to call it by." Admittedly, the difficulties are there in either case: "the deeper we go into the question of how Bach should be performed, the more complicated it becomes." But,—let a church be used for a Bach performance by all means, if suitably constructed: if not, then a concert room: in neither case can the essentially religious character of the performance be impaired.

How can Bach help it if churches are often so built today that no chorus and no orchestra can be placed in them, or only in such a way that the chorus sings into the backs of the audience? The great point is that Bach, like every lofty religious mind, belongs not to the church but to religious humanity, and that any room becomes a church in which his sacred works are performed and listened to with devotion.[2]

That a scholar engrossed in original research in two distinct fields of learning should turn to the advanced study of the theory of music for mental recreation and spiritual refreshment, is in itself remarkable; but that he should turn to it, not as an amateur, but as a specialist in the most intricate and subtle domain of that art, and contribute to its elucidation a classic work, this reaches the summits of scientific and artistic achievement..

[1] *J. S. Bach*, vol. i, p. 207.   [2] *Ibid.* p. 264.

It was a necessity of Schweitzer's inmost being to interpret, so that others might understand, the essential meaning of Bach's music as well as the correct method of rendering it. Fortunately for the intelligence of the less gifted, scientific invention has made it possible for him to effect his purpose not only by means of the printed word, but also in sound. Since the publication of his *Bach*, gramophone records of his rendering of the master have been made at the Queen's Hall by "His Master's Voice"; by the Columbia Corporation, at All Hallows, Barking, from the organ which he loved best of all in this country; and at St. Aurélie, Strasburg, from the organ built by the famous organ-maker Silbermann, a contemporary of Bach. Restored and modernized several times since it was first constructed, it had nevertheless retained its fine deep tone. These two last organs have been demolished by war. But the records have fulfilled their purpose in preserving with perfect fidelity the colourful tone, the clarity of detail, and the wonderful plasticity of Bach's music.

Yet only a soul that is already in tune with the soul of a master-musician can ever truly interpret his work. That is why Schweitzer, after summarizing the principles that should govern the minds of producers and performers of Bach's orchestral works, concludes:

> These are the external requirements for the rendering of Bach's music. But above and beyond them, that music demands of us men and women that we attain a composure and an inwardness that will enable us to raise to life something of the deep spirit that lies hidden within it.[1]

NOTE

In *Music and Letters* of October 1942 there appeared a violent attack by Dr. Gordon Sutherland on Schweitzer's theory of aesthetic in general and on his application of it to the music of Bach in particular, on the ground that it is "not only false but pernicious," and that it is a tangle of "inconsistencies, contradictions, confusions, and ambiguities."

This extraordinary onslaught was countered by an admirably clear and convincing reply in the same periodical in April 1945 by Mr. A. B. Ashby. In it he demolishes the whole argument by showing

[1] *My Life and Thought*, p. 84.

that it misrepresents all that Schweitzer wrote and meant. The tables are thus completely turned on the prosecution, and it is convincingly shown that the accuser is himself guilty of the charges which he brings against the defendant.

In all his criticisms Sutherland disregards or overlooks the fact that there are two different categories of music to be discussed in any theory of aesthetics, corresponding to two forms of music which Bach wrote: namely, his free instrumental works and general organ music on the one hand, and his cantatas, choral works, and organ chorale preludes on the other. The former are a supreme model of formal perfection, "pure" music. The latter are those which may be called his "associative" or "representative" music, where form is determined by the subject matter, so much so that without its context much of the music remained incomprehensible to even so great a musician as Widor and to others, until Schweitzer's revealing aesthetic was applied to it. It is with this special branch of applied aesthetics that Schweitzer's valuable interpretation of Bach's music is primarily concerned. Sutherland's criticisms are beside the point because they ignore this fundamental distinction; for he writes throughout as if Schweitzer were always referring without qualification to all music and to the whole of Bach's music.

Sutherland first accuses Schweitzer of holding the theory of one "universal art." He holds nothing of the kind; he holds a theory of the *co-operation* of the several arts, which is a totally different thing. From this false premiss Sutherland develops a gratuitous line of argument, which is shown to be fallacious at each step. Mr. Ashby then shows how a repeated process of perversion, following upon this, actually reverses the meaning of the quotations from Schweitzer's book which Sutherland borrows for his purpose. He points to one instance, for example, where Sutherland has, from one of Schweitzer's closely qualified particular propositions (given as an exception to a general rule), drawn an inference that Schweitzer is propounding a quite different general rule; which general rule Sutherland then proceeds to condemn, having unwarrantably ascribed its proposition to Schweitzer himself.

There is a certain plausibility, even brilliance, about Sutherland's presentation of the case which might well prove disconcerting to admirers of Schweitzer as a musician who have not carefully read his book. Mr. Ashby's exposure of its fallacies and misrepresentations is all the more welcome since it comes from one who combines the acumen of a trained logician with the experience and sensibility of a musical critic.

CHAPTER XVII

INDIAN THOUGHT AND ITS DEVELOPMENT

THOUGHT, for Schweitzer, is as strenuous an activity as life itself. Constantly in his writings he speaks of the truth as something "for which we should strive." Nowhere perhaps is this mental strife more apparent than in his *Civilization and Ethics* where he delves like a bold explorer into the deep mines of western philosophy to discover, if it be discoverable there, the essential thought that shall give an answer to the meaning and purpose of existence. But, because he is a serious explorer, he is not content to rest there, but sets his pick to quarry in the mines of Asiatic thought as well, both near and far. The fact that he has chosen the Thought of India as a subject for another of his major works by no means implies that he is attracted by it more than by the other philosophies of the East. In fact, he is far more attracted by the thought of China: this is evident whenever in *Civilization and Ethics* he has occasion to make a comparison between European and Asiatic thought. The reason that he has chosen Indian Thought rather than Zoroastrian or Mohammedan, for example, is that it on the whole represents the clearest antithesis to European. That he has made no similar contribution to the study of the Thought of China is due to his never yet having found the time to complete it for publication.

Since the year 1900 he had set himself to study, as far as time allowed, all the great philosophies and all the great religions of the world, as well as the writings of the mystics. He had intended to devote a chapter in his third volume of the Philosophy of Civilization to a sketch of the general trend of human thought in religion, mysticism, and philosophy, with the aim of showing how these three forms of thought supplement, complete, and interpenetrate one another—in their quest for that ultimate truth which gives purpose and direction to our existence. The several sketches which he made of these three forms of thought, extending as they did over a period of years and expanding beyond the limits of reduction into a single chapter, compelled him to the decision to make a separate publication of *Indian Thought and its Development*, though in a much abridged compass; and to treat his researches into the Thought of China in the same way, as its sequel.

The literatures of both Indian and Chinese philosophies are of course enormous; beside them that of Europe is as it were a drop in a bucket; and yet Schweitzer, with his penetrating instinct for essentials, seems to have possessed himself of the substance of them both.

Indian Thought and its Development[1] should be read as a sequel to *Civilization and Ethics*, and its first chapter "Western and Indian Thought" should be read in conjunction with the preface to the latter. The impression left upon the reader is that he has studied Indian Thought in a spirit of detachment, objectively; it is only rarely that he can express enthusiasm for any aspect of it, and when he does so this is qualified by a criticism. In this respect his treatment of it contrasts markedly with that of Keyserling, a thinker whose insight into all the philosophical systems of the world is touched with sympathetic feeling. Nevertheless, if Schweitzer's treatment of Indian Thought is critical rather than sympathetic, it is also just;[2] and more important, it is, like all his other work, of a character that is wholly original.

Foreseeing that "the purely critical nature of his investigation" may give offence to Indian readers, Schweitzer in his preface—with that respect for the feelings of others which is second nature to him —asks their pardon in advance. He acknowledges his consciousness of the profundity of Indian thought as well as of an affinity of mind which he shares with its great representative thinkers, ancient and modern; and adds: "The highest honour one can show to a system of thought is to test it ruthlessly with a view to discovering how much truth it contains, just as steel is assayed to try its strength."

He forestalls two further criticisms. First, on the score of "the deliberate brevity of his treatise" which sets forth, not to describe Indian philosophy in detail, but to demonstrate its approach to the fundamental problems of living and the solutions which it attempts. Secondly, on the score of his deliberate omission of reference to Indian religious beliefs, since "all arguments from History are only of relative importance where thought is concerned." That is to say,

---

[1] Translated by Mrs. C. E. B. Russell (1936).
[2] Except, in this writer's opinion, on the subject of primitive Buddhism.

his treatise excludes Indian metaphysics on the one hand, and Indian theology on the other. It also excludes Indian psychology. Its concern is with ethics, which is after all the fundamental problem for man: how he ought to live, how realize his place and purpose in the universe and his union with infinite Being. Schweitzer explains that he was first drawn to study Indian thought through his acquaintance with the philosophy of Schopenhauer (this was actually as far back as his student days).

> From the very beginning I was convinced that all thought is really concerned with the great problem of how man can attain to spiritual union with infinite Being. My attention was drawn to Indian thought because it is busied with this problem and because by its nature it is mysticism. What I liked about it also was that Indian ethics are concerned with the behaviour of man to all living beings and not merely with his attitude to his fellow-man and to human society.[1]

But as his study of it deepened he found himself "assailed with doubts" as to whether Schopenhauer's account of Indian philosophy (and the accounts of other Europeans also), that it is entirely pessimistic (world- and life-denying), could be correct; but was compelled to recognize that there are, from its very origins, "optimistic" elements (world- and life-affirming) interwoven with its pessimism, and that it is this fusion of the two which constitutes its special characteristic and has determined its development.

Some sentences of the conclusion of his preface must be quoted:

> When Western and Indian philosophy engage in disputation, they must not contend in the spirit that aims at the one proving itself right in opposition to the other. Both are the guardians of valuable treasures of thought. But both must be moving along the path towards a way of thinking which shall pass beyond all the differences of the historical past and eventually be shared in common by all mankind. . . .
>
> For there must indeed arise a philosophy profounder and more living than our own, and endowed with greater spiritual and ethical force. . . . It is for this that we must strive.[2]

"We know very little about any thought except our own, especi-

---

[1] Preface to *Indian Thought*, p. vi.   [2] *Ibid.* pp. ix–x.

ally about Indian thought." With this sentence the book opens and it is a salutary reproof to European intellectual complacency. The chapter of which this sentence forms the text is a very close and careful analysis of the distinctive features of Indian thought, and of the complexities involved in it for Western comprehension.

For the sake of brevity European thought has been classified as optimistic, and Indian thought as pessimistic. "But these expressions do not define the distinction in its essential nature."—Optimistic thought may be defined as a conviction that life is worth living; it asserts the value of existence in general and of one's own existence within it; it seeks to promote and enhance life; it is therefore "world- and life-affirmation." Pessimistic thought is convinced that life is not worth living; it denies any value to existence; it seeks to discourage the impulse to live (though it does not encourage the actual destruction of life); it is therefore "world- and life-negation." But neither of these attitudes is determined by circumstances, whether favourable or unfavourable: each rests upon an inner determination of the will. And when the will is in control, then the optimistic attitude manifests itself outwardly in the active ethic of self-devotion ; and the pessimistic attitude inwardly as the passive ethic of self-perfection.

> The most profound world- and life-affirmation is that which has been hard won from an estimate of things unbiassed by illusion and even wrested from misfortune; whilst the most profound world- and life-negation is that which is developed in theory in despite of a naturally serene disposition and happy outward circumstances.[1]

In Indian thought both these attitudes are found to exist side by side, though pessimism predominates. In certain periods of European thought the same parallelism is apparent, notably in Neo-Platonism, Gnosticism, and Stoicism, though optimism on the whole predominates.

The world-view of Jesus is unique and distinct from either, by the fact that although it is pessimistic (in expectation of the imminent end of the natural world and the supervention upon it of the supernatural), it nevertheless enjoins an activist ethic of self-devotion as well as a passive ethic of self-perfection, and both in an absolute sense.

[1] *Indian Thought*, p. 20.

In the profoundest form of world- and life-affirmation, in which man lives his life on the loftiest spiritual and ethical plane, he attains to inner freedom from the world and becomes capable of sacrificing his life for some end. This profoundest world- and life-affirmation can assume the appearance of world- and life-negation. But that does not make it world- and life-negation: it remains what it is—the loftiest form of world- and life-affirmation. He who sacrifices his life to achieve any purpose for an individual or for humanity is practising life-affirmation. He is taking an interest in the things of this world and by offering his own life wants to bring about in the world something which he regards as necessary. The sacrifice of life for a purpose is not life-negation, but the profoundest form of life-affirmation placing itself at the service of world-affirmation.[1]

The pessimism of world- and life-negation is an attitude which is in the last resort untenable. Unless it takes the logical course of quitting existence by a self-chosen death, it finds itself bound to make concessions to the optimism of world- and life-affirmation. It may endeavour to avoid this course by adopting a purely passive ethic of self-perfection; that is, by cultivating a spirit which is completely free from enmity, and refraining from inflicting destruction or damage to any living thing; but this sort of renunciation is immature; when ethics comes to full self-consciousness it is bound to manifest itself in activity.

And as a fact the development of Indian thought follows the line of ever greater concessions [to world- and life-affirmation], until at last, as ethics gradually expand, it is forced either to unconfessed or to admitted abandonment of world- and life-denial. But on the circuitous paths which it follows, the thought of India encounters questions and forms of knowledge which we who follow the straight road of our modern world- and life-affirmation either do not meet at all or do not see so plainly. . . . Our world- and life-affirmation needs to try conclusions with the world- and life-negation which is striving after ethics, in order that it may arrive at greater clarity and depth.[2]

Again: whereas the thought of India is monistic and mystical, ours is dualistic and rationalistic. In this we have much—most of all—to learn from India.

[1] Ibid. pp. 6-7.   [2] Ibid. pp. 9-10.

If in the last resort the aim of a world-view is our spiritual unity with infinite Being, then the perfect world-view is of necessity mysticism. Mysticism alone corresponds to the ideal of a world-view. All other world-views are in their very nature incomplete, and fail to correspond with the facts. . . .[1]

The forms which the dualistic interpretation of the Universe has presented are many and various; but on examination each one of them is shown to be fallacious. It is a habit of thought which is based upon ethical belief, and it strives, but in vain, to make the Universe conform to this belief. For the world-process is *not* ethical. "No ethics can be won from knowledge of the Universe. Nor can ethics be brought into harmony with what we know of the Universe." Hence the emergence of a remarkable paradox in European thought. It is one in which naïve thought can rest satisfied, but which deeper thought must seek to resolve. This is the real secret of the monistic mysticism of Spinoza, and also of the monism (which was mysticism unconfessed) of the German Idealists. But this kind of mysticism proves ineffective because what it understands as spiritual unity with infinite Being is really no more than passive absorption into that Being.

The paradox for Indian thought is unrolled, so to speak, from the opposite end of the same scroll. Starting with the passivity of confessed monistic mysticism it finds itself obliged, as ethics takes hold upon it, to make ever greater concessions to dualism, and finally arrives at a position which it originally avoided. Ethical world- and life-affirmation thus finds a footing in its passive mysticism of life-denial. Nevertheless, in spite of this, Indian thinkers have remained faithful to their mysticism. "It is true that they cannot make a reality of the ideal of which they confess themselves adherents. Their mysticism is inadequate, in its nature, as to its content. But what a magnificent thing it is that they do not abandon the ideal!"

What is required is a synthesis between European and Indian thought which will result in the attainment of a mysticism of ethical world- and life-affirmation. Can such a consummation be realized? In *Civilization and Ethics* Schweitzer has already shown that it can.[2]

How did Indian thought arrive at the attitude of world- and life-negation? There is but little trace of it in the earliest literature—the Vedic hymns. These, on the contrary, are for the most part full of a simple joy in existence. The gods, Indra, Angi, Varuna, Mitra, and

---

[1] *Indian Thought*, p. 11.   [2] *Op. cit.* chap. xix.

the rest, are propitious to man and can be placated by sacrifices [it is a polytheism somewhat similar in character to the early Greek]. But there is also in them an independent element of life-negation at a crude level. This is apparent in the practices of the Shamans (the magicians) to attain to a state of ecstasy artificially induced through intoxication, mortification of the flesh, and self-hypnosis. "Thus possessed, they regard themselves as beings into whom the gods have entered, and believe themselves in possession of supernatural powers. This consciousness of being uplifted above the world is the condition determining Indian world- and life-negation." It is to be noted that it was the privilege of the few, and also that it was sought only after the first part of life had been spent in the ordinary way. The origin of world- and life-negation in India is therefore associated with ideas of magic. "It belonged to a sacerdotal form of thought which was developed alongside popular thought."

There is no mention of the Brahmins (the priests) in the earliest Vedic hymns (the Rig-Veda); this occurs only in the latest (the Atharva-Veda), and with it also the first mention of caste. With the ancient Brahmins the idea of magic is fully developed: by sacrificial acts and incantations they, united with the supra-sensuous Power, become superior to the gods whom they can make subservient to their will. Here was a period pregnant with possibilities for the future development of Indian thought: the evolution from polytheism to ethical monotheism. But it failed to take this course. No prophet, no Zarathustra, arose in India to transform and complete the early faith. There was no recoil from the traditional ceremonialism towards an inward religion of the will. A development did occur, however; it proved to be a development from crude magical mysticism into a mystical—but as yet unethical—world-view. Great minds set about the task of a spiritual interpretation of the Vedas, based upon natural observation and reflection. A spiritual world was now believed to underlie the world of sense.

> From being a force exercising control over existence by magic, the Transcendental became for them something which belongs to existence in the ordinary course of Nature. So the doctrine was developed that the real essence of all things is something immaterial and eternal which derives from the primal cause of the Immaterial, from the World-Soul, and that it participates in the World-Soul and returns to it.[1]

[1] *Indian Thought*, p. 29.

This World-Soul they called the Brahman (Power).

But now the word Atman (Breath) is also used to denote the Immaterial, the Supra-sensuous; at first only in connection with the individual entity; later, the word is applied to the whole universe. This means that henceforth union with infinite Being is conceived of —no longer as the privilege of the priestly few—but as a possibility for all men. Thus the mystical world-view of the Upanishads—with its famous *Tat twam asi* (Thou art That)—comes in to displace the magical mysticism of the Brahminic caste. "From this time on world- and life-negation is valid for man as man." Ecstasy is no longer thought of as attainable by the old, crude, materialistic methods of the Shamans, but as a concentration of the Spirit on the Supra-sensuous. It has its definite and prescribed psychical exercises. Schweitzer will not allow that the Upanishads are to be understood as if union with the Brahman can result from reflection by the light of reason, although some passages in them do lend colour to such an interpretation.

Although the Upanishads teach universalism in respect of the possibility of mystical union with the Infinite, there seems to be no anticipation in them that numerous members of other castes might devote themselves to world- and life-negation. The "double standard of morality" as between priesthood and laity (to borrow a phrase from Mediaeval Christendom) persisted, and it persisted also in the personal life of the Brahmin, divided as it was between life-affirmation in youth and life-negation in old age.

> Because Brahmanism had set up for itself an ideal of life containing world- and life-negation and world- and life-affirmation side by side, it became a dam which stemmed the flood-waters of world- and life-negation which burst forth in Jainism and Buddhism.[1]

Although the body of doctrine presented in the Brahmanas and the Upanishads has no ethical content, and being essentially a doctrine of non-activity, makes no pretence to being ethical—it nevertheless prescribes unfailingly one duty of paramount importance: this is the duty of absolute truthfulness. Schweitzer notes this as the test, all the world over, of advance from lower to higher ethics. "The Brahmins do not merely teach truthfulness; they observe it as well."

[1] *Indian Thought*, p. 42.

The Brahmins therefore may be credited with this great and exceedingly rare achievement, that as priests they are altogether intent on truth! Truthfulness blooms as a marvellous flower in the glacier landscape of their chilly world-view. Inadequate as is their morality, it has an essentially distinguished quality.[1]

Thus far Schweitzer would appear to have little to say about the teaching of the Upanishads that has not been noticed by other critical European commentators, though few would be found capable of disentangling their ravelled threads with such skill and precision. But when he comes to deal with the doctrine of reincarnation, and its adoption into Brahmanic teaching, he has some strikingly original observations to make. In the first place he shows that this doctrine is really incompatible with the Brahmanic mystical world-view and therefore cannot be indigenous to it. True, "it has something Brahmanic about it in so far as it assumes that the souls of men, animals, and plants are of like nature"; but it does not presuppose, as Brahmanic mysticism does, the identity of individual souls with the World-Soul. Brahmanic mysticism teaches a continuous emanation of soul-stuff from Brahma, and re-absorption into Brahma, comparable to the rhythmic act of breathing. Reincarnation, however, starting from the premises that all souls are imprisoned and enmeshed in the world of sense, teaches emancipation through a cycle of rebirths in which each soul, preserving the indestructible core of its own individuality, works out its own salvation and earns its own redemption. The first is universalistic (at least in theory), the other is particularistic. The one is supra-ethical, the other ethical. Schweitzer's explanation of the reason why Brahmanism was obliged, despite itself, to incorporate this alien doctrine into its system, and his account of the modification which the doctrine underwent in the process, would seem to be an important contribution to the study of Indian thought. He concludes this extremely informative section of his book by posing a series of six "problems" which the teaching of the Upanishads by implication raises, but does not solve. Summarized very briefly, they are as follows:

(1) What is really to be understood by the Brahman?—According to the genuine Brahmanic teaching, the Brahman is the impersonal Absolute without attributes (*Neti-neti*, that is, beyond

---

[1] *Ibid.* p. 46.

definition). But the Brahman is also described as the highest spiritual Being that unites all forms of perfection in itself. Occasionally
also as the Primal Force that indwells and maintains all Being.
Sometimes even as the highest divine Person.

Samkara tried to explain these vacillations of thought by assuming the Upanishads to present an esoteric truth which covers the
first definition, and an exoteric truth which suffices for the rest.
But this is to read into the Upanishads an interpretation which
was not in the mind of the Brahmins.

(2) In what relationship does the World-Soul stand to the world
of sense?—The more ancient Upanishads accept the world of sense
as something real. But they later regard the World-Soul as en-
veloped in the sense-world as in a veil. This veil is an illusion, a
phantom shadow-play (*Maya*), from which the individual soul
must free itself by the force of right reflection.

But man cannot engage in ethical activity in a world which has
no meaning. The Brahmins therefore cannot logically justify even
the little which they demand from ethics.

(3) How do individual souls come into existence from the
World-Soul and how are they re-absorbed into it?—The earlier
Upanishads evade this question or answer it by the use of metaphors.
But when the doctrine of reincarnation is introduced, the theory
of emanation and re-absorption becomes no longer tenable. The
individual soul is no longer a mere spectator of the stage-play in
the world of sense, but an active participator in it. His final destiny
is no longer passive absorption in the impersonal World-Soul, but
active individual persistence in a realm of eternal bliss.

(4) What is the connection between the individual soul and its
physical manifestation?—According to the original Brahmanic
teaching the soul is unaffected by its physical manifestation. But
according to the later teaching the soul participates in the corporeal and is affected by its experiences therein. Indian thought here
encounters in fact exactly the same problems that confronted
Descartes: to make comprehensible how soul and body, if by
their nature they have nothing in common, can stand in any
relationship to each other whatever.

(5) According to the Brahmins the only value attaching to ethics
is as preparation for deliverance from the cycle of re-births. The
actual deliverance is affected, not by good deeds, but by knowledge, renunciation of the world, and self-submergence.—But can
ethics rest in such a one-sided limitation of its activity?

(6) The Brahmins concede to world- and life-affirmation the
fulfilment in early life of the obligations dictated by caste. This is

the recognized preliminary to world- and life-negation in old age, and is equally meritorious. But now that members of other castes —warriors and agriculturalists—are entering in on the same path of ultimate union with the Brahman, and assuming the right to do so from youth up, what becomes of the obligations dictated by caste? The Upanishads are silent upon this; but the challenge is met centuries later in the courageous mode of thought which finds expression in the Bhagavad-Gita.[1]

With such complexities implicit thus early in Indian thought, it is no cause for wonder that revolutions of thought as non-mystical as the Samkhya doctrine, Jainism, and Buddhism, could co-exist with the original mystical world-view of the Brahmins. The concern of these three is with liberation from the cycle of re-births, and of the two latter with its relation to ethics. Yet they could only maintain themselves for a time in the mystical atmosphere of Indian thought. The mysticism of identity with the Primal Origin of Being was to prove victorious in the end.

The Samkhya doctrine is a development out of the later Brahmanism, as influenced by the doctrine of reincarnation, and it therefore abandons monism. It represents a transitional stage in the history of Indian thought which is of great importance. In its dualistic interpretation of existence it has strong affinities with Graeco-Oriental Gnosticism. Spirit has need of matter as a mode of manifestation in order to arrive at full self-consciousness: there is a partial anticipation of Hegel's thought in this. In its pluralistic explanation of matter-entities and soul-entities united each to each there is also a distinct resemblance to the thought of Leibnitz. [In its theory of unending cycles of existence it would appear also to anticipate an aspect of Stoic philosophy, though Schweitzer does not notice this.] Both modern theosophy and modern anthroposophy owe their ideas to it. But, seen in its own place and time, its importance lies in the fact not only that it paved the way for the exalted ethics of Jainism and Buddhism, but also because many of its doctrines have become the common spiritual heritage of India: for example, "Every villager is familiar with the teaching contained in the three *Gunas*." Schweitzer finds himself able to say of it: "Rarely in human thought has a theoretical problem been so clearly recognized; rarely has a solution been undertaken and achieved with such clear judgment."

[1] *Indian Thought*, pp. 56-64.

In ancient Indian thought there are two kinds of world- and life-negation to be discerned which are really distinct from one another, —a fact which is constantly overlooked. There is 'first the supra-ethical mysticism of the Brahmins for whom world- and life-negation is an end in itself; here, no ideas of redemption are present; the immaterial spirit returns intrinsically unchanged by its pilgrimage in the flesh to its source, the World-Soul. There are secondly a variety of ethical systems in which world- and life-negation is a means to an end, namely redemption, attainable through purification of the psychic *ego* during its cycle of re-births.

In Jainism the stress is on the purificatory aspect of the whole ethical redemptive process. This represents a departure, in a practical direction, from the theoretical doctrine of the Samkhya. "The idea of being exalted above the world is replaced by that of keeping pure from the world—an event full of significance for the thought of India!" In Jainism the purely ethical aspect of world- and life-negation first comes to light as something of more vital import than ceremonial rite or traditional *gnosis*. And the injunction not to hurt nor destroy any living creature now takes precedence as the great commandment—*Ahimsa*. This commandment did not, however (as Schweitzer is careful to point out), originate in India out of a natural feeling of compassion, as it did so originate in China centuries later, but merely from the motive of avoidance of defilement. "It belongs originally to the ethic of becoming more perfect, not to the ethic of action." But when once *Ahimsa* has been generally accepted it operates with an educative effect; it awakens sympathy. Hence the Jains' abstention from the age-old ceremonial sacrifices of the Brahmins (an advance comparable to that of the Hebrew prophets upon the Levites' sacrificial butcheries). This is "one of the greatest events in the spiritual history of mankind" and it remains "the great merit of Indian thought." It remains so in spite of the fact that the Jains did not realize the complexity which this problem involves for ethics, or perceive that its application without limits and without qualification is an impossibility.

However seriously man undertakes to abstain from killing or damaging, he cannot entirely avoid it. He is under the law of necessity, which compels him to kill and to damage both with and without his knowledge. In many ways it may happen that by slavish adherence to the commandment not to kill, compassion is less served than by breaking it. When the suffering of a living creature cannot be alleviated, it is more ethical to end its life by killing it mercifully than it is to stand aloof. It is more cruel to let domestic animals, which can no longer feed, die a painful death by starvation than to give them a quick and painless end by violence. Again and again we see ourselves placed under the necessity of saving one living creature by destroying or damaging another.[1]

But Jainism, though it has endured down to the present day, has lost much of the importance which it had, since its tenets are embraced and far developed in Buddhism.

By many minds—and those not necessarily of professed adherents of Buddhism—the personality of its Founder is felt to be too tremendous to be approached without veneration, and his teaching so exalted as to place it on a plane beyond criticism. This is not the case with Schweitzer. He subjects this phase of Indian thought to the same keen analytical examination as he does the rest. Although he is conscious of traversing a region far beyond that which even the loftiest aspirations of the Upanishads attained, he is not conscious of treading upon holy ground. His admiration for the Buddha's spiritual achievement is qualified by several criticisms of his ethical system which ultimately resolve themselves into one: that it stops short in what he elsewhere (in dealing with Stoicism) describes as only "the vestibule of ethics"—renunciation.

In the Buddha he sees affinities with Luther. Both were religious reformers; both struggled with the problem of redemption; both were champions of the principle of freedom; both had sought redemption by the path of "works," and both had abandoned it for the path of "inwardness"; in both there is an elemental "naturalness." But what he fails to observe is that the insights of Luther were derived; the repository of his spiritual illumination was the Bible. But those of the Buddha were entirely original: as Schweitzer says himself, "The Buddha broke with the sacred writings of the Brahmins just as he broke with their doctrine. The four Vedas, the Brahmanas and the Upanishads were nothing to him."

He sees also affinities between the Buddha and St. Paul. Neither were social reformers, because for both of them the terrestrial world is something that was doomed to pass away. Just as St. Paul does not

---

[1] *Indian Thought*, pp. 83-84. This passage should be read in conjunction with the chapter "The Ethic of Reverence for Life" in *Civilization and Ethics*.

demand the abolition of slavery, so neither does the Buddha attack the validity of caste. Both regard the eating of flesh (the Buddha, if placed in his alms-bowl; St. Paul, if slaughtered for heathen sacrifices) with the same kind of tolerance. [There is another obvious affinity also: St. Paul received not his tradition from men, but by direct revelation, as did also the Buddha.]

Such comparisons are legitimate, even though (in this writer's view) they are unessential and somewhat irrelevant. But when an essential comparison is drawn between the Christ and the Buddha, and when it is made in order to point a contrast—this is another matter.

Jesus and the Buddha have this in common, that their form of ethics, because it is under the influence of world- and life-negation, is not an ethic of action, but an ethic of inner perfection. But in both the ethic of inner perfection is governed by the principle of love. It therefore carries within it the tendency to express itself in action, and in this way has a certain affinity with world- and life-affirmation. With Jesus the ethic of the perfecting of the self commands active love: with the Buddha it does not get so far.[1] . . . The ethic of action in the spirit of love remains outside the circle of his vision. It is only what is spiritual in the world that he wants to alter, not earthly conditions. It does not occur to him to abandon the principle of non-activity, although the thought of action is already present in his ethics.[2]

Now in the first place it might be argued that this is a comparison which ought not to be made (for it is made in contravention of the first sentence of the conclusion to his preface above quoted); and also that it is a straining of a comparison. It is very debatable whether the Buddha's ethic of love was in fact so passive as it is represented. Indeed, Schweitzer himself refers to "cases in which the Buddha in person allowed himself to be carried away, and acted from the motive of love." He mentions the Buddha's personal care of the monk suffering from dysentery, and his exhortation: "Whoever would nurse me should nurse the sick." But Schweitzer would maintain that such cases are exceptional, that they really do not form an integral part of the Buddha's ethic.

[1] *Indian Thought*, p. 113. But on p. 153 where the same comparison is made again, in order to show that both Buddhism and Christianity, despite their world- and life-negation, contain the germs of world- and life-affirmation,—the derogation in respect to Buddhism is omitted.
[2] *Ibid.* p. 108.

In the personality of the Buddha, so great in its humanity, ethics are so strong and so living that they really find no place in the inactivity demanded by world- and life-negation. But they do not revolt against it and shatter it, but, wherever occasion offers, as is the natural result, go beyond it, just as pent-in water overflows the dam at one spot and another.[1]

In the second place, to judge from the principle that a tree is known by its fruits, there is evidence of a spirit of active self-devotion inspired by primitive Buddhism (not only by later Buddhism) in the enormous number of philanthropic institutions and beneficent activities in Ceylon and elsewhere in Asia. These surely cannot be disregarded in any estimate of the abiding influence of the Buddha's own teaching.

In the third place there is the effect which the Buddha's personality produced upon his contemporaries. Schweitzer acknowledges this. There was "a power that went forth from him"—it was "a radiation of kindliness" that was said to have affected not only human beings, but also animals. "It constitutes the secret of his powerful and simple personality." And yet Schweitzer says in another place: "He was no Francis of Assisi,"—and maintains that the Buddha's compassion was "a compassion of the understanding, but not of the heart." By this he would imply that the Buddha was overwhelmed by the spectacle of the universal tragedy of existence, but that he held aloof from personal contact with it and sought for its remedy solely in the intellectual sphere; in other words, that his concern about the Problem of Pain was (like Schopenhauer's) theoretical, not practical.

He, the acute investigator of the theory of knowledge, passes by the elementary problem whether ethics can really be limited to non-activity, or whether they must not also enter the domain of action, as if he were smitten with blindness. World- and life-negation is a solid certainty for him as a matter of course. He is unconscious that compassion means a protest against it coming from the very depths of human nature.[2]

While it must be fully admitted that this is the impression which the Buddha's teaching leaves upon us, it leaves unexplained the impression produced upon us of his personality. How could so powerful

[1] *Ibid.* p. 114.   [2] *Ibid.* p. 109.

a radiation of goodness have proceeded from a will that knew only renunciation and from a heart devoid of compassion?

There is evidently something about the Buddha and his teaching which Schweitzer finds baffling. He cannot make the Buddha completely accord with his own view of primitive Buddhism as entirely world- and life-denying. He admits that a similar difficulty exists with regard to the teaching of the Christ.

> For us Europeans—and for modern Indians no less—there is a certain difficulty in visualizing the historical Buddha and his teaching as they really were. We cannot reconcile ourselves to the fact that the great teacher of compassion in theory was still so completely governed by world- and life-negation and the principle of non-activity which results from it. This will not fit into the ideal portrait which we should like to paint of him. It gives to his character some quality which seems alien to us. And his ethics trouble us because they are incomplete.
>
> With the Buddha we have a similar experience to that which we pass through when we study Jesus. It is difficult for us to admit that the thought and ethics of Jesus were influenced by a longing expectation of the end of the world. But we have sufficient reliable information to compel us to see both teachers as they really were.[1]

Thus Schweitzer sees the Buddha as "the creator of the ethic of inner perfection"—and of no more.

> He gave to India something it did not yet possess: an ethic derived from thought. Up to then it only knew a traditional morality of virtues and duties, and such an ethic as that is only capable of development up to a certain point. . . . When the Buddha exalted compassionate love to be the fundamental principle of morality, he breathed into Indian ethics a new breath of life.
>
> In this sphere he gave expression to truths of everlasting value, and advanced the ethics—not of India alone—but of humanity. He was one of the greatest ethical men of genius ever bestowed upon the world.[2]

He might also have added—"one of the most penetrating intelligences." For the intellectual stature of the Buddha is surely something quite outstanding—not only in India—but also in the world.

---

[1] *Indian Thought*, pp. 115-116.   [2] *Ibid.* pp. 117 and 119.

The Buddha is too great a teacher to be classed as but one among the teachers of India, and primitive Buddhism is too vast a subject to be treated as but a phase in the development of Indian thought. The Buddha is unique in that he is the pioneer in the quest and discovery of *cosmic law*. His teaching is elementally simple and profound. His utterances have a ring of finality and inevitability about them—nowhere is it possible to detect in them inconsistency or ambiguity. Indian Thought in general is concerned with an abstract theoretical world-view; Semitic Thought, and also European Thought in the main, are concerned with an abstract theoretical theodicy. The Buddha is concerned with neither of these—in fact, he rejects them; his concern is with the law that governs the universe, man's place therein, and how he should conform to it in the practical conduct of his life. Stoicism is the nearest approximation to this in European Thought, but its ethic is mixed up—as the Buddha's never is—with speculative theories about the nature of the Universe. Of the two, primitive Buddhism is by far the profounder, and it is strange that Schweitzer, who was so strongly attracted by Stoicism, should have allowed Buddhism to pass him by.

Lastly, is it true that the Buddha was no mystic?—It is certainly true that he utterly repudiated any theoretical mystical world-view, but was he not himself in the highest sense a practical mystic? (Schweitzer is himself a supreme example of a practical Christian mystic who repudiates the pre-suppositions of theoretical Christianity.) What was his experience of enlightenment and deliverance under the Bo-tree but an experience of mysticism in the intensest degree? and what is *Nirvana* to him, in the last resort, but the eternal consummation of the same experience?

In general, it must be said that Schweitzer looks at Buddhism too much through the eyes of a European, and his account of it suffers from his desire to contrast it unfavourably with Christianity. For, in the last resort and when all is said, does the Buddha's doctrine of the "extinction of the will-to-live" and of *Nirvana* differ essentially from the magnificent paradox of Jesus, "He that loveth his life loseth it, and he that loseth it keepeth it unto life eternal"?

Schweitzer sees Mahayana-Buddhism as the logical outcome of primitive Buddhism.—"In Buddha the ethical is so strongly developed that it is already an end in itself. He does not admit this, but leaves ethics still in the service of the redemption dominated by world- and life-negation." But the Mahayana does admit it, and no longer regards personal redemption as the highest good. Hence those who have attained redemption—the Bodhisattvas, of whom the Buddha himself is one—voluntarily renounce entrance into *Nirvana* in order to reincarnate for the purpose of rescuing all those who as yet are unredeemed.

> How profound is the saying, "As long as living creatures suffer, there is no possibility of joy for those who are full of compassion." For the first time in the thought of mankind, world-view is dominated by the idea of compassion.[1]

But, like primitive Buddhism, the Mahayana is still tied to the idea of world- and life-negation, and its way of redemption is the way of knowledge, not of practical mercy. It indulges in the "imaginary activity" of compassionate desires, long intercessory supplications and the like, but refrains itself from the positive ethic of self-devotion. Nevertheless—"How wonderful that there was once a time when there were in the world millions of people so entirely dominated by feelings of compassion"!

The Buddha had denied the existence or identity of the psychic ego (Atman), along with his denial of the metaphysical Primal Source of Being (Brahma). But it is only from the epistemological point of view that he is agnostic. "Without embarrassment he premises the Self for the purpose of ethics, the Self whose existence he denies in his theory of knowledge." On the basis of this, Mahayana-Buddhism denied any distinction between the I and the Thou. The Upanishads had explained all love as self-love on the ground that, because the same Brahman dwells in others as in ourselves, that which seems to be neighbour-love is only the profoundest self-love. Mahayana-Buddhism explains all love as neighbour-love on the ground of a similar identity. As Schweitzer justly observes:

> These contrary assertions come to the same thing in the long run. By both of them ethics are reduced to nothing by the explanations given. True ethics presume the absolute difference of one's own ego and those of others and accentuate it. The difference, however, is not a plain matter of course, but an enigma.[2]

Again: in the opinion of the teachers of the Mahayana, the Buddha

[1] *Indian Thought*, p. 125.   [2] *Ibid.* p. 131.

had denied the existence of the external world apart from consciousness, for which however it exists only as illusion (*Maya*). Enlightenment delivers consciousness from the delusion that the world of the senses is a reality. In the Mahayana, this opinion was given the force of a dogma: "All is Nothing."

> But what (asks Schweitzer) is compassion doing in an unreal world? How can Mahayana-Buddhism combine its ethics with its nihilistic doctrine of existence?—This is only possible on the hypothesis of a twofold truth. For if our existence and the existence of the Universe are merely the vision of a dream, they nevertheless as such have for us a relative reality. We must behave in a way which corresponds with the imagined world and our supposed existence in it. As this world seems to us full of suffering, it is our duty to strive to bring the suffering in it to an end.[1]

Buddhism eventually disappeared from India because it could not sustain itself in competition with the mystical world-view of Brahmanism, and later of Hinduism, which are congenital to Indian thought. That it was able to do so at all, and for so many centuries, is due to the fact that it was "the creation of a great mind," and because its ethics are superior to theirs. "After long hesitation the spirit of India was obliged in the main to reject the Buddha's world- and life-negation. But it kept his ethic."

Schweitzer's account of the passage of Buddhism from India to the Far East—to China, Tibet, Mongolia, and Japan—and of the changes it underwent in the process, is a further testimony to the range and thoroughness of his learning. Though his treatment of this subject provides no new contribution to the study, it is distinguished as always by the sure touch of an original mind.

Meanwhile the Brahmanic doctrine was pursuing its independent course in India with the formulation of the Vedanta, which stereotypes the main doctrine of the Upanishads—identity with the World-Soul. It receives its final fixation in the Brahmasutras. These essay the impossible task of reconciling identity of the soul and the World-Soul with the doctrine of deliverance through incarnation, and represents the beginnings of Brahmanic scholasticism. Samkara is in fact "the Thomas Aquinas of Brahmanism." Schweitzer's exposition of this obscurantist movement of thought—"The Doctrine of Two-

[1] *Ibid.* p. 132.

fold Truth," esoteric and exoteric—is penetrating, but it cannot be followed here.

Samkara is called the completer of the Brahmanic doctrine. He is that, but at the same time he is the beginning of its end. He thinks out in detail the Brahmanic mysticism of union with the Universal Soul, and preserves for it its majestic greatness. But at the same time he admits another mysticism to a place beside it.[1]

This is the *bhakti* mysticism of Hinduism. It represents the trend of popular religion in the direction of monotheism, which, though for centuries retarded by the Brahmanic mysticism, could no longer be ignored by it. Hinduism is of course a term that is used to cover every conceivable variety of Indian religious thought, but is here used in its more properly specific sense to denote the doctrine of personal manifestations (*avataras*) of divinities incarnate in human guise, for the purpose of redemption through the way of knowledge. In its zeal for activity Hinduism contains within it impulses towards world- and life-affirmation, but this wholesome impulse was checked by the influence of Brahmanic authority that underlay it. "It nowhere makes the demand that love to God shall be actively realized as love to man."

So this is what happens in Hindu thought—that world- and life-affirmation with ever-increasing strength rises in rebellion against the world- and life-negation forced upon Indian thought by the Brahmins, and finally carries the day. But it does not accomplish this by its own intrinsic power. It only becomes capable of victory through the alliance it has made with ethics.[2]

The first signs of the conflict appear in the Bhagavad-Gita. Some eminent European thinkers (among them von Humboldt)—captivated by the matchless beauty of its phrasing concerning inner detachment from the world, loving-kindness, and self-devotion to God—have regarded this famous poem as the high-water mark of personal mysticism, not only in Indian but in world literature, comparable with, if not indeed surpassing, that flower of ethical Christian world- and life-affirmation which might have blossomed but for the blighting frost of scholasticism. Schweitzer takes a soberer view.

[1] *Indian Thought*, p. 164.   [2] *Ibid.* p. 180.

In reality the Bhagavad-Gita has nothing of such a spirit. It is only an attempt undertaken by magnificent, unimpassioned thought to gain recognition for the idea of self-devotion to God by activity within the world-view of world- and life-negation. . . . It grants recognition to activity, but only after activity has renounced natural motives and its natural meaning. . . . The charm of the Bhagavad-Gita is due to this idea of spiritualized activity which springs only from the highest of motives. . . . It is not merely the most read, but also the most idealized, book in world-literature.[1]

For others, it represents the finest flowers of Indian mysticism thrown together as it were in a wild disordered cluster, from which any and every devotee may cull his particular choice. But Schweitzer discerns a consistent plan and purpose in its arrangement. In masterly fashion he disentangles the medley, and is able to explain each apparent inconsistency as it arises. "If one would rightly understand the Bhagavad-Gita, one must not forget the Brahmanic narrowness of its horizon."

Here, then, the age-old conflict between the affirmative and negative attitudes to life reach a culminating point. It is age-old, because elements of affirmation had been present in Indian thought since the earliest Vedic hymns and had existed ever since subterraneously in the popular world-view, for it is after all the natural attitude to life. But does the poem succeed in resolving this difference?

It begins by professing unreservedly the Brahmanic belief that life in the world is only a phantom shadow-play that God acts with himself; for us, the marionettes, it has no meaning. But it will not admit the Brahmanic deduction from this that we should withdraw ourselves as inactive spectators of the scene. Man should play his part as an active participant in this play that God has 'staged. (Here Schweitzer sees a remarkable anticipation of the thought of Fichte.) Yet inactivity, too, may lead to salvation, though activity is better. In either case it is the inner motive that counts, not the ulterior aim. (Here is an obvious anticipation of Kant.) But absolute inactivity is not the will of God; nor is it practicable. God himself is active in creating and sustaining the universe; man is active by the very fact of living. But, it is to be observed, whenever Krishna speaks of activity in the poem, no more and no less is intended than "the exercise of the activity dictated by caste," and he defines it as "the

[1] *Ibid.* p. 195.

totality of the obligations which naturally belong to a man's station in life." And yet it is not man, but God, who works—and who worketh all in all. "All that a man does is a happening sent by God. Krishna finds the reconciliation of the bondage and the freedom of the will in the fact that man in spiritual self-surrender accomplishes what God does by means of him." Evil as well as good is therefore the act of the selfsame God: evil, that is to say, which by human standards is judged to be evil.

> The ultimate question man has to ask himself is whether the work he resolves on comes to him as a task which must be fulfilled, and whether he accomplishes it in purest self-surrender to God. . . . Krishna then dares to confess the simple truth that if the freedom of the will be denied, there can be no question of guilt.[1]

In criticism of this supra-ethical ethic Schweitzer points out that activity which is not purposive in a natural way has no significance. The only activity which is really worth the name is that which sets natural aims before it and realizes these in self-devotion to a supreme end. The ethic contained in the Bhagavad-Gita is not natural. There is in it no genuine loving self-devotion to the God of Love. God is for it a value completely exalted above good and evil.

> In the struggle for the true world-view as it is enacted in the thought of humanity, the ultimate question is always this—how can man, not only in thinking and in suffering, but also in acting, become one with infinite Being? How can he combine the part of being the instrument of incomprehensible supra-ethical necessity, and at the same time of being an ethical personality?[2]

The great unknown thinker of the Bhagavad-Gita does not answer this. He cannot solve the great problem—the problem of the mysticism of action.

Far higher than the Bhagavad-Gita, or than any of the ethical philosophies which preceded it, Schweitzer ranks the simple natural ethic of activity as we find it expressed in the Kural. This is indeed "the living ethic of love."—"There hardly exists in the literature of the world a collection of maxims in which we find so much lofty wisdom." This is world- and life-affirmation at its best, and we find it voiced again in the teaching of Ramananda where "at last the

---

[1] *Indian Thought*, p. 189.   [2] *Ibid.* p. 194.

thought is developed that devotion to God must be manifested in love to man."

Schweitzer devotes a concluding chapter to a series of appreciative biographical sketches of several modern Indian thinkers, especially to the life and thought of Gandhi and Rabindranath Tagore, of both of whom he writes with admiration. This is qualified to a slight extent, in the case of the former, by a criticism of Gandhi's interpretation of the doctrine of *Ahimsa* as non-resistance.

> Gandhi places Ahimsa at the service of world- and life-affirmation, directed to activity within the world, and in this way it ceases to be what in essence it is. Passive resistance is a non-violent use of force. The idea is that, by circumstances brought about without violence, pressure is brought to bear on the opponent and he is forced to yield. Being an attack that is more difficult to parry than an active attack, passive resistance may be the more successful method. But there is also a danger that this concealed application of force may cause more bitterness than an open use of violence. In any case the difference between passive and active resistance is only quite relative. . . . All mixing up of what is different in essence is an unnatural and dangerous proceeding.[1]

In Gandhi, the affirmative and negative attitudes to life, "which go back to the Buddha," exist side by side. In Tagore, the affirmative has completely triumphed. Tagore condemns passive mysticism as an aberration of Oriental thought, but he also condemns European activity as a loss of inwardness. "He demands both together: that man should belong to God with his soul, and serve Him actively in the world." But Schweitzer maintains that Tagore, in proclaiming this as the ancient Indian wisdom, is doing violence to the texts, and especially to the Upanishads.

> Truth requires no other authority than that which it contains within itself. If the witness of the past can be brought forward to support it, it more easily finds recognition than without that witness. But the truth must never be violently interpolated into the thought of an earlier period in order that it may there find justification. In itself truth possesses such power of carrying conviction that it has no need to turn to history for a recommendation.[2]

These sentences are of the first importance for an understanding

Ibid. pp 231-232.   *Ibid.* pp. 243-244.

of Schweitzer's whole philosophy. Compare his words quoted on p. 70 of this book: "Truth has no special time of its own. Its hour is now—always."

Tagore is in the wrong, too, in his endeavour to interpret the universe ethically. "In Tagore's magnificent thought-symphony the harmonies and modulations are Indian. But the theme reminds us of those of European thought. . . . He has not yet studied the question whether ethical idealism must not renounce the claim that its foundations rest on knowledge of the Universe." Nevertheless, and in spite of inaccuracies of thinking, Tagore—"the Goethe of India"—has expressed the affirmative world-view "in a manner more profound, more powerful, and more charming, than any man has ever done before him. This completely noble and harmonious thinker belongs not only to his own people, but to humanity."

It is a noteworthy feat of exposition to have surveyed the whole field of essential Indian thought, as Schweitzer has done, in the compass of 265 pages. Several aspects of his elucidation of the subject are necessarily omitted in this all too brief review of it. There are several others also with which he has deliberately refrained from dealing. Among these are the problems connected with the distinctively religious beliefs of India. Had he dealt with these, he would no doubt have traced in the cult of Amidha-Buddha, for example (ensuing from the deification of the man who had utterly repudiated theism), a remarkable parallel with the theological interpretation of the Christian faith as it unfolded itself in the first centuries of our era and beyond them: especially adumbrations of the Augustinian doctrine of Grace, and the Lutheran doctrine of Justification by Faith. The parallel extends itself into an equally remarkable similarity in ecclesiastical practices and beliefs. In "The Lotus of the Buddha," and again (quite independently of that) in the cult of Krishna among the Vishnuite sects, he might have pointed to adumbrations of the doctrine of the incarnation of the Logos. In these and in other respects he might have found support for his own contention, that all theologies are in the end but human ways of thinking about God.

This great book concludes with a chapter in which its author sums up the relationship in which European and Indian thought stand to one another. They seem to confront one another over an as yet unabridged abyss. Neither has yet solved the ultimate problem,—how to attain union with infinite Being, and at the same time engage actively in the finite world of sense. This chapter should be read in its entirety as an introduction to Schweitzer's own philosophy as he expounds it in *Civilization and Ethics*. To select any extracts from it for quotation would be to interrupt the sequence of its thought, and to mar the symmetry of its expression. And as it represents his latest published reflections on the subject (although so long ago as 1935), it is all the more important. So far from being out of date, it is the thought of the world at large—not his—which is a decade behind-hand.

NOTE

Recognition of the importance of this book is attested by the fact that so great an authority as Radhakrishnan, whose wide learning is luminous with fine mystical insight, makes it the main topic of a chapter in his *Eastern Religions and Western Thought* (1940). This chapter is devoted to a (somewhat too discursive) criticism of Schweitzer's estimate of Indian thought, based wholly on the pre-miss that he regards it as entirely world- and life-denying. But, with all due deference to the critic, it must be said that this is precisely what Schweitzer does not do. From the outset of his enquiry, as he distinctly tells us, he was "assailed with doubts" as to whether the usual Western estimate of Indian thought as entirely pessimistic could be really true; his whole interest in the subject lay in his dis-covery of optimistic elements interwoven with its pessimism, from the Vedas to the Bhagavad-Gita and thence to the present day; his search, which ended negatively, was for a principle which would fuse these elements into a mysticism deserving to be called ethical. Radhakrishnan rightly says: "The life and work of Dr. Schweitzer are themselves an example of disciplined asceticism at a time when both purpose and discipline are lacking in the world," but his criti-cism of Schweitzer's appraisal of Indian thought is based on a mis-understanding.

This is not by any means to claim that Schweitzer is always right; he would be the first to admit that his ideas are open to correction. When his friend Father Andrews, acknowledging the fairness of his conclusions as derived from a study of Indian sacred texts, urged that personal contact with India itself might modify them, Schweitzer answered: "You have lived with the Indians, I have only read about them; your judgment is perhaps the truer."

CHAPTER XVIII

THE ETHIC OF REVERENCE FOR LIFE

But in truth it is by much longer than a decade that modern thought is outdistanced by this prophetic thinker. For the conclusions of his book on Indian Thought are but a summing-up of those which he had ventilated in *Civilization and Ethics* nearly a quarter of a century ago; and these again are but the mature expression of reflections that had been stirring in his mind as far back as the 'nineties.

Even then he had divined that our vaunted civilization was doomed because it was no longer rooted in a stable world-view, and had drawn attention to the symptoms of its decay. Scientific inventions and achievements, advancing at unprecedented speed, were already outstripping the power of man to control or direct them, and resulted in the inevitable catastrophe of the first World War. Thereafter, modern thought would appear to have abandoned in despair the search for a stable world-view (that is, for an understanding of man's place and purpose in the universe of which he forms a part), and betook itself instead to the formulation of rival ideologies (that is, conceptions of his place and purpose as a denizen of that particular fragment of the earth's surface in which he happened to be). Mechanization, already the bane of his daily life and occupation, now began to invade the province of man's mind; personality became the victim of organized state-craft and state-machinery; the last vestiges of respect for human values were brushed aside, and in the second World War humanity was well on the way to self-extermination. With the collapse of any stable world-view, civilization itself collapsed and is now in ruins.

There had been a time in the history of European thought when there was a good hope that sanity and humane counsels might prevail which would result in the birth of a civilization as truly civilized as the world had ever seen. This was the Age of Reason in the eighteenth century. The men of the Enlightenment combined an optimistically affirmative attitude to life with the cultivation of an active ethic of enthusiastic self-devotion. This hope was short-lived, however. For when it was found that the world-process itself is not susceptible to an ethical interpretation at all, thought was baffled. If the world-process is indifferent to human behaviour, why should human beings any longer cherish ideals of the highest good? And as a fact idealism fell out of favour: from the middle of the nineteenth century and onwards behaviour came more and more to be guided by actuality, by happenings, by events (miscalled "realism")—by what appears, rather than by what ought to be.

Meanwhile, in this resultant epoch of ethical chaos and confusion, abstract thought has not been idle. "Clever men who stumble about in seven-league boots in the History of Civilization"—have been at work trying to persuade us, as if on the ground of an evolutionary theory, that all civilizations are destined to blossom and perish like leaves on the tree, and because no civilization in the past has endured none in the future ever can. Metaphysicians, too, have been at work, no longer in blazing new trails to the goal of knowledge concerning the nature of the ultimate Reality, but in repairing or side-tracking the old ones, all which, new or old, are "roads that lead nowhere." And now the theologians (though their reappearance on the scene has taken place noticeably since Schweitzer wrote)—concerned with equally abstract notions about the nature of the Supreme Being and of His providential direction of the course of events in human history —have also been busy, not so much in constructing any new edifice for their theodicies, however, as in tinkering with the old ones long since outworn beyond repair—all which, like the systems of metaphysics from which they borrow their precarious foundations, are but "cloud-castles" of their own conceiving. For when one comes to consider the number and variety of metaphysical systems, it is manifest that if one of them is right the others must be wrong, and the choice of which is right must depend upon a subjective preconception. And the preconceptions and subsequent conclusions of theology—whether Christian, Mahayana-Buddhist, or Hindu—are seen on critical examination to have so much in common that all alike, however "dogmatic" their assertions or however "systematic" their scheme of redemption, must be judged as no more than speculative and theoretical flights of the discursive reason.

No thinker—philosopher, theologian, or sociologist—has yet dared to come to terms with the fundamental problem for thought; how to realize union with infinite Being and at the same time to engage actively in the world of sense. The honest mind, bewildered by the abstruse complexities of metaphysics, repelled by the pseudo-rationalistic subtleties and arrogant pretensions of theology, disappointed with the mechanistic propositions of sociology, turns in despair to scepticism, only to find that there is no rest there.

It is here that Schweitzer comes to the rescue of the modern mind with an elemental thought, as simple as it is profound. But before explaining what this thought is, it is necessary to consider the extent of his own intellectual agnosticism.

A historian,—he realizes that historical documents, however well authenticated, can afford us only the most partial glimpses of what really happened in the past; and that sacred history, even were it a hundred-fold completer and more accurate than it is, can never claim —by its very nature as history—to be "revelation."—For "historical knowledge cannot call spiritual life into existence. . . . Spiritual life is independent of any historical confirmation or justification," and knows no limitations of time or space.

A scientist,—he sees no purpose in the world-process, nor any justification for drawing inferences of spiritual law in the natural world, or conversely. Instances where these can be traced are exceptional, they are not the rule. The world as we see it presents a puzzling spectacle of meaningless destructive amid meaningful creative forces: there is nothing ethical about it.—"There is (in the world-process) no knowledge and no hope that can give to our lives either stability or direction."

A theologian,—he sees in the unveiling of the figure of the historical Jesus (an unveiling as objectively true to fact as genuine historical research can make it) a Personality inimical to theology, that escapes logical definition, One whom no words can describe, and who can only be known by active participation in the fellowship of suffering. —"Those who are fond of talking about negative theology" (so he writes at the end of *The Quest*) "can find their account here. There is nothing more negative [for theology] than the result of the critical study of the Life of Jesus."

A philosopher,—he sees the Truth as something which is beyond the power of abstract thought either to discover or to comprehend, and finds that the more systematized any philosophical system is (for example, the immensely imposing systems of an Aristotle or a Hegel), so much the more fallacious it can be shown to be.—"To understand the meaning of the whole—and that is what a world-view demands —is for us an impossibility."

From any one of these purely intellectual standpoints which view the world, and life in the world, detachedly from the standpoint of a spectator, it is impossible to extract any intelligible meaning. "What our thinking tries to proclaim as knowledge is never anything but an unjustifiable interpretation of the world."

> Against the admission of this, thought guards itself with the courage of despair, because it fears it will find itself in that case with no idea of what to do in face of the problem of life. What meaning can we give to human existence, if we must renounce all pretence of knowing the meaning of the world?—Nevertheless, there remains only one thing for thought to do, and that is to adapt itself to facts. . . .[1]
>
> I believe I am the first among Western thinkers who has ventured to recognize this crushing result of knowledge, and who is absolutely sceptical about our knowledge of the world, without at the same time renouncing with it belief in world- and life-affirmation and ethics.[2]

Whether this be so or not (Kraus thinks that he was anticipated by the blind German-Moravian poet Lorm[3]), he is certainly the first who has combined so vast an erudition with so profound a scepticism. It is all the more important to stress this aspect of Schweitzer's thought —this (in his own words) "pessimistic result of knowledge"—in order to contrast it with the enthusiastic optimism of his ethics. Therefore, we must follow him in his scepticism to its ultimate depth.

When thought has reached rock-bottom; when the mind has dared to disabuse itself of its last illusions; when reason has cleared its eyes of all its self-engendered truth-obscuring mists and confronts a sky of brass,—the will-to-live begins to question what value it can any longer assign to its own existence. Since the world is unintelligible, is life itself worth while?

When one looks closely into life, as most people are bound to do before they get to the end of it, there is one reflection above all that presses on the mind with increasingly disturbing force: that life promises more than it fulfils, that it suggests a good which it somehow fails to impart. Some deep disease seems rooted in the world's

---

[1] *Civilization and Ethics*, p. 207.   [2] *Ibid.* p. xi.
[3] Kraus quotes Lorm: "A starving man seizes greedily the food offered him: that is natural. He gives the food to a starving fellow-creature and goes without himself: that is supernatural"—and comments: "It is as if Schweitzer were speaking."

very constitution. More seems to be wrong with the world than can be accounted for by the fact of human sin; there seems to be a radical evil, that everywhere perversely baffles the loftiest human aspirations.[1] No facile optimism, no wishful thinking or fondly cherished preconceptions, can burke these stark, inexorable facts. The pages of history and of biography alike are blurred with the record of lost causes, quenched enthusiasms, frustrated hopes. Schweitzer puts it thus:

> Life attracts us (say the facts) with a thousand expectations, and fulfils hardly one of them. And the fulfilled expectation is almost a disappointment, for only anticipated pleasure is really pleasure; in pleasure which is fulfilled its opposite is already stirring. Unrest, disappointment, and pain are our lot in the short span of time which lies between our entrance upon life and our departure from it. The spiritual is in a dreadful state of dependence on the bodily. Our existence is at the mercy of meaningless happenings and can be brought to an end by them at any moment. The will-to-live gives me an impulse to action, but the action is just as if I wanted to plough the sea, and to sow in the furrows of the waves. What did those who worked before me effect? What significance in the endless chain of world-happenings have their efforts had? With all its illusive promises, the will-to-live only means to mislead me into prolonging my existence, and allowing to enter on existence,— so that the game may go on without interruption—other beings to whom the same miserable lot has been assigned as to myself.[2]

This is indeed a picture of the case as it presents itself to serious reflection, and has tempted many a spiritual athlete to step aside in his running and fall out of the track. The course seems too long, the struggle too hard, the goal too far,—if indeed there be a goal. Recognition of the impotence of the theoretical reason to establish a world-view in which life-view can find a meaning results, for some minds, in a paralysis of the will, because it seems as if the springs of action were frozen at their source.

But it is to be observed that, in Schweitzer's case, his intellectual agnosticism has never affected his enthusiasm for life. It has haunted his mind, but it has never depressed his spirit. It is evident indeed that his intellectual agnosticism never came upon him as a shock,

---

[1] The point is well developed, for example, in the chapter on "Gnosticism" in Rainy's *Ancient Catholic Church*.
[2] *Civilization and Ethics*, p. 213.

but that it steadily grew upon him from his youth up until it became a settled conviction. But side by side with it there grew up a steadily increasing enthusiasm for life and active effort in the world. His search was for a principle which would justify world- and life-affirmation and ethics—despite the manifest unintelligibility of the world—a principle which must become a necessity for thought. And it was not till his fortieth year that he found it.

Hitherto he had set his immense intellectual energies and imaginative insight to the task of interpreting, revealing, and expounding the dynamic inspiration that informs the apocalyptic utterances of the historical Jesus and His great Apostle. In them he had found sufficient impulse to give to his own life its purpose and meaning. But now, for the sake of others whose faith might be shocked and even disastrously shaken by these radical disclosures, he embarked upon a yet more original voyage of discovery. This was to track through uncharted seas of thought in quest of one single elemental intuition that would establish Truth, not on the derivative extrinsic revelation of holy writ, but on immediate experience universally recognizable as such, and to show it to be a necessity both for thought and for action.

He was travelling, as he tells us, slowly in a tug-steamer upstream on the Ogowe River—a long journey—to bring medical help to the wife of a friend, sharing with the natives their cooking-pot; and as the familiar antediluvian landscape slid past his view, hour after hour, his mind was engaged as often before on this unsolved problem; the riddle of existence.

With the endless panorama, constantly unfolding, of life-in-death in tropical vegetation before his eyes; and in his mind's eye the endless panorama of life-in-death in the long history of mankind—mankind that had never yet attained to a civilization worthy of the name; both equally unintelligible, and apparently leading nowhere but to endless repetition; and as subconscious background to his thoughts, the welfare of his hospital and the well-being of each one of its totally uncivilized inmates, for the preservation of whose apparently worthless lives he had dedicated his own—against all obvious reason and in the teeth of every obstacle,—we may perhaps imagine his reflections on existence taking shape somewhat as follows. What is the most elementary thought of which consciousness is capable? It is certainly not this: "I think, therefore I am." For the concept of thought involves the prior consciousness of existence. Besides, that rationalistic approach to the problem leads nowhere but to abstract theories, as the history of thought has shown. The primary concept is obviously, "I am." But what? The subject demands a predicate. "I am life that wills-to-live."—But that is not all; I do not exist in isolation. The corollary is equally obvious—"in the midst of life that wills-to-live." Not "of other life," for the life without me is in some sense an extension of the life within me. It is true that the life I see about me presents the dreadful spectacle of life struggling for its own existence at the expense of other life, and the world of nature is very much a reproduction of the course of human history: the Other is obtruded as something alien to the Self. And yet within me, and in spite of all, is this mysterious urge to enter into life, to save life, to enhance its value.

The world is a ghastly drama of will-to-live divided against itself. One existence makes its way at the cost of another; one destroys the other. One will-to-live merely exerts its will against the other, and has no knowledge of it. But in me the will-to-live has come to know about other wills-to-live. There is in it a longing to arrive at unity with itself, to become universal.[1]

Then there suddenly flashed upon his mind, "unforeseen and unsought," the phrase, "Reverence for Life." A simple phrase no doubt; and yet for Schweitzer it has proved the key to unlock the door of all philosophy.

The iron door had yielded; the path in the thicket had become visible. Now I had found my way to the idea in which world- and life-affirmation and ethics are contained side by side! Now I knew that the world-view of ethical world- and life-affirmation, together with its ideals of civilization, is founded in thought.[2]

For if, from the primary datum, "I am life that wills-to-live in the midst of life that wills-to-live," thought proceeds to address itself to the question, "To what end?"—the mysterious urge of the life-force within the will-to-live makes answer: "To attain spiritual unity with infinite Being." [This, in religious language, is expressed as "the knowledge and love of God."] But union with infinite Being cannot be attained in abstraction from the manifestations thereof in the plane of phenomena. [That is, "to love one's neighbour as oneself."]

[1] *Civilization and Ethics*, p. 249.   [2] *My Life and Thought*, pp. 185-186.

There is no Essence of Being, but only Infinite Being in infinite manifestations. It is only through the manifestations of Being, and only through those with which I enter into relations that my being has any intercourse with infinite Being. The devotion of my being to infinite Being means devotion of my being to all the manifestations of being which need my devotion, and to which I am able to devote myself.[1]

What then is the determining factor of this ethical mysticism, to which "all deep philosophy, all deep religion, are ultimately a struggle,"—that which gives it its power and its inspiration? It is not duty externally imposed; it is pity.

Ethics are pity. All life is suffering. The will-to-live which has attained to knowledge is therefore seized with deep pity for all creatures. It experiences not only the woe of mankind, but that of all creatures with it. What is called in ordinary ethics "love" is in its real essence pity. In this powerful feeling of pity the will-to-live is diverted from itself. Its purification begins.[2]

And is it not this after all which was the very motive power of the life of Jesus, of which his "absolute ethic of love" was the expression in action? This is the victory that overcomes the world, the only force in the universe that is ultimately invincible. He came to be the Healer of men's bodies and the Saviour of their souls. "I am come that they might have life, and that they might have it more abundantly."—But it is inconceivable that such divine compassion, touched as it was to the last extremity by the feeling of our infirmities, should have stopped short there, and have remained indifferent to, and untouched by, the sufferings of all creation. That is why Schweitzer can find it possible to write: "The ethic of Reverence for Life is the ethic of Jesus brought to philosophical expression, extended into cosmical form, and conceived of as intellectually necessary."

For no one who pretends to the least sentiment of pity, no one who is sensitive to pain, no one who, in short, claims to be human,—can remain unmoved by the spectacle of suffering in anything that lives. To take it as a matter of course, or to regard it as a circumstance divinely ordained because it "happens" and therefore as something outside one's consideration or right to interfere, is to be false to one's truest instincts, to blunt the finest sensibilities of one's nature.

[1] *Civilization and Ethics*, p. 242.   [2] *Ibid.* p. 169.

This widespread indifference to creaturely pain may be due either to callousness or thoughtlessness, but, as often as not, it is due to the moral cowardice of being considered sentimental. But once a man accepts his kinship with, and responsibility for, all creatures great and small; once he realizes that they too are the concern of the same Creator and the objects of His care, he experiences within him an unburdening, a release, and a sense that he has a right to his own place in the same universe.

To the world in which he finds himself man stands in the relation of passivity and of activity. Of passivity, that is the world-denying principle of true resignation: thereby he wins his way to inward freedom from the fortunes and misfortunes that shape the outward side of his existence. Of activity, that is the world-affirming principle of ethics: thereby he affects the life of all that comes within his reach.

> He will feel that all life's experiences are his own, he will give it all the help that he possibly can, and will feel all the saving and promotion of life that he has been able to effect as the deepest happiness that can ever fall to his lot. . . .
> Existence will thereby become harder for him in every respect than it would be if he lived for himself, but at the same time it will be richer, more beautiful, and happier. It will become, instead of mere living, a real experience of life.[1]

The ultimate problem, the problem of pain—and of the vicarious sacrifice of the lower orders of creation which is bound up with it— is one which the man who is truly ethical must be content to leave unsolved. He only knows that, finding himself in a world of evil, he must go about doing good, "and thus step for a moment out of the incomprehensible horror of existence." There are so many ills that call for curing that he can but strive in his infinitesimal degree to lessen the vast sum-total of human and of creaturely misery.

A theism which is not also pantheistic is incomplete.

> Every form of living Christianity is pantheistic in that it is bound to envisage everything that exists as having its being in the great First Cause of all being. But at the same time all ethical piety is higher than any pantheistic mysticism, in that it does not find the God of Love in Nature, but has knowledge of Him only from the

fact that He announces Himself in us as Will-to-Love. The First Cause of Being, as He manifests Himself in Nature, is to us always something impersonal. But to the First Cause of Being who becomes revealed to us as Will-to-Love, we relate ourselves as to an ethical personality. Theism does not stand in opposition to pantheism, but emerges from it as the ethically determined out of what is natural and undetermined.[1]

"From the crystal to the medusa, from the grass-blade to the flowering tree," from the lowest to the highest forms of life, "in everything that exists there is at work an imaginative force, which is determined by ideals, and strives to reach the perfection with which it is endowed." In man this striving becomes conscious. But only in the man who is capable of deep reflection and of conduct which is truly ethical, does a contradiction to this principle of merely individual self-assertion make its presence felt. The extension of the will-to-live within him into the midst of the will-to-live outside him involves him in a world- and life-affirmation which militates against his individual will-to-live. Yet, paradoxically, his individual will-to-live is not thereby diminished, rather it is enhanced. The primary instinct of self-preservation, on the natural subhuman level, is on the natural human level transformed into a will to enhance and promote the life of all that lives.

I am thrown, indeed, by Reverence for Life into an unrest such as the world does not know, but I obtain from it a blessedness which the world cannot give. I begin to learn the secret of spiritual self-assertion. I win an unsuspected freedom from the various destinies of life. At moments in which I had expected to find myself overwhelmed, I find myself in an inexpressible and surprising happiness of freedom from the world, and I experience therein a clearing of my life-view.[2]

The unrest is occasioned by the fact that, in the practical application of the principle of Reverence for Life, ethical man is called upon from day to day, almost from hour to hour, to exercise intelligence and discrimination. He finds himself the inhabitant of a world which is not ethical, which is utterly indifferent to ethics. No sooner do creative and life-conserving energies arise than destructive and death-disfiguring forces are at work among them. And man is obliged

[1] *Ibid.* p. 278.   [2] *Civilization and Ethics*, pp. 250-251.

himself to prey on other life, either animal or vegetable, in order to maintain his own, and even as he walks he crushes the lowly organisms of herb and of insect unwittingly beneath his tread.

He is subject to the puzzling and horrible law of being obliged to live at the cost of other life, and to incur again and again the guilt of destroying and injuring life. But as an ethical being he strives to escape whenever possible from this necessity, and as one who has become enlightened and merciful to put a stop to this disunion of the Will-to-live, so far as the influence of his own existence reaches. He thirsts to be permitted to preserve his humanity, and to be able to bring to other existences release from their sufferings.[1]

There is no objective code of moral behaviour to guide him; he must deal with each concrete situation as it arises, guided only by the reflection: Is this particular injury or destruction to life necessary to the preservation of life which is more valuable?

To the man who is truly ethical all life is sacred, including that which from the human point of view seems lower in the scale. He makes distinctions only as each case comes before him, and under the pressure of necessity, as, for example, when it falls to him to decide which of two lives he must sacrifice in order to preserve the other. But all through this series of decisions he is conscious of acting on subjective grounds and arbitrarily, and knows that he bears the responsibility for the life that is sacrificed.[2]

In *Civilization and Ethics* Schweitzer has written at length and with care on these considerations. But it is more fitting in this place to illustrate them by instances taken from his own example.

Soon after his first arrival in West Africa, when journeying by canoe, he incurred the reproaches of his native paddlers for refusing to shoot the monkeys in the overhanging boughs or the birds that circled over the river. They compared him unfavourably with one of his missionary friends who was "a great sportsman." He willingly endured their reproaches, and they gradually accepted his lack of "sportsmanship."

Birds which circle above the water I never like shooting; monkeys are perfectly safe from my weapon. One can often bring

[1] *My Life and Thought*, p. 189. [2] *Ibid.* p. 271.

down or wound three or four in succession and yet never secure their bodies. They get caught among the thick branches or fall into the undergrowth which covers an impenetrable swamp; and if one finds the body, one often finds also a poor little baby monkey which clings, with lamentations, to its dying mother. My chief reason for keeping a gun is to be able to shoot snakes, which swarm on the grass around my house, and the birds of prey which plunder the nests of the weaver-birds in the palm-trees in front of it.[1]

When clearing the site of his new hospital he constantly came across oil-palms which could neither flower nor fruit because of the matted creeper-vines which clung to them and stifled their growth. He cut the creepers at their root; but not so the oil-palms.

We burden ourselves with some extra work out of compassion for the palm-trees with which the site of our future home is crowded. The simplest plan would be to cut them all down. An oil-palm is valueless, there are so many of them. But we cannot find it in our heart to deliver them over to the axe just when, delivered from the creepers, they are beginning a new life. So we devote some of our leisure hours to digging up carefully those which are transplantable and setting them elsewhere, though it is heavy work. Oil-palms can be transplanted when they are 15 years old and quite big. . . . How thankful the palms are when the sun can at last shine upon them!

To this he adds whimsically:

That one should feel compassion for animals my natives can understand (but only after long and oft-repeated exhortations and example). But that I should expect them to carry heavy palm-trees about so that they may live instead of being cut down, this seems to them a perverted philosophy![2]

When setting the piles in position for the foundations of the hospital:

Before the pile is lowered into the pit I look whether any ants or toads or other creatures have fallen into it, and if so I take them out with my hands so that they may not be maimed by the pile,

---

[1] On the Edge of the Primeval Forest, p. 72.
[2] More from the Primeval Forest, p. 157.

or crushed to death later by the earth and stones, and I explain why I do this to those who are standing by. Some smile in embarrassment; others pay no attention at all to what they have heard so often. But one day a real savage who was working with me was fetched to work in the plantation at cutting down the undergrowth. A toad being espied in it, his neighbour wanted to kill it with his bush-knife; but the first one seized his arm and unfolded to him and to a listening group the theory that the animals were like ourselves created by God, and that He will some day hold a great palaver with the men who torment or kill them. This savage was the very last on whom I should have expected my deeds and words to make any impression.[1]

This is the man who as a doctor and surgeon describes himself as "a mass-murderer of bacteria"; who carries on a ceaseless war with mosquitoes, spiders, scorpions, snakes, leopards, and all the noxious vermin that endanger human life—and none more vigorously, determinedly, and deliberately than he; and yet who goes out of his way to lift a parched earthworm from the dust and put it safely in the grass, or stoops to rescue a struggling insect from a puddle, who tears no leaf from a tree and plucks no flower, and who prefers to work in the stuffy atmosphere of a shuttered room rather than let a moth flutter to its death round a lamp.

Reverence for Life indeed awakens a heightened sensitivity which to conventional morality may well appear extravagant, and calls for decisions which may appear over-scrupulous.

I rejoice over the new remedies for sleeping sickness, which enable me to preserve life, whereas I had previously to watch the painful disease. But every time I have under the microscope the germs which cause the disease, I cannot but reflect that I have to sacrifice this life in order to preserve other life.

I buy from the natives a young fish-eagle which they have caught on a sand-bank in order to rescue it from their cruel hands. But now I have to decide whether I shall let it starve, or kill every day a number of small fishes in order to keep it alive. I decide on the latter course, but every day I feel it hard that this life must be sacrificed for the other on my own responsibility.[2]

Hurrying afoot with a companion along an English country lane, to catch a train and keep an appointment, his bulky rucksack slung

[1] *More from the Primeval Forest*, pp. 152-153.
[2] *My Life and Thought*, pp. 271-272.

between them on a walking stick, a sudden jerk brought his companion to a standstill whilst Schweitzer stooped to lift a worm from its peril in the roadway and drop it safely in the grass.

One of his colleagues at Lambaréné recalls that while working late at night, when a grape-fruit was brought in to him, he would always drop a spoonful of the juice on the floor beside him, and when it was surrounded by a thirsty crowd of little black ants, he would look up with a smile and say, "Look at my ants! Just like cows round a pond!"

Mrs. C. E. B. Russell, in her delightful little book *My Monkey Friends*, tells how the maimed and the young of animals and birds are as warmly welcomed and as carefully treated at Lambaréné as its human inmates; indeed, one gains the impression that there are times when the establishment resembles a menagerie as much as an infirmary.

The principle of Reverence for Life indeed extends itself beyond the realm of animal and bird and fish and insect life to the humblest forms of the vegetable creation and even to forms of beauty which are inanimate.

> That man is truly ethical who shatters no ice-crystal as it sparkles in the sun, tears no leaf from a tree, cuts no flower. . . . The farmer who has mown down a thousand flowers in his meadow to feed his cows, must be careful on his way home not to strike off in heedless pastime the head of a single flower by the roadside, for he thereby commits a wrong against life without being under the pressure of necessity.

"Love thou the rose, but leave it on its stem."—The line, from a great poem by our own Lord Lytton, would, did he know it, greatly appeal to Schweitzer. Once, when walking with one of his colleagues from Lambaréné across St. James' Park, the paths of which were regravelled and rough to tread, he met her suggestion that they should follow the example of those who were walking on the grass with vehement protest, "What! do you think that I would trample on the *grass* when there is any sort of a path to walk on!"

But great as are the responsibilities of ethical man to the rest of creation, they are small in comparison with those which Reverence for Life imposes on him in respect to his fellow-man. Here his responsibility is "so unlimited as to be terrifying."—Reverence for Life is more than sympathy, because sympathy does not include ethics.

Sympathy denotes no more than emotional or intellectual compassion, no more than an "interest," however deep and genuine, in "suffering will-to-live." But Reverence for Life is love in action: it includes "fellowship in suffering, in joy, and in effort; it includes feeling as one's own all the circumstances and all the aspirations of the will-to-live, its pleasures too, and its longing to live itself out to the full, as well as its urge to self-perfecting."

In its zeal to preserve, promote, and enhance the values of life beyond its own life, "it is unconcerned with the significance of its activity in the total happenings of the world-process." As it is not deterred by failure, so also it is not unduly elated by success. "It sows as one who does not count on living to reap the harvest." It is not anxious for results. "It is not a flame which burns only when events provide suitable fuel; it blazes up, and that with the purest light, when it is forced to feed on what it derives from within itself." It is not weary of well-doing, and in well-doing it does not allow weariness to overcome it. In the moments when ethical man longs for "rest"—to escape from sharing and helping to bear the weight of the universal tragedy—love and pity drive him out again into the path of service to his fellow-men.

> At the moments when I should like to enjoy myself without restraint, it awakens in me reflection about the misery which I see around me or which I suspect, and it does not allow me to drive away the uneasiness thereby caused to me. Just as the wave cannot exist for itself, but is ever a part of the heaving surface of the ocean, so must I never live my life for myself, but always in the experience which is going on around me.
>
> It is an uncomfortable doctrine which the true ethic whispers into my ear. You are happy, it says; therefore you are called upon to give much. Whatever more than others you have received in health, natural gifts, working capacity, success, a beautiful childhood, harmonious family circumstances, you must not accept as being a matter of course. You must pay a price for them. You must show more than an average devotion to life.
>
> To the happy the voice of the true ethic is dangerous, if they venture to listen to it. . . .
>
> Reverence for life is an inexorable creditor! [1]

The will-to-live which has become ethical, and expresses itself as Reverence for Life and all things living, is nothing but veracity to

[1] *Civilization and Ethics*, pp. 259-260.

self. To be content with less than that is to be untrue to self, to exist on a lower level of life than that of which the will-to-live is capable; and that is sin. "A good conscience," says Schweitzer, "is an invention of the devil."

Reverence for Life pretends to no knowledge of the world or of what the world may mean; it formulates no "world-view." It has no love for "faith" (that is, for theoretical belief); but it has faith (that is, has trust) in Love. This is its "life-view." Not knowledge, but the will, is the true organ of spiritual understanding. "Whosoever doeth the will shall know of the doctrine." Acceptance of creed is easy: pursuit of ideals is hard.

What are the implications of this for theology? Schweitzer does not enlarge upon them, yet it is necessary that they should be most emphatically stressed. Confronted with the fact of moral evil, dogmatic theology goes back to the fall of man to account for it, and deduces therefrom a doctrine of original sin. Admitting the fact of universal moral evil and the fall of man, ethical mysticism goes back to a prior state of grace from which man fell and reaffirms his original righteousness. Sin is not natural or indigenous to man; it is unnatural. What is called the "supernatural" is really the most truly natural. Plato (who taught—and more convincingly than any moralist—the doctrine of the fall of man) was the first among European thinkers (as Schweitzer points out) to realize that the ethical is also the supernatural in man; and after him Kant. Dogmatic theology separates man from God. It seeks to hypostasize, objectivize, exteriorize God, making Him wholly other from man, and in so doing it of necessity worships, not God, but its own concepts of Him. It makes of Him an Object external to consciousness. Ethical mysticism is aware of God only as experienced, as the very Ground and Source of our being. Spatial or temporal ideas of Transcendence or Immanence are unknown to ethical mysticism.

Again, ethical mysticism differs from dogmatic theology in this, that it walks by faith and not by sight. Theology depends for its beliefs upon criteria, extrinsic to faith: sacred books, creeds, dogmas, history, tradition; its gaze is directed upon the past. Ethical mysticism cares nothing for the past, and receives not its traditions from men. "Even though I had known the incarnate Christ, yet now no more." The voice of the historical Jesus is for it but a faint and far-heard echo of the same voice as it speaks in clarion tones today. It is the Spirit of Jesus risen in the hearts of men that calls us and "sets us to the tasks that He has to fulfil for our time." Ethical mysticism is free from all conditions of space or time; from all ideas of cosmology or theodicy; it begins here and now; it is conditioned by nothing external to faith. Its life is rooted, not in the past, but in the present. "Everyone that is of the Truth heareth my voice."

Again, the concern of dogmatic theology is with abstract propositions not rooted in experience; its whole world is a world of theory. The concern of ethical mysticism is with concrete life, with activity in the world, with experience both in action and in passion. It knows only one thing needful,—to heal and help, to fling down all the barriers between the self and the other; to overcome—as far as its influence can reach—all that now makes for division and disunion in the separately striving wills-to-live.

But although ethical mysticism has nothing to do with dogmatic theology (so-called Christian "apologetic" being, as Schweitzer truly says, "a crooked and fragile way of thinking"), it has much to do both with religion and with moral philosophy.

The essential element in Christianity as it was preached by Jesus and as it is comprehended in thought, is this, that it is only through Love that we can attain to communion with God. All living knowledge of God rests upon this foundation: that we experience Him in our lives as Will-to-Love.

Anyone who has recognized that the idea of Love is the spiritual beam of light which reaches us from the Infinite, ceases to demand from religion that it shall offer him complete knowledge of the supra-sensible. He ponders indeed on the great questions: what is the meaning of the evil in the world; how in God, the great First Cause, the will-to-create and the will-to-love are one; in what relation the spiritual and the material life stand to one another, and in what way our existence is transitory and yet eternal. But he is able to leave these questions on one side, however painful it may be to give up all hope of answers to them. In the knowledge of spiritual existence in God through love he possesses the one thing needful.—"Love never faileth; but whether there be knowledge, it shall be done away." The deeper piety is, the humbler are its claims with regard to knowledge of the supra-sensible.[1]

And on the side of moral philosophy it is to be observed that ethical mysticism is the only life-view which completes and connects

[1] *My Life and Thought*, p. 277.

the two mutually antagonistic schools of moral philosophy: the ethic of Self-Devotion (which we in England know as Utilitarianism or Altruistic Hedonism) on the one hand, and the ethic of Self-Perfection (which we know as Intuitionism or Perfectionism) on the other. The standard of the first is external and objective; it is Happiness; looking to the goal of action, it asks the question: what is the ultimate *Good*,—what do I *want* to do? It is essentially active and life-affirming. The standard of the other is internal and subjective; it is Duty; looking to the motive of the agent, it asks the question: what is the absolute *Right*,—what *ought* I to do? It is essentially passive and life-denying. But until a man can say, "I want to do what I ought to do," and conversely, "I ought to do what I want to do," he falls short of the standard which he has set himself. Hence Mill, the greatest exponent of the former method, is obliged in the last resort to introduce the concept of Duty into his definition of Happiness. And hence Kant, the greatest exponent of the latter, is bound to see Happiness in the end as the inevitable concomitant of Duty. They seem to be tightly clutching opposite ends of the same stick; yet neither can bring their theories of the ethical standard to completion on their own premises; each depends on the other, the one for its form, the other for its content. The one looks afar and beyond to the lodestar of the Good; the other looks anigh and within to the compass-needle of the Right. Only in ethical mysticism are these differences resolved. For Love is the only power in the universe that can magnetize the one, and polarize the other.

The becoming-one of the finite will with the Infinite acquires a content only when it is experienced both as quiescence in it and at the same time as a being-taken-possession-of by the Will of Love, which in us comes to consciousness of itself, and strives in us to become act. Mysticism only takes the road to life when it passes through the antithesis of God's Will of Love with His Infinite enigmatic creative will, and transcends it. Since human thinking cannot comprehend the eternal in its true nature, it is bound to arrive at dualism and be forced to overcome it, in order to adjust itself to the Eternal. It must, no doubt, face all the enigmas of existence which present themselves to thought and harass it, but in the last resort it must leave the incomprehensible uncomprehended, and take the path of seeking to be certified of God as the Will of Love, and finding in it both inner peace and springs of action.

... In Jesus Christ, God is manifested as Will of Love. In union
with Christ, union with God is only realized in the only form
attainable by us.[1]

The ethic of Reverence for Life provides a theme which is capable
of infinite expansion. As a principle of conduct it is of course by
no means new; it is the "old commandment"—that we should love
God with all our powers, and love our neighbours as ourselves.
That "we are members one of another" is no figure of speech, but
a literal statement of fact. But as a principle of thought it has claims
to be called original. For first, as Schweitzer formulates it, it is extended cosmically; since Reverence for Life would be a foreshortened
view of life unless it brought within the focus of its vision the whole
world of living things. And second, it is a necessity for thought;
since it alone is capable of combining into one comprehensive
life-view two separate world-views, the life-affirming and the life-
denying, held fast together by the sheet-anchor of the ethical.

Amid the babel of tongues that supervenes upon this period of
humanity's most poignant distresses, the ethic of Reverence for Life,
if heard and heeded in its gentle undertones, would prove a far more
efficacious remedy for the whole world's pain than all the panaceas
advocated in strident tones by the politicians, or the sociologists, or
the theologians; but whether it will be so is a matter for doubt, since
it would cost much more in personal effort and personal sacrifice.

Much could be written to amplify and interpret what Schweitzer
has written so tersely and with such chiselled sentences upon the
theme of ethical mysticism, expressed as Reverence for Life, in the
concluding chapters of his *Civilization and Ethics* and again in the
corresponding sections of *My Life and Thought*. These meditations
must, without qualification, be reckoned among the profoundest
reflections in the whole history of human thought. Nothing that he
has himself written, even in the finest passages of his *Quest* or of
his *Paul*, can compare with them for depth of spiritual insight, for
they are original and personal in a sense that no exposition, however
penetrating and sympathetic, can be. In the former, his thought is
so condensed, and is expressed with such restraint, that it requires
to be read several times before its meaning can be fully grasped.
Like all great artistic expression it says less than it suggests. But

[1] *Mysticism of Paul the Apostle*, p. 379.

underneath the austerity and the matter-of-factness of its phrasing there is a cadence in the diction which eventually sings its way into the mind of the attentive reader, like a fugue of Bach. In the latter, it is his heart that gives utterance to his thought; therefore it should be read first.

But perhaps nothing could be written more fittingly to reveal the inner meaning of his thought than is written by other spiritual adventurers who have trodden the path to the same goal. In the anthology of Christian mysticism many utterances spring to the mind to illuminate that ethical mysticism, expressed as Reverence for Life, of which Schweitzer is the modern advocate and to the truth of which his whole life is the noblest witness. Two such are chosen here, partly because their very familiarity testifies to their universal appeal, and partly because they each respectively voice the yearning of the will-to-live to live its life out to perfection in action and in passion.

The first is from Ignatius Loyola, the motive of whose spiritual discipline, very far removed from Schweitzer's though its method was, is akin to his and finds expression in the prayer:

To give and not to count the cost; to fight and not to heed the wounds; to toil and not to seek for rest; to labour and not to look for any reward save that of knowing that I do Thy Will.

The second is from Francis of Assisi, that lover of Christ and of men, and birds, and animals, and flowers, who washed the feet of lepers and was the friend of all the outcast and oppressed:

Lord, make me an instrument of Thy Peace. Where there is hatred, let me sow love; where there is injury, pardon; where there is doubt, faith; where there is despair, hope; where there is darkness, light; where there is sadness, joy.
O Divine Master, grant that I may not so much seek to be consoled, as to console; to be understood, as to understand; to be loved, as to love. For it is in giving that we receive, it is in pardoning that we are pardoned; it is in dying that we are born to eternal life.

Lastly there is this, though less well known perhaps, which expresses as no other words have done the relation in which the true disciple stands to the Saviour of the world. It comes from the pen of a modern seer and mystic, Anna Kingsford, who more than any in her day and generation raised her voice to succour the cause of the suffering dumb creation.

The wrongs of others wound the Son of God, and the stripes of others fall on his flesh.

He is smitten with the ·pains of all creatures and his heart is pierced with their wounds.

There is no offence done and he suffers not, nor any wrong and he is not hurt thereby.

For his heart is in the breast of every creature, and his blood in the veins of all flesh.

For to know perfectly is to love perfectly, and so to love is to be a partaker in the pain of the beloved.

And inasmuch as a man loves and succours and saves even the least of God's creatures, he ministers unto the Lord.

Christ is the perfect lover, bearing the sorrows of all the poor and oppressed.

And the sin and injustice and ignorance of the world are the nails in his hands and in his feet.

O Passion of Love that givest thyself freely, even unto death!

For no man can do Love's perfect work unless Love thrust him through and through.

But if he love perfectly, he shall be able to redeem; for strong Love is a net which shall draw all souls unto him.

Because unto Love is given all power, both in heaven and on earth;

Seeing that the will of Him who loves perfectly is one with the Will of God:

And unto God and Love, all things are possible.

CONCLUSION

To every one of the several branches of knowledge which Schweitzer has enriched by his learning, he has imparted a wholly original contribution, of a kind which may be called revolutionary. By his refusal to take established opinions for granted; by the new light he has thrown upon subjects whose conclusions were considered as long since foreclosed; by the freshness and vitality of his approach to every field of study that his genius has touched; by the manner in which he reopens each field of scientific or artistic exploration, and invests his researches with the illumination of a great discovery,—he shows himself a pioneer, with a passion for ultimate truth. Old conceptions, as has been truly said, show an extraordinary tenacity for existence at any price; they allow the infiltration of new knowledge to flow past them; and even when their cast-iron theories, their concrete gun-emplacements and pill-boxes, have been by-passed and engulfed in the forward march of new enlightenment,—they linger on, however ineffectually, in the fond belief that their age-old positions are impregnable.

If one seeks for the denominator which is common to all Schweitzer's "heresies," the quality which gives to each one its peculiar distinction, one finds it, I think, in a desire, amounting to an intellectual necessity, to give substance to form. But this necessity in him is more than merely intellectual; it is spiritual, it forms the warp and woof of character, it touches the mainsprings of action. His life and thought and work are all of one piece. Just as nature abhors a vacuum so it would seem does Schweitzer, himself the most natural of men, abhor abstractions. Unless form has, or can be provided with, substance, for him it is meaningless.

Thus, to a doctrinal formula which, investing the historical Jesus with a "supernatural nimbus," would make of him at best a metaphysical abstraction, at worst a psychological monstrosity,—Schweitzer opposes the sharp delineation of a figure clothed with human flesh and blood, not different from us in kind, though immeasurably different in degree. But in His historical setting He is of necessity beyond our comprehension; and if we would truly know Him we must know Him as He is, no longer as He was.

In the apostle Paul he sees—not the propounder of a Christological conundrum to which four centuries of argument could only find an ambiguous solution; not the founder of doctrines which should provide Augustinian and Thomist and Lutheran divines with matter for endless speculation—but a religious genius fired and inspired with the single experience of mystical union with Christ, an experience so intense that he could only express it in terms of corporeity.

To the aesthetic interpretation of Bach as the creator of "pure lines of sound" only, the master-geometrician of music,—he presents a Bach whose art is symbolical and significant of actuality, whose music is the perfection of pictorial tone-painting, the ideal representation of conceptual images embodied in pure lines of sound with "the utmost possible vitality and clearness."

And it is because in Kant he can discover no concrete content to give life and colour to his impersonal Categorical Imperative, that he abandons Kant as a thinker who had not thought out his formal philosophy to a conclusion, and himself supplies the lack of it with substance. For what is Reverence for Life but self-veracity, which is the keystone of Kant's ethic, and what is self-veracity but Reverence for Truth itself?

Now whether form without substance can have meaning or not may be a matter for academic debate; but it very certainly can have no value. And what Schweitzer asks from philosophy is not a world-view (that is, "knowledge of the meaning of the whole, which for us is an impossibility"), but a wisdom, which is wisdom-for-life. What he asks from religion is not a faith once delivered, derivative, traditional, dependent upon hearsay evidence, received at second hand,—but a faith contemporaneous with existence, immediate, universal, absolute, authoritative because true, not true because authoritative, valid for each moment, independent of the past, a faith which is rooted in the spirit's vital and conscious experience of its Source. Not *Credo ut intelligam* would be his maxim; rather, *Ago ut credam*— in the sense, not of intellectual belief, but of personal trust.

But if the desire to give substance to form is a necessity for his mental life, it is *a fortiori* a necessity for his life-work which is the expression of his thought in action. To succour mankind, to bring the light of the knowledge of the glory of God to those who sit in darkness and the shadow of death, and to guide their feet into the way of peace,—that is his vocation. But to take shape, to prove effective, solid, substantial, this evangel must come not from his lips only, but from his hands; not in word only, but in deed. To be a missionary, yes, that is something; but to be a medical missionary, that is more. To preach the word, that is something; but simultaneously to heal the sick, that is more. Both in his life and thought, therefore, it is his constant aim to vindicate, in a concrete way, the primacy of the practical over the theoretical reason.

Rationalistic theology, with its insistence on the vitiation and impotence of the practical human will which original sin has poisoned at the root, is, strange to say, by no means so pessimistic about the effect of the same sin upon the health and potency of the theoretical human reason. On the contrary, it makes reason, assisted by "revelation," the organ for the apprehension of spiritual truth. But it mistakes the nature of revelation. It takes revelation to be equivalent to information about the purposes of God and the destiny of man imparted through the pages of sacred books. This information having been imparted and duly assimilated by the mind, the will can thereafter be restored to health and vigour by the infusion of supernatural grace—but not before. Dogma takes precedence of morals; right conduct is dependent upon correct belief. But the belief thus arbitrarily presented as a truth-claim to the consciousness of the believer is of an origin extraneous to his "nature"; it is also, and for that very reason, a theoretical belief, an abstraction of the understanding, because it lies outside experience. Moreover, experience itself contradicts the assumption that conduct invariably results from conscious theoretical belief. Practice by no means accords with profession. Invariably it proceeds from a life-view, whether consciously recognized as such or not; men act first, as it is truly said, and give their reasons afterwards.

Schweitzer's position is an entire reversal of the accepted view. He is a free-thinker who takes his stand upon the intellectual integrity of the older Rationalism, when thought was free and unentangled with the yoke of bondage to any dogma; he starts, that is, without any presuppositions or assumptions save the facts that are immediately present to consciousness, or can be ascertained by rational enquiry; and arrives at the conclusion that any world-view envisaged by reason is valueless because it rests upon an inadmissible interpretation of the facts. (After all, any such world-view is based upon a selection of known facts which can be contradicted by other known facts; and what are the known facts, both those which are selected and those which are ignored, beside the incalculable number of facts which are not known?) Thought, then, when it honestly thinks itself out to a conclusion, leads to scepticism, but it does not end there. What is required is not the abandonment of thought, but deepened thinking. If the question, "What is the meaning of the world?" remains insoluble, this is because it is posing a concept abstracted from consciousness. But let thought seek an answer to the deeper question, "What am I?"—and it may yet find an answer to the first question, from the subjective, though not from the objective, point of view; and thus cross the "desert" of scepticism to the "oasis" that lies beyond. "I am life that wills-to-live"—to bring to fruition all the fullness of my powers, physical, mental, spiritual. But my life is not independent; it interpenetrates and is interpenetrated by the life that wills-to-live around me. I perceive much of the life around me maimed and thwarted in the same struggle for self-fulfilment; and because I am bound up with it, because I feel it as my own, I am seized by the altruistic pain which is called pity. This deepened reflection upon life awakes in me the desire to engage actively in the furtherance and enhancement of all that lives. Schweitzer thus rejects the need for any supernatural adventitious aids either to enlighten reason or to reinforce the will. Both are already inherent in human nature. The supernatural is the most truly natural; human nature when it is most truly human is most divine.

"Brother, in thine own heart seek wisdom; there shalt thou find it." The words, attributed to Francis of Assisi, would be echoed by Schweitzer. Thought, when it thinks itself to a conclusion, must end in ethical mysticism, which is another name for Love: that is, in man's aspiration to union with infinite Being on the one hand, and on the other in his forth-giving service to all the manifestations of Being which come within the range of his influence. These are the two Great Commandments, and they stand or fall together. They are not extraneously superimposed upon conscience; they are the deepest promptings of man's innermost heart, his human nature, his essential humaneness.

Every great creative thinker is open to criticism, especially if his thought offers a challenge to accepted views, if it reopens discussions which were considered foreclosed, if it refuses to regard orthodox opinions as finally established. Examination of all the criticisms that have been levelled against Schweitzer, in whatever field of learning his mind has travelled, shows that in every case they are two: one-sidedness and inconsistency. The first of these he anticipates in *The Quest*, boldly claiming it as the distinguishing merit of his method: "Progress always consists in taking one or other of two alternatives, in abandoning the attempt to combine them." But this is not to say that he is blind to the other alternative; he fully recognizes it, but finds it impossible to reconcile with the one which he has chosen. One-sidedness may mean a perverse refusal to see what is to be said on the other side of a question. But if one-sidedness signifies a faculty —after having grasped the whole field of the problem to be investigated and comprehended in one view all its details—to seize on the one point that is essential and that gives significance and cohesion to all the rest, and with this clue in hand to follow it undeviatingly to the end,—then Schweitzer is one-sided, but in a very different sense.

What critics of *The Quest*, for example, have all without exception failed to do is to present a portrait of Jesus as positive or compelling, as conclusive or convincing as Schweitzer's "Sketch." Admittedly it is no more than a sketch, but it is the most authentic that can be drawn, objectively and scientifically, from the records available. Admittedly it does not explain or account for all the data, but more than have ever been explained before or since. Admittedly it contains lines which bear traces of subjective interpretation, but these are the fewest possible, and, from the sources available, to delineate a sketch without them would be an impossibility. No human mind can pretend to fathom the full depths of the consciousness of Jesus; that lies beyond the range of human ken, but His commandment to follow Him does not lie beyond the capacity of human response.

Similarly in his study of the apostle Paul. In this case the investigation is simpler in that the data are fuller, but harder in that the personality appears more complex. It is not true, as one critic, Professor Mackinnon, suggested, that Schweitzer is "a man of one idea which he works out with persistent determination and compels the evidence to corroborate." But once the thread of eschatological mysticism is firmly grasped, every other thread (or nearly every other) in the apostle's thought is at once unravelled, and an amazingly clear picture of his mind comes to light. The fact that the mysticism of St. Paul happens to be congenial to Schweitzer's is beside the point; there are aspects in it which Schweitzer can by no means accept, because a changed historical situation has put them out of focus. Admittedly one mind, however finely attuned to another, cannot explore all the recesses of that other; but as St. Paul could say, "Be ye imitators of me as I am of Christ," so there are few who have earned a better right to interpret the mind of the first great Christian missionary than one who has so faithfully followed him in practice.

When we pass from the field of historical criticism—in this case as it affects the history of individual religious thought and experience —to that of music and art, we are passing from the realm of objective fact in which the barest minimum of subjective interpretation is permissible, to that of aesthetic appreciation in which subjective interpretation is not only permissible but unavoidable. The former relate to judgments of fact; the latter to judgments of value. The former are capable of scientific verification; the latter are not. And though there is much diversity of opinion as to what is true (historically), there is considerably more diversity of opinion as to what is beautiful. —As against Schweitzer's interpretation of Bach and his theory of music in general, it is urged by the orthodox that he is one-sided in regarding all art as symbolical representation, and in maintaining that music—and especially the music of Bach—not only *is*, but that it has *significance*. Admittedly there is here introduced what may be called a psychological determinant, and whether the interpretation by an admirer of any work of art corresponds always and in every respect with the inspiration which prompted the genius of the creator to compose it, is something which can never be known; but the fact remains that Schweitzer's interpretation of Bach has taught thousands of musicians who revered him to revere him as never before, and thousands of others who never understood him at all to appreciate him for the first time.

The other criticism—of inconsistency—is found on examination to be rooted in the objection that Schweitzer's ethical philosophy is not systematic. But this is precisely what, for good reasons, it disclaims to be.

There is an irresponsible kind of pseudo-criticism which misunderstands the nature of Schweitzer's inconsistency. A specimen of this type is to be found in a somewhat supercilious review contributed to a theological quarterly[1] in which the critic, after premising that *The Quest* is "already for most scholars a museum piece," and con-

---

[1] By Vincent Turner, S.J., in the *Dublin Review* for July 1944. The article is intended as a review of Kraus' study of Schweitzer.

cluding that its author is "manifestly a warm-hearted, nice man, and a fine musician" (!)—has this to say of his philosophy: "Sometimes mysticism of the will seems to be equiparated with ethical reflection and contrasted with ethics based on scientific knowledge; sometimes sheer will to action is awarded a unique validity of its own." The first sentence, though confusedly expressed, is substantially correct; the second is quite mistaken. Sheer will to action, undirected by ethical reflection, is a feature of subhuman behaviour and one which, as practised by human beings, is the very thing which, on Schweitzer's own showing, has laid civilization in ruins.

This critic, whilst appreciating fully as he does the heroic quality in Schweitzer's life, says further: "There is here nobility of heart and of action. Nevertheless, the relation of thought to conduct is rarely of such sort that the excellence of the latter can be taken, without a further close inspection, to guarantee the excellence of the former."—With far more justice the terms of this proposition might be inverted; and a sufficient answer to it is this: "By their fruits ye shall know them. Do men gather grapes of thorns, or figs of thistles?"

The most informed and penetrating study of Schweitzer's life and thought that has yet appeared in English is undoubtedly that by Magnus C. Ratter. The chief excellence of this study (apart from its literary brilliance) is that it shows with sympathetic insight precisely how these two aspects of his personality, thought and conduct, weave themselves together into an integral unity. Its author deals, and deals effectively, with sundry criticisms that have been directed against Schweitzer's thought. He has one criticism of his own to make which events have, sadly, failed to justify. He writes: "Disaster will not come as he threatens, and further the most potent force compelling to truer righteousness, and so avoiding the catastrophe, will be the urge to devotion that comes from his life and the inspiration that flows from his ethic." Here, alas, the prophet was right; his critical admirer wrong.

But there are other criticisms with which he does not deal, and these are in the opinion of the present writer the most searching that have been made. They come from the pen of Professor Kraus,[1] the chief merit of whose study is that it combines unqualified admiration for Schweitzer as a man with the advocacy of a philosophical

[1] *Albert Schweitzer: His Work and his Philosophy*, 1926. Tr. by E. G. McCalman. (A. & C. Black, 1944.)

position diametrically opposed to Schweitzer's. Kraus was a thorough-going exponent of a systematic philosophy of psychological deter-minism, a type of thought with which mysticism, ethical or other, can obviously have nothing in common. Nevertheless Kraus with the utmost sincerity sets himself to try to understand Schweitzer's position and even, where possible, to justify it. For example, in replying to Theodor Lessing's wholly unwarrantable aspersion of Schweitzer's ethic of Reverence for Life as "scholastic philosophy, which has not been gained by personal suffering and personal sacri-fice,"—Kraus rejoins, "A more unjust accusation than this can hardly be imagined," and points out that Schweitzer's philosophy can only be rightly understood and appreciated *after* an estimate has been formed of his personality and activities; adding: "Schweitzer *lives* his life of self-surrender, and it is just this which characterizes him above all else."

The present writer, while totally disagreeing with Kraus' philo-sophical standpoint and being wholly in agreement with Schweitzer's, is bound to say that there is one particular—and in his view only one —in which Kraus has detected a serious inconsistency in Schweitzer's thought. Kraus finds an "oscillation" in Schweitzer's thought firstly between rationalism and mysticism; secondly, between pantheism and theism; and thirdly, between optimism and pessimism in his application of these terms to the world-view of Jesus.

With regard to the first of these antinomies, Schweitzer has written:

If rational thought thinks itself out to a conclusion, it comes to something non-rational which, nevertheless, is a necessity of thought. This is the paradox which dominates our spiritual life. If we try to come through without this non-rational, the result is views of the world and of life which are without life and without value.

All valuable conviction is non-rational and has an emotional character, because it cannot be derived from knowledge of the world, but arises out of the thinking experience of our will-to-live, in which we stride out beyond all knowledge of the world. This thought it is which the rational thought that thinks itself out to a conclusion comprehends as the truth by which we must live. The way to true mysticism leads up through rational thought to deep experience of the world and of our will-to-live. We must all venture once more to be thinkers, so as to reach mysticism, which is the only direct and the only profound world-view. We must all wander in the field of knowledge to the point where knowledge passes over into experience of the world. We must all, through thought, become religious.[1]

The truth is that Schweitzer's mind, though eminently logical, is not the mind of a pure logician. Rather, he is an imaginative thinker with a strongly rationalistic background to his thought. But there comes a point when thought, if it is to be creative, must transcend logic: this is where it crosses the boundary between rationalism and mysticism. To borrow a phrase from Schweitzer's own estimate of Bach's music, it finds itself obliged to sacrifice tonal design for clarity of representation.—To the published comment of Professor Kraus that "his sceptical repression of the metaphysical impulse finds an outlet in mystical emotionalism," Schweitzer replied in a private letter, "Yes, I have experienced this, though I have not experienced ethics emotionally,[2] but as a logical necessity—or super-logically, if you like." This is by no means a begging of the question. Judged by the standard of pure logic Schweitzer's ethical mysticism is inconsistent by virtue of its being, as he frankly says, "non-rational" (though "supra-rational" is a fairer description of it).

With regard to the second antinomy, Schweitzer wrote to Kraus:

Hitherto it has been my principle never to express in my philosophy more than I have experienced as a result of absolutely logical reflection. That is why I never speak in philosophy of "God" but only of the "universal will-to-live," which I realize in my consciousness in a two-fold way: firstly, as a creative will outside myself, and secondly, as an ethical will within me. . . . That is why I prefer to content myself with a description of the experience of reflection, leaving pantheism and theism as an unsolved conflict in my soul. For that is the actuality to which I am always being forced to return.

But if I speak the traditional language of religion, I use the word "God" in its historical definiteness and indefiniteness, just as I speak in ethics of "Love" in place of Reverence for Life. For I am anxious to impart to others my inwardly experienced thought

[1] *Civilization and Ethics*, pp. xv–xvi.

[2] Here is an obvious inconsistency (not remarked by Kraus), though not a serious one. For it is clear that Schweitzer has experienced ethics both emotionally and as a logical necessity: for him the sentiment of compassion is the emotional factor which provides the determinant for the rational thought which becomes a necessity.

in all its original vividness and in its relation to traditional religion. . . .

I do not seem able to get beyond this renunciation of knowledge of the universe, nor beyond the conflict between pantheism and theism. . . . It is my fate and my destiny to reflect and to live, to ponder on the question of how much of ethics and religion can be comprised in a world-view which dares to be inconclusive. . . .

On this there is perhaps more to be said. Definite acceptance of theism would seem to involve the acceptance of a metaphysical dualism; pantheism, that of a metaphysical monism. Schweitzer has since shown (in the first chapter of his *Indian Thought*, 1935) that neither of these positions is philosophically tenable: dualism because, influenced as it is by an ethical habit of thought, it cannot include in its world-view those features of the world-process which are non-ethical; monism because, seeking a single comprehensive world-view, it is obliged to borrow its account of the ethical from the world-view of dualism.—God, the author of all Good only; or God, who is eternally All in All: that is the problem which the mind of man has never solved.

Let me express it by a simile. There is an ocean—cold water without motion. In this ocean, however, is the Gulf Stream —hot water, flowing from the Equator towards the Pole. Enquire of all the scientists how it is physically imaginable that a stream of hot water flows between the waters of the ocean, which, so to speak, form its banks, the moving within the motionless, the hot within the cold: no scientist can explain it. Similarly there is the God of Love within the God of the Forces of the Universe—one with Him, and yet so totally different. We let ouselves be seized and carried away by that vital stream.[1]

Thus Schweitzer abandons any theoretical solution of the problem, objectively. He seeks only union with Infinite Being, that is, with God as experienced subjectively. Ethical mysticism must remain a paradox for thought, and yet it is a necessity for thought. Ethically it leans towards theism and dualism; mystically towards pantheism and monism.

But it is the third of these antinomies which is the most important and the most difficult of all. On the one hand, according to Schweitzer, the world-view of Jesus is optimistic in that it presupposes the

[1] *Christianity and the Religions of the World.*

existence of an other-worldly principle already inherent in man, which is the guarantee of man's ultimate perfectibility. On the other hand it is pessimistic because it envisages a supernatural catastrophe as the prerequisite for the Kingdom, having the appearance of an act of grace, and so presumably beyond the natural capacity of man. As Kraus justly observes, whether the event comes to pass by natural or supernatural means is of minor importance compared with the fact of ultimate perfection itself. Schweitzer's reply to Kraus was as follows:

> You are quite right when you refer to my wavering between the terms optimistic and pessimistic when it is a question of forming a judgment on the world-view of Jesus. Only when I was working at my Philosophy of Civilization did I eventually find the right definition. Before that I was still working with the old traditional terminology.

It must be observed in the first place that there is an ambiguity in Schweitzer's use of the term "world-view." It may have a general or a special reference. Schweitzer himself defines it in a very comprehensive sense as to cover "the sum-total of the thoughts which the community or the individual think about the nature and purpose of the universe and about the place and destiny of mankind within the world." But such thoughts may have a metaphysical or a cosmological reference. In the former sense the term is properly applicable to all forms of philosophic thought and to any habits of thinking which can be generalized; but it is in the latter specialized sense that the world-view of Jesus is to be understood.

Secondly, and as a consequence of this, there is an ambiguity in his use of the term "pessimistic" to describe the world-view of Jesus. Pessimism may signify world- and life-denial, the logical outcome of which is the extinction of the will-to-live, and in this sense it is generally understood. Or it may bear the more specialized meaning of despair of the natural perfectibility of man, a consummation which can only be brought about on his behalf by supernatural intervention. It is in this latter sense that Schweitzer interprets the "pessimistic world-view" of Jesus. Nevertheless, as Schweitzer himself with great cogency pointed out in his original Sketch of the Life of Jesus, it was the natural capacity of man—his capacity for repentance— which was to hasten the cosmic catastrophe; and this was in fact the secre of the Mystery of the Kingdom of God. The incidence of the supernatural event depended on man's response to the call for repentance, which it was open to all men to hear and to heed. Those who refused to do so were guilty of what one might call a treasonable betrayal of their own nature. Those who responded (the Elect) were "the men of violence who would take the Kingdom by force." It was this activist world- and life-affirmation which above all distinguished the world-view of Jesus from that of His contemporaries who waited as passive spectators for the supernatural event.

Kraus states his own personal conviction that Our Lord's world-view was in fact optimistic, "being founded in the first place on the perfection of the Father, and secondly on the natural capacity of man —that is, on his capacity for repentance." To the present writer it seems that if Schweitzer could accept this interpretation, his own philosophy of world- and life-affirmation and ethics would be enormously strengthened thereby. For once again—and it cannot be too emphatically asserted—the divine principle is already inherent in human nature, and in so far as man falls short of it he is unnatural and false to himself.

In the Epilogue to his book *My Life and Thought*, written from Lambaréné as far back as 1931, Schweitzer in moving words explains his own attitude with regard to this matter.

> To the question whether I am a pessimist or an optimist, I answer that my knowledge is pessimistic, but my willing and hoping are optimistic.
>
> I am pessimistic in that I experience in its full weight what we conceive to be the absence of purpose in the course of world-happenings. Only at quite rare moments have I felt really glad to be alive. I could not but feel with a sympathy full of regret all the pain that I saw around me, not only that of men but that of the whole creation. From this community of suffering I have never tried to withdraw myself. It seemed to me a matter of course that we should all take our share of the burden of pain which lies upon the world. Even while I was a boy at school it was clear to me that no explanation of the evil in the world could ever satisfy me; all explanations, I felt, ended in sophistries, and at bottom had no other object than to make it possible for men to share in the misery around them, with less keen feelings. That a thinker like Leibnitz could reach the miserable conclusion that though this world is, indeed, not good, it is the best that was possible, I have never been able to understand.
>
> But however much concerned I was at the problem of the misery

in the world, I never let myself get lost in brooding over it; I always held firmly to the thought that each one of us can do a little to bring some portion of it to an end. Thus I came gradually to rest content in the knowledge that there is only one thing we can understand about the problem, and that is that each of us has to go his own way, but as one who means to help to bring about deliverance.

In my judgment, too, of the situation in which mankind finds itself at the present time I am pessimistic. I cannot make myself believe that that situation is not so bad as it seems to be, but I am inwardly conscious that we are on a road which, if we continue to tread it, will bring us into "Middle Ages" of a new character. The spiritual and material misery to which mankind of today is delivering itself through its renunciation of thinking and of the ideals which spring therefrom, I picture to myself in its utmost compass. And yet I remain optimistic. One belief of my childhood I have preserved with the certainty that I can never lose it: belief in truth. I am confident that the spirit generated by truth is stronger than the force of circumstances. In my view no other destiny awaits mankind than that which, through its mental and spiritual disposition, it prepares for itself. Therefore I do not believe that it will have to tread the road to ruin right to the end.

If men can be found who revolt against the spirit of thoughtlessness, and who are personalities sound enough and profound enough to let the ideals of ethical progress radiate from them as a force, there will start an activity of the spirit which will be strong enough to evoke a new mental and spiritual disposition in mankind.

Because I have confidence in the power of truth and of the spirit I believe in the future of mankind. Ethical world- and life-affirmation contains within itself an optimistic willing and hoping which can never be lost. It is, therefore, never afraid to face the dismal reality, and to see it as it really is.

Naturalness. That is the keynote of Schweitzer's thought, life, and personality. The ultimate thought, the thought which holds the clue to the riddle of life's meaning and mystery, must be the simplest thought conceivable, the most natural, the most elemental, and therefore also the most profound. To find it one must needs be an explorer. And Schweitzer is before all else an explorer, a spiritual adventurer, an intellectual pioneer. In seeking his life's vocation among primitive men in Equatorial Africa he is, as has been said of a famous Polar explorer, "an elemental sort of person going to an elemental sort of place." His massive intellect, his robust frame, his brusque direct manner, are the visible expression of a grand, rugged, rock-like personality. His acute sensitivity to the sufferings of others, and disregard of his own, is the expression of a soul of gentleness. So deep and genuine is his sense of gratitude for even the smallest services rendered to his cause that sometimes, for lack of words in which to express it, he will say: "It is a good thing that there is a hereafter, since I could never thank you enough on earth!" Gifted as he is with rare and various endowments, and conscious as he cannot help being of powers far beyond the ordinary, he is also the soul of modesty. This latter characteristic in him resembles that which he ascribes to Bach: "His modesty was not the hypocritical and conceited thing in which celebrities love to drape themselves in order to bulk still larger in the eyes of the world, but the sane and healthy modesty that comes from the simple consciousness of one's own worth."

Simplicity. This quality is apparent in his workaday life in which he has reduced his own necessities to the barest minimum. It is apparent in all his writing, in which he abjures technicalities and abstractions, and succeeds in matching profundity of thought with the utmost possible lucidity of expression. It is apparent in his intercourse with his fellow-men, in the directness of his address and the homely idiom of his speech. It is apparent also in another way. For even more remarkable than the many-sidedness of his interests is the single-mindedness with which he has harnessed them to one end; "the striking fact" (to borrow his own words about Goethe) "that these various activities, mental and practical, bear no relation to one another, but are quite distinct, and only united in his personality."

Two things, he tells us, have cast their shadows over his existence. One is the perception that "the world is inexplicably mysterious and full of suffering"; the other, "the consciousness of having been born into a period of spiritual decadence in mankind." But each of these depressing thoughts he has been enabled to meet and overcome by steadily deepening reflection on the principle of world- and life-affirmation embodied in the ethic of Reverence for Life. His one concern is how best as a faithful steward to use the talents committed to his trust, both in word and in deed, to the welfare of his fellow-men; and so to prove worthy of the highest privilege to which the soul of man can aspire, the privilege of fellowship with Jesus.

Reticence. The lad who never wore his heart upon his sleeve; who could not tell his mother how much he loved her, or his friends how much he owed them; who hid his deepest feelings from his spiritual counsellor and his artistic sensibility from his music master; the youth who at 21 made a momentous resolve for life but kept it to himself, and carried it into effect at 30 without advice or consultation; the medical administrator who hid from his colleagues his decision to build a new hospital in the teeth of every obstacle, and also the anguish he had felt for the sufferings of his patients,—is the thinker and the man of action to whom respect for the personality of others is an obligation as sacred as reverence for life itself.

United in his single personality, thought and action have marched always side by side: the one the necessary complement and fulfilment of the other. It was his sense of the inexplicable both in natural life and human destiny that first led him to the study of physical science and of history, and finding no solution in them, to the study of philosophy—at the same time putting it to pragmatic test by going out of his way to relieve distress. Finding the discursive reason value-less for his quest, he turned to a thorough and radical examination of historical religion. The result was a confirmation of his intuitive con-viction that the secret of life's mystery is revealed not to the rational but to the mystic consciousness, but only as it finds expression in sacrificial service. To establish this discovery and fulfil it, he devoted his life and talents to the service of the least and lowest of mankind, to personal experience of life in the raw, stripped of all the veneer of civilization. Having found his own inspiration for this service in the command of Jesus and the example of a great apostle, he yet had not found obedience to it a necessity for thought. So he betook himself again to the study of philosophy with an intenser purpose than ever before, till he found at last the key to unlock the iron door of thought. And through every stage of his intellectual and practical labours he has found in music the truest expression and most satisfying release for his own spiritual aspiration.

Those who tread the heights of spiritual experience must needs be lonely. In the last words of *My Life and Thought* Schweitzer has revealed the character of his loneliness, and, though they were written fifteen years ago, there are none fitter with which to end this present record of his life.

In my own life anxiety, trouble, and sorrow have been allotted to me at times in such abundant measure that had my nerves not been so strong, I must have broken down under the weight.

Heavy is the burden of fatigue and responsibility which has lain upon me without a break for years. I have not much of my life for myself, not even the hours I should like to devote to my wife and child.

But I have had blessings too: that I am allowed to work in the service of mercy; that my work has been successful; that I receive from other people affection and kindness in abundance; that I have loyal helpers, who identify themselves with my activity; that I enjoy a health which allows me to undertake most exhausting work; that I have a well-balanced temperament which varies little, and an energy which exerts itself with calmness and deliberation; and, finally, that I can recognize as such whatever happiness falls to my lot, accepting it also as a thing for which some thank-offering is due from me.

I feel it deeply that I can work as a free man at a time when an oppressive lack of freedom is the lot of so many, as also that, though my immediate work is material, yet I have at the same time opportunities of occupying myself in the sphere of the spiritual and intellectual.

That the circumstances of my life provide in such varied ways favourable conditions for my work, I accept as something of which I would fain prove myself worthy.

How much of the work which I have planned and have in mind shall I be able to complete? . . .

I look back with thankfulness to the time when, without needing to husband my strength, I could get through an uninterrupted course of bodily and mental work. With calmness and humility I look forward to the future, so that I may not be unprepared for renunciation if it be required of me. Whether we be workers or sufferers, it is assuredly our duty to conserve our powers, as being men who have won their way through to the peace which passeth all understanding.

APPENDICES

CIVILIZATION AND COLONIZATION

In January 1928 Schweitzer contributed to the *Contemporary Review* a paper on "The Relations of the White to the Coloured Races," in which he expressed his mature considerations on the problems connected with colonization among primitive races in general. This is too important to be omitted from any complete record of his life. It is also too concisely expressed for abbreviation. His observations on the same problems as they affect the negro in particular are of course to be found extensively in all his books on Africa; but the most concise account of them is in the chapter entitled "The Book of African Reminiscences" of his book *My Life and Thought*. In order to give force to his contention, as well as to illustrate the general by the particular, extracts from the latter are here introduced in square brackets into the text of the former.

The Relations of the White and Coloured Races

I WISH to discuss Colonization, and the relations of the White and Coloured Races which it involves, as a peasant talks of his cabbages, and not as an artist or a poet would depict the same cabbages. It is the point of view of the man who is in the work, who has to dig and sow, manure, and tend the plants. Let us concentrate upon the essential problems of Colonization, which is the conservation and protection and the exercise of the rights of man.

[Have we white people the right to impose our rule on primitive and semi-primitive peoples? No, if we only want to rule over them and draw material advantage from their country. Yes, if we seriously desire to educate them and help them to attain to a condition of well-being.]

The independence of primitive or semi-primitive peoples is lost at the moment when the first white man's boat arrives with powder or rum, salt or fabrics. The social, economic, and political situation at that moment begins to be turned upside down. The chiefs begin to sell their subjects for goods. From that point the political work of a State in colonizing is to correct, by its actions, the evils developed through unrestrained economic advance.

Independence, then, is not lost by primitive peoples from the moment when a Protectorate or other form of government is proclaimed; but has

already been lost in the commercial advance of which the political colonization must be a corrective.

[If there were any sort of possibility that these peoples could live really
by and for themselves, we could leave them to themselves. But as things
are, the world trade which has reached them is a fact against which both
we and they are powerless. They have already through it lost their
freedom. Their economic and social relations are shaken by it. An inevitable development brought it about that the chiefs, with the weapons and
money which commerce placed at their disposal, reduced the mass of the
natives to servitude and turned them into slaves who had to work for
the export trade to make a few select people rich. It sometimes happened,
too, that as in the days of the slave trade, the people themselves became
merchandise, and were exchanged for money, lead, gunpowder, tobacco,
and brandy. In view of the state of things produced by world trade there
can be no question with these peoples of real independence, but only
whether it is better for them to be delivered over to the mercies, tender
or otherwise, of rapacious native tyrants or to be governed by officials
of European states.]

The question for us, therefore, is not—"Have we a right there?"—the
question is simply one of alternatives. Are we, on the one hand, the masters
of these folk and lands, simply as raw material for our industries; or are
we, on the other hand, responsible for developing a new social order, so
as to create the possibility among those peoples of resisting the evils,
and of developing themselves a new political organization? We have, I
hold, the right to colonize if we have the moral authority to exercise
this influence.

[That, of those who were commissioned to carry out in our name the
seizure of our colonial territories, many were guilty of injustice, violence,
and cruelty, as bad as those of the native chiefs, and so brought on our
heads a load of guilt, is only too true. Nor of the sins committed against
the natives today must anything be suppressed or whitewashed. But
willingness to give these primitive and semi-primitive people of our
colonies an independence which would inevitably end in enslavement to
their fellows, is no way of making up for our failure to treat them properly.
Our only possible course is to exercise for the benefit of the natives the
power we actually possess, and thus provide a moral justification for it.
Even the hitherto prevailing imperialism can plead that it has some
qualities of ethical value. It has put an end to the slave trade; it has stopped
the perpetual wars which the primitive peoples used to wage with one
another, and has thus given a lasting peace to large portions of the world;
it endeavours in many ways to produce in the colonies conditions which
shall render more difficult the exploitation of the population by world
trade. I dare not picture what the lot of the native lumbermen in the
forests of the Ogowe district would be if the Government authorities

which at the present time preserve their rights for them in opposition to the merchants, both white and black, should be withdrawn.

What so-called self-government means for primitive and semi-primitive peoples can be gathered from the fact that in the Black Republic of Liberia, domestic slavery and what is far worse, the compulsory shipment of labourers to other countries, have continued down to our own day. They were both abolished on 1st October 1930—on paper.]

The idea of the rights of man was formed and developed in the eighteenth century, when society was an organized and stable thing. Whatever the fundamental rights of men are, they can only be fully secured in a stable and well-ordered society. In a disordered society the very well-being of man himself often demands that his fundamental rights should be abridged. We have, then, to start in our discussion from an empirical rather than a philosophical basis.

The fundamental rights of man are, first, the right to habitation; secondly, the right to move freely; thirdly, the right to the soil and sub-soil, and to the use of it; fourthly, the right to freedom of labour and of exchange; fifthly, the right to justice; sixthly, the right to live within a natural, national organization; and, seventhly, the right to education. We now ask ourselves how far are these safeguarded by existing colonization?

The power to safeguard the rights of man varies in direct relation with the social order. If the social order is normal, the rights can be complete; but if it is abnormal, they are menaced and limited. For instance, the sense in which our life is less normal since the war than before it, has its effect on our freedom of movement in Europe, and a consequent development of the passport difficulties as against freedom of movement. For this reason, in order to develop and establish in practice the rights of man in the colonies, our fundamental aim is to develop a social State more normal than that which exists today.

[The tragic fact is that the interests of colonization and those of civilization do not always run parallel, but are often in direct opposition to each other. The best thing for primitive peoples would be that, in such seclusion from the world trade as is possible, and under an intelligent administration, they would rise by slow development from being nomads and semi-nomads to be agriculturists and artisans, permanently settled on the soil. That, however, is rendered impossible by the fact that these peoples themselves will not let themselves be withheld from the chance of earning money by selling goods to the world trade, just as on the other hand world trade will not abstain from purchasing native products from them and depositing manufactured goods in exchange. Thus it becomes very hard to carry to completion a colonization which means at the same time true civilization.]

Let us now examine one by one these rights on the spot, face to face with the existing situation in primitive societies under colonization.

1. THE RIGHT TO HABITATION

Man has the right to live where his life has been developed, and not to be displaced. This is a burning point in primitive and semi-primitive society. Yet in colonization the right is constantly menaced; often not by ill-will in any degree, but by the sheer force of facts. For instance, a large, modern white city grows up round a small, primitive village, or the creation and development of an arterial road on which the very lives of the inhabitants depends, involves living by that road. The future development of the good of the people may necessitate the movement of villages, yet, if it is done without long foresight, careful planning and adequate warning, with provision for the creation of new plantations, and if any violence enters into it, a fatal impression will be created in the mind of the native that he is delivered up to the working of an arbitrary will. Any movement that is ordered must always be on a rational basis for the future good.

[In the interest of the development of the country it may become necessary to transplant remote villages to the neighbourhood of the railway or the road. But only when no other course is possible should there be encroachment in this and other ways on the human rights of the natives. How much disaffection is provoked again and again in the colonies by the compulsory application of measures which are expedient only in the imagination of some official who wants to draw attention to himself.]

2. THE RIGHT TO CIRCULATE FREELY

The right of emigration and immigration is today surrounded by every kind of difficulty. For instance, vast cocoa plantations exercise a very strong economic pull for labour on the population of the neighbouring territories. To allow that economic pull to have free play would rob neighbouring colonies of the essential labour. Therefore there is restriction on movement. In the collection of taxes again, there is a strong temptation to the natives to disappear into the forest and move to another area to escape taxes. So the administration insists that he stays in his own canton. From the State's point of view and from that of the development of the country this is reasonable; but the right to circulate is limited.

[With regard to the question, much discussed today, of the justifiableness or not of forced labour, my standpoint is that the natives may under no circumstances be compelled by the authorities to work for any period either long or short, for any private undertaking, not even if the labour is accepted as a substitute for a tax or for statutory labour due to the state. The only labour which may be imposed on the natives is what has to be done in the interests of the public well-being and is done under the supervision of state officials.

Nor must it be thought that the native can be trained to labour by requiring him to pay ever-increasing taxes. He is indeed obliged to work to obtain the money needed for such taxes, but this concealed forced labour will not, any more than the unconcealed, change him from an indolent to an industrious man. Injustice cannot produce a moral result.

In every colony in the world the taxes are today already so high that they can only with difficulty be paid by the population. Colonies everywhere have, for want of thought, been burdened with loans, the interest on which can hardly be raised.]

3. The Right to the Soil and to its Development and Use

There is a right to the natural riches of the soil and sub-soil; and to dispose of it as one will. But here, again, two very strong factors enter in. First, the development of the value of the whole land by enterprises from without. Few things are more difficult to foresee on a long view than what lands and sub-soils should remain in the hand of the native, and how much should be placed in the hands of enterprises that will develop their values.

Again, on the other hand, a chief is offered money to sell his land. The money is put into his hands. He spends it on clothes, and trinkets, and tools and other things for himself and his wives. The land is gone and the money is gone; and his descendants find themselves pariahs—landless labourers. It is, therefore, in the interests of the people themselves to restrict the right of the chief to dispose of his land.

[The real wealth of the peoples would consist in their coming to produce for themselves by agriculture and handicrafts as far as possible all the necessities of their life. Instead of that they are exclusively bent on providing the materials which world trade requires and for which it pays them good prices. With the money thus obtained they procure from it manufactured goods and prepared foodstuffs, thereby making home industry impossible, and often endangering the stability of their own agriculture. This is the condition in which all primitive and semi-primitive peoples find themselves who can offer to world trade rice, cotton, coffee, cocoa, minerals, timber, and similar things.

Whenever the timber trade is good, permanent famine reigns in the Ogowe region, because the natives neglect the making of new plantations in order to fell as many trees as possible. In the swamps and the forest in which they find this work they live on imported rice and imported preserved foods, which they purchase with the proceeds of their labour.

Colonization, then, in the sense of civilization, means trying to ensure that among the primitive and semi-primitive peoples who are in danger in this way, only so much labour power is allowed to be engaged for the export trade as is not needed for home industry and for that proportion of their agriculture which produces the foodstuffs needed at home. The more thinly any colony is populated, the more difficult it is to reconcile the interests of a sound development of the country with those of world trade. A rising export trade does not always prove that a colony is making progress; it may also mean that it is on the way to ruin.]

4. THE RIGHT TO FREE WORK AND FREE EXCHANGE

No right is more fundamental or more essential than that of the free disposal by a man of his labour. In the present condition of things, however, we are confronted from time to time by circumstances and conditions that seem to make it essential for the State to demand labour. The State has the right to impose taxes to be collected in money or in kind. Has it also the right to collect service in actual labour? To take two instances. A famine occurs in a certain area to which food must be transported if life is to be saved. The men will not carry that food for simple payment. (Payment, of course, is always made whether labour is forced or not.) Is it not then essential actually to command labour?

Again, the destruction of human life by long porterage is in Africa terrible. The only way to stop it is by the engineering of long, arterial roads capable of taking motor-wagon traffic. In order to save life, therefore, it may become essential both to make the road by forced labour and to insist that along that road villages shall maintain the area of the road within their neighbourhood clean from the forest, which in six months would completely overgrow it; for a road left for that period disappears in the undergrowth. The labour of those villages is paid for, but is enforced. Directly we attempt that, however, we are faced by the problems of time and space. If men are taken long distances, leaving their families and villages, with consequent problems of food, sanitation and so on, great injustice can be done. The African loses his vitality and his elasticity directly you take him from his village. He is the most rooted of men.

[Again, road and railway construction shows itself as a difficult problem amid a primitive population. Roads and railways are necessary in order that the horror of transport by carriers may be ended; that in times of famine foodstuffs may be conveyed into the threatened regions; and that trade may prosper. At the same time there is a danger that they may imperil the beneficial development of the country. They do that when they call for more labour-power than the country can normally spare for them. Account must be taken, too, of the fact that colonial road and railway construction involves great loss of human life, even when—and this is unfortunately not always the case—the best possible provision is made for the lodging and provisioning of the labourers. It may happen, too, that the district which the road or the railway was meant to serve is ruined by it. The opening-up of any region must therefore be undertaken only after full consideration. The public works which are taken in hand because they are held to be necessary and also possible, must be carried on slowly, in some cases even with occasional cessations of work, for in that way, as experience has shown, many lives can be saved.]

The African primitive man who is accustomed to seeing his womenfolk at the plantation work, cannot see why they should not do the road work; and women are used on the roads to some extent.

In the control, therefore, of what forced labour is needed I would lay down these principles:—

(1) That it should only be used by the State and under stress of absolute need. (2) That the sharing of women in such labour should only be (a) when it is near their own village to which they can return to sleep; (b) when plantation work is not needed (this time is in practice quite clear and sharply defined); (c) when they are not nursing a child. (3) That no children should be allowed to work. (4) That where the men live while working away from their villages, proper preparation shall be made in the way of sanitation, food, habitation; and (5) That the pace of the labour shall never be forced.

In the matter of the right to free exchange face to face with private enterprise, we confront a difficult problem. Experiments have been made in two directions of giving a particular company a monopoly of a certain area, or of allowing competition. Each process has its own advantages and disadvantages. If you give one company a monopoly of an area, it is to its interest to look after the natives there, to see that the clothes and hatchets, etc., that they buy are good; to refrain from introducing alcohol and so on. The disadvantages are that the company, having a monopoly, can sell to the native at its own fixed price.

The State now comes into alliance with commerce for developing the value of these areas, and here again we confront a problem of forced labour. Rubber or palm-oil grown a long distance from the coast is absolutely useless unless it can be transported; and often the only way to transport it is by forced porterage by the State from the plantations to the point at which commerce on the coast can send up its steamers or its railways or motor-wagons. There is no other way of development, and it has desperately dangerous tendencies in it. Frankly, it is better to leave them undeveloped, in a certain number of cases, rather than develop along abnormal lines and with injustice. Where development is proceeded with, the State must exercise the most strict supervision. The indolence and inconsequence of the African may often be infuriating, and I personally suffer greatly from it; but I do not believe at all in the educative value of forced labour. That is not the way to educate him to work.

5. THE RIGHT TO JUSTICE TO AND FOR THE NATIVE

Primitive tribal justice has the great quality that it is justice for everybody face to face with his adversary, administered locally and swiftly by the chief. Attempts to administer justice by Europeans, with a judge either infrequently there or at a long distance, not knowing the language or the people individually, and unable to penetrate behind the lives of the witnesses, is often long, slow, difficult and inefficient. Furthermore, the natives' own law (often more severe than ours) has been developed to meet their own conditions. Therefore in order to secure the great need for a settlement on the spot at a man's own door, we must have travelling judges or administrators who will move from place to place giving justice on the spot, in co-operation with the authority of the chiefs. One of the best administrators that I know always passes his judgment with the aid of three well-known and universally-respected older men on whom he puts the responsibility for judgment.

The greatest bar set up between the races on the spot comes less from the big, spectacular injustices that appear in the press than from the little repeated cases of violence on the part of immature, untested and inexperienced white men, exasperated beyond expression by the ways of primitive man. Before condemning even these acts of violence we should ask whether we ought not in fact really to condemn the governments and commercial enterprises that send young, untested, inexperienced men of inadequate moral calibre into the interior to difficult posts. The interior should also be subject to regular visitation by inspectors to investigate cases. This system must be accompanied by very careful protection for the witnesses. The inspectors must in all cases be experienced men who know the land and the folk, and the chief's authority must be strengthened. To do away with that authority is to destroy your one intermediary between the administration and the multitude. In Europe the intermediary between government and the people is the office. That process is impossible with primitive peoples. It is always the man that matters. We have to do not with peoples but with tribes; not with organized governments but with chiefs. We are thus brought to

6. The Right to Natural, National Organization

The only way to defend and extend the other rights already enumerated is to develop a new stable social organization. To go back to the very beginning of what I have here said—the rights of man are a direct function of the normal organization of Society. We have, therefore, to create a social organization and economic conditions in which the native can flourish face to face with Western commerce. To do this, we need a stable population, possessing houses, fields, orchards, workshops, and the requisite capacity to create and use them. This can only be achieved by the exercise of the last right on our list—the right to education.

7. THE RIGHT TO EDUCATION

The education so far undertaken has been incomplete—in fact, usually the only educational work yet done has been that contributed by the missionaries. If, for instance, I want (or any man wants) an artisan—someone who can really work skilfully with his hands, a carpenter, for instance —I cannot find any save those educated by the missionary societies. When the modern State talks about doing an educational work among the natives, I say to it: "Do not make phrases; show me your work. How many educators have you in fact exported to your colony?"

[The problems of native education are mixed up with economic and social problems, and are not less complicated than the latter. Agriculture and handicraft are the foundations of civilization. Only where that foundation exists are the conditions given for the formation and persistence of a stratum of population which can occupy itself with commercial and intellectual pursuits. But with the natives in the colonies—and they themselves demand it—we proceed as if not agriculture and handicraft, but reading and writing, were the beginnings of civilization. From schools which are mere copies of those of Europe they are turned out as "educated" persons, that is, who think themselves superior to manual work, and want to follow only commercial or intellectual callings. All those who are unable to secure acceptable employment in the offices of the business houses or of the Government sit about as idlers or grumblers. It is the misfortune of all colonies—and not only of those with primitive or semi-primitive populations—that those who go through the schools are mostly lost to agriculture and handicraft instead of contributing to their development. This change of class, from lower to higher, produces thoroughly unhealthy economic and social conditions. Proper colonization means educating the natives in such a way that they are not alienated from agriculture and handicraft, but attracted to them. Intellectual learning should in every colonial school be accompanied by the acquisition of every kind of manual skill; for their civilization it is more important that the natives should learn to burn bricks, to build, to saw logs into planks, to be ready with hammer, plane, and chisel, than they should be brilliant at reading and writing, and even be able to calculate with $a + b$ and $x + y$.]

The work of education among a primitive people must be a blend of the intellectual and the manual adapted to the needs of citizenship in a primitive society. We must send out to such areas not only ordinary teachers, but artisan educators; in fact, a central problem of education there is how to make a craft loved and practised among primitive peoples. The native is in danger of cutting out the stage between primitive life and professional. That is, he tends to eliminate the stages of agriculture and handicraft. He has a certain antagonism to the use of tools, and a desire to sit in an office with a cigarette in his mouth and a pen in his hand. I am constantly hearing the phrase "I want to be a writer." At my hospital, recently, I was helping to carry things to the garden, partly in order to create this impression of the dignity of labour. I saw a native in white clothes standing by the fence, and asked him to join in and help. His reply was—"No, I am an intellectual; a brain-worker." I went to a store, run by a native for natives, and could not get a single tool that I wanted, but found masses of silk stockings. We cannot, therefore, build a proper social organization until the native himself is skilled in making the essentials of his life—that is, growing his food and building his habitation. All independence, and therefore all capacity to face economic stress and to secure justice, is rooted there. If from the European side we want through our administration to hasten this end, our work is not to elaborate minute regulations for guarding the native, and so build up in Europe a façade out of justice that really conceals injustice out there; but to send out as administrators tested men of humane feeling and goodwill, making them take all responsibility on the spot face to face with the natives on the one side, and with their own superior on the other; to increase the initiative of the officer and the authority of the chief; and establish our control by regular visitation through skilled, experienced men. The native moves under patriarchal authority. He does not understand dealing with an office, but dealing with a man in whom he has confidence and who understands him.

Many commercial men and administrators whom I know do their work among the natives with idealism, and it is after all on the character of such men that our success depends. It is on the development of manhood in the native craftsman and cultivator that a new social order can alone be built, and it is in manhood in the administrator and educator from the West that we can alone find the means of helping the native to re-create a new civilization on his own soil.

[But the most important thing of all is that we cry "Halt" to the dying-out of the primitive and semi-primitive peoples. Their existence is threatened by alcohol, with which commerce supplies them, by diseases which we have taken to them, and by diseases which already existed among them, but which, like sleeping sickness, were first enabled to spread by the intercourse which colonization brought with it. Today that disease is a peril to millions.

The harm which the importation of alcohol means for these people cannot be counteracted by forbidding brandy and rum while allowing wine and beer as before. In the colonies wine and beer are much more dangerous beverages than in Europe, because, to enable them to keep good in tropical and sub-tropical regions, pure alcohol is always added to them.

The absence of brandy and rum is amply made up for by an enormously increased consumption of wine and beer of this description. The share that alcohol has in the ruin of these peoples can, therefore, only be prevented by absolute prohibition of the importation of all alcoholic drinks, of whatever sort.

In nearly all colonies the struggle against disease has been undertaken with too little energy and was begun too late. That it can be carried on today with some prospect of success we owe to the weapons which the latest medical science has put into our hands.

The necessity for taking medical help to the natives in our colonies is frequently argued on the ground that it is worth while to preserve the human material without which the colonies would become valueless. But the matter is in reality something much more important than a question of economics. It is unthinkable that we civilized peoples should keep for ourselves alone the wealth of means for fighting sickness, pain, and death, which science has given us. If there is any ethical thinking at all among us, how can we refuse to let these new discoveries benefit those who, in distant lands, are subject to even greater physical distress than we are? In addition to the medical men who are sent out by the governments, and who are never more than enough to accomplish a fraction of what needs doing, others must go out, too, commissioned by human society as such.

Whoever among us has through personal experience learnt what pain and anxiety really are must help to ensure that those, who out there are in bodily need, obtain the help which came to him. He belongs no more to himself alone; he has become the brother of all who suffer. On the "Brotherhood of those who bear the mark of pain" lies the duty of medical work, work for humanity's sake, in the colonies. Commissioned by their representatives, medical men must accomplish among the suffering in far-off lands what is crying out for accomplishment in the name of true civilization.

In reliance upon the elementary truth which is embodied in the idea of the "Brotherhood of those who bear the mark of pain," I ventured to found the Forest Hospital at Lambaréné. That truth was recognized and is now spreading.

Finally, let me urge that whatever benefit we confer upon the peoples of our colonies is not beneficence, but atonement for the terrible sufferings which we white people have been bringing upon them ever since the day on which the first of our ships found its way to their shores. Colonial problems, as they exist today, cannot be solved by political measures alone. A new element must be introduced; white and coloured must meet in an atmosphere of the ethical spirit. Then only will mutual understanding be possible.

To work for the creation of that spirit means helping to make the course of world politics rich in blessings for the future.]

NOTE

As one who for five years lived in close contact with the negroes, often spending many weeks together alone with them in the bush—not as a missionary, but as an official in the Civil Service, nor in West Africa, but in the triangle of territory that lies between the Zambesi, the Loangwa, and Lake Nyasa—the present writer may be perhaps allowed to say that every word of Dr. Schweitzer's contention was again and again confirmed in his own experience. He is sure that it would be endorsed by his colleagues in Northern Rhodesia as well as by other British Civil Servants in south central Africa. Unfortunately it is not by those who work in closest contact with the primitive races that laws for their amelioration, or otherwise, are passed.

GOETHE PRIZE ADDRESS [1]

I WILL narrate shortly how I came into touch with Goethe, and how he reacted on my life.

It was in the field of philosophy that I had first to take up a position with regard to Goethe. When my revered Strasburg teachers, Wilhelm Windelband and Theodore Ziegler, had introduced me to the new philosophy, and I was glowing with enthusiasm for the great speculative systems, I could not but feel it almost incomprehensible that Goethe, who had lived through the powerful influence of a Kant, a Fichte, a Hegel, stood comparatively coldly on one side and let this influence pass by, while he remained within the circle of a nature-philosophy as he had learnt it from the Stoics and Spinoza, coming to believe in it with complete confidence and to attempt himself to develop it further. This astonishment at his remaining loyal to the apparently insignificant, and allowing something so powerful to pass by him, had a great effect on me. I can say that it was for me my first and longest-lasting incitement to come to an understanding with the new philosophy, and to develop my own thought. It thus became in the course of years clear to me that there are two philosophies which exist side by side. The object of all philosophy is to make us, as thinking beings, understand how we are to place ourselves in an intelligent and inward relation to the universe, and how we are to be active under the impulses which come to us from it.

The first of these philosophies brings man and the universe together only by doing violence to nature and the world, and putting men into connection with a world which has been made to bend itself to their thought.

The other philosophy, the insignificant nature-philosophy, leaves the world and nature as they are and compels man to find his place in them, and to assert himself in them as a spirit triumphant over them and working upon them.

The first is a work of genius, the other is elemental. The first progresses by means of mighty eruptions of thought such as appear in the great speculative systems of German philosophy and compel our admiration. But it has its day, and then disappears. The other, the homely, simple

[1] Delivered at Frankfort, August 28, 1928. Translated by C. T. Campion for the *Hibbert Journal*, July 1928.

nature-philosophy, remains current. In it there comes into its own an elemental philosophizing which first sought to realize itself in the Stoic doctrine, but then shared the latter's ruin because it could not find its way through to an affirmative view of the world and of life. This nature-philosophy has been handed down to us incomplete. In Spinoza and in the rationalism of the eighteenth century it tried again to think itself through to world- and life-affirmation, but when it proved unable to do this, force took the place of tentative effort. The great speculative philosophy produced its systems of compulsion. But at a time when everyone was blinded by the sight of a world that was bent to human thought there was one man who was not blinded, but held to the elemental, homely nature-philosophy, recognizing that it had not yet indeed—that is, in the eighteenth century in which he lived—succeeded in thinking itself through to the end as affirmative, but knowing that it must somehow do so, and labouring on at that task in the plain and simple way which is the essence of his genius.

When I came to myself again and, returning to this nature-philosophy, recognized that what is demanded of us is to think it through to its goal of world- and life-affirmation in so simple a way that every thoughtful person in the world should have to take part in this thinking and thereby find himself at peace with the infinite, while at the same time obtaining an effective impulse to creative activity, then I saw in Goethe the man who had held out at the abandoned post where we were now mounting guard again, and resuming the interrupted work.

Meanwhile I had found contact with him in another way. At the end of my student days I re-read, almost by chance, the account of his Harzreise in the winter of 1777, and it made a wonderful impression on me that this man, whom we regarded as an Olympian, set out amid November rain and mist to visit a minister's son who was in great spiritual difficulties, and give him suitable help. A second time there was revealed to me behind the Olympian the deep but homely man. I was learning to love Goethe. And so whenever it happened in my own life that I had to take upon me some work or other in order to do for some fellow-man the human service that he needed, I would say to myself, "This is a Harzreise for you."

I came once more on the real Goethe when it struck me in connection with his activities that he could not think of any intellectual employment without practical work side by side with it, and that the two were not held together by their character and object being similar, but were quite distinct and only united through his personality. It gripped me deeply that for this giant among the intellectuals there was no work which he held to be beneath his dignity, no practical employment of which he ever said that others on account of their natural gifts and of their profession could do it better than he, and that he was always ready to prove the unity of his personality by the union of practical work with intellectual activity.

I was already a minister when I first had to arrange my daily work, and when I sighed over the fact that through the much walking and the manifold duties entailed by my new office—which I had persisted in taking upon me to satisfy an inward need—I lost time which would have been available for intellectual labour, I comforted myself with Goethe, who, as we know, with mighty plans of intellectual activity in his head, would sit studying accounts and trying to set in order the finances of a small principality, examining plans so that streets and bridges should be constructed in the most practical way, and exerting himself year in, year out, to get disused mines at work again. And so this union of homely employment with intellectual activity comforted me concerning my own existence.

And when the life-course I had chosen led me to the point where I was compelled to embrace an activity which lay far from the natural endowment in which I had hitherto proved myself—far, too, from the employment for which I had prepared myself—then Goethe was the comforter who provided the words which helped me through. When other people, and even those who knew me best, found fault with my decision and tormented me with reproaches for wanting to study medicine, a subject for which (they said) I was not suited, declaring it to be a quixotic adventure, then I was able to reflect that this quixotic proceeding would perhaps not have been for him, the great man, so entirely quixotic, seeing that he finally allows his Wilhelm Meister, little prepared as he seemed to be for it, to become a surgeon in order that he may be able to serve. And at this point it struck me what a meaning it has for us all that Goethe in his search for the final destiny of man allows those characters in which he has depicted himself, viz. Faust and Wilhelm Meister, to end their days in a quite insignificant activity that they may thereby become men in the fullest sense in which, according to his ideas, they can become so.

Then when I began preparing myself for this new activity I met Goethe again. For my medical course I had to busy myself with natural science, though as a learner, not, like him, as an investigator. And how far removed, alas, lay natural science from what I hoped to complete in the way of intellectual production before I became immersed in practical work! But I was able to reflect that Goethe, too, had left intellectual work to return to the natural sciences. It had almost excited me that, at a time when he ought to have been bringing to its final shape so much that was stirring within him, he lost himself in the natural sciences. And now I myself, who had hitherto been engaged only in intellectual work, was compelled to occupy myself with them. It deepened my nature, and it became clear to me why Goethe devoted himself to them and would not give them up. It was because it means for everyone who produces intellectually, enlightenment and enormous gain, if he who has hitherto created facts now has to face facts, which are something, not because one has imagined them, but because they exist. Every kind of thinking is helped, if at any particular moment it can no longer occupy itself with what is imagined, but has to find its way through reality. And when I found myself under this "On through reality!" compulsion, I could look back at the man who had done it all before us.

And when my laborious years of study had ended, and I left them behind as a qualified doctor, I once more met Goethe, seeming even to converse with him in the primeval forest. I had always supposed that I went out there as a doctor, and in the first years, whenever there was building or similar work to be done, I took care to put it on the shoulders of those who seemed to me to be specially adapted for it, or who had been engaged for it. But I had to acknowledge that this would not do. Either they did not turn up or they were so ill-suited for the work that no progress was made. So I accommodated myself to the work, far removed though it was from my duties as a doctor. But the worst came last. When at the end of 1925, owing to a severe famine which endangered the existence of my hospital, I was compelled to get a plantation made for it, so that during any famine in the future we might be able to keep our heads above water to some extent through our own resources, I was obliged to superintend the clearing of the forest myself. The very miscellaneous body of workers, which the chance of the moment produced from among the willing ones of the friends of our patients, would bow to no authority but that of "the old Doctor," as I was called. So I stood for weeks and months in the forest, worrying over refractory labourers, in order to wrest from it land that would produce food for us. Whenever I got reduced to despair I thought how Goethe had devised for the final activities of his Faust the task of winning from the sea land on which men could live and feed themselves. And thus Goethe stood at my side in the swampy forest as my smiling comforter, and the man who really understood.

There is one more point which I should like to mention of Goethe's influence on me, and it is this: that I found him everywhere haunted by anxiety about justice. When about the end of the last century the theory began to prevail that whatever is to be realized must be realized without regard to right, without regard to the fate of those who are hard hit by the change, and I myself did not know how these theories should be met, it was to me a real experience to find everywhere in Goethe the longing to avoid realizing any design at the cost of right. And I have again and again with real emotion turned over the final pages of *Faust* (which both in Europe and in Africa I always re-read at Easter) where Goethe represents as the last experience of Faust, and that in which he is for the last time guilty of wrongdoing, his attempt to remove the hut which disturbs him in his possession—by a slight and well-intentioned act of violence—being, as he himself says, tired of righteousness. But in the execution of it this well-intentioned act of violence becomes a cruel act of violence in which more than one person loses his life, and the hut goes up in flames. That Goethe at the conclusion of his *Faust* should insert this episode which holds up the action of the poem gives us a deep insight into the way in which there worked within him anxiety about justice, and the strong desire to realize any plan that has to be carried out without causing any kind of injury.

My final lasting contact with Goethe arose out of my recognition of the living and vigorous way in which he shared the life of his age in its thought and in its activity. Its billows were ever surging within him. That is what impresses one, not only in the young and in the fully ripe Goethe, but in the aged Goethe also. When the mail-coach was still crawling along the high road, and we should have thought that the industrial age could be announcing its arrival merely by uncertain shadows cast in advance, it was for him already there. He was already concerning himself with the problem it put before the world, viz. that the machine was now taking the place of the man. If in his *Wilhelm Meister* he is no longer master of his material, it is not because the old man no longer has the power to shape it which he formerly had at his command, but because the material had grown till it could be neither measured nor moulded; it was because the old man was putting into it the whole of his experience and of his anxiety about the future; it was because this old man was so concerned about being among men of his age as one who understands the new age and has grown to be a part of it. That is what impresses one so deeply in the ageing Goethe.

Such were the contacts with Goethe through which I came nearer and nearer to him. He is not one who inspires. He puts forward in his works no theories which rouse to enthusiasm. Everything that he offers is what he himself has experienced in thought and in events, material which he has worked up into a higher reality. It is only through experience that we come nearer to him. Through experience which corresponds with his he becomes to us, instead of a stranger, a confidant with whom we feel ourselves united in reverential friendship. My own destiny has brought it about for me that I can experience with a vividness that goes to the very marrow of my soul the destinies of our time and anxiety about our manhood. That in an age when so many whom we need as free personalities get imprisoned in the work of a profession, I, as such a free personality, can feel all these things and, like Goethe, can through a happy combination of circumstances serve my age as a free man, is to me an act of grace which lightens my laborious life. Every task or piece of creative work that I am allowed to do is to me only a return of gratitude to destiny for that act of grace.

Similar anxiety about his age and similar work for it Goethe went through before us. Circumstances have become more chaotic than he, even with his clear vision, could foresee. Greater then than circumstances must our strength be, if in the midst of them we are to become men who understand our age and grow to be a part of it.

A spirit like Goethe's lays upon us three obligations. We have to wrestle with conditions so as to secure that men who are imprisoned in work and are being worn out by it may nevertheless preserve the possibility of a spiritual existence. We have to wrestle with men so that, in spite of being continually drawn aside to the external things which are provided so abundantly for our age, they may find the road to inwardness and keep in it. We have to wrestle with ourselves and with all and everything around us, so that in a time of confused ideals which ignore all the claims of humanity we may remain faithful to the great humane ideals of the eighteenth century, translating them into the thought of our own age, and attempting to realize them today. That is what we have to do, each of us in his life, each of us in his profession, in the spirit of the great Frankfort child whose birthday we are celebrating today in his birthplace. I myself think that this Frankfort child does not move further away from us with the course of time, but comes nearer to us. The further we travel forward the more certainly we recognize Goethe to be the man who, as our own duty is, amid the deep and widely varied experience of his age cared for his age and laboured for it; the man who would become a man who understood his age and grew to be a part of it. He did this with the abounding talents which were laid in his cradle here by destiny. We have to do it as men who have received only one small pound, but who in our trading with that pound wish to be found faithful.

RELIGION IN MODERN CIVILIZATION [1]

I AM going to discuss religion in the spiritual life and civilization of our time. The first question to be faced, therefore, is: "Is religion a force in the spiritual life of our age?" I answer, in your name and mine, "No!" There is still religion in the world; there is much religion in the church; there are many pious people among us. Christianity can still point to works of love and to social works of which it can be proud. There is a longing for religion among many who no longer belong to the churches. I rejoice to concede this. And yet we must hold fast to the fact that religion is not a force. The proof? The war!

Religion was powerless to resist the spirit through which we entered the war. It was overcome by this spirit. It could bring no force against the ideals of inhumanity and unreasonableness which gave birth to the war, and when war had broken out, religion capitulated. It became mobilized. It had to join in helping to keep up the courage of the peoples. To give each people courage to go on fighting, one had to explain that they were fighting for their existence and for the spiritual treasures of humanity. Religion helped to give this conviction. It is easy to understand why it did this. It seemed a necessity. It remains true, however, that in the war religion lost its purity, and lost its authority. It joined forces with the spirit of the world. The one victim of defeat was religion. And that religion *was* defeated is apparent in our time. For it lifts up its voice but only to protest. It cannot command. The spirit of the age does not listen. It goes its own way.

How did it come about that ethical ideals could not oppose the inhuman ideals of the war? It was due to the spirit of practical realism. I place at opposite extremes the spirit of idealism and the spirit of realism. The spirit of idealism means that men and women of the period arrive at ethical ideals through thinking, and that these ideals are so powerful that men say: We will use them to control reality. We will transform reality in accordance with these ideals. The spirit of idealism desires to have power over the spirit of realism. The spirit of practical realism, however, holds it false to apply ideals to what is happening. The spirit of realism has no power over reality. If a generation lives with these ideas, it is subject to reality. This is the tragedy which is being enacted in our age. For what

[1] *The Christian Century* (New York), Nov. 21st and 28th, 1934.

is characteristic of our age is that we no longer really believe in social or spiritual progress, but face reality powerless.

The religion of our age gives the same impression as an African river in the dry season—a great river-bed, sand-banks, and between, a small stream which seeks its way. One tries to imagine that a river once filled that bed; that there were no sand-banks but that the river flowed majestically on its way; and that it will some day be like that again. Is it possible, you say, that once a river filled this bed? Was there a time when ethical religion was a force in the spiritual life of the time? Yes, in the eighteenth century. Then ethical religion and thinking formed one unity. Thinking was religious, and religion was a thinking religion. Because it was conditioned by ethical religious ideas, the thinking of that period undertook to represent reality to itself as it should be. It possessed ethical ideals in accordance with which it transformed reality.

And as a matter of fact because it was filled with ideals of this kind, it had power over reality. It undertook a great work of reform. It waged war against superstition and ignorance. It obtained recognition for humanity in the eyes of the law. Torture was abolished, first in Prussia in the year 1740 through a cabinet order of Frederick the Great. It was demanded of the individual that he should place himself at the service of the community. English emigrants formulated in America for the first time the rights of man. The idea of humanity began to gain in significance. People dared to grasp the thought that lasting peace must reign on earth. Kant wrote a book on "Everlasting Peace" (1795), and in it represented the thought that even politics must submit to the principles of ethics. Finally, an achievement which the spirit of the eighteenth century brought about in the nineteenth century, came the abolition of slavery.

The religious-ethical spirit of the eighteenth century desired then to make the kingdom of God a reality on earth.

Then in the nineteenth century the spirit of realism rose against this spirit of idealism. The first personality in which it was realized was Napoleon I. The first thinker in whom it announced itself was the German philosopher Hegel. Men have not, Hegel maintained, to transform reality in order to bring it into accord with ideals devised by thinking. Progress takes place automatically in the natural course of events. The passions of ruling personalities and of peoples in some way or other are in the service of progress—even war is. The view that ethical idealism is a form of sentimentality of which no use can be made in the world of reality, began with Hegel. He was first to formulate the theory of rationalism. He wrote: "What is reasonable is real, and what is real is reasonable." On the night of June 25, 1820, when that sentence was written, our age began, the age which moved on to the world war—and which perhaps some day will end civilization!

Hegel dares to say that everything serves progress. The passions of rulers

and of peoples—all are the servants of progress. One can only say that
Hegel did not know the passions of people as we know them, or he would
not have dared to write that!

One truth stands firm. All that happens in world history rests on something spiritual. If the spiritual is strong, it creates world history. If it is
weak, it suffers world history. The question is, shall we make world
history or only suffer it passively? Will our thinking again become ethical-
religious? Shall we again win ideals that will have power over reality?
This is the question before us today.

In religion there are two different currents: one free from dogma and
one that is dogmatic. That which is free from dogma bases itself on the
preaching of Jesus; the dogmatic bases itself on the creeds of the early
church and the reformation. The religion free from dogma is to some
extent the heir of rationalistic religion. It is ethical, limits itself to the
fundamental ethical verities, and endeavours, so far as is in its power, to
remain on good terms with thinking. It wants to realize something
of the kingdom of God in the world. It believes itself identical with the
religion of Jesus. All the efforts of historical-theological science in the
nineteenth century are aimed at proving that Christian dogma began
with St. Paul and that the religion of Jesus is non-dogmatic, so that it
can be adopted in any age.

But it constituted a great difficulty for the non-dogmatic religion when
theological science at the end of the nineteenth century was forced to
admit that the ethical religion of Jesus shared the supernatural ideas of
late-Jewish belief in the messianic kingdom, and indeed that it also shared
with it its expectation of the approaching end of the world. Here it
becomes clear that there is no purely historical foundation for religion.
We must take the ethical religion of Jesus out of the setting of his world-
view and put it in our own. Whereas he expected the kingdom of God
to come at the end of the world, we must endeavour, under the influence
of the spirit of his ethical religion, to make the kingdom of God a reality
in this world by works of love.

Dogmatic religion is based on the creeds, the early church, and the
reformation. It has no relations with thinking, but emphasizes the difference
between thinking and believing. This religion further is more dominated
by the thought of redemption than by that of the kingdom of God. It
has no wish to influence the world. That is the characteristic of all the
ancient creeds—that the idea of the kingdom of God finds no expression
in them.

Why did the idea of the kingdom of God have no significance in the
early church? It was closely connected with the expectation of the end of
the world. And when hope of the coming of the end of the world had
faded, the idea of the kingdom of God lost its force as well. So it came
about that the creeds were not at the same time preoccupied with the

idea of redemption. Only after the reformation did the idea gradually arise that we men and women in our own age must so understand the religion of Jesus that we endeavour to make the kingdom of God a reality in this world. It is only through the idea of the kingdom of God that religion enters into relationship with civilization.

In recent times a tendency has appeared in dogmatic religion which completely turns its back on thinking and at the same time declares that religion has nothing to do with the world and civilization. It is not its business to realize the kingdom of God on earth. This extreme tendency is mainly represented by Karl Barth.

Karl Barth, who is the most modern theologian, because he lives most in the spirit of our age, more than any other has that contempt for thinking which is characteristic of our age. He dares to say that religion has nothing to do with thinking. He wants to give religion nothing to do with anything but God and man, the great antithesis. He says a religious person does not concern himself with what happens to the world. The idea of the kingdom of God plays no part with him. He mocks at what he calls "civilized Protestantism." The church must leave the world to itself. All that concerns the church is the preaching of revealed truth. Religion is turned aside from the world.

Yet Karl Barth—whom I, personally, value greatly—came to the point when he had to concern himself with the world, which in theory he did not want to do. He had to defend the freedom of religion against the state. And he did it with courage. But it shows that his theory is false! It is something terrible to say that religion is not ethical. Karl Barth is a truly religious personality, and in his sermons there is much profound religion. But the terrible thing is that he dares to preach that religion is turned aside from the world and in so doing expresses what the spirit of the age is feeling.

The spirit of the age dislikes what is simple. It no longer believes the simple can be profound. It loves the complicated, and regards it as profound. It loves the violent. That is why the spirit of the age can love Karl Barth and Nietzsche at the same time. The spirit of the age loves dissonance, in tones, in lines, and in thought. That shows how far from right thinking it is, for right thinking is a harmony within us.

If one reviews the development of religion since the middle of the nineteenth century, one understands the tragic fact that although really living religion is to be found among us, it is not the leaven that leavens the thinking of our age.

Let us examine four "paths" along which thinking seeks to arrive at a religion. The first is the path of materialism—the religion of natural science. Materialism proclaims war against metaphysics. It wants only the positive—what one can really know—and by that it declares its intention of living. The ethics of materialism consists in saying: You must live for the good of the community. Has this form of ethics really the significance of a religion? Can a man understand the purpose of his life when he says: I live for the good of the community? No! The ethics of materialism is incomplete. It hangs in the air.

Further, the ethics of materialism is unnecessary. Society has no need that the individual should serve it. Society does not need his morality; it can force upon him the sociology which it holds to be best. Herbert Spencer was not only a great thinker but a great prophet. He expressed anxiety lest the state should by violence force the individual to submit to it. He was right. The ethics of materialism has not triumphed, for in our days we have experienced the state destroying the individual in order to make the individual its servant. Therefore, the ethics of materialism is no religion.

The second path is that followed by Kant and by nearly all the major philosophers of the latter half of the nineteenth century. What do they seek in order to arrive at religion? They no longer venture to say that from ethics we derive the idea of the existence of God and the immortality of the soul. They are more cautious. They ask: Does thinking arrive at anything we can call God? They seek to show that the existence of an ethical God is necessary in some way, and try to prove to the materialist that without this idea he cannot rightly live.

But this ethical religion of the philosophers of the second half of the nineteenth century is not firmly grounded. Its idea of God is quite incomplete. What is ethical in such teaching has no force. It lacks compulsive power and enthusiasm, and so this fine philosophical religion has had no significance for the thinking of the world in general. It is something which cannot be placed in the centre of things; it is too delicate, too cautious, it utters no commands.

The third path is that of the philosophy of values and pragmatism. The philosophy of values resorts to a type of thinking which becomes dualistic. It asserts that there are spiritual truths alongside theoretical truths, and that all valuable conviction has truth in itself—a dangerous assertion. The real father of this doctrine of double truth is Hume. To escape scepticism Hume says, we need convictions, which will help us to live, and in regard to which we ask, not, Are they true? but, Are they necessary for our life?

What is pragmatism compared with this philosophy of values? It is a philosophy of values which has given up the criterion of ethics. Pragmatism says: Every idea that helps me to live is truth. Europeans got this pragmatism sent, all ready for use, from America, in William James. So modern thinking arrives at the doctrine of double truth. The theory of double truth is a spiritual danger. If there is a double truth, there is no truth. The sense of sincerity is blunted and the last thing that thinking can give humanity is a feeling for truth—for sincerity is fundamental in all spiritual life, and when this fundamental is shaken, there is no spiritual life remaining. In pragmatism, not only sincerity and truth, but ethics is in danger. For ethics is no longer the criterion of what is valuable. Pragmatism is filled with the spirit of realism. It permits men to take their ideals from reality.

The fourth path is that trodden by modern thinkers emancipated from Kant. They are obscure thinkers—their thinking is obscure and, moreover, they have a talent of writing obscurely! They want to get at religion by saying: All this knowledge of the world through science is only a description of the world, from which man derives nothing. What we must know is the essential nature of the universe. The thing we must be preoccupied with is the mystery of our life. How we understand the mystery of our life is the mystery of the universe. They say: We know the universe by intuition, not by reason. Our life knows the life in the world, and through our life we become one with the life of the universe. This thinking therefore is mysticism.

But ethics plays no part in this form of thought. The great problem of what man is aiming at plays no part in it.

In modern thinking the same thing happens as in religion. Thinking drops the tiller from its hand in the middle of the storm. It renounces the idea of giving to human beings ideals by the help of which they can get on with reality. It leaves them to themselves, and that in a most terrible moment. For the present moment *is* terrible. Man has won power over the forces of nature and by that has become superman—and at the same time most miserable man! For this power over the forces of nature is not being used beneficially, but destructively.

Because he has power over the forces of nature, man built machines which took work away from man, and this makes social problems of such magnitude that no one would have dreamed of them forty years ago. In some cities now air-raid practices are held, with sirens shrieking and all lights out. People shove something over their heads which makes them look like beasts, and rush into cellars, while flying through the air appears the superman, possessing endless power for destruction.

Humanity has always needed ethical ideals to enable it to find the right path, that man may make the right use of the power he possesses. Today his power is increased a thousandfold. A thousandfold greater is now the need for man to possess ethical ideals to point the way. Yet at the very moment when this happens, thinking fails. In this period of deepest need thinking is not giving to humanity the ideals it needs so that it may not be overwhelmed. Is that our destiny? I hope not. I believe not. I think that in our age we are all carrying within us a new form of thought which will give us ethical ideals.

All thinking must renounce the attempt to explain the universe. We cannot understand what happens in the universe. What is glorious in it is united with what is full of horror. What is full of meaning is united to what is senseless. The spirit of the universe is at once creative and destructive—it creates while it destroys and destroys while it creates, and therefore it remains to us a riddle. And we must inevitably resign ourselves to this.

Thinking which keeps contact with reality must look up to the heavens, it must look over the earth, and dare to direct its gaze to the barred windows of a lunatic asylum. Look to the stars and understand how small our earth is in the universe. Look upon earth and know how minute man is upon it. The earth existed long before man came upon it. In the history of the universe, man is on the earth for but a second. Who knows but that the earth will circle round the sun once more without man upon it? Therefore we must not place man in the centre of the universe. And our gaze must be fixed on the barred windows of a lunatic asylum, in order that we may remember the terrible fact that the mental and spiritual are also liable to destruction.

Only when thinking thus becomes quite humble can it set its feet upon the way that leads to knowledge. The more profound a religion is, the more it realizes this fact—that what it knows through belief is little compared with what it does not know. The first active deed of thinking is resignation—acquiescence in what happens. Becoming free, inwardly, from what happens, we pass through the gate of recognition on the way to ethics.

The deeper we look into nature, the more we recognize that it is full of life, and the more profoundly we know that all life is a secret and that we are united with all life that is in nature. Man can no longer live his life for himself alone. We realize that all life is valuable and that we are united to all this life. From this knowledge comes our spiritual relationship to the universe.

In the mysticism of the middle ages there was this wonderful phrase, *docta ignorantia*—"knowing ignorance." That is our condition. This *docta ignorantia* has been brought to us by natural science. Have no fear of natural science—it brings us nearer to God.

There is a development under way by which the circle of ethics always grows wider, and ethics becomes more profound. This development has been in progress from primitive times to the present. It is often halted, hindered by the absence of thought among men—I dare to say through that absence of thought which characterizes thought! But yet the development goes on to its end. The circle described by ethics is always widening. Primitive man has duties only toward his nearest relations. All other living beings are to him only things; he mistreats them and kills them, without compunction. Then the circle widens to the tribe, to the people, and grows ever wider until at last man realizes his ethical association with the whole of humanity. This represents an enormous act of thinking.

Consider Plato and Aristotle. Their ethics is narrow-hearted. They were occupied only with their fellow-citizens. Slaves and foreigners did not concern them. Then with Stoicism the circle begins to widen. That was the greatest manifestation of Greek thought. (Forgive me this heresy!) Then in Seneca, Epictetus, Marcus Aurelius, the idea suddenly crops up that ethics is concerned with all humanity. Thought arrives at that intuitive knowledge which you find already in the prophets of Israel and which is explained by Jesus.

Surely, ethics thinks, the circle is wide enough. But no! The force that causes the circle to enlarge enlarges it further. Slowly in our European thought comes the notion that ethics has not only to do with mankind but with the animal creation as well. This begins with St. Francis of Assisi. The explanation which applies only to man must be given up. Thus we shall arrive at saying that ethics is reverence for *all* life.

Let me give you a definition of ethics: It is good to maintain life and further life; it is bad to damage and destroy life. However much it struggles against it, ethics arrives at the religion of Jesus. It must recognize that it can discover no other relationship to other beings as full of sense as the relationship of love. Ethics is the maintaining of life at the highest point of development—my own life and other life—by devoting myself to it in help and love, and both these things are connected.

And this ethic, profound, universal, has the significance of a religion. It *is* religion.

Today there is an absence of thinking which is characterized by a contempt for life. We waged war for questions which, through reason, might have been solved. No one won. The war killed millions of men, brought suffering to millions of men, and brought suffering and death to millions of innocent animals. Why? Because we did not possess the highest rationality of reverence for life. And because we do not yet possess this, every people is afraid of every other, and each causes fear to the others. We are mentally afflicted one for another because we are lacking in rationality. There is no other remedy than reverence for life, and at that we must arrive.

Thinking has not given us that, but thinking is preparing it—in natural science, which allows us to know the inner nature of being; and in ethics, which is developing in a direction by which it reaches its conclusion in reverence for life. Reverence for life dwells within our thought. We have only to go deep enough through absence of thought until we come to this profound ethic which is already a religion.

We wander in darkness now, but one with another we all have the conviction that we are advancing to the light; that again a time will come when religion and ethical thinking will unite. This we believe, and hope and work for, maintaining the belief that if we make ethical ideals active in our lives, then the time will come when peoples will do the same. Let us look out toward the light and comfort ourselves in reflecting on what thinking is preparing for us.

INDEX

343

THE END